Accounting, Finance, Sustainability, Governance & Fraud: Theory and Application

Series Editor

Kıymet Tunca Çalıyurt,
Business Administration Department & Accounting and Finance Department, Faculty of Business Sciences and Economics,
Trakya University, Edirne, Türkiye

This Scopus indexed series acts as a forum for book publications on current research arising from debates about key topics that have emerged from global economic crises during the past several years. The importance of governance and the will to deal with corruption, fraud, and bad practice, are themes featured in volumes published in the series. These topics are not only of concern to businesses and their investors, but also to governments and supranational organizations, such as the United Nations and the European Union. Accounting, Finance, Sustainability, Governance & Fraud: Theory and Application takes on a distinctive perspective to explore crucial issues that currently have little or no coverage. Thus the series integrates both theoretical developments and practical experiences to feature themes that are topical, or are deemed to become topical within a short time. The series welcomes interdisciplinary research covering the topics of accounting, auditing, governance, and fraud.

Ganite Kurt • Özkan Sarısoy
Editors

Recent Advancements in Auditing

Theory, Practice, and Innovation

Springer

Editors
Ganite Kurt
Department of Finance and Banking
Ankara Hacı Bayram Veli University
Ankara, Türkiye

Özkan Sarısoy
Accounting and Tax Practices
Tekirdağ Namık Kemal University
Tekirdağ, Türkiye

ISSN 2509-7873 ISSN 2509-7881 (electronic)
Accounting, Finance, Sustainability, Governance & Fraud: Theory and Application
ISBN 978-981-95-5810-0 ISBN 978-981-95-5811-7 (eBook)
https://doi.org/10.1007/978-981-95-5811-7

This Springer imprint is published by the registered company Springer Nature Singapore Pte Ltd.
The registered company address is: 152 Beach Road, #21-01/04 Gateway East, Singapore 189721, Singapore

This book is part of the *International Group on Governance, Fraud, Ethics, Sustainability and Corporate Reporting (IGonGFESR),* which was founded at the *1st International Conference on Governance, Fraud, Ethics, and CSR* in 2009 in Edirne. (Between 2009 and 2024, our group title was *International Group on Governance, Fraud, Ethics and CSR.*)

IGonGFESR
since 2009

INTERNATIONAL GROUP ON GOVERNANCE, FRAUD, ETHICS,
SUSTAINABILITY AND CORPORATE REPORTING

Contents

Editors and Contributors

About the Editors

Ganite Kurt is a distinguished professor of accounting at Ankara Haci Bayram Veli University, with over 30 years of academic experience. Her research interests span a wide range of topics, including accounting theory, auditing, accounting ethics, audit fraud, financial accounting, International Financial Reporting Standards (IFRS), International Standards on Auditing (ISA), family businesses, corporate governance, and internal control systems. Prof. Kurt has authored numerous publications in both national and international peer-reviewed journals, as well as book chapters in the field of accounting. In addition to her academic contributions, she has actively participated in the design, management, and execution of various national and international research projects. Throughout her career, she has held key academic and administrative positions, including serving as an instructor and as an administrator at a vocational school, gaining extensive experience in both teaching and institutional leadership. In addition, Prof. Kurt currently serves as the founding president of the Assurance Services Association (GHD), a prominent organization operating in Türkiye, and she is also one of the leading coordinators of the Accounting and Audit Researchers' Platform (MUDEP), which brings together numerous accounting scholars across the country.

Özkan Sarisoy, CPA, began his undergraduate studies in Business Administration at Trakya University in 2006. He completed the final semester of his undergraduate education in Germany through a student exchange program and earned his bachelor's degree in 2010. He obtained his M.A. in Accounting and Auditing from the Institute of Social Sciences at Trakya University in 2012, with a thesis focusing on International Financial Reporting Standards. In 2018, he received his Ph.D. in Accounting from Istanbul University, with a dissertation analyzing the presentation of Key Audit Matters in independent auditor reports. Dr. Sarisoy's research interests include independent auditing, financial fraud, behavioral accounting, and accounting culture. He has served as a reviewer for various national and international academic journals. He is currently working as an academic at Tekirdağ

Namik Kemal University. He was an active member of the Accounting and Audit Researchers Platform (MUDEP), ACFE Trakya University Student Club, and a contributing member of the International Group of Governance, Fraud, Ethics, and Corporate Social Responsibility.

About the Contributors

Fevzİ Serkan Özdemİr is a professor of accounting at Ankara University, Faculty of Political Sciences, and a postdoctoral research scholar at New York University's Stern School of Business. He earned his B.A. in Economics from Anadolu University, his M.A. in Accounting from Gazi University, and his Ph.D. in Accounting from Ankara University. His research focuses on sustainability accounting, the ESG–financial performance nexus, assurance services, and the integration of artificial intelligence into accounting education. At NYU Stern, he has developed the concept of Born Sustainable Firms (BSFs) to examine how early strategic adoption of sustainability influences firms' financial outcomes. Prof. Özdemir has published extensively in national and international journals and has edited several academic volumes. He is also the founding president of the Assurance Services Association (GHD) and a leading coordinator of the Accounting and Audit Researchers Platform (MUDEP)—two prominent initiatives advancing sustainability, assurance, and accounting scholarship in Türkiye. He is currently working on enhancing the effectiveness and innovation of accounting education in higher education through interdisciplinary and technology-driven approaches.

Ayşegül Ciğer, CPA, completed her undergraduate studies in Business Administration at Gazi University in 1994. She earned her master's degree in 2000 from Gazi University, Institute of Social Sciences, Department of Accounting and Finance, with a thesis titled "National and International Standards in Inflation Accounting and an Application." In 2006, she received her Ph.D. from Selçuk University, Institute of Social Sciences, Department of Business Administration, with a dissertation titled "The Implementation of New Cost Approaches in Hospitality Businesses and an Application." Dr. Ciğer began her academic career at Akdeniz University in 1994 and has held various positions in the fields of accounting and finance. Since 2018, she has been serving in the Department of Banking and Finance at the Faculty of Applied Sciences. Her academic research interests include independent auditing, KAM in audit reports, financial statement analysis, financial reporting, and cost accounting. She has contributed to numerous national and international articles, conference papers, and book projects. She also teaches undergraduate and graduate courses in general accounting, cost accounting, financial statement analysis, and auditing. She currently serves as the Head of the Department of Accounting and Auditing in the Department of Banking and Finance at the Faculty of Applied Sciences, Akdeniz University.

Özgür Teraman is a distinguished tax advisor and financial auditor with nearly two decades of expertise as a partner and consultant. He has also worked as a part-time and full-time lecturer at universities in the past, and holds licenses as a CPA, Independent Auditor, and CFA Level 3. He is also a member of the Association of International Accountants (AIA) in the UK. Dr. Teraman holds a Bachelor's degree in Economics from Istanbul University (2002), a Master's degree in Accounting from Dokuz Eylül University (2011), and a PhD in Accounting and Finance from Marmara University (2015). His career spans a diverse range of clients, including multinational corporations, financial institutions, and government agencies. Dr. Teraman is not only an accomplished advisor but also a skilled trainer who has nurtured auditors and other professionals in the audit field. In addition, with his expertise in the field of valuation. Dr. Teraman has been working on appraising various intangible assets. He has significant expertise in the field, having been involved in numerous company and brand valuations. Between 2020 and 2023, Dr. Teraman served as Chief Financial Officer (CFO), providing leadership, direction, and management of finance and accounting teams. He also developed strategic recommendations for the CEO/president and members of the executive management team, managed the processes for financial forecasting and budgeting, and oversaw the preparation of all financial reporting. He currently continues his advisory and auditing profession as a partner.

Fatma Temelli graduated from Atatürk University, Faculty of Economics and Administrative Sciences, Department of Business Administration in 2008. In 2011, she completed her master's degree at Atatürk University's Institute of Social Sciences, Department of Accounting and Finance, and in 2015, she completed her doctorate. In 2015, Temelli was appointed as Assistant Professor at Ağri İbrahim Çeçen University, Faculty of Economics and Administrative Sciences, Department of Business Administration, Department of Accounting and Finance. Since 2020, he has been working as an Associate Professor at the Department of Accounting and Finance, Department of Business Administration of the same faculty. Main fields of study: her main fields of study are financial accounting, accounting education, accounting professional ethics and corporate social responsibility, cost and management accounting, and accounting auditing.

Gizem Çopur Vardar began her undergraduate studies in the Department of Business Administration at Gazi University. After completing her undergraduate education, she pursued a further academic career by earning her MBA master's degree at the Institute of Social Sciences of Mersin University in 2007. Her master's thesis focused on valuation in accounting. In her doctoral dissertation, completed in 2013 at the Department of Business Administration at Gazi University, she examined accounting and reporting for Build-Operate-Transfer (BOT) arrangements by International Financial Reporting Standards (IFRS) and International Accounting Standards (IAS). Dr. Çopur Vardar has made significant contributions to academia, particularly in the areas of independent auditing, international accounting, financial reporting, KAM in audit reports, financial statement analysis, and the principle of prudence in financial accounting. She serves as a faculty member in the Department of Accounting and Finance at Mersin University Faculty of Business Administration, where she shares her knowledge and inspires future professionals in the field.

Zafer Anadolu, CPA, earned an associate degree in Accounting and Taxation from Bülent Ecevit University in 2006, followed by a bachelor's degree in Business Administration from Anadolu University in 2008. He obtained a master's degree in Accounting and Auditing from Okan University in 2015. Anadolu has continued his professional career, focusing on financial consulting and independent auditing. He has held senior auditor and tax auditor positions at various institutions, including Ecovis Değer Independent Audit, Toluen YMM, and Sinpaş Holding. His areas of expertise include independent auditing, Turkish Financial Reporting Standards (TFRS), BOBİ FRS, IFRS reporting, deferred tax calculations (TMS 12), valuation, capital increase audits, and tax planning. He is deeply involved in comprehensive certification, incentive, and exemption audits while enhancing financial processes. Anadolu possesses certifications in SAP FI and logistics modules and has undergone pedagogical training. He advances.

Ömer Faruk Demirkol completed his undergraduate education in Business Administration at Selçuk University in 1994. He completed his master's degree in 1999 at İnönü University, Department of Accounting and Finance, with a thesis titled "Suggestions for Agricultural Policies and Financing in the Southeastern Anatolia Region". He completed his doctorate at Gazi University, Department of Accounting and Finance, with a thesis titled" Calculation of Product Costs According to International Accounting Standards in Greenhouse Agriculture" in 2006. He currently serves as a faculty member in the Department of Business Administration at Harran University, Faculty of Economics and Administrative Sciences. Prof. Demirkol 's research areas include Cost Calculation Methods, Auditing Techniques, Agricultural Activity Accounting, and Turkish Financial Reporting Standards.

Abdulrezzak İkvan completed his undergraduate education at Gazi University, Department of Accounting and Finance Education in 2006. He completed his master's degree at Gaziantep University, Department of Business Administration, with his thesis titled "Lending Behavior and Analysis of Deposit Banks in Türkiye" in 2017. He completed his doctorate at Harran University, Department of Business Administration, with his thesis titled "Possible Effects of Digital Developments on Independent Audit Process: Evaluation from the Perspective of Independent Auditors" in 2023. He currently serves as a faculty member at Adiyaman University. Dr. İkvan's research interests include Accounting and Auditing Standards, Forensic Accounting, and Key Auditing Issues.

Hayrettin Uzunoğlu completed his undergraduate education at Istanbul University, Department of Business Administration in 2007. He obtained his M.A. in Business Administration from the Institute of Social Sciences at Yeditepe University in 2012. He completed his Ph.D. in Business Administration from Hacettepe University with his thesis titled "Financial Information Manipulation: An Application of BIST

Industrials Index" in 2018. He is a faculty member in the Department of Accounting and Finance Management at the Faculty of Applied Sciences, Kayseri University. Dr. Uzunoğlu's research interests include independent auditing, financial fraud, and auditing standards.

Beyhan Beller Dikmen completed her undergraduate education in Accounting and Finance Teaching at Gazi University in 2008. She earned her master's degree in 2011 from the Department of Accounting and Finance at Niğde University with a thesis titled "Calculation of Environmental Costs in Production Companies and a Case Study". In 2017, she completed her Ph.D. at Niğde Ömer Halisdemir University, also in the Department of Accounting and Finance, with a dissertation titled "Calculation of Passenger Transportation Costs in State Railway Enterprises According to Activity-Based Costing Method and an Application". She is currently a faculty member in the Department of International Trade and Logistics at Tarsus University's Faculty of Applied Sciences. Dr. Beller Dikmen's research interests include cost calculation methods, agricultural accounting, and Turkish Financial Reporting Standards.

Musa Özçelik was born in Ankara in 1993. He graduated with a bachelor's degree from Gazi University's Banking Department in 2015 and completed his master's degree in 2019. Özçelik, who has four years of experience in the banking sector, was appointed as a research assistant at Tarsus University in 2019. In 2023, he earned his doctorate from Ankara Haci Bayram Veli University and currently serves as an Assistant Professor at Tarsus University. His research interests include auditing, financial and non-financial reporting, international accounting, and the application of artificial intelligence and digitalization. He has numerous scientific studies in his field.

Murat Karahan completed his high school education at Ankara Finance Vocational High School in 1992. He completed his undergraduate education in the Department of Economics at Hacettepe University in 1998. After graduating from university, he was appointed as a lecturer at Gaziantep University Gölbaşi Vocational School, Accounting and Tax Department in 1999. He completed his master's degree in the Department of Economics at Gaziantep University, Institute of Social Sciences in 2002. He completed his doctorate at Akdeniz University, Institute of Social Sciences, Department of Tourism and Business Administration in 2014. In January 2018, he was appointed as an Assistant Professor at Gaziantep University, Faculty of Economics and Administrative Sciences, Department of Business Administration, Accounting and Finance Department. He received the title of Associate Professor of Accounting in 2021. Throughout his career, he has taught accounting, auditing, and tax law courses at the associate, undergraduate, graduate, and doctoral levels. He has many works published nationally and internationally. He is currently working as an Associate Professor in the Department of Business Administration, Accounting and Finance, Faculty of Economics and Administrative Sciences, Gaziantep University.

İlkay Ejder Erturan Department of Accounting and Tax Applications – Düzce University, Türkiye. Dr. Erturan received his Bachelor of Science degree in Business Administration from Anadolu University in 1993, followed by his Master of Science degree in Accounting and Finance from the same institution in 1996. She continued his academic career in 1995 as the first appointed Accounting Assistant at the Osmangazi University Faculty of Economics and Administrative Sciences. She began his doctoral studies at Anadolu University in 1996. Dr. Erturan resided in Cincinnati, Ohio, between 2000 and 2003, where she pursued advanced academic development and cross-cultural studies in the fields of accounting, auditing, and organizational management. After returning to Türkiye in 2003, she faced a serious health problem and was diagnosed with Multiple Sclerosis (MS). After a long and determined recovery process, she returned to academic life in 2013 and joined Düzce University School of Higher Education as a faculty member. Dr. Erturan primarily works in the field of auditing, with research topics including Auditing and the Internet of Things (IoT), Digital Twins in Auditing, and the Philosophical and cultural dimensions of Auditing. Her doctoral thesis is the first academic study to investigate the impact of cultural values on auditors' professional judgments, an interdisciplinary study that integrates sociology and auditing. Dr. Erturan served as the Director of Düzce University School of Higher Education from 2017 to 2024. She is also the founding advisor and executive member of Çilimli Women's Labor Association, which promotes women's participation in education and the workforce, and a member of MUDEP.

Selçuk Gülten, CPA, began his undergraduate education at the Department of Finance at Gazi University in 1995. In 2012, he received his master's degree in finance from Sakarya University's Institute of Social Sciences, with a thesis that focused on comparing the tax systems of Azerbaijan and Turkey. He graduated from Ankara University, Department of Computer Programming in 2019. In 2022, he completed his second master's degree in cybersecurity at Hoca Ahmet Yesevi University. He received his Information Systems Independent Auditing License in 2025. Selçuk Gülten's research areas include independent auditing, forensic accounting, digitalization and artificial intelligence. He has published articles in various national and international academic journals. He currently works as an Independent Auditor. He is an active member of MUDEP.

Yasemin Acar Uğurlu completed her undergraduate studies in 2008 at Başkent University's Department of Accounting and Financial Management, supported by a full scholarship. In 2010, she began her academic career as a lecturer at Istanbul Arel University. She obtained her master's degree in 2013 from Marmara University, Accounting Auditing Program, with a thesis titled "Applications to the Court in Forensic Accounting Profession and Research." In 2014, she received her Certified Public Accountant (CPA) license. In 2019, she earned her Ph.D. in Accounting from Istanbul University with her dissertation titled "The Role of the Use of Different Sources in Internal Audit to Detect and Deter Fraud." Dr. Acar Uğurlu currently serves as a faculty member in the Department of Accounting and

Financial Management at the Faculty of Economics and Administrative Sciences, Istanbul Arel University. Her research focuses on internal auditing and independent auditing.

Yasemin Ertan is a faculty member in the Department of Accounting and Finance at the Faculty of Business Administration, Bursa Uludağ University. She earned her undergraduate degree in Business Administration from Gazi University and completed both her master's and Ph.D. in the same field at Bursa Uludağ University. Dr. Ertan has published extensively on financial analysis, auditing, and financial performance. She has broad experience in both national and international projects. In addition to her academic teaching and research activities, she is actively involved as a researcher in the European Union-funded projects that focus on sustainability, innovative business models, digitalization, and environmental, social, and governance (ESG) principles.

Recep Güneş started his undergraduate education at the Higher Teacher Training School of Commerce and Tourism. After completing his undergraduate education, he continued his academic career by obtaining his master's degree at Gazi University Institute of Social Sciences (MBA). In his doctoral thesis, which he completed at Gazi University Institute of Social Sciences in 1991, he analyzed the subject of 'Cost-based pricing and its evaluation in terms of applications in Turkey'. Between 1990 and 1992, he earned his MBA degree in Finance from the University of Nottingham Business School in England. Prof. Dr. Recep Güneş has made significant contributions to academic studies in independent auditing, international accounting standards, financial reporting, financial statement analysis, and cost and management accounting. After working at Malatya Faculty of Economics and Administrative Sciences, he is currently working at Artvin Çoruh University, Faculty of Business Administration, Department of Finance and Banking.

List of Figures

List of Tables

Part I
About Accounting and Audit Researchers' Platform (MUDEP) and Assurance Services Association (GHD)

Chapter 1
Introduction: An Innovative Dual Structure for Academic Engagement in Accounting: The Association-and-Platform Model

Ganite Kurt, Fevzi Serkan Özdemir, and Özkan Sarısoy

Abstract This paper introduces and analyzes the GHD–MUDEP model, a dual-structured initiative fostering academic engagement and professional development among accounting scholars in Türkiye. Comprising the formal Assurance Services Association (GHD) and the informal Accounting Audit Employees Platform (MUDEP) platform, the model offers a decentralized, voluntary alternative to traditional, bureaucratic faculty development systems. While GHD provides institutional stability and legitimacy, MUDEP encourages grassroots academic interaction, peer learning, and rapid response to professional needs. Together, they form a hybrid mechanism that identifies and addresses skill gaps, supports early-career scholars, democratizes knowledge-sharing, and generates sustainable academic outputs such as books and journal publications. Through webinars, workshops, field visits, and participatory conferences, the model cultivates inclusivity, mentorship, and cross-institutional collaboration. Positioned within a rigid higher education context, this framework demonstrates how civil society can reimagine academic development as a dynamic, inclusive, and community-led process with potential applicability beyond the accounting field.

G. Kurt (✉)
Ankara Hacı Bayram Veli University, Ankara, Türkiye
e-mail: ganite.kurt@hbv.edu.tr

F. S. Özdemir
Ankara University, Ankara, Türkiye
e-mail: fsozdemir@ankara.edu.tr

Ö. Sarısoy
Tekirdağ Namık Kemal University, Tekirdağ, Türkiye
e-mail: osarisoy@nku.edu.tr

G. Kurt, Ö. Sarısoy (eds.), *Recent Advancements in Auditing*, Accounting, Finance, Sustainability, Governance & Fraud: Theory and Application,
https://doi.org/10.1007/978-981-95-5811-7_1

Keywords Assurance services association (GHD) · MUDEP · Accounting culture · Case-based learning · Academic solidarity · Voluntary organization

1.1 Introduction

In Türkiye, the professional development of academics—particularly in practice-based disciplines like accounting—often unfolds in an unstructured and highly individualized manner. Despite the increasing complexity of higher education and the growing expectations of professionals, systemic support for ongoing academic training remains limited. Public institutions typically rely on top-down, bureaucratic models of in-service education, which tend to be rigid, uniform, and disconnected from the lived realities of faculty members.

Against this backdrop, the GHD–MUDEP framework introduces an innovative dual structure that challenges conventional models of academic development. Through a combination of formal association (Assurance Services Association—GHD) and an informal platform (Accounting Audit Employees Platform—MUDEP), this initiative fosters a grassroots, horizontal, and voluntary community of scholars. It not only provides responsive and flexible training opportunities but also redefines the role of civil society in shaping academic capacity building, extending its influence beyond the accounting field.

Importantly, the success of this model cannot be explained by funding mechanisms or institutional mandates alone. Its strength lies in a genuine commitment to shared academic growth, anchored in a collective spirit of solidarity. GHD–MUDEP has:

- Given early-career scholars a meaningful voice,
- Enabled senior faculty to transfer institutional memory through mentorship and co-learning, and
- Transformed insights into publications, ideas into action, and peer interactions into a living archive of academic engagement.

This paper examines the structure, evolution, and broader implications of the GHD–MUDEP model, offering a compelling case for how civil society can play a transformative role in reimagining faculty development in Türkiye and beyond.

1.2 Foundational Structure: Distinguishing Between the Association (GHD) and the Platform (MUDEP)

The institutionalization of civil society's contribution to the professional development of accounting faculty in Turkey has not followed a conventional, single-entity model. Instead, it has evolved into a dual and complementary structure—one that combines formal legal standing with the agility of an informal, community-driven platform. This innovative model is embodied in the relationship between the **Assurance Services Association (GHD)** and the **Accounting and Audit Researchers' Platform (MUDEP)**.

1.2.1 GHD: Formal Organization With Institutional Endurance

Founded in 2016, GHD is a legally recognized non-governmental organization operating under Turkish civil law. It brings together academics, practitioners, and professionals under a shared ethical and professional vision. GHD provides institutional continuity and formal representation, making it suitable for managing structured processes such as training programs, publications, academic panels, and international collaborations. Its legal identity enables the organization to interact with public institutions and formal structures in a credible and sustainable way.

1.2.2 MUDEP: Informal Platform With Voluntary Participation

Established on November 13, 2021, MUDEP was initiated by GHD as an informal academic platform. While it operates under the broader umbrella of the Association, it is structurally flexible and does not require any formal membership. Participation is granted through a simple WhatsApp group, creating a space where volunteerism, accessibility, and spontaneous collaboration thrive. MUDEP's rapid growth—reaching over 595 accounting academics from across Turkey—attests to its inclusive and dynamic character.

This dual arrangement is far from accidental; rather, it is a conscious design choice.

- **GHD** fulfills the role of a formal institution, offering legal accountability, administrative continuity, and outward-facing legitimacy.
- **MUDEP**, in contrast, provides a fluid, grassroots environment for academic interaction and rapid mobilization.

Together, they enable a hybrid system that is both durable and responsive. In a field like accounting, where regulatory and technological changes occur frequently, such structural flexibility allows for early recognition of professional skill gaps and swift intervention. This model supports a form of academic engagement that is legally sound, socially inclusive, and operationally agile.

1.3 Identifying and Addressing Professional Skill Gaps Through Voluntary Engagement

One of the most pressing structural challenges facing accounting faculty members in Turkey is the limited availability of continuous professional development opportunities. Amid accelerating shifts in technology, global standards, and interdisciplinary expectations, most higher education institutions have struggled to keep pace with the evolving training needs of academic staff. This misalignment has led to growing disparities in both curriculum content and individual faculty members' pedagogical and technical competencies.

1.3.1 Structural Causes of the Professional Development Gap

- Lack of systematic training in new technologies such as Python, data analytics, and AI.
- Delayed integration of changes in international standards (e.g., IFRS) into course syllabi.
- Overemphasis on academic publishing for promotion, often at the expense of teaching quality and instructional development.
- Limited, shallow, or outdated in-service training opportunities within public universities.

1.3.2 A Voluntary Solution: The GHD–MUDEP Model

The GHD–MUDEP model operates without any formal mandate yet succeeds in identifying and addressing professional gaps through grassroots academic observation and peer coordination. Its impact stems from:

- Early recognition of unmet needs based on informal academic dialogue and tacit signals.
- Participant-driven design of webinars, workshops, and training programs.
- Freedom from bureaucratic delay, allowing for agile content creation and rapid delivery.

1.3.3 Community-Driven Content Development

Unlike traditional top-down training models, the GHD–MUDEP structure functions as a peer-to-peer learning ecosystem:

- Training topics emerge from the needs and feedback of members, not from administrative directives.
- Sessions are interactive and grounded in applied problem-solving.
- Access is open, free of charge, and unconstrained by geography or academic rank.

In sum, this volunteer-led structure offers a practical, inclusive, and responsive solution to the often-invisible professional development gaps faced by accounting faculty in Turkey. It democratizes capacity-building by placing trust in academic communities to recognize and resolve their own evolving needs.

1.4 Key Activities and Programs

The dual-structure model established by GHD and MUDEP not only identifies gaps in professional development but also implements a range of practical and innovative solutions. These include webinars, technical workshops, case-based learning platforms, field visits to businesses, and participatory "search conferences." Collectively, these initiatives represent a forward-looking approach to academic enrichment in accounting education.

1.4.1 Webinars: Broad Access to Relevant Knowledge

Since 2020, MUDEP has organized more than 40 webinars, each designed to address critical topics that lie outside the boundaries of conventional accounting curricula:

- International Financial Reporting Standards (IFRS)
- Inflation accounting and implementation techniques
- Data science tools: Python, artificial intelligence, and machine learning
- Academic publishing ethics and digital tools (e.g., Zotero)
- Research project design and international collaboration strategies

These sessions do not simply transfer technical knowledge; they create a space for dialogue between junior academics and experienced experts.

1.4.2 Technical Training and Skill Workshops

GHD and MUDEP have developed hands-on training programs to address disparities in technical knowledge across institutions:

- Excel in accounting applications targets instructors in applied roles.
- Artificial neural networks and decision trees serve research-oriented faculty.

These workshops are delivered in a practical format, using real datasets, interactive software screens, and guided exercises.

1.4.3 Case-Based Learning: The Case Platform

MUDEP's Case Platform bridges the gap between academic theory and real-world accounting practices. Participants:

- Visit companies to observe operations firsthand,
- Conduct a structured academic analysis of their findings,
- Develop case studies that are later published as teaching materials.

This approach promotes experiential learning while enriching the pool of context-specific educational content.

1.4.4 Business Field Visits: Grounded Academic Observation

Since 2022, field visits have been conducted in diverse cities such as Sivas, Mardin, Kayseri, Gaziantep, and Van. These visits allow faculty to:

- Examine regional business models and accounting practices,
- Identify cultural and regulatory variations in implementation,
- Transform field experiences into publishable academic outputs.

By linking classroom theory with real-world dynamics, the initiative enhances both curriculum relevance and research impact.

Accounting Search Conferences: Collaborative Educational Design

The *Muhasebe Arama Konferansları*—referred to by their Turkish acronym **MAK**—represent a distinctive departure from conventional academic meetings. Rather than centering on formal presentations or passive knowledge transfer, these conferences are structured as participatory design workshops in which faculty members collectively rethink core components of accounting education.

Key features of the MAK model include:

- A **station-based format** that encourages rotation and cross-pollination of ideas across thematic tables,
- The positioning of participants as **co-creators**, not just consumers, of educational strategies,
- A clear focus on **generating tangible outputs**, such as redesigned course modules, competency-based learning plans, and pedagogical roadmaps.

Each conference is built around a central theme and oriented toward practical solutions. For instance:

- **MAK I** (Konya, 2023) addressed the strategic direction of accounting research and sought to identify shared priorities for the academic community.
- **MAK II** (Eskişehir, 2024) explored the role of artificial intelligence in accounting pedagogy, producing scenario-based modules for classroom use.
- **MAK III** (Tokat, 2025) is devoted to reimagining the *Financial Accounting I* course through a collaborative, experience-driven approach that emphasizes pedagogical innovation and contextual adaptation.

As a collective academic practice, the MAK conferences exemplify how peer-led initiatives can build both **pedagogical infrastructure** and **community solidarity** in higher education. They stand as a testament to the power of grassroots academic organizations in fostering meaningful change.

1.5 Participant Profile and Inclusivity: Creating Space for Early-Career Academics

The volunteer-based model implemented by GHD and MUDEP is notable not only for the content of its programs but also for the inclusiveness of its participation structure. In particular, it has opened new pathways for early-career academics, many of whom face structural and social barriers in traditional academic networks.

Barrier-Free Participation: A WhatsApp-Based Entry Point

MUDEP's membership mechanism is strikingly simple: anyone can join by being added to a WhatsApp group. No application forms, no dues, no formal registration. This low-threshold model ensures that:

- Participation is accessible regardless of institutional rank or title.
- Young scholars with limited academic networks can gain entry without gatekeeping.
- Academics from under-resourced or geographically isolated universities can join and contribute actively.

Visibility Opportunities: First Talk, First Publication, First Panel

For many participants, MUDEP has been the venue for significant professional firsts:

- Delivering a webinar for the first time
- Publishing a book chapter
- Contributing to a peer-reviewed journal
- Serving as a panelist or session moderator

These experiences not only build visibility but also foster confidence, skill development, and professional identity.

Mentorship and Intergenerational Knowledge Sharing

In the absence of rigid hierarchies, the platform organically facilitates mentorship:

- Senior academics support junior colleagues in writing, project management, and curriculum development.
- Co-authorship and co-presentation opportunities are encouraged.

This informal, collaborative ethos fosters sustained academic growth and continuity.

Embracing Diversity Across Institutions

The platform maintains an ethos of institutional neutrality:

- No distinction is made between public and private universities.
- Geographical centrality (urban vs. rural) carries no weight.
- Academic hierarchy does not determine speaking time or leadership roles.

This horizontal structure has resulted in a rare form of equity and openness in the Turkish academic landscape—one in which inclusion is not a principle to aspire to but a reality already in practice.

1.6 Publication-based Sustainability: Book Series, Journal Themes, and Knowledge Generation

A key driver of long-term impact within the GHD–MUDEP model is its commitment to converting experiential knowledge into durable academic outputs. Rather than allowing insights from webinars and conferences to fade with time, the platform systematically transforms them into published works—books, special journal issues, and conceptual frameworks that contribute to broader disciplinary literature.

From Experience to Literature: Book Publications

Insights gathered from platform activities are compiled and published as edited volumes through GHD's publishing collaborations. Examples include:

- *Artificial Intelligence in Accounting Education*
- *Proceedings of the Accounting Search Conference*
- *Practice-Oriented Instruction in Introductory Accounting*

These are not merely reports—they are citable, peer-reviewed academic resources that formalize shared learning.

Thematic Journal Issues and Refereed Articles

Outcomes from collective academic efforts are regularly published as themed issues in peer-reviewed journals, with editorial roles filled by MUDEP-affiliated scholars. This structure:

- Provides early-career academics with entry points into scholarly publishing,
- Encourages co-authorship and interdisciplinary dialogue,
- Bridges the gap between practical engagement and academic discourse.

Generating New Frameworks: Conceptual Models from Conferences

Thematic dialogues within search conferences serve as a fertile ground not only for instructional design but also for:

- Advancing conceptual frameworks in areas like entrepreneurship, pedagogy, and AI-integration,
- Developing theoretical models with research potential,
- Enabling testable hypotheses that grow organically from practice.

By rooting its academic output in lived experience and collaborative learning, the GHD–MUDEP structure ensures that sustainability in education is not an abstract goal but a concrete and cumulative reality.

1.7 Conclusion

The collaboration between the Güvence Hizmetleri Derneği (GHD) and its affiliated MUDEP platform represents a novel approach to professional development in the Turkish academic landscape, particularly in the field of accounting education. This dual structure:

- Relies on a **formal organization** (GHD) for institutional grounding,
- Operates through an **informal platform** (MUDEP) for flexibility and ease of access.

This arrangement has enabled hundreds of scholars across academic ranks, regions, and institutional affiliations to converge around shared academic values in a voluntary and collaborative ecosystem. The activities are not limited to information transfer; they foster peer learning, co-creation, and sustainable academic engagement rooted in trust and shared purpose.

What makes this model particularly noteworthy is its ability to thrive within the highly centralized and bureaucratic structure of Turkish higher education. By combining the legitimacy and continuity of a registered association with the adaptability and inclusiveness of a grassroots platform, GHD–MUDEP challenges the assumption that academic capacity building must be state-driven or hierarchically imposed. Instead, it offers a bottom-up, community-centered alternative that is dynamic, inclusive, and responsive to real-time needs in the field.

This initiative also serves as a **transferable model** for other disciplines and contexts, both within and beyond Türkiye. In an era when faculty development is increasingly seen as a strategic priority, yet often lacks agile and inclusive delivery mechanisms, the GHD–MUDEP framework demonstrates how civil society can play a proactive and enabling role.

Looking ahead, the continued evolution of this model will depend on its ability to sustain collaborative energy, foster intergenerational learning, and remain thematically open to the expanding scope of academic and professional challenges. Its core strength—voluntariness, flexibility, and shared intellectual labor—will be vital not only for its longevity but also for its potential to inspire similar initiatives elsewhere.

In short, the GHD–MUDEP experience exemplifies how trust-based, community-driven efforts can lead to meaningful and lasting contributions to academic life. It turns informal collaboration into structured value, shared intention into enduring impact, and a professional need into a collective mission.

Reference

The references in this chapter have been compiled by the authors.

Chapter 2
In Memoriam: The Scholarly Legacy of Mehmet Özbirecikli – a Bibliometric Reflection

Ganite Kurt and Özkan Sarısoy

Abstract This study aims to examine the scholarly legacy of Prof. Dr. Mehmet Özbirecikli, who passed away in the 2023 earthquake centered in Kahramanmaraş, Türkiye, and who left a profound impact on the accounting community through both his academic work and personal character. Following his sudden and deeply saddening death, a comprehensive evaluation was undertaken to make his contributions to the field of accounting more visible and to transmit them to future generations. A total of 39 academic articles published between 2000 and 2022 were analyzed in detail, and his works were classified under seven thematic categories: accounting education, independent auditing, cost accounting, professional ethics, accounting standards, historical-theoretical approaches, and other complementary subfields. The findings reveal that Prof. Dr. Özbirecikli adopted an academic approach that integrated theoretical frameworks with practical applications, with particular emphasis on ethical awareness, quality in education, and alignment with regulatory frameworks. His research on accounting education and professional ethics reflects a vision aimed at cultivating qualified and responsible practitioners. The study concludes that Prof. Dr. Özbirecikli left behind an academic legacy that not only holds quantitative significance but also provides qualitative guidance to the accounting field.

This chapter was previously published in Turkish by Gazi Kitabevi with the ISBN: 978-975-7727-16-7.

G. Kurt (✉)
Ankara Hacı Bayram Veli Üniversitesi, Ankara, Türkiye
e-mail: ganite.kurt@hbv.edu.tr

Ö. Sarısoy
Tekirdağ Namık Kemal Üniversitesi, Tekirdağ, Türkiye
e-mail: osarisoy@nku.edu.tr

G. Kurt, Ö. Sarısoy (eds.), *Recent Advancements in Auditing*, Accounting, Finance, Sustainability, Governance & Fraud: Theory and Application,
https://doi.org/10.1007/978-981-95-5811-7_2

Keywords Mehmet Özbirecikli · Academic heritage · Accounting education · Ethics · Accounting history

2.1 Introduction

Accounting is not merely a process of producing numerical information; it is also an area of ethical responsibility that prioritizes transparency, accountability, and the public interest. The reliability of economic systems largely depends on the accuracy, timeliness, and objectivity of accounting information. Therefore, accounting is not only a technically oriented applied field but also a discipline deeply intertwined with the social sciences and inseparable from its cultural and societal context. The development of this discipline is made possible not only by legislation and market dynamics but also by the production of scientific knowledge—that is, through the contributions of academics.

In Türkiye, the academic field of accounting has undergone a rapid transformation since the 1980s. Especially from the 1990s onward, the spread of independent auditing, the emergence of international reporting standards, and the increasing visibility of ethical issues led accounting education and research in a new direction. Within this shift, Prof. Dr. Mehmet Özbirecikli held a significant place as a distinguished scholar who made original contributions to the field through both his academic productivity and ethical sensitivity. Throughout his nearly thirty-year academic career, he conducted numerous studies on a wide range of topics, including accounting education, professional ethics, cost accounting, financial reporting standards, independent auditing, and the history of accounting.

The death of Prof. Dr. Mehmet Özbirecikli in the earthquake disaster that struck Kahramanmaraş, Türkiye, in 2023 and caused widespread devastation across the country was a profound loss for the accounting academia. The primary aim of this study is to systematically evaluate his academic legacy, analyze the extent of his contributions to the literature through thematic categories, and explore how these contributions may inspire future research. Furthermore, the impact he made on the development of young researchers through the graduate theses he supervised has also been taken into consideration.

In this context, the study examines 39 academic articles published by Prof. Dr. Özbirecikli between 2000 and 2022, categorizing them under seven main themes and providing a comprehensive evaluation in terms of content, methodology, and outcomes. The objective is not merely to provide a numerical inventory but to holistically present his qualitative contributions, including his emphasis on ethics, social responsibility, and educational engagement, that stood out in his research.

2.2 Life of Integrity: The Personal and Human Story of Prof. Dr. Mehmet Özbirecikli

Prof. Dr. Mehmet Özbirecikli was born on August 24, 1967, in Gaziantep. Throughout his primary, secondary, and high school education, which he completed in Gaziantep, he was raised with values such as honesty, diligence, and social responsibility, instilled in him by his family and environment. These values became firmly embedded in his character from an early age.

Özbirecikli graduated in 1985 from the Department of Business Administration at Bursa Uludağ University's Faculty of Economics and Administrative Sciences. During his student years, he distinguished himself through his intellectual curiosity, academic discipline, and critical thinking. He did not settle for theoretical knowledge alone; instead, he began to construct a scholarly identity rooted in critical thinking.

He pursued his master's degree at the Institute of Social Sciences at Çukurova University. His thesis, defended in 1990 and titled "The Role of Quality Costs in Accounting Systems and Their Effects on Managerial Decisions in Businesses," attracted attention with its holistic approach to integrating quality management into the accounting system. This study offered significant insights not only in accounting but also in the field of strategic management.

Later, returning to Çukurova University for his doctoral studies, Özbirecikli completed his dissertation in 1997, titled "The Relationship Between Internal Control Systems and Internal Auditing in Businesses: A Model Proposal." In this work, he analyzed the functionality of internal audit systems within institutions in Türkiye, both theoretically and practically. Beyond its academic contribution, the dissertation offered practice-oriented suggestions and models that shed light on the profession and served as a foundational reference for subsequent research. His doctoral work stood out for its interdisciplinary approach, methodological rigor, and academic originality.

Özbirecikli began his academic career in 1993 as a research assistant at Hatay Mustafa Kemal University. Over time, he became recognized within his professional circle as a trustworthy scholar, dedicated to knowledge and committed to collaborative work. Although he achieved the titles of associate professor in 2003 and full professor in 2009, these academic promotions were, for him, merely instruments of learning rather than goals in themselves (Fig. 2.1).

One of the most defining characteristics of Prof. Dr. Özbirecikli was his modesty in the face of success. He never sought to assert authority nor used his position as a symbol of superiority. In both his work and interpersonal relationships, values such as sharing, fairness, and openness were always at the forefront. Conversations with him conveyed more than just the transfer of knowledge—they offered a sense of mentorship and companionship. Those close to him, including his students, often described him with attributes such as "objective," "fair," "transparent," "positive," "inquisitive," "investigative," and "scientific," which genuinely reflect the legacy he left behind.

Fig. 2.1 Prof. Dr. Mehmet Özbirecikli

Just as he upheld ethical principles in his academic publications, he also made them a cornerstone of his daily life. He believed that sharing knowledge was a moral duty and was frequently recognized for his willingness to share information with young academics and practitioners. In every educational setting where he taught, he emphasized the importance of professional ethics, personal integrity, and intellectual honesty. The most enduring impact he had on those who admired him was not only his scholarly competence but also his profound moral stance (Fig. 2.2).

Fig. 2.2 Prof. Dr. Mehmet Özbirecikli

Tragically, this exemplary life came to an end on February 6, 2023, when the apartment building where he resided in Hatay collapsed due to the devastating earthquake centered in Kahramanmaraş, Türkiye. He and his beloved wife, Rana Özbirecikli, lost their lives in the disaster. This loss created a profound void for his family, students, colleagues, and the entire accounting community. In the messages of remembrance written in his honor, what stood out were not only his scholarly contributions but also the deeply human qualities he embodied—his sincerity, integrity, and passion for his work.

This section reflects on the life of Prof. Dr. Mehmet Özbirecikli, not merely as an academic profile but as a life story defined by conviction, ethical integrity, and a deep respect for humanity. He is remembered not just as a name counted by his publication but as a figure who illuminated the present and the future through the values he lived by, the students he mentored, and the bridges he built.

2.3 Scope, Method, and Selection Criteria for the Analysis

This study aims to analyze the scholarly contributions of Prof. Dr. Mehmet Özbirecikli through a qualitative approach, focusing directly on the academic articles he authored. The scope of the analysis consists of a total of 39 articles listed on his Google Scholar profile, all categorized as journal publications. Only those articles for which the complete texts were accessible have been included in the research. Some of his earlier works, published in the early stages of his academic career, were excluded due to their unavailability on digital platforms or lack of open access. Therefore, the scope of this review does not represent the entirety of Prof. Dr. Özbirecikli's publication record but rather a qualified sample of works that could be accessed.

Qualitative research techniques were employed in this study. Each article was examined individually, with summaries provided regarding its subject matter, significance, co-authors (if any), and main findings. Through this systematic evaluation, the study aims to provide a comprehensive overview of Prof. Dr. Özbirecikli's academic orientation, research domains, and scholarly contributions.

2.3.1 General Assessment: Mapping Prof. Dr. Özbirecikli's Publications by Years, Collaborations, Journals, and Themes

Throughout his academic career, Prof. Dr. Mehmet Özbirecikli made significant contributions to the fields of accounting, auditing, and ethics—not only through journal articles and thesis supervision but also through numerous theoretical and practical books. Particularly, his books, which have become essential reference sources in the literature, are widely used in both graduate education and professional practice. These works are notable for bridging the gap between theoretical frameworks and practical applications. In addition, the papers he presented at various international congresses and symposiums contributed to the global representation of the Turkish accounting academia and facilitated participation in current scholarly debates. Although these books and papers are not examined within the scope of this study, they represent valuable academic outputs that merit separate, in-depth investigations. In this regard, Prof. Dr. Özbirecikli's academic legacy is noteworthy not only in terms of quantity but also in terms of its breadth, impact, and contribution to the literature.

The 22 graduate theses supervised by Prof. Dr. Mehmet Özbirecikli between 2000 and 2022 demonstrate his capacity for academic mentorship and his skill in guiding research. An examination of the thesis topics reveals a strong alignment with his areas of expertise, such as accounting, auditing, internal control systems, cost accounting, and ethics. The emphasis on field research conducted in Antakya and Hatay indicates that he encouraged his students to engage in applied studies within local economic contexts, thereby reflecting a dual aim of transferring theoretical knowledge to practice and contributing to regional development. Moreover, the fact that some of these theses were later transformed into academic articles is evidence that his supervision was not superficial but rather part of a high-quality process culminating in scholarly output. In this respect, Prof. Dr. Özbirecikli left a lasting impact not only through his academic achievements but also through his efforts in cultivating new generations of researchers (Council of Higher Education [YÖK], n.d.).

An examination of Table 2.1, which presents citation information, reveals that Prof. Dr. Mehmet Özbirecikli was not only a prolific scholar but also one whose work consistently demonstrated high quality and was frequently cited. The fact that both his h-index and i10-index values are high—both in total and in recent years—demonstrates the sustained impact of his research and its enduring presence in the literature. This influence within academic circles points to the existence of a scientific foundation that serves as a guide in both educational and practical accounting studies.

A review of Prof. Dr. Mehmet Özbirecikli's academic publication history indicates a consistent and long-term pattern of scholarly output. His publications

Table 2.1 Citation and indexing metrics of Prof. Dr. Özbirecikli

Google scholar	All	Since 2020
Citations	1134	410
h-index	22	11
i10-index	31	13

Source (Google Scholar, n.d.)

began in 1995 and continued without interruption until 2023. The years in which he published the highest number of articles were 2006 and 2018, with five articles published in each of those years. (It should be noted that Prof. Dr. Özbirecikli also authored numerous books, conference papers, and theses beyond the 39 articles examined in this study. Since the present research is limited to these 39 articles, the assessment should be interpreted within that scope.) He published four articles in 2016 and two articles each in 2004, 2005, 2009, 2020, and 2022. These data indicate a notable increase in research productivity in the mid-2000s and the late 2010s. The rise in publications during these periods coincides with years in which academic accumulation became institutionalized and interdisciplinary approaches gained prominence (Table 2.2).

In terms of journal preferences, it is evident that Prof. Dr. Mehmet Özbirecikli primarily focused on academic journals with themes centered on accounting and finance. The journal in which he published the most articles is the *Journal of Accounting and Finance*, with a total of 11 publications. This is followed by "*The World of Accounting Science*," where eight of his studies were published. In third place is the *Accounting and Auditing Review*, which includes 3 of his articles. This distribution indicates that his scholarly interests within the field of accounting were particularly concentrated on topics such as cost accounting, ethics, independent auditing, educational processes, and institutional structuring. In addition, several of his works have appeared in other outlets, including the *Journal of Economics, Business and Finance*, the *Journal of Business Research–Turk*, the *Karadeniz Technical University Journal of Social Sciences*, and internationally indexed publications. This diversity reflects both his strong presence in the national academic community and his intent to engage with international scholarly audiences.

An examination of his co-authored works reveals that Prof. Dr. Özbirecikli valued collaborative research as much as individual scholarship—notably, his partnership with İ. Kıymetli Şen stands out, with four co-authored publications. He also collaborated with scholars such as T. Ural, B.A. Adana, C. Süslü, G. Mayil, Y. Karaömer, and O. Güvemli. These academic partnerships demonstrate his ability to find common ground with both experienced colleagues and emerging academics from different institutions. Moreover, most of these collaborations are concentrated in thematic areas such as ethics, accounting education, auditing, and financial structures. In this regard, Özbirecikli contributed to the field of accounting not only through his research but also through knowledge sharing and academic mentorship.

In conclusion, Mehmet Özbirecikli's publication profile throughout his academic career is characterized by disciplinary depth, methodological diversity, and institutional engagement. His sustained scholarly output over many years, combined with his continuous contributions to the accounting and finance literature, had a significant impact on both the development of the field and the shaping of professional practice.

Table 2.2 Included in the Analysis

No	Year	Author(s)	Title	Journal
M1	1995	Özbirecikli, M.	A new approach in cost accounting: activity-based costing system	Journal of Çukurova University Faculty of Economics and Administrative Sciences
M2	1998	Özbirecikli, M., Kakilli, S.	A Study on the effectiveness of accounting education and methodological suggestions for accounting instruction	Journal of Management and Economics
M3	2002	Özbirecikli, M., Ölçer, F.	Strategy-focused performance measurement system: balanced scorecard-BSC	Istanbul University Journal of the School of Business Administration
M4	2004	Özbirecikli, M., Mayıl, G.	A study to determine the extent to which stock market rumors about price changes materialize in stocks traded on the Istanbul Stock Exchange (ISE)—Part I	Journal of Accounting and Finance
M5	2004	Özbirecikli, M., Mayıl, G.	A Study to determine the extent to which stock market rumors about price changes materialize in stocks traded on the Istanbul Stock Exchange (ISE)—Part II	Journal of Accounting and Finance
M6	2005	Özbirecikli, M., Süslü, C.	Auditing firms' fraud risk assessment practices and comparative research on the auditing firms in Turkey-I	Journal of Accounting and Finance
M7	2005	Özbirecikli, M., Süslü, C.	Auditing firms' fraud risk assessment practices and a comparative research on the auditing firms in Turkey-II	Journal of Accounting and Finance
M8	2006	Özbirecikli, M.	Environmental, ethical, and social auditing: a comparative review on global initiatives and practices in Türkiye	Journal of Accounting and Finance
M9	2006	Özbirecikli, M., Ural, T.	Determination and evaluation of the unethical behaviors encountered in the accounting profession: the case of Turkey	Economics, Business, Finance
M10	2006	Özbirecikli, M.	Behavior of independent auditor against fraudulence of client: a review from perspectives of corporate fraudulent cases and legal regulations	Accounting and Auditing Review

(continued)

Table 2.2 (continued)

No	Year	Author(s)	Title	Journal
M11	2006	Ural, T., Özbirecikli, M.	Is ethical judgement influenced by social desirability İn responding? An analyze on Turkish accountants.	Çukurova University Social Sciences Institute Journal
M12	2007	Özbirecikli, M., Ural, T.	Perception of the importance of ethics and social responsibility in accountants' decision-making process: the study of Turkey	Economics, Business, Finance
M13	2007	Özbirecikli, M.	The framework of International Education Standards for Professional Accountants	Journal of Accounting and Finance
M14	2008	Özbirecikli, M., Coşkun, A.A.	Is tax amnesty a palliative solution or permanent problem source? An investigation on the tax amnesty law no: 4811: the example of Hatay	Journal of Accounting and Finance
M15	2009	Özbirecikli, M.	Education levels of professional accountants: an investigation on changes from 1992 to present	Journal of Accounting and Finance
M16	2009	Özbirecikli, M., Pastacıgil, A.	The development process of accountants education in Turkey: a comparative analysis with the IFAC standards	Journal of Accounting and Finance
M17	2010	Özbirecikli, M.	The institutions forming the socioeconomic structure of Turkish private enterprises between the 13th and the nineteenth centuries: Akhism, The Lonca System and the Gedik System	Pecunia: Revista de la Facultad de Ciencias Económicas Empresariales
M18	2011	Özbirecikli, M.	The first course books on double-entry accounting in the Ottoman era	Centro Studi Mario Pancrazi
M19	2011	Özbirecikli, M., Güvemli, B.	Can the regulations prevent the unethical behaviors of in accounting profession? A philosophical approach on the case of Türkiye	International Journal of Economics and Accounting
M20	2011	Güvemli, O., Özbirecikli, M.	The development process of external audit in Turkey: 1990–2010	Accounting and Financial History Research Journal
M21	2012	Sanlı, N., Özbirecikli, M.	The development process of the auditing profession in Türkiye: a historical and future-oriented study	Accounting and Auditing Review
M22	2015	Özbirecikli, M., Tüm, K., Keskin, İ.	A research study on the applications of the internal control system in manufacturing companies: the case of Antakya	The World of Accounting Science

(continued)

Table 2.2 (continued)

No	Year	Author(s)	Title	Journal
M23	2016	Özbirecikli, M., Öksüz, N.	A research study on the institutional errors enabling occupational fraud and abuse in manufacturing companies: the case of Hatay	The World of Accounting Science
M24	2016	Özbirecikli, M., Karaömer, Y.	The role of operational audit on institutionalization of family companies: the case of a company	Karadeniz Technical University Journal of Social Sciences
M25	2016	Özbirecikli, M., Jinnai, J., Cika, N.	Can types of wrongdoings and the corruption perception scores be criteria to define audit thresholds for non-listed companies? the cases of Turkey, Japan and Albania	The World of Accounting Science
M26	2016	Özbirecikli, M., Güven, G.	A research study on the costing methods used by the restaurants: the case of Antakya	The World of Accounting Science
M27	2018	Kırıtoğlu, C., Özbirecikli, M.	A survey on the effects of ethics training for auditors on auditors' perception of accounting fraud	Journal of Accounting & Taxation Studies
M28	2018	Özbirecikli, M., Kıymetli Şen, İ.	Ethics education and vocational training process of accounting and auditing professions in Turkey: A historical perspective	The World of Accounting Science
M29	2018	Özbirecikli, M., Tüfekçi, L.M.	A research study on cost accounting practices in the furniture sector: the case of Antakya	Journal of Business Research
M30	2018	Kıymetli Şen, İ., Özbirecikli, M.	Changes the FRS for LMSE FRS has brought to accounting practices: an investigation on FRS for LMSE, IAS/IFRS and current local accounting system	Journal of Accounting & Taxation Studies
M31	2018	Özbirecikli, M., Kıymetli Şen, İ.	The education-related developments in accounting profession in Turkey: a comparative review with international education standards	The World of Accounting Science
M32	2019	Karaömer, Y., Özbirecikli, M.	Effects of financial reporting differences in between FRS for LMSE and MSUGT on financial statement analysis: an investigation on financial structure ratios	Journal of Accounting and Finance
M33	2020	Kıymetli Şen, İ., Özbirecikli, M.	The potential benefits the IFRS for SMEs can ensure for businesses: a comparative investigation on FRS for LMSE, IAS/IFRS and current local accounting system	The World of Accounting Science

(continued)

Table 2.2 (continued)

No	Year	Author(s)	Title	Journal
M34	2020	Adana, B., A., Özbirecikli, M.	Evaluation of independent audit process in terms of effects of COVID-19 pandemic	Journal of Business Research
M35	2021	Adana, B.A., Özbirecikli, M.	An investigation on the legal regulations for transfer pricing practices during the COVID-19 pandemic	International Journal of Business, Economics and Management Perspectives
M36	2022	Özbirecikli, M., Kaya, M.	A research study on the institutional structure and cost accounting applications of shoe manufacturing enterprises: the case of Antakya	Journal of Accounting and Finance
M37	2022	Özbirecikli, M., Sayar, A.R.Z., Türkoğlu, A. E.	A research study on the education need of accounting professionals for accounting standards and independent audit activity	Accounting and Auditing Review
M38	2023	Kırıtoglu, C, Özbirecikli, M.	A scale development study: ethical training for independent auditor types of accounting fraud perception scale of independent auditors	International Social Sciences Studies Journal
M39	2023	Adana, B.A., Özbirecikli, M.	evaluation of concord between financial performance and the footnote explanations on the effects of the COVID-19 pandemic for the year 2020: a comparative investigation on publicly held companies in food and retail sectors and the tourism sector	The World of Accounting Science

2.3.2 Research Topics of the Reviewed Studies

The 39 academic articles authored by Prof. Dr. Mehmet Özbirecikli cover a wide range of content; however, they also reveal strong research tendencies clustered around specific themes (Table 2.3).

The 39 academic articles authored by Prof. Dr. Mehmet Özbirecikli encompass a broad and in-depth range that reflects both the theoretical and practical dimensions of the accounting discipline. His work is particularly concentrated in core areas such as accounting education, auditing, ethics, and cost accounting, while also being enriched by contemporary developments and historical perspectives. Below, these studies are analyzed in detail under seven main categories based on their thematic content:

Table 2.3 Topics of the Reviewed Studies

No	Research Subject
M1	The challenges in allocating indirect costs to products in manufacturing firms were identified, and the Activity-Based Costing (ABC) system was examined.
M2	The effectiveness of accounting education at universities was evaluated, and suggestions for instructional methods were developed.
M3	The fundamental dimensions of strategic performance measurement were analyzed using the Balanced Scorecard (BSC) approach.
M4	The impact of stock market rumors on share prices was examined, and the extent to which the rumors materialized was analyzed.
M5	The influence of news published in stock exchange magazines on ISE-listed stock prices was assessed through frequency analysis.
M6	Methods used by independent audit firms to assess fraud risks were compared through examples from both domestic and international contexts.
M7	The practices developed by audit firms in response to fraud risks were discussed in a cross-country context.
M8	The evolution of environmental and social auditing practices and their implementation in Türkiye and developed countries were compared.
M9	Unethical behaviors observed in the accounting profession were identified and evaluated in light of ethical principles.
M10	The attitudes of independent auditors toward fraud and their reporting responsibilities were examined.
M11	The effect of social desirability on the ethical judgments of Turkish accountants was measured, and a culturally adapted scale was developed.
M12	The perceptions of accountants regarding ethics and social responsibility in decision-making processes were analyzed.
M13	International Education Standards for Accountants were introduced and evaluated in terms of professional competencies.
M14	The impact of the Tax Amnesty Law on tax collection and the judicial burden in Hatay was analyzed.
M15	The educational levels and professional development of accounting professionals after 1992 were examined.
M16	The historical development of accounting education in Türkiye was compared with international standards.
M17	The effects of the Ahi-order, guild, and "gedik" systems on private enterprise structures were historically analyzed.
M18	The first double-entry bookkeeping book published during the Ottoman period was examined.
M19	Unethical behaviors in Türkiye's accounting profession were evaluated from a philosophical perspective.
M20	The development of independent auditing in Türkiye between 1990 and 2011 was examined across five dimensions.
M21	The historical development of the independent auditing profession and its alignment with regulatory frameworks was evaluated.

(continued)

Table 2.3 (continued)

No	Research Subject
M22	Internal control system practices and compliance with auditing standards in manufacturing firms in Antakya were investigated.
M23	Employee fraud and institutional error sources were identified in manufacturing firms.
M24	Performance evaluation criteria and the effectiveness of implementation in family businesses were analyzed.
M25	The relationship between types of fraud and perceptions of corruption, as well as audit thresholds, was examined in Türkiye, Japan, and Albania.
M26	Cost calculation methods, control techniques, and pricing decisions in restaurants located in Antakya were analyzed.
M27	The knowledge and awareness levels of accounting professionals regarding accounting ethics principles were measured.
M28	The historical development of ethics education in the accounting and auditing professions was evaluated.
M29	Cost calculation and control methods in furniture manufacturing firms in Antakya were analyzed.
M30	The innovations brought to accounting practices by the Financial Reporting Standard for Large and Medium-Sized Enterprises (FRS for LMSE) were discussed by comparing them with existing systems.
M31	The transformation in accounting education between 1992 and 2018 was compared with IES standards.
M32	The impact of reporting differences between FRS for LMSE and MSUGT/VUK systems on financial ratios was analyzed.
M33	The potential benefits of IFRS for SMEs were evaluated by comparing them with FRS for LMSE and other systems.
M34	The effects of COVID-19 on the independent audit process and audit reports were analyzed.
M35	The impact of COVID-19 on transfer pricing and legal regulations was examined through a cross-country comparison.
M36	The relationship between the corporate structures of shoe manufacturers and their cost accounting practices was evaluated.
M37	The training needs of accountants in the Eastern Mediterranean regarding IAS/IFRS for LMSE and auditing practices were analyzed.
M38	The effect of ethics education on auditors' ability to perceive types of accounting fraud was measured, and a new scale was developed.
M39	The implications of COVID-19 on financial reporting and audit disclosures in publicly traded companies were examined.

- **Accounting Education (7 articles):** The area most frequently studied by Özbirecikli is accounting education. His work examines both student competencies and the alignment of educational programs with international standards—particularly those set by IFAC and the IES. These studies focus on multidimensional aspects, including ethics education, internship systems, and communication skills. This thematic concentration highlights his contributions not only to the practice of accounting but also to its pedagogical foundations. A total of seven articles explore the training processes of accounting professionals, their educational levels, ethical awareness, and the degree of compliance with international standards. Key issues addressed include the comparison of curricula with IFAC and IES standards, evaluation of teaching effectiveness based on student feedback, the insufficiency of ethics education, problems in internship systems, and deficiencies in communication skills. These studies emphasize that professional education should be reinforced not only with technical knowledge but also with values of ethical and social responsibility.

- **Professional Ethics and Related Sub-Themes (7 articles):** A total of seven articles address the relationship between accounting professionals and ethical values, categorized under "Professional Ethics" (3), "Ethics" (2), "Fraud and Ethics" (1), and "Ethical/Fraud Perceptions" (1). The most violated ethical values in the Turkish accounting profession were found to be integrity and objectivity. These studies also examine the relationship between ethical judgments and social desirability, the impact of ethics education on auditors' perception of fraud and provide philosophical analyses of unethical behavior. They argue that ethical values should be addressed through moral and educational frameworks rather than merely legal ones. This reflects Özbirecikli's high ethical sensitivity and his normative academic orientation.
- **Independent Auditing (6 articles):** The theme of independent auditing is approached through sub-topics such as practical issues, comparisons with international standards, and historical development. This indicates Özbirecikli's strong academic contributions toward the institutionalization of audit culture and its integration with ethical foundations. The six articles focus on both the historical evolution and current practices of the auditing profession. Key focal points include the transformation of Türkiye's audit system from a tax-oriented structure to one aligned with international standards, how audit firms assess fraud risk, and how auditing activities are affected by crises such as COVID-19. The inadequacies of internal control systems and the boundaries of auditor responsibilities are also analyzed. The studies within this theme highlight the crucial role of independent auditing in maintaining institutional trust and promoting economic transparency.
- **Cost Accounting (4 articles):** This theme encompasses topics such as costing systems, activity-based accounting, and sector-specific practices in the manufacturing industry. Field studies conducted primarily in the Antakya region provide a strong empirical dimension and demonstrate the practical relevance of academic research to local businesses. A total of four articles focus on activity-based costing, traditional methods, and strategic cost tools. Applied studies in sectors such as restaurants, furniture manufacturing, and footwear manufacturing in Antakya evaluate the accuracy of cost calculation, pricing, cost control, and the relationship between cost systems and institutional structures. The studies observe the limited use of modern costing systems and the dominance of traditional methods, revealing a gap between academic knowledge and practical application.

- **Accounting Standards (3 articles):** These studies provide comparative analyses of systems such as FRS for LMSE, IFRS for SMEs, MSUGT, and TMS/TFRS. They offer significant insights into Türkiye's compliance with international accounting standards. A key focus is the need for financial reporting standards tailored to small and medium-sized enterprises, highlighting the contributions of FRS for LMSE in terms of consistency and transparency. The comparative analyses question the extent to which Türkiye's accounting system aligns with international norms.
- **Accounting History (2 articles):** These two studies examine the historical development of accounting information systems from the Ottoman era to the present, analyzing traditional organizational forms such as the Ahi order and guild systems. This approach underscores the importance of understanding accounting systems not only in technical terms but also within sociological and historical contexts.

2.4 Other Themes

- *Financial Markets (2 articles):* The effects of stock market rumors on ISE share prices were examined.
- *Performance Measurement (2 articles):* Topics include the Balanced Scorecard and performance criteria in family businesses.
- Topics such as internal control, social and ethical auditing, international comparisons, taxation, transfer pricing, and the effects of COVID-19 are each represented by individual studies. Notably, the recent analyses of post-COVID-19 developments reflect Özbirecikli's strong academic responsiveness to contemporary issues.

This thematic analysis demonstrates that Prof. Dr. Mehmet Özbirecikli adopted a systematic and in-depth research approach, particularly in the areas of accounting education, independent auditing, and ethics. The distribution of his work across theoretical frameworks and practical domains highlights the multidimensional and sustainable nature of his contributions to the accounting academy and professional culture.

2.5 Findings of the Reviewed Studies

The concluding statements of Prof. Dr. Mehmet Özbirecikli's 39 academic publications reveal how theoretical approaches in the field of accounting align with practical applications and identify areas that require further development. A thematic analysis based on these findings is presented below (Table 2.4).

Table 2.4 Findings of the Reviewed Studies

No	Research Results
M1	The ABC system enables more accurate cost calculation in complex production processes.
M2	The effectiveness of accounting instruction is low; it should be improved through the use of updated content and practice-oriented methods.
M3	Compared to traditional measurement systems, the Balanced Scorecard provides a more comprehensive and strategic approach to performance evaluation.
M4	Stock market rumors can influence investment decisions; however, the market does not function with full efficiency.
M5	News containing rumors has been observed to cause short-term effects on stock prices.
M6	Audit practices require further development and structural organization to align with international standards.
M7	Methodological differences in auditing indicate a lack of standardization in practice.
M8	Strong risk management and control systems are vital for corporate success and investor confidence.
M9	Honesty and objectivity are the most frequently violated ethical values; there is a need to strengthen professional oversight.
M10	Auditors should follow a gradual and careful process in detecting fraud.
M11	Ethical judgments are generally unaffected by social desirability; however, personal interests may occasionally influence them.
M12	Accountants with high ethical awareness make more informed ethical decisions; as experience increases, so does their judgment strength.
M13	IFAC standards are partially implemented in Türkiye; however, deficiencies persist, particularly in ethics education.
M14	Although tax amnesties yield short-term benefits, their effects are not lasting, and the same problems tend to re-emerge.
M15	Education levels have increased over time, and legal regulations have had a positive effect on professional quality.
M16	Accounting education in Türkiye has moved closer to IFAC standards, but structural shortcomings remain.
M17	Historical systems have shaped business ethics and educational approaches, and their impact is still evident today.
M18	The first accounting book contained fundamental elements of the double-entry system but did not fully reflect modern practices.
M19	Unethical behaviors often contradict professional principles, and awareness among practitioners remains low.
M20	Independent auditing has evolved from a tax-oriented structure into a broad-based system aligned with international standards.
M21	Over time, auditing has become an indispensable tool for economic transparency and institutional trust.

(continued)

Table 2.4 (continued)

No	Research Results
M22	Significant deficiencies have been identified in internal control systems, with key components inadequately implemented.
M23	Lack of trust in employees and insufficient internal controls increase the risk of fraud; these controls are not being effectively applied.
M24	Unclear performance criteria reduce motivation and make evaluations more subjective.
M25	Although fraud types vary by country, they are not directly applicable as audit threshold indicators.
M26	Restaurants make limited use of cost calculation methods; raw material costs are the most decisive factor.
M27	General knowledge of ethical principles is high, but implementation is lacking in certain areas.
M28	Ethics education should be supported not only by legislation but also through value-based and applied approaches.
M29	Furniture manufacturers primarily use traditional costing methods; strategic cost tools are rarely employed.
M30	FRS for LMSE is primarily compatible with international standards, enhancing the quality of financial reporting.
M31	Accounting education has improved overall, but areas such as communication and ethical reasoning still need enhancement.
M32	There are significant differences among systems, and these differences directly affect financial analysis.
M33	IFRS for SMEs provides straightforward, transparent, and comparable reporting options for small and medium-sized enterprises.
M34	The pandemic disrupted audit processes, which now require restructuring following the International Standards on Auditing (ISA).
M35	During the COVID-19 pandemic, many countries implemented temporary regulations, including digitalization and reporting deadline extensions.
M36	A meaningful relationship was found between the level of institutionalization and cost control methods.
M37	Training programs supported by practice-oriented examples increase effectiveness; experience enhances knowledge levels.
M38	Auditors who received ethics training demonstrated a higher awareness of various types of accounting fraud.
M39	Despite the pandemic, audit reports generally reflected the actual financial status of businesses.

Prof. Dr. Özbirecikli's studies yielded multifaceted findings shaped by both quantitative and qualitative approaches and made significant contributions to both the theoretical and practical domains of accounting science.

Primarily, research focused on education and ethics revealed that accounting professionals exhibit limited ethical awareness and that ethical behavior must be supported not only through legal regulations but also through value-based and practice-oriented education (M11, M12, M27, M28, M38). These findings suggest that professional and ethical challenges are more closely tied to awareness and value systems than to technical knowledge deficiencies.

Studies related to accounting education emphasize that the effectiveness of instruction remains low (M2), complete alignment with international standards such as those of IFAC has not been achieved (M13, M16), and further development is needed in areas like communication skills and ethical reasoning (M31, M37). On the other hand, it has been noted that educational levels have improved over time, positively influencing professional quality (M15). This suggests that, despite efforts toward improvement, structural problems persist.

Studies on independent auditing demonstrate that the auditing system in Türkiye has evolved from a tax-focused structure toward alignment with international standards (M20), that variations in practice create issues of standardization (M6, M7), and that regulations such as International Standards on Auditing (ISA) need to be reconsidered, particularly in times of crisis such as during the Covid-19 pandemic (M34, M39). The responsibility and caution required of auditors in fraud detection are also emphasized (M10).

In cost accounting and practice-based studies, particularly those involving manufacturing enterprises (e.g., restaurants, furniture, footwear), it has been observed that traditional methods are predominant, and modern, strategic systems are used only to a limited extent (M26, M29, M36). This highlights the need for more advanced accounting systems to support decision-making processes in businesses.

Findings related to accounting standards and financial reporting indicate that Türkiye's regulatory frameworks (e.g., FRS for LMSE, IFRS for SMEs) are essentially in alignment with international practices (M30, M33). However, differences among these systems can significantly impact financial analysis and decision-making (M32).

The identification of unethical behavior (M9, M19), deficiencies in internal control systems (M22, M23), cross-country differences in fraud perceptions (M25), and the effectiveness of legal adjustments made during the pandemic (M35) all point to important gaps in practical implementation.

Finally, historical studies (M17, M18) serve as a reminder that the accounting system in Türkiye is not merely a technical framework but is also built upon historical and cultural foundations. In summary:

- Most studies are practice-oriented, supported by field data, and include normative evaluations.
- Ethics, auditing, and education are the most frequently discussed themes in the findings.
- Academic responsiveness to current crises, such as COVID-19, reflects the scholar's scientific sensitivity.
- The findings support not only professional development but also provide data that can inform policymakers in the pursuit of systemic transformation.

2.6 Conclusion and Evaluation

This study aimed to examine the scholarly legacy of Prof. Dr. Mehmet Özbirecikli—an influential figure in the development of accounting science in Türkiye, known for his academic productivity and humanistic stance—through thematic and methodological lenses. The 39 academic articles he published between 2000 and 2022 reflect not only quantitative significance but also a comprehensive, ethics-based, and reform-oriented scholarly approach.

The analyzed works primarily focus on accounting education, independent auditing, and professional ethics. They critically address practical challenges and offer solution-oriented and normative recommendations. Prof. Dr. Özbirecikli's research contributed to aligning accounting education with international standards (particularly those of IFAC and IES), enhancing the ethical sensitivity of accounting professionals, and promoting transparency in audit processes. His applied studies on cost accounting, internal control systems, and financial reporting standards are exemplary cases of field-based knowledge production, addressing real-world issues faced by local enterprises from an academic perspective.

The theses he supervised further reflect his pedagogical orientation, his role as a mentor to young researchers, and his unwavering commitment to scientific ethics. Most of these theses are based on fieldwork and are of a quality that contributes not only to academic literature but also to practitioners. In this respect, Prof. Dr. Özbirecikli generated scholarly impact not only through his research performance but also through the researchers and professionals he helped shape.

Tragically, Prof. Dr. Özbirecikli passed away prematurely in the devastating earthquake that struck Türkiye in 2023. However, he left behind more than just published works—he bequeathed a scientific stance shaped by principle and a profoundly human legacy. Beyond his academic contributions, he is remembered for his ethical conduct, humility, and genuine care for his students. The purpose of this study has been to honor his name, document his contributions, and provide inspiration for future generations of researchers.

In conclusion, the scholarly legacy of Prof. Dr. Mehmet Özbirecikli—grounded in theoretical depth, practical awareness, and an ethics-based approach—will continue to illuminate the future of the accounting academy. Honoring his memory is not only a gesture of gratitude but also a commitment to sustaining an academic perspective that is qualified, responsible, and oriented toward the public good.

References

Adana BA, Özbirecikli M (2020) Bağımsız denetim sürecinin Covid-19 salgınının etkileri açısından değerlendirilmesi. İşletme Araştırmaları Dergisi 12(2):2080–2093

Adana BA, Özbirecikli M (2021) COVID-19 salgını sürecinde transfer fiyatlandırması uygulamalarına yönelik yasal düzenlemeler üzerine bir inceleme. In *VI. International Symposium on Accounting and Finance ISAF 2021*. 127

Adana BA, & Özbirecikli M (2023) COVID-19 SALGINININ ETKİLERİNE YÖNELİK 2020 YILI DİPNOT AÇIKLAMALARI İLE FİNANSAL PERFORMANS ARASINDAKİ UYUMUN DEĞERLENDİRİLMESİ: GIDA VE PERAKENDE İLE TURİZM SEKTÖRLERİNDEKİ HALKA AÇIK ŞİRKETLER ÜZERİNE MUKAYESELİ BİR İNCELEME. Muhasebe Bilim Dünyası Dergisi 25(MODAVICA Özel Sayısı):413–434

Google Scholar. (n.d.). *Mehmet Özbirecikli – Citations profile*. Retrieved June 18, 2025, from https://scholar.google.com/citations?user=Wm1P9LgAAAAJ&hl=en

Güvemli O, & Özbirecikli M (2011) The development process of external audit in Turkey: 1990–2010. Accounting and Financial History Research Journal 1:146–180

Karaömer Y, Özbirecikli M (2019) Effects of financial reporting differences in between BOBİ FRS and MSUGT on financial statement analysis: an investigation on financial structure ratios. Muhasebe ve Finansman Dergisi 84:233–250

Kırıtoğlu C, Özbirecikli M (2018) Bağımsız denetçilere yönelik etik eğitiminin bağımsız denetçilerin muhasebe hilelerini algılamalarına etkisi üzerine bir araştırma. Muhasebe Ve Vergi Uygulamaları Dergisi 11(1)

Kırıtoğlu C, Özbirecikli M (2023) Bir ölçek geliştirme çalışması: bağımsız denetçilere yönelik etik eğitiminin bağımsız denetçilerin muhasebe hile türleri algı ölçeği. Int Soc Sci Stud J 9 (107):4952–4960. https://doi.org/10.29228/sssj.67544

Kıymetli Şen İ, & Özbirecikli M (2018) Changes the FRS for LMSE FRS has brought to accounting practices: an investigation on FRS for LMSE, IAS/IFRS and current local accounting system. Muhasebe ve Vergi Uygulamalari Dergisi (MUVU)/Journal of Accounting & Taxation Studies (JATS), April (2018):462–484

Kıymetli Şen İ, & Özbirecikli M (2020) KÜMİ FRS'nin iş dünyasına sağlayabileceği yararlar: BOBİ FRS, TMS/TFRS ve mevcut muhasebe sistemi ile mukayeseli bir inceleme. Muhasebe Bilim Dünyası Dergisi, ÖS 1:1–19

Kurulu Y (YÖK). (n.d.). *National Thesis Center*. Retrieved June 18, 2025, from https://tez.yok.gov.tr/UlusalTezMerkezi/tezSorguSonucYeni.jsp

Özbirecikli M (1995) Maliyet muhasebesinde yeni bir yaklaşım: faaliyet esasına dayalı maliyetleme sistemi. Çukurova Üniversitesi İİBF Dergisi 5(1)

Özbirecikli M (2006) Çevresel etik ve sosyal denetim: küresel girişimler ve Türkiye'deki uygulamalar üzerine mukayeseli bir inceleme. Muhasebe ve Finansman Dergisi 31:62–77

Özbirecikli M (2007) Ana hatlarıyla IFAC muhasebeci eğitimi standartları. Muhasebe ve Finansman Dergisi 33:73–80

Özbirecikli M (2009) Muhasebe meslek mensuplarının eğitim düzeyleri: 1992'den günümüze bir inceleme. Muhasebe ve Finansman Dergisi 43:80–84

Özbirecikli M (2010) The institutions forming the socioeconomic structure of Turkish private enterprises between the 13th and the nineteenth centuries: akhism, the lonca system and the gedik system. Pecunia Rev Fac Cienc Econ Empres 11:135–152

Özbirecikli M (2011) The first course was on double-entry accounting in the Ottoman era. *Before and After Luca Pacioli*. https://www.centrostudimariopancrazi.it/images/pubblicazioni/before_and_after_luca_pacioli/28.pdf

Özbirecikli M, Coşkun AA (2008) Vergi affı geçici bir çözüm mü yoksa kalıcı bir sorun kaynağı mı? 4811 sayılı VBK çerçevesinde bir inceleme: hatay örneği. Muhasebe ve Finansman Dergisi 37:39–50

Özbirecikli M, Güvemli B (2011) Can the regulations prevent the unethical behaviours in accounting profession? A philosophical approach on the case of Türkiye. Int J Econ Account 2(4):314–334

Özbirecikli M, Güven G (2016) Lokantalarda kullanılan maliyet hesaplama yöntemleri üzerine bir araştırma: Antakya örneği. Muhasebe Bilim Dünyası Dergisi 18(4)

Özbirecikli M, Jinnai J, Cika N (2016) Can types of wrongdoings and the corruption perception scores be criteria to define audit thresholds for non-listed companies? The cases of Turkey, Japan and Albania. Muhasebe Bilim Dünyası Dergisi 18(1):99–126

Özbirecikli M, Kakilli S (1998) Muhasebe öğretiminin etkinliği üzerine bir araştırma ve muhasebe öğretiminde yöntem önerileri. Yönetim Ve Ekonomi Dergisi 4(1):393–414

Özbirecikli M, Karaömer Y (2016) Faaliyet denetiminin aile şirketlerinin kurumsallaşmasındaki rolü: Bir şirket uygulaması. Karadeniz Teknik Üniversitesi Sosyal Bilimler Dergisi 6(11):33–46

Özbirecikli M, Kaya M (2022) Ayakkabı üretim işletmelerinin kurumsal yapısı ve maliyet muhasebesi uygulamaları üzerine bir araştırma: antakya örneği. Muhasebe ve Finansman Dergisi 94:133–150

Özbirecikli M, Mayıl G (2004) İMKB'deki hisse senetlerinin fiyat değişimine ilişkin borsa söylentilerinin gerçekleşme düzeyini tespite yönelik bir araştırma-I. Muhasebe ve Finansman Dergisi

Özbirecikli M, Mayıl G (2004) İMKB'deki hisse senetlerinin fiyat değişimine ilişkin borsa söylentilerinin gerçekleşme düzeyini tespite yönelik bir araştırma-II. Muhasebe ve Finansman Dergisi

Özbirecikli M, Öksüz N (2016) Üretim işletmelerinde çalışan hilelerine imkân sağlayan kurumsal hatalar üzerine bir araştırma: Hatay örneği. Muhasebe Bilim Dünyası Dergisi 18

Özbirecikli M, Ölçer F (2002) Strateji odaklı performans ölçüm sistemi: balanced Scorecard-BSC. İstanbul Üniversitesi İşletme Fakültesi Dergisi 31(2)

Özbirecikli M, Pastacıgil A (2009) Türkiye'de muhasebeci eğitiminin gelişim süreci: IFAC standartları ile mukayeseli bir inceleme. Muhasebe ve Finansman Dergisi 41:82–97

Özbirecikli M, Şen İK (2018). Ethics education and vocational training process of accounting and auditing professions in Turkey: a historical perspective

Özbirecikli M, Şen İK (2018) The education-related developments in accounting profession in Turkey: a comparative review with international education standards. Muhasebe Bilim Dünyası Dergisi 20:266–293

Özbirecikli M, Süslü C (2005) Bağımsız denetim firmalarının yolsuzluk riski faktörlerini değerleme uygulamaları ve Türkiye'deki bağımsız denetim firmaları üzerine karşılaştırmalı bir araştırma-I. Muhasebe ve Finansman Dergisi 27:67–85

Özbirecikli M, Süslü C (2005) Bağımsız denetim firmalarının yolsuzluk riski faktörlerini değerleme uygulamaları ve Türkiye'deki bağımsız denetim firmaları üzerine karşılaştırmalı bir araştırma-II. Muhasebe ve Finansman Dergisi 28:48–66

Özbirecikli M, Tüfekçi LM (2018) Mobilyacılık sektöründe maliyet muhasebesi uygulamaları üzerine bir araştırma: antakya örneği. İşletme Araştırmaları Dergisi 10(2):512–533

Özbirecikli M, Tüm K, Keskin İ (2015) Üretim işletmelerinde iç kontrol sistemi uygulamaları üzerine bir araştırma: antakya örneği. Muhasebe Bilim Dünyası Dergisi 17(3):497–524

Özbirecikli M, Ural T (2006) Muhasebe mesleğinde yaşanan etikdışı davranışların tespiti ve etiksel değerlendirmesi: türkiye örneği. Iktisat, Işletme Ve Finans 21(248):102–119

Özbirecikli M, Ural T (2007) Muhasebecilerin mesleki kararlarında etik ve sosyal sorumluluğun önemini algılama düzeyleri ve etiksel karar alma süreci: türkiye örneği. Iktisat, Işletme Ve Finans 22(254):104–127

Özbirecikli M, Zafer Sayar ARZ, Türkoğlu AE (2022) Muhasebe meslek mensuplarının muhasebe ve bağımsız denetim standartlarına yönelik eğitim ihtiyacı üzerine bir araştırma. Muhasebe Ve Denetime Bakış 67:1–20. https://doi.org/10.55322/mdbakis.1120509

Sanlı N, & Özbirecikli M (2012) TÜRKİYE'DE DENETİM MESLEĞİNİN GELİŞİM SÜRECİ: GEÇMİŞTEN GELECEĞE BİR ARAŞTIRMA. Muhasebe ve Denetime Bakış 38:1–28

Part II
Audit Theory Through the Eyes of MUDEP Academics

Chapter 3
Audit Procedures Disclosed Under Key Audit Matters: An Analysis of Auditor Reports From Bist-listed Manufacturing Companies

Ayşegül Ciğer

Abstract This study examines the audit procedures disclosed under Key Audit Matters (KAMs) in the independent auditor reports of manufacturing companies listed on Borsa Istanbul (BIST). The primary aim is to identify and classify the audit procedures applied to the five most frequently reported KAMs: Revenue, Trade Receivables, Inventories, Property, Plant and Equipment (PPE), and Investment Properties. The sample consists of 169 companies and covers audit reports for the fiscal years 2018 and 2019. The originality of the study lies in its dual-method approach. Unlike many prior studies that focus merely on the quantity or presence of KAMs, this research conducts a two-tier analysis: (1) a qualitative content analysis of the audit procedures disclosed in each KAM, and (2) a systematic classification of these procedures based on ISA 500 audit procedure types (e.g., inspection, inquiry, external confirmation, recalculation). This framework allows for the evaluation of how auditors apply risk-based thinking in practice and whether their disclosures reflect firm-specific responses and professional judgment. Property, Plant and Equipment (PPE) emerged as one of the most technically complex KAMs, with frequent use of recalculation, impairment analysis, and reliance

Throughout the chapter, the audience should refer to the following standard for the International Standards on Auditing (ISAs). International Federation of Accountants (IFAC, 2025), Handbook of the International Quality Management, Auditing, Review, Other Assurance and Related Service Pronouncements, 2025 Edition, September 24, 2025, https://www.iaasb.org/publications/2025-handbook-international-quality-management-auditing-review-other-assurance-and-related-services (Accessed on Jan 3rd, 2026). For access to the standard, please link to https://ifacweb.blob.core.windows.net/publicfiles/2025-09/IAASB-2025-Handbook-Volume-1.pdf

This chapter was previously published in Turkish by Gazi Kitabevi with the ISBN: 978–975-7727-16-7.

A. Ciğer (✉)
Faculty of Applied Sciences, Department of Finance and Banking, Akdeniz University, Antalya, Türkiye
e-mail: aysegulc@akdeniz.edu.tr

G. Kurt, Ö. Sarısoy (eds.), *Recent Advancements in Auditing*, Accounting, Finance, Sustainability, Governance & Fraud: Theory and Application,
https://doi.org/10.1007/978-981-95-5811-7_3

on expert valuations. It also ranked second in terms of procedural diversity—reporting 24 distinct audit procedures—following inventories. This indicates that PPE auditing requires more sophisticated techniques and reflects higher levels of auditor involvement. The findings reveal a high level of standardization and repetition in the way audit procedures are presented, regardless of company, sector, or fiscal year. While some disclosures are specific and clear, others are vague or formulaic, diminishing the communicative value of KAMs and falling short of ISA 701's transparency goals. Overall, the study offers a novel lens for evaluating audit reporting quality and provides practical insights into enhancing transparency and auditor accountability in emerging capital markets.

Keywords Audit disclosure quality · Auditor judgment · Audit procedures · Audit reports · Emerging market auditing · Key audit matters

3.1 Introduction

According to Independent Auditing Standard (IAS) 200, *"Overall Objectives of the Independent Auditor and the Conduct of an Audit in Accordance with International Standards on Auditing"*, the objective of an audit is to enhance the degree of confidence of intended users in the financial statements. This is achieved by expressing an opinion on whether the financial statements are prepared, in all material respects, in accordance with the applicable financial reporting framework. In other words, the auditor is expected to provide an impartial opinion on the validity of the company's financial statements and to offer reasonable assurance that the financial statements are free from material misstatement.

Accordingly, the auditor bears the responsibility to plan the audit (risk assessment); to design a program, collect audit evidence, and evaluate it (responding to assessed risks); and finally, to report the conclusions appropriately and express an audit opinion. In this respect, the audit process is a systematic and dynamic undertaking, which requires the auditor to design audit procedures based on professional judgment in order to establish a reasonable assurance level that is both objective and accurate. Essentially, the audit process can be described as a set of audit procedures. These procedures consist of the actions, tests, and processes planned and performed by the auditor to obtain sufficient and appropriate audit evidence. Audit procedures may vary depending on the sector in which the entity operates and the auditor's specific approach.

In recent years, particularly following the global accounting and auditing scandals of the 2000s, *Independent Auditing Standards* were developed and issued with the aim of restoring trust in financial statements and enhancing audit quality. Within this framework, audit procedures hold a critical place. In addition to the standards specifically dedicated to audit procedures—such as ISA 330 *"The Auditor's Responses to Assessed Risks"*, ISA 500 *"Audit Evidence"*, ISA 501 *"Audit Evidence—Specific Considerations for Selected Items"*, ISA 505 *"External*

Confirmations", and ISA 520 *"Analytical Procedures"*—several other standards also incorporate audit procedures as part of their broader application. One such standard is ISA 701 *"Communicating Key Audit Matters in the Independent Auditor's Report."*

ISA 701 falls under the category of *"Reporting on the Results of an Audit"* and requires the auditor to include a separate section in the auditor's report titled *Key Audit Matters (KAMs)*. The International Auditing and Assurance Standards Board (IAASB) introduced this standard in 2015 to enhance trust in the audit process and in financial reporting, and to improve the communicative value of the auditor's report (Yanık & Karataş, 2017, p. 7). ISA 701 obliges auditors to disclose the key areas of focus (i.e., significant and high-risk areas) identified during the audit, along with the procedures applied in those areas (KPMG 2018, p. 8). In order to foster greater transparency, audit quality, and entity-specific informational value, it is essential that the auditor clearly articulates the significant matters and the related audit procedures within the KAM section.

In conclusion, audit procedures not only generate the evidence upon which the auditor's opinion is based, but also significantly contribute to the quality, transparency, clarity, and communicative value of the auditor's report through the disclosure of KAMs.

The aim of this study is to identify the *audit procedures* disclosed in the *Key Audit Matters* sections of auditor reports issued for manufacturing companies listed on Borsa Istanbul (BIST), and to evaluate their compliance with the criteria outlined in the standard. The study is based on 2019 company data and focuses on the areas most frequently reported as high-risk in both 2018 and 2019: Revenue, Trade Receivables, Inventory, Property, Plant and Equipment, and Investment Property.

The study consists of three main parts. The first section explores the concept, types, and purposes of audit procedures within the framework of auditing standards. The second section explains the purpose of KAMs, how auditors identify and determine KAMs based on specific criteria, and how these matters should be communicated, in accordance with the relevant standard. The third section presents the findings of the empirical research.

3.2 Audit Procedures

The term *procedure* originates from the French language and is defined as a method or a process (Turkish Language Association, n.d.). Another definition describes it as a series of actions that enable something to be done in a usual or correct way—in other words, it is a method for performing a task (Cambridge Dictionary, n.d.; Oxford Learner's Dictionary, n.d.). More concisely, a procedure can be defined as the techniques and instructions required to carry out a process.

Independent auditing is a systematic process that begins with the selection and acceptance of a client engagement and proceeds through planning, gathering audit evidence, and documenting audit work, concluding with the formation of an audit opinion and the communication of the audit report to information users. To carry out the activities within each stage of this process, audit procedures must be developed. Thus, auditing is essentially a process composed of procedures. By applying audit procedures, auditors obtain reasonable assurance that the information presented in the financial statements is accurate and free of material misstatement.

To better understand audit procedures, it is helpful to begin with their definition. In the literature, the terms *audit techniques* and *audit procedures* are often used interchangeably; however, these concepts are distinct. To clarify this distinction, it is useful to define the term *technique* as well. A *procedure* refers to a series of techniques or actions performed in a specific order, while a *technique* refers to specific activities that are observable, measurable, and implemented by users. Moreover, a technique is often a component of a broader procedure (Andiappan and Wan 2020, p. 552). In this context, techniques are practical applications that demonstrate how procedures are executed. Since this study relies on the terminology used in International Standards on Auditing (ISA), the term *audit techniques* will not be used to avoid conceptual confusion.

Audit procedures refer to the methods and actions used by auditors to evaluate management assertions and obtain sufficient appropriate evidence to support their audit opinion on the financial statements (Kaval 2005, p. 141; Kavut et al. 2009, p. 149; Bory 2020). According to another definition, audit procedures are the actions taken by the auditor during the audit to comply with auditing standards (ACCA Global, n.d.). Arens et al. (2014) define audit procedures as detailed instructions for gathering audit evidence during the audit. Karacan and Uygun (2016) describe them as the methods used in tests of control and substantive procedures. Johnstone et al. (2014) define them as the processes, techniques, and methods applied by auditors to obtain audit evidence that enables them to reach conclusions and express their opinion. Another definition describes audit procedures as the steps performed by auditors to gather all necessary information regarding the quality of the financials provided by the company, to determine whether the financial statements fairly present the financial position of the entity (Jain, n.d.). Based on these definitions, audit procedures can be concisely described as actions that demonstrate how audit tasks should be performed.

The efficiency expected from audit procedures and the decision on which procedures to apply are based on the auditor's professional judgment. Assessing risks and designing audit procedures that respond appropriately to those risks requires the application of professional judgment. As a result, the scope, nature, and evaluation of the outcomes of audit procedures may vary according to the auditor's judgment. Furthermore, audit procedures may also vary from client to client and from period to period due to differences in internal control systems over financial reporting and changes in those systems over time.

Well-designed audit procedures not only help auditors carry out their work more effectively, but also contribute to minimizing audit risks (particularly detection risk). Clearly defined procedures assist auditors in obtaining relevant and reliable audit evidence, while also specifying the time and effort required to gather such evidence (Jain, n.d.). Moreover, audit procedures play a crucial role in determining the quality of information presented in the financial statements (Bragg 2019a).

When designing an audit procedure, the auditor must ensure that it includes: the management assertion being tested (see Table 3.1), the procedure itself, and the rationale for performing that procedure (ACCA Global, n.d.). For example, to confirm the physical existence of inventory recorded in the account balance, selected inventory items can be traced back to raw materials through sampling. This procedure provides evidence regarding the existence assertion for inventory.

When documenting audit procedures, auditors should (ACCA Global, n.d.):

- Clearly state the purpose of the procedure;
- Include a relevant assertion term as the basis for performing the procedure;
- Write specific and comprehensible procedures;
- Avoid ambiguous or misleading statements;
- Exclude irrelevant procedures;
- Focus on describing what needs to be done rather than merely restating internal control functions.

In addition to these points, audit procedures must be clear enough for all members of the audit team to fully understand what is required.

The first step in developing an audit procedure is correctly identifying the management assertions to be tested. Procedures designed to obtain audit evidence can be linked to financial statement assertions as shown below. The auditor's ability to assess and respond appropriately to audit risk depends significantly on a thorough understanding of these assertions.

3.2.1 Management Assertions Tested in Audit Procedures

Management assertions refer to the representations made by management concerning *classes of transactions, account balances, and disclosures* presented in the financial statements (see Table 3.1). To provide assurance on an entity's financial statements, the auditor obtains these assertions from management. In essence, the information presented in the financial statements prepared by management constitutes implicit assertions. However, auditors do not rely solely on these assertions; instead, they gather sufficient and appropriate audit evidence to verify the accuracy of such representations.

The auditor must design audit procedures in a manner that reflects the specific risks of the audit engagement and the nature of the management assertions. When structuring the audit procedures according to these assertions, it should be noted that a single audit procedure may provide evidence for one or more management assertions related to an account balance (Johnstone et al. 2014, p. 224).

İşlem sınıfları, hesap bakiyeleri ve sunum ve açıklamalara ilişkin denetim kanıtlarının toplanabilmesi için denetçi gerekli denetim prosedürlerini uygular.

Table 3.1 Management assertions

Assertions Related to Classes of Transactions and Events	Assertions Related to Account Balances	Assertions Related to Presentation and Disclosure (Footnotes)
Occurrence: Recorded transactions and events have occurred and pertain to the entity.	**Existence:** Assets, liabilities, and equity interests exist as of the balance sheet date	**Occurrence, Rights, and Obligations:** Disclosed events, transactions, and other matters have occurred and pertain to the entity.
Completeness: All transactions and events that should have been recorded have been included.	**Rights and Obligations**: The entity holds or controls rights to assets, and liabilities are the obligations of the entity	**Completeness:** All necessary information is disclosed, including footnotes.
Accuracy: Amounts and other data relating to recorded transactions and events have been recorded appropriately.	**Completeness:** All assets, liabilities, and equity interests that should have been recorded have been included.	**Classification and Understandability:** Financial information is appropriately presented, clearly described, and disclosures are adequately explained.
Cut-off: Transactions and events have been recorded in the correct accounting period.	**Valuation and Allocation**: Assets, liabilities, and equity interests are included in the financial statements at appropriate amounts.	**Accuracy and Valuation:** Financial and other information is disclosed fairly and at appropriate amounts.
Classification: Transactions and events have been recorded in the proper accounts.		

Source Adapted Uyar (n.d.); ISA 315

Hangi prosedürlerin nasıl uygulanacağı denetçinin mesleki muhakemesine göre yapacağı değerlendirmeye bağlıdır. (Sağlam ve Yolcu, 2014: 230).

3.2.2 Objectives of Audit Procedures

The objectives of audit procedures are summarized in Fig. 3.1. Audit Procedures

3.2.2.1 Risk Assessment Procedures

The audit procedures adopted by the auditor to gain an understanding of the entity and its environment are referred to as *risk assessment procedures*, and they are primarily used for planning the audit. Fundamentally, these procedures serve as a source of audit evidence to support the assessment of risks of material misstatement in the financial statements (Soltani 2007, p. 228). However, risk assessment

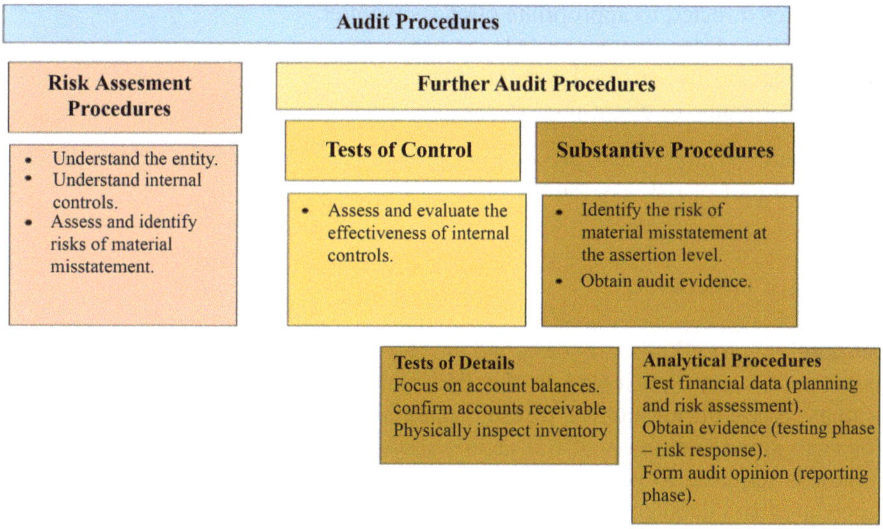

Fig. 3.1 Audit procedures (Created by the author)

procedures alone do not constitute sufficient and appropriate audit evidence. They must be complemented by subsequent audit procedures, such as tests of controls and substantive procedures (Soltani 2007, p. 285; Johnstone et al. 2014, p. 166; Cömert et al., n.d., p. 9).

A substantial portion of the auditor's risk assessment procedures is applied to gain an understanding of internal control (Arens et al. 2014, p. 402). In accordance with ISA 315, risk assessment procedures include inquiry, analytical procedures, observation, and inspection.

3.2.2.2 Further Audit Procedures

Further audit procedures refer to the audit procedures applied by the auditor following the completion of the risk assessment phase (ISA 200). These procedures are classified into two categories: tests of controls and substantive procedures.

Tests of Controls

Tests of controls are audit procedures designed to obtain evidence regarding the effectiveness of an entity's internal controls. In other words, they are applied to evaluate the operating effectiveness of controls implemented by the client entity to prevent or detect material misstatements (Bragg 2019b).

According to Arens et al. (2014, p. 403), tests of controls (TOC) may involve the following four types of procedures:

- Inquiries directed to appropriate client personnel,
- Inspection of documents, records, and reports,
- Observation of control-related activities,
- Reperformance of client procedures.

It should be noted that procedures designed to understand controls are also considered part of risk assessment procedures.

Substantive Procedures

Substantive procedures are designed to test for material misstatements in the monetary amounts presented in the financial statements. Auditors rely on two primary types of substantive testing: analytical procedures and tests of details. For each significant class of transactions, account balances, and disclosures, the auditor is required to perform substantive procedures (ISA 330). Both analytical procedures and detailed tests should be performed in conjunction.

Analytical Procedures

Analytical procedures are defined in ISA 520, as *"the evaluation of financial information through analysis of plausible relationships among both financial and non-financial data."* Additionally, analytical procedures include *"investigating identified fluctuations or relationships that are inconsistent with other relevant information or deviate significantly from expected values."*

Analytical procedures are applied at three stages of the audit:

- During the planning phase as risk assessment procedures (ISA 315),
- During the substantive testing phase in response to assessed risks (ISA 330),
- And at the conclusion of the audit to support the audit opinion (ISA 520).

Because analytical substantive procedures are typically more cost-effective than other forms of evidence-gathering, many auditors apply them across all engagements.

Tests of Details

Tests of details focus on the balances of specific accounts in the financial statements, and they are primarily applied to balance sheet accounts (Arens et al. 2014, p. 406).

When deciding which audit test to use in order to obtain sufficient appropriate audit evidence, cost is a significant consideration. Analytical procedures are generally the least costly due to their computational and comparative nature, whereas tests involving confirmations and physical inventory counts are among the most expensive.

Typically, the scope of audit procedures increases as the assessed risk of material misstatement increases. However, it is essential to recognize that the *nature* of the procedure is of paramount importance. Expanding the scope of a procedure is only effective if the procedure is both reliable and relevant to the specific risk being addressed.

In order to reduce the extent of substantive procedures, the auditor must obtain sufficient evidence through tests of controls that the relevant controls are operating effectively at the level of the assertion and with the desired level of assurance (McConnell Jr. & Schweiger, 2007).

Audit procedures aimed at obtaining audit evidence are generally carried out during the evidence-gathering stage and may include both tests of controls and substantive procedures.

3.2.3 Types of Audit Procedures

When determining which audit procedures to apply, the auditor selects from eight distinct types, commonly referred to as 'types of audit procedures'. Although the types of audit procedures are occasionally referred to in the literature as types of evidence or evidence-gathering techniques, ISA 500 explicitly defines them as 'audit procedures'. Therefore, in order to ensure terminological consistency with the standard, this study adopts the term 'audit procedures' as used in ISA 500, and presents these procedure types in Table 3.2.

Table 3.2 Types of audit procedures (audit procedures for obtaining audit evidence)

Audit Procedures	Description
Inspection	It involves the examination of records or documents—whether obtained from within or outside the entity—and whether in printed, electronic, or other formats, as well as the physical inspection of assets.
Observation	It is the observation of a process or procedure being performed by others.
External Confirmation	It refers to audit evidence obtained as a written response—whether in paper form, electronic format, or another medium—directly from a third party (the confirming party) to the auditor.
Recalculation	It is the verification of the mathematical accuracy of documents or records.
Reperformance	It refers to the independent execution by the auditor of procedures or controls that were originally performed as part of the entity's internal control.
Analytical Procedures	It involves the evaluation of financial information through the analysis of meaningful relationships between financial and non-financial data.
Inquiry	It is the process of obtaining information, throughout the audit, from knowledgeable individuals within or outside the entity regarding financial and non-financial matters.

Source ISA 500

The audit procedures presented in the table may be used by the auditor as risk assessment procedures, tests of controls, or substantive procedures, depending on their area of application and objective (ISA 500). The higher the assessed risk of material misstatement, the more audit procedures the auditor is expected to perform, thereby obtaining more audit evidence (KGK, n.d., p. 20).

Auditors can obtain evidence by employing less costly procedures such as inquiry, recalculation, and analytical procedures. However, they are also expected to avoid unnecessary procedures and strive to conduct the audit efficiently.

The information discussed thus far regarding audit procedures is summarized in Table 3.3. The table outlines which procedures are applied and what types of procedures are selected at the level of management assertions within both traditional and risk-based audit processes.

3.3 Audit Procedures in Key Audit Matters

The purpose of the standards is to produce auditor's reports that enhance users' confidence not only in the audit process itself but also in the financial statements of companies. The International Auditing and Assurance Standards Board (IAASB) further believes that improving auditor reporting will enhance communication between auditors and both investors and those charged with governance.

However, the audit process is inherently complex, and it requires the auditor to assess the risks of "material misstatement" in the financial statements in order to effectively guide audit performance (Almond 2015). To enable intended users to understand where the auditor perceives the areas of greatest audit risk, the independent auditor's report must include a section titled *"Key Audit Matters" (KAM)* in accordance with ISA 701 *"Communicating Key Audit Matters in the Independent Auditor's Report."*

KAM appears as a distinct section within the auditor's report and is considered one of its core components

Under ISA 701, one of the standards concerning audit conclusions and reporting, the primary objective is to enhance the communicative value of the auditor's report by providing more information to intended users and promoting greater transparency. In addition, the standard aims to improve communication between auditors and those charged with governance, increase the usefulness of financial statement disclosures, deliver clearer and more informative insights on significant matters, and ultimately support better decision-making and strengthen confidence through meaningful information.

The disclosure of Key Audit Matters (KAMs), as determined through the professional judgment of the auditor and those charged with governance, provides additional insight to users of financial statements by highlighting the issues of greatest significance.

Table 3.3 Audit procedures and types applied by stage of the audit process and level of management assertions

Traditional Audit	Risk-Based Audit	Relevant ISAs Underlying the Procedures	Management Assertions	Procedures Applied	Types of Procedures
1. Client Acceptance and Engagement 2. Audit Planning	1. Risk Assessment	**ISA 315** Identifying and Assessing the Risks of Material Misstatement through Understanding the Entity and Its Environment **ISA 330** The Auditor's Responses to Assessed Risks **ISA 520** Analytical Procedures		Risk Assessment Procedures Procedures to understand the client's business and industry Procedures to Understand Internal Control Planning of Analytical Procedures	• Inspection • Inquiry • Analytical Procedures
3. Audit Execution	2. Responding to Assessed Risks	**ISA 330** The Auditor's Responses to Assessed Risks **ISA 500** Audit Evidence **ISA 501** Audit Evidence—Specific Considerations for Selected Items **ISA 505** External Confirmations	**Assertions Related to Classes of Transactions and Events** • Occurrence • Completeness • Accuracy • Classification • Cut-off Assertions Related to Account Balances • Existence	Tests of Controls Substantive Tests of Transactions Analytical Procedures Tests of Details	• Inspection • Observation • Inquiry • Reperformance • Recalculation • Physical Inspection • External Confirmation • Inspection • Inquiry • Reperformance • Analytical Procedures • Recalculation

(continued)

Table 3.3 (continued)

Traditional Audit	Risk-Based Audit	Relevant ISAs Underlying the Procedures	Management Assertions	Procedures Applied	Types of Procedures
		ISA 520 Analytical Procedures	• Completeness • Accuracy • Classification • Cut-off • Valuation and Allocation • Rights and Obligations		
4. Completion of the Audit and Issuance of the Audit Report	3. Forming an Opinion and Reporting	**BDS 520** Analytical Procedures	• Assertions Related to Presentation and Disclosure • Occurrence, • Rights and Obligations • Completeness • Accuracy • Classification and Understandability	• Analytical Procedures • Tests of Details	• Analytical Procedures • Inspection • Inquiry (of the Client)

Source Adapted from Çetinkaya (2017, p. 113) and Arens et al. (2014, p. 421)

In order to identify the audit procedures applied to KAMs, the matters themselves must first be determined. For this reason, the discussion will begin with how KAMs are identified.

3.3.1 Identification of Key Audit Matters

Key Audit Matters (KAMs) are defined as those matters that, in the auditor's professional judgment, were of most significance in the audit of the current period's financial statements and were communicated with those charged with governance. Determining whether a matter is a KAM requires significant judgment and is specific to the circumstances of each audit.

According to ISA 701, the concept of 'matters of most significance' in acknowledges the risk-based nature of the audit. In this context, the auditor focuses on identifying and assessing the risks of material misstatement in the financial statements, designing and performing audit procedures responsive to those risks, and obtaining sufficient and appropriate audit evidence to form the audit opinion.

The higher the assessed risk of material misstatement at the assertion level for a specific class of transactions, account balance, or disclosure, the more judgment the auditor must exercise in planning and performing audit procedures and in evaluating their results. The greater the risk identified during risk assessment, the more persuasive the audit evidence that must be obtained (ISA 330).

In response to higher assessed risks, the auditor may increase the quantity of evidence or seek more relevant and reliable audit evidence. For example, the auditor may place greater emphasis on third-party confirmations or obtain corroborative evidence from multiple independent sources (ISA 330). Accordingly, matters that present significant challenges in obtaining sufficient appropriate audit evidence or in forming the audit opinion may be particularly relevant in determining KAMs (ISA 701).

At the planning stage, it may be beneficial to develop a preliminary view of matters likely to be KAMs and to communicate them during the initial planning meeting with those charged with governance. However, the final determination of KAMs is based on the audit evidence obtained and the outcome of the audit, and may evolve throughout the audit process (ISA 701).

KAMs help the auditor focus on areas that require the most careful judgment, thereby contributing to higher audit quality (ACCA 2018, p. 20). Areas involving significant management judgment or unusual transactions may be associated with risks of material misstatement (ISA 701). However, not every such risk will necessarily be determined to be a KAM, depending on its nature (ISA 701; Ryen 2018).

Additionally, the auditor may determine that a matter is a KAM even if it does not involve a risk of material misstatement. For instance, if the company holds a material goodwill balance, the auditor's evaluation of goodwill impairment may constitute a KAM—even when no impairment has been recorded (Ryen 2018).

The auditor's reassessment of risks and the reconsideration of planned procedures for a particular area of the financial statements may lead to its identification as an area of most significance (ISA 701). Such areas often involve complex financial reporting or significant management judgment and may require particularly challenging or subjective audit judgments (ISA 701).

In determining the matters of most significance, the auditor considers the following criteria (ISA 701):

- Areas of higher assessed risk of material misstatement or those identified as significant risks in accordance with ISA 315.
- Significant auditor judgments relating to areas in the financial statements involving significant management judgment, including accounting estimates with high estimation uncertainty.
- The effect on the audit of significant events or transactions that occurred during the period.

Additional considerations in determining whether a matter communicated with those charged with governance is a KAM include (ISA 701; Stamford and Murray 2016, p. 6):

- Matters requiring the most communication and audit effort with those charged with governance (areas where significant time was spent).
- Matters that are of particular importance to understanding the financial statements and to intended users.
- Matters involving adjustments or accumulated uncorrected misstatements that are significant in nature or amount.
- The nature and extent of audit effort needed to address the matter, including the need for specialized skills or knowledge.
- The nature of consultations outside the engagement team regarding the matter.
- The complexity and subjectivity involved in the accounting policy, particularly in comparison to industry peers.
- Difficulties encountered in applying audit procedures, evaluating results, or obtaining relevant and reliable evidence—especially where subjective judgment is involved.
- Whether the matter involved multiple, separate but related audit considerations.
- Areas affected by significant control deficiencies.

The identification of a matter as a KAM indicates that it was a key area of audit focus and typically one of the areas of greatest audit risk (Almond 2015).

3.3.2 Communicating Key Audit Matters

Each Key Audit Matter (KAM) must be described in a separate section under the heading 'Key Audit Matters' in the auditor's report. The content should be entity-specific and audit-specific, avoiding boilerplate language, excessive technical jargon, or audit-specific terminology. The auditor is expected to provide concise and understandable disclosures rather than revealing confidential information, in order to meet the expectations of intended users (ISA 701). Otherwise, the usefulness and clarity of KAMs would be diminished.

When presenting a KAM, it is required to refer, where relevant, to disclosures in the financial statements and to explain why the matter was considered to be of most significance in the audit and therefore determined to be a KAM. Additionally, the auditor must describe how the matter was addressed during the audit. Referring to the related financial statement disclosure helps users understand management's treatment of the matter (ISA 701).

The rationale for identifying the matter as a KAM may be linked to the auditor's risk assessment, and the description of how the matter was addressed may relate to the auditor's response to the assessed risk. In practice, the 'how it was addressed' section typically includes the audit procedures performed. The auditor should clearly describe the procedures applied and the types of procedures used in response to the matter identified as a KAM.

Identifying and articulating a KAM is not straightforward. For example, summarizing why a matter was a KAM and describing the procedures performed in an informative yet accessible way can be challenging (Burns 2019, p. 3).

To ensure the information is relevant and understandable, each KAM should be tailored to the specific circumstances of the entity and the audit. This helps minimize the risk of standardized wording across reporting periods (ISA 701).

According to ISA 701, the explanation of how the KAM was addressed should include:

- The most relevant response or approach taken by the auditor.
- A brief summary of the audit procedures performed.
- An indication of the outcome of those procedures, where appropriate.
- Key observations related to the matter.

To ensure that intended users understand both the significance of the KAM in the context of the audit and its relationship with the auditor's opinion and other elements of the report, careful wording must be used (ISA 701):

- The wording should not imply that the matter was not appropriately resolved in forming the auditor's opinion.
- Generic or boilerplate language should be avoided, and the matter should be clearly linked to the specific circumstances of the entity.
- Any related disclosure(s) in the financial statements should be considered in describing how the matter was addressed.
- The explanation should not constitute or imply a separate opinion on individual elements of the financial statements.

The standard explicitly allows flexibility in communication to avoid standardized language. The level of detail and scope of explanation regarding how the matter was addressed depends on the auditor's professional judgment (Stamford and Murray 2016, p. 9).

When the auditor significantly tailors their approach to the specific circumstances of the entity, it helps users better understand the nature of the auditor's judgment in addressing unusual circumstances and material risks (ISA 701). Furthermore, in evaluating accounting estimates involving high uncertainty, the auditor may consider it appropriate to consult with a specialist (ISA 701).

Auditors may face difficulties in articulating how they addressed areas involving complex or subjective audit judgment. In particular, clearly and concisely describing the nature and scope of responses to risks of material misstatement and significant judgments made by the auditor can be challenging. Nonetheless, to adequately communicate how the matter was addressed, it may be necessary to disclose specific procedures performed—even if such descriptions are more detailed. However, the explanations should remain concise (ISA 701).

Consequently, the identification of KAMs and the application of audit procedures is a process that continues throughout the audit. In fact, the same risk assessment and substantive audit procedures that support the audit opinion also form the basis for identifying and addressing KAMs. In certain cases, matters that do not involve risks of material misstatement may still be designated as KAMs if they are of particular significance to the entity.

3.4 Research

3.4.1 Objective of the Research and General Information on the Manufacturing Sector

The primary objective of this study is to identify the audit procedures and their types disclosed under Key Audit Matters (KAMs) in the auditor's reports of companies listed in the BIST manufacturing sector. Another aim is to analyze whether the disclosed procedures align with the criteria specified in ISA 701—namely, being entity-specific, non-boilerplate, and clearly understandable.

To this end, KAM procedures from the auditor's reports for the 2018 and 2019 fiscal years were examined for 175 companies listed in the BIST manufacturing sector as of 2020. However, since 2019 reports were unavailable for 6 companies, the final sample includes data from 169 companies. The analysis focused on the five most frequently reported and high-risk KAM topics in order to identify the most common and clearly articulated audit procedures.

Because there was no significant variation between the years 2018 and 2019 in terms of KAM content, procedures were evaluated as a whole across both years. The auditor's reports were obtained from the official website of the Public Disclosure Platform (KAP) (KAP, n.d.).

The audit procedures identified in the findings section are presented exactly as stated in the original auditor's reports. This approach was adopted to ensure the

Table 3.4 Distribution of companies in the manufacturing sector by sub-sectors

Sub-Sector Name	Sub-Sector	
	N	%
Chemicals, Pharmaceuticals, Petroleum, Rubber, and Plastic Products	33	19
Metal Products, Machinery, Electrical Equipment, and Transportation Vehicles	33	19
Food, Beverage, and Tobacco	27	15
Textiles, Wearing Apparel, and Leather	23	13
Non-Metallic Mineral Products	22	13
Basic Metal Industry	18	10
Paper, Printing, and Publishing	13	7
Forest Products and Furniture	5	3
Other Manufacturing Industries	1	1
Total	**175**	**100**

accuracy of interpretation and to enhance the transparency and clarity of the analysis in line with the research objective.

The BIST manufacturing sector comprises the following sub-sectors Table 3.4.

The distribution of audit firms and types of audit opinions across sub-sectors is presented in Table 3.5 An adverse opinion was issued only in the 'Textiles, Wearing Apparel, and Leather' sub-sector.

The top five Key Audit Matters (KAMs) identified in the sectors examined within the scope of the research are as follows Table 3.6.

3.4.2 Research Findings

The research findings are presented in order from the most frequently reported to the least frequently reported Key Audit Matters (KAMs). Accordingly, the order is as follows:

- Revenue
- Trade Receivables
- Property, Plant and Equipment
- Inventories
- Investment Properties

Table 3.5 Distribution of audit firms and reported types of audit opinions by sub-sector

Sub-Sector	Audit Firm				Opinion Type			
	Big4 n	%	Other n	%	Unqualified n	%	Qualified n	%
Chemicals, Pharmaceuticals, Petroleum, Rubber, and Plastic Products	17	20	13	16	26	18	4	20
Metal Products, Machinery, Electrical Equipment, and Transportation Vehicles	19	22	13	16	29	20	3	15
Food, Beverage, and Tobacco	12	14	14	17	21	14	5	25
Textiles, Wearing Apparel, and Leather	6	7	16	19	15	10	6	30
Non-Metallic Mineral Products	15	17	7	8	22	15	–	0
Basic Metal Industry	8	9	10	12	17	11	1	5
Paper, Printing, and Publishing	8	9	5	6	13	9	–	0
Forest Products and Furniture	–	0	5	6	4	3	1	5
Other Manufacturing Industries	1	1	–	0	1	–	1	0
Total	**86**	**100**	**83**	**100**	**148**	**100**	**20**	**100**

Big4: KPMG, Deloitte, EarnstYoung, PricewaterhouseCoopers

3.4.2.1 Common Audit Procedures Disclosed in KAMs-Revenue

In order to identify frequently used audit procedures related to revenue, the procedures disclosed in 115 KAMs reported under the "Revenue" category were examined. The identified procedures and their respective types are presented in Table 3.7.

As shown in the table, the most frequently used audit procedure type in relation to revenue is "inspection." This involves the examination of documents and records. In addition to inspection, the auditor may also apply the procedure of "reperformance

3.4.2.2 Common Audit Procedures Disclosed in KAMs-Trade Receivables

In order to identify the frequently used audit procedures related to "Trade Receivables," a total of 96 KAMs classified under this category were examined. The identified procedures and their respective types are presented in Table 3.8.

In the area of "Trade Receivables", the prominent audit procedures include inspection of documents and records, external confirmations, recalculation, and

Table 3.6 Number of the most frequently reported high-risk key audit matters in 2019 by sub-sector

Sub-Sector Name	Revenue		Trade Receivables		Property, Plant and Equipment		Inventories		Investment Properties	
	2019	2018	2019	2018	2019	2018	2019	2018	2019	2018
Basic Metal Industry	13	6	7	4	3	3	5	4	1	-
Chemicals, Pharmaceuticals, Petroleum, Rubber, and Plastic Products	12	5	15	8	5	6	5	6	1	1
Food, Beverage, and Tobacco	9	7	9	5	8	5	6	9	5	2
Forest Products and Furniture	5	3	0	–	1	2	1	1	–	–
Metal Products, Machinery, Electrical Equipment, and Transportation Vehicles	13	7	9	9	6	7	6	7	-	1
Non-Metallic Mineral Products	9	5	5	2	4	9	4	1	2	2
Other Manufacturing Industries	–	–	0	1	–	–	–	–	–	–
Paper, Printing, and Publishing	5	3	8	2	5	7	3	2	2	1
Textiles, Wearing Apparel, and Leather	10	9	5	7	7	8	6	6	3	2
Total	**76**	**45**	**58**	**38**	**40**	**47**	**36**	**36**	**14**	**9**

Table 3.7 Common audit procedures disclosed in KAMs-Revenue

	Description of Audit Procedure	Type of Audit Procedure Applied
1	Examination of the design, implementation, and operating effectiveness of internal controls (with the assistance of IT specialists)	ToC & SAP • Inquiry • Inspection
2	Evaluation of the Company's accounting policies by reviewing selected contracts for compliance with IFRS 15	SAP • Inspection
3	Review of supporting sales documents to determine the timing of transfer of control	SAP • Inspection
4	Assessment of the timing of revenue recognition in the financial statements (cut-off and appropriateness)	SAP • Inspection
5	Obtaining external confirmations for trade receivables and checking consistency with financial statements.	SAP • External Confirmation
6	Performing analytical procedures to identify the existence of non-recurring transactions.	SAP • Analytical Procedure
7	Reviewing the timing and appropriateness of discounts and turnover premiums granted to customers in line with the Company's discount policies	SAP • Inspection
8	Evaluating the adequacy and appropriateness of disclosures related to revenue	SAP • Inspection
9	Performing substantive testing on returns occurring after the reporting period to assess whether revenue was recognized in the correct period	SAP • Inspection

SAP: Substantive Audit Procedures; ToC: Tests of Controls

analytical procedures, depending on the nature of the audit activity performed (Table 3.9).

3.4.2.3 Common Audit Procedures Disclosed in KAMs—Property, Plant and Equipment

A total of 87 audit procedures related to Property, Plant and Equipment (PPE), as disclosed in the Key Audit Matters (KAMs), were examined. The audit procedures most commonly observed across auditor reports are presented in Table 3.9.

In the area of Property, Plant and Equipment (PPE), audit procedures appear to be more numerous and complex. The most commonly used types of procedures include inspection, analytical procedures, recalculation, and inquiry. Mathematical calculations and detailed examinations are more extensively applied in PPE-related procedures. In other words, it can be stated that the procedures used in this KAM are predominantly technical in nature.

Table 3.8 Common audit procedures disclosed in KAMs-Trade Receivables

	Description of Audit Procedure	Type of Audit Procedure Applied
1	Understanding the Company's process related to collection monitoring and credit risk of trade receivables, and evaluating the operational effectiveness of internal controls within this process,	ToC & SAP • Inspection • Inquiry
2	Assessing the compliance of applied accounting policies with IFRS 9, the Group's historical performance, and local and global practices	SAP • Inspection
3	Testing collections made in the subsequent period through sampling,	SAP • Inspection
4	Performing analytical review of aging schedules and comparing the collection turnover rate with the prior year,	SAP • Analytical Procedure
5	Testing trade receivable balances by sending confirmation letters on a sample basis,	SAP • External Confirmation
6	Testing collateral received for receivables through sampling and evaluating their liquidity,	SAP • Inspection • Analytical Procedure
7	Reviewing legal disputes and lawsuits related to receivables to audit the appropriateness of provisions for doubtful receivables, and obtaining confirmation letters from legal counsel regarding ongoing litigation,	SAP • External Confirmation • Inquiry
8	Inquiring into the assumptions used in calculating impairment of trade receivables,	SAP • Inspection • Recalculation
9	Evaluating the reasonableness and appropriateness of management's key judgments, estimates, methods, and data sources used in impairment calculations under IFRS 9—Financial Instruments,	SAP • Inspection
10	Verifying foreign currency valuation of trade receivables.	SAP • Recalculation
11	Performing physical count of promissory notes in the receivables portfolio	SAP • Fiziki İnceleme
12	Assessing the assumptions used in the model developed for expected credit loss calculation	SAP • Inspection
13	Auditing valuation transactions such as receivable discounts (deferred interest income) and other adjustments	SAP • Recalculation
14	Evaluating collection risk by reviewing the past payment performance of customers whose payment terms have been exceeded	SAP • Analytical Procedure
15	In related party transactions, comparing prices of sales to related parties with sales to third parties using the comparable uncontrolled price method and evaluating transfer pricing implications	SAP • Analytical Procedure
16	Assessing the adequacy and IFRS compliance of disclosures related to trade receivables and associated impairment losses	SAP • Inspection

SAP: Substantive Audit Procedures; ToC: Tests of Controls

Table 3.9 Common audit procedures disclosed in KAMs—Property, Plant and Equipment

	Description of Audit Procedure	Type of Audit Procedure Applied
1	Testing of internal controls related to property, plant and equipment	ToC & SAP • Inspection
2	Verification of all items of fixed assets through supporting documents such as invoices, and reassessment of their useful lives	SAP • Inspection
3	Recalculation of depreciation amounts for property, plant and equipment to verify accuracy	SAP • Recalculation
4	Assessment of compliance with IAS 16 in recognition, classification, and disclosure of fixed assets	SAP • Inspection
5	Examination of the scrap values of fixed assets considering whether they reflect current market conditions	SAP • Inspection
6	Substantive testing of capitalized costs, including supporting documentation and calculations, for ongoing investments and borrowing costs, as well as assessing whether subsequent investments in completed projects were capitalized properly	SAP • Inspection
7	Assessment of the frequency of revaluation and compliance with the conditions and intervals specified in IAS 16 and relevant audit standards	SAP • Inspection
8	Evaluation of inputs used in the average comparable value per square meter calculated by the valuation company through sample testing, and assessment of sensitivity to negotiation margin, location adjustments, etc	SAP • Inspection
9	Assessment of management's estimates and assumptions regarding the fair value of land, buildings, and improvements as of 31 December 2018 in collaboration with external experts, in accordance with auditing standards	SAP • Inspection • Inquiry
10	Engagement of external specialists for review of valuation reports sampled for evaluating the assumptions and methods used by management and independent professional appraisers in accordance with ISA 620	SAP • Inspection • Inquiry
11	Obtaining property valuation reports prepared by real estate appraisers authorized by the Capital Markets Board and applying relevant audit procedures under ISA 620—Using the Work of an Auditor's Expert,	SAP • Inspection • Inquiry
12	Evaluation of the professional qualifications and independence of the valuation company that conducted the valuation of land, buildings, and site improvements,	SAP • Inquiry
13	Joint assessment with our valuation experts of the appropriateness of the methods and data used in the valuation study,	SAP • Inspection
14	Checking the mathematical accuracy of calculations presented in the valuation study,	SAP • Recalculation
15	Verification of the consistency between the fair value amounts determined by the appraisers and those disclosed in Note 14 of the financial statements.	SAP • Inspection

(continued)

Table 3.9 (continued)

	Description of Audit Procedure	Type of Audit Procedure Applied
16	Evaluation of licenses, qualifications, and impartiality of valuation experts, as well as the appropriateness of valuation methods applied in the report,	SAP • Inspection
17	Comparison of assumptions used by valuation experts (e.g., growth rates, discount rates) with market data and the Company's historical performance	SAP • Analytical Procedure
18	Assessment of whether the high-level estimates and judgments used in the valuation report are within an acceptable range, including the reasonableness of appraised values	SAP • Inspection
19	Review of the consistency of the Group's estimates for property, plant and equipment with those used in prior periods	SAP • Inspection
20	Verification of the valuation report prepared by an independent expert for Ünye CEM SRL, including assessment of the appropriateness of the model, valuation methodology, depreciation analysis, and disposal cost estimations	SAP • Inspection • Recalculation • Analytical Procedure
21	Analysis of replacement cost or escalated purchase cost assumptions used in the valuation report and assessment of the reasonableness of abandonment cost estimates	• Analytical Procedure
22	Critical evaluation of the Group's impairment testing model, including discounted cash flow projections by business unit and historical financial performance, along with recalculation of the impairment model to assess sensitivity of assumptions such as growth and discount ratesı.	SAP • Inspection • Recalculation • Analytical Procedure
23	Assessment of the adequacy and appropriateness of disclosures in the consolidated financial statement notes regarding the determination of fair value of the assets	SAP • Inspection
24	Verification of the accuracy and presentation of the deferred tax impact arising from revaluation differences on fixed assets	SAP • Inspection

SAP: Substantive Audit Procedures; ToC: Tests of Controls

3.4.2.4 Common Audit Procedures Disclosed in KAMs—Inventories

A total of 72 Key Audit Matters (KAMs) related to inventories were examined. The audit procedures commonly observed across different audit firms are presented in Table 3.10.

A total of 26 audit procedures were identified as commonly applied in relation to inventories. Among the five Key Audit Matters (KAMs) examined in the study, the inventory-related KAM contained the highest number of distinct procedures. As seen in the table, the most frequently applied procedure types include analytical procedures, recalculation, observation, inspection of documents and records, and inquiry. Unlike other areas, procedures related to inventories also involved the use of physical examination and inquiry techniques that appear to be specific to the nature of this topic.

Table 3.10 Common audit procedures disclosed in KAMs—Inventories

	Description of Audit Procedure	Type of Audit Procedure Applied
1	Internal control procedures performed based on the results of our risk assessment	KT ve SAP • Inquiry • Inspection
2	Understanding and evaluating the appropriateness of the accounting policy related to the Group's import practices	SAP • Inspection
3	Understanding and evaluating the appropriateness of the accounting policy related to inventory impairment,	SAP • Inspection
4	Comparing delivery notes with sales invoices recorded in the Group's accounting system to verify the reflection of sales and deliveries in the legal records,	SAP • Inspection
5	Comparing current and prior period inventory quantities and verifying whether adjustments related to idle inventory items have been reflected in the financial statements.	SAP • Inspection
6	Applying alternative verification techniques and conducting detailed substantive testing related to purchase and sales transactions.	SAP Ambiguous (possibly confirmation, inspection, or recalculation)
7	Testing the appropriateness of the components of inventory costs and the net realizable values,	SAP • Inspection • Recalculation
8	Participating in physical inventory counts and verifying the quantities and net realizable values of selected inventory items through sampling	SAP • Physical Examination • Observation • Recalculation
9	Confirming the physical existence of inventories through inventory counts conducted with the participation of in-house experts.	SAP • Physical Examination • Observation
10	During the year-end physical inventory count we observed, verifying the physical presence of relevant inventory items, identifying any unrecorded stock outflows, and assessing storage conditions and usability,	SAP • Physical Examination
11	For raw materials, comparing unit prices in current inventory with those in purchase invoices and verifying whether the identified impairments are reflected in the financial statements.	SAP • Inspection • Recalculation
12	Testing the mathematical accuracy of data used in valuation analyses.	SAP • Recalculation
13	Comparing the cost of sales to sales ratio, inventory turnover rate, and cost of sales with prior period figures,	SAP • Analytical Procedure

(continued)

Table 3.10 (continued)

	Description of Audit Procedure	Type of Audit Procedure Applied
14	Assessing whether a provision for net realizable value loss is necessary based on gross margin changes at the general or product level,	SAP • Analytical Procedure
15	Conducting profitability analyses by product category in the net realizable value calculation to assess whether there is any impairment.	SAP • Analytical Procedure
16	Reviewing inventory aging reports.	SAP • Inspection
17	Reviewing borrowing costs capitalized to inventories during the current period and whether such capitalization occurred	SAP • Inspection
18	Testing whether exchange rate differences have been capitalized	SAP • Inspection
19	Comparing inventory carrying amounts with market prices.	SAP • Inspection
20	Performing analytical reviews and substantive testing related to the recording and valuation of inventories.	SAP • Analytical Procedure • Recalculation
21	Comparing the inventory turnover rate with that of the prior year,	SAP • Analytical Procedure
22	Observing during year-end counts whether there are obsolete or damaged inventory items	SAP • Observation
23	Evaluating the adequacy of inventory impairment provisions recognized during the current period,	SAP • Recalculation
24	Reviewing all inventory items potentially subject to impairment through observation and inquiry.	SAP • Observation • Inquiry
25	Discussing with Group management the risk of impairment due to changing circumstances,	SAP • Inquiry
26	Evaluating the adequacy of disclosures related to inventories in the notes to the financial statements.	SAP • Inspection

SAP: Substantive Audit Procedures; ToC: Tests of Controls

3.4.2.5 Common Audit Procedures Disclosed in KAMs—Investment Property

A total of 23 audit procedures applied in relation to Investment Property were examined. The identified procedures are presented in Table 3.11.

Investment Property, similar to Property, Plant and Equipment, is an area where technically detailed procedures are frequently applied. Although fewer in number compared to other KAMs, a relatively high number of audit procedures were identified for this category. The most commonly used procedure types include inspection, analytical procedures, and recalculation.

Table 3.11 Common audit procedures disclosed in KAMs– Investment Property

	Description of Audit Procedure	Type of Audit Procedure Applied
1	Evaluation of the design and implementation of key controls related to valuation reports prepared by the valuation expert appointed by the Group	ToC
2	Review of licenses, contracts, and declarations concerning the technical competence and independence of the valuation company	SAP • Inspection • Inquiry
3	Assessment of the qualifications, competencies, and objectivity of the appointed real estate valuation experts	SAP • Inspection • Inquiry
4	Verification of the consistency between fair values determined by valuation experts in the reports and the amounts disclosed in Notes 13 and 14	SAP • Inspection
5	Obtaining valuation reports for each investment property, and focusing audit procedures on those with significant fair value increases	SAP • Inspection • Recalculation
6	Review of the appropriateness of the applied valuation methodology by considering the intended use of the related investment properties	SAP • Inspection • Recalculation
7	Verification of the square meters used in fair value calculations against title deed records of the respective properties	SAP • Inspection • Teyit
8	Evaluation of the sensitivity of average comparable values per square meter used by the valuation company to market conditions, including assumptions like negotiation margin and location adjustments	SAP • Inspection • Recalculation
9	Confirmation that there were no significant changes in comparable unit prices, sales prices of similar units, or occupancy rates of leased investment properties during the period	SAP • Confirmation
10	Observation of whether each investment property was evaluated considering its specific characteristics, geographic location, and cash flow generation	SAP • Inspection
11	Comparison of the variance in comparable rental rates stated in valuation reports with housing price index values and assessment of the reasonableness of such variances	SAP • Analytical Procedure
12	Obtaining valuation reports prepared by real estate valuation experts authorized by the Capital Markets Board, and performing relevant audit procedures in accordance with ISA 620—Using the Work of an Auditor's Expert,	SAP • Inspection • Inquiry (under ISA 620)
13	Testing the accuracy of cost values of properties with invoices and validating comparable values through sampling	SAP • Analytical Procedure
14	Comparison of the assumptions used by valuation experts (e.g., growth expectations, discount rates) with market data and the Group's historical performance	SAP • Analytical Procedure

(continued)

Table 3.11 (continued)

	Description of Audit Procedure	Type of Audit Procedure Applied
15	Assessment of accrued rental income through lease agreements and evaluation of any unaccrued rental receivables	SAP • Inspection
16	Comparison of leased investment properties with lease agreement terms	SAP • Inspection
17	Review of controls over the collection of rental receivables	SAP • Inspection
18	Verification of compliance of disclosures related to investment properties in the financial statement notes with IAS requirements	SAP • Inspection
19	Assessment of the appropriateness and relevance of the information disclosed in the financial statements and explanatory notes, considering their significance for users of financial statements	SAP • Inspection

SAP: Substantive Audit Procedures; ToC: Tests of Controls

An important cross-cutting finding was identified across all procedures in the study. Specifically, the audit procedures disclosed under each KAM were almost identical in wording between 2018 and 2019. This consistency was observed regardless of the audit firm or the industry in which the entity operates. In fact, certain procedures were reused across different sectors without any modification. One illustrative finding related to this issue is presented in Table 3.12.

In addition to all the findings above, it was observed that among both the commonly applied audit procedures and all reviewed procedures, some were described clearly and specifically, outlining the audit steps in an understandable manner, while others were presented in more general and non-specific terms. A few examples are listed below:

(a) Clear and Specific Procedures

- Obtaining external confirmations for trade receivables and verifying consistency with financial statements (Table 3.7, Item 5).
- Testing the depreciation amounts calculated for property, plant and equipment using the recalculation method (Table 3.9, Item 3).
- Sending confirmation letters by sampling to test the trade receivable balances (Table 3.8, Item 5).
- Performing profitability analysis by product categories in the calculation of net realizable value to assess potential impairment (Table 3.10, Item 15).
- Reviewing all inventory items potentially subject to impairment through observation and inquiry (Table 3.10, Item 24).

(b) General and Non-Specific Procedures

- Alternative verification techniques were applied, and detailed tests were performed for purchase and sales transactions (Table 3.10, Item 6).

Table 3.12 Example of a "Standardized" audit procedure used by the same audit firm across different sectors

Audit Girm	Sector (2019)	Audit Procedure Description
X1	Y1	During our audit, the following audit procedures were applied regarding the recognition of revenue in the financial statements: • The design and implementation of controls related to the revenue process were evaluated. The Company's sales and delivery procedures were analyzed. • The appropriateness of the Company's accounting policy for revenue recognition was assessed. • Substantive procedures focused on evaluating cases where revenue was invoiced but not yet earned. High-volume and high-risk customers were selected from among existing customers, and sales lists covering the relevant date range were obtained from the respective departments and defined as the population. The completeness and accuracy of these lists were verified. • Sales selected through sampling were tested to determine whether they were recorded in the correct period by comparing sales contracts, delivery terms, shipment and delivery documents, and invoices. • In designing procedures to address this key audit matter, consideration was given to whether the revenue recognition policies applied by the Company's management complied with IFRS and relevant regulations. • In our risk assessment procedures, the effectiveness of the Company's internal controls related to revenue was evaluated. • Transactions selected from those executed during the reporting period were tested individually by comparing revenue amounts to supporting documentation. • As a result of our audit procedures on the revenue process, no material misstatements or errors were identified in the recognition of revenue.
	Y2	• The design and implementation of controls related to the revenue process were evaluated. The Group's sales and delivery procedures were analyzed. • The appropriateness of the Group's accounting policy for revenue recognition was assessed. • Substantive procedures focused on evaluating cases where revenue was invoiced but not yet earned. High-volume and high-risk customers were selected from among existing customers, and sales lists covering the relevant date range were obtained from the respective departments and defined as the population. The completeness and accuracy of these lists were verified. • Sales selected through sampling were tested to determine whether they were recorded in the correct period by comparing sales contracts, delivery terms, shipment and delivery documents, and invoices. • In designing procedures to address this key audit matter, consideration was given to whether the revenue recognition policies applied by the Group's management complied with IFRS and relevant regulations. • In our risk assessment procedures, the effectiveness of the Group's internal controls related to revenue was evaluated. • Transactions selected from those executed during the reporting period were tested individually by comparing revenue amounts to supporting documentation. • As a result of our audit procedures on the revenue process, no material misstatements or errors were identified in the recognition of revenue.

- Obtaining valuation reports prepared by real estate valuation experts authorized by the Capital Markets Board and conducting the necessary audit procedures in accordance with ISA 620—Using the Work of an Auditor's Expert (Table 3.11, Item 12).

3.5 Conclusion

Audit procedures can be defined as the actions, tests, and techniques designed by the auditor based on professional judgment and in accordance with ISAs, in order to carry out the audit process effectively. These procedures play a significant role in forming the auditor's opinion, enhancing the communicative value of the audit report, ensuring its comprehensibility, and increasing its level of transparency. They also reflect how the auditor responds to and approaches the audit.

The Key Audit Matters (KAM) section, which is required to be disclosed in the auditor's report, must be determined with care in order to increase the communicative value of financial statements, bridge the expectation gap between the entity and users, and strengthen users' confidence in the financial reports. For each identified KAM, the auditor is expected to describe the audit procedures in a company-specific and understandable manner, avoiding boilerplate language. Therefore, audit procedures are not only essential but must be continuously improved to ensure audit quality and enhance the value of the audit report.

In this study, five KAMs identified as the most significant risk areas in BIST-listed manufacturing companies were analyzed: Revenue, Trade Receivables, Property, Plant and Equipment (PPE), Inventories, and Investment Property.

Although revenue was the most frequently reported KAM, it was the one with the fewest distinct procedures applied by auditors. It also lacked variety in procedure types. Revenue-related procedures primarily focused on whether revenue was recognized in the correct period and at the correct amount. The most common procedure types were inspection of documents and records and, due to its relation to sales, external confirmations linked to receivables.

For trade receivables, procedures mostly targeted impairment assessment, doubtful receivables, and collectability. The most applied procedure types were external confirmation, recalculation, and analytical procedures.

Procedures for PPE and Investment Property were longer and more complex due to the technical nature of these items. In both areas, procedures often involved experts hired for valuation work and relied heavily on technical procedures.

Inventories were found to be the area with the highest diversity of procedures. Most of these addressed inventory impairment and included analytical procedures, recalculation, observation, inspection of documents and records, and inquiry.

Audit procedures generally reflect transactions arising from the nature, operation, and use of accounts (e.g., impairment testing, inventory turnover, invoice inspection, depreciation recalculation). These procedures are applicable across companies and sectors. In the manufacturing sector, no procedures were observed that were unique to the industry. Moreover, procedures did not vary by auditor or sector. In many cases, the same procedures were used verbatim across different periods and industries.

While previous studies suggest that engagement with a Big Four firm (KPMG, Deloitte, Ernst & Young, PwC) positively impacts audit quality, this study found no significant difference in the nature of procedures disclosed by these firms compared to others. Even among the Big Four, standardized explanations were frequently observed.

Furthermore, some procedures were found to be described in vague and general terms, which contradicts the nature of audit procedures that are expected to be specific, concise, clear, and tailored to the company. This highlights the importance of the auditor's professional judgment in defining appropriate procedures. However, no evidence was found indicating that such professional judgment was reflected in the KAM disclosures. The prevalence of standardized procedures in KAMs may reduce audit quality and diminish the communicative value of the auditor's report, ultimately reducing user engagement over time.

Alternatively, auditors might refrain from disclosing subjective or tailored procedures due to concerns about revealing their audit strategy, or due to time and cost constraints limiting audit effort.

In conclusion, it can be said that audit procedures related to balance sheet accounts are more detailed and varied than those related to income statement accounts, despite the latter having a higher number of total procedures. Moreover, the use of standardized language across sectors, companies, and periods in the manufacturing industry—without employing company-specific or tailored language—raises concerns about how much value users actually derive from audit reports.

In addition, this study contributes to the literature not only by examining the audit procedures disclosed in KAMs from a content perspective, but also by classifying them according to the procedure types defined in ISA 500. This dual-layered approach is significant as it enables an assessment of the diversity, technical depth, and degree of standardization in the reported procedures, while also revealing strengths and weaknesses in terms of the communicative value of audit reports. In this respect, the study provides original findings based on empirical data from the Turkish context and critically addresses the formalistic tendencies observed in auditor reporting practices.

References

ACCA (2018, March). Key audit matters: unlocking the secrets of the audit.Retrieved August 20, 2020 from https://www.accaglobal.com/content/dam/ACCA_Global/professional-insights/Key-audit-matters/pi-key-audit-matters.pdf. Erişim Tarihi: 20/08/2020

ACCA Global (n.d.) Audit Procedures. | ACCA Qualification | students | ACCA Global.Retrieved August 9, 2020 from https://www.accaglobal.com/in/en/student/exam-support-resources/fundamentals-exams-study-resources/f8/technical-articles/audit-procedures.html.

Almond S (2015) Key audit matters: wha tthey are and why they are important. Retrieved August 20, 2020, from https://www.ey.com/en_gl/assurance/key-audit-matters–what-they-are-and-why-they-are-important

Andiappan V, Wan YK (2020) Distinguishing approach, methodology, method, procedure and technique in process systems engineering. Clean Technol Environ Policy 22(3):547–555. https://doi.org/10.1007/s10098-020-01819-w

Arens AA, Elder RJ, Beasley MS, Hogan C (2014) Auditing and assurance services an integrated approach, Fifteenth Edition, Pearson

Bory (2020, July 30) Audit procedures. Retrieved August 5, 2020 from https://accountinguide.com/audit-procedures/

Bragg S (2019a) Audit procedures definition—accountingTools. Retrieved August 5, 2020 from https://www.accountingtools.com/articles/audit-procedures.html

Bragg S (2019b) Audit procedures definition—accountingTools. Retrieved August 5, 2020 from https://www.accountingtools.com/articles/audit-procedures.html

Burns J (2019, April) What to expect from auditor reporting of critical audit matters. *On The Board's Agenda | US*. Retrieved August 15, 2020 from https://www2.deloitte.com/content/dam/Deloitte/us/Documents/center-for-board-effectiveness/otba-what-to-expect-from-auditor.pdf

Çetinkaya N (2017) Risk Odaklı Denetimde Denetim Kanıtının Kalitesinin Önemi ve Bir Araştırma. World Account Sci 19(1):109–133. Retrieved from https://research.ebsco.com/c/oxraz4/viewer/pdf/uvo3tbv5pv

Cömert N, Uzay Ş, UYAR S (n.d.) *Denetimde Risk Değerlendirme Yöntemlerinin Uygulanması*. Retrieved August 08, 2020 from http://www.dt-audit.com/dosyalar/Kutuphane/DENET%C4%B0MDE%20R%C4%B0SK%20DE%C4%9EERLEND%C4%B0RME%20Y%C3%96NTEMLER%C4%B0N%C4%B0N%20UYGULANMASI.pdf

International Federation of Accountants (IFAC, 2025) International Standards on Auditing ISA 330 the auditor's responses to assessed risks. *Handbook of the International Quality Management, Auditing, Review, Other Assurance, and Related Services Pronouncements*, p. 327–341, September 24, 2025, https://www.iaasb.org/publications/2025-handbook-international-quality-management-auditing-review-other-assurance-and-related-services, Accessed on Jan 3rd, 2026). To access the standard, please link to https://ifacweb.blob.core.windows.net/publicfiles/2025-09/IAASB-2025-Handbook-Volume-1.pdf

International Federation of Accountants (IFAC, 2025) International Standards on Auditing ISA 520 Analytical Procedures. *Handbook of the International Quality Management, Auditing, Review, Other Assurance, and Related Services Pronouncements*, p. 402–406, September 24, 2025, https://www.iaasb.org/publications/2025-handbook-international-quality-management-auditing-review-other-assurance-and-related-services, Accessed on Jan 3rd, 2026). To access the standard, please link to https://ifacweb.blob.core.windows.net/publicfiles/2025-09/IAASB-2025-Handbook-Volume-1.pdf

International Federation of Accountants (IFAC, 2025) International Standards on Auditing ISA 701 (New), Communicating Key Audit Matters İn The Independent Auditor's Report. *Handbook of the International Quality Management, Auditing, Review, Other Assurance, and Related Services Pronouncements*, p. 629–642, September 24, 2025, https://www.iaasb.org/publications/2025-handbook-international-quality-management-auditing-review-other-assurance-and-related-services, Accessed on Jan 3rd, 2026). To access the standard, please link to https://ifacweb.blob.core.windows.net/publicfiles/2025-09/IAASB-2025-Handbook-Volume-1.pdf

International Federation of Accountants (IFAC, 2025) International Standard on Auditing 200 Overall Objectives of the Independent Auditor and the Conduct of an Audit in Accordance With International Standards on Auditing. *Handbook of the International Quality Management, Auditing, Review, Other Assurance, and Related Services Pronouncements*, p. 99–116, September 24, 2025, https://www.iaasb.org/publications/2025-handbook-international-quality-management-auditing-review-other-assurance-and-related-services, Accessed on Jan 3rd, 2026). To access the standard, please link to https://ifacweb.blob.core.windows.net/publicfiles/2025-09/IAASB-2025-Handbook-Volume-1.pdf

International Federation of Accountants (IFAC, 2025) International Standard on Auditing 200 Identifying and Assessing the Risks of Material Misstatement, *Handbook of the International Quality Management, Auditing, Review, Other Assurance, and Related Services Pronouncements*, p. 242–320, September 24, 2025, https://www.iaasb.org/publications/2025-handbook-international-quality-management-auditing-review-other-assurance-and-related-services, Accessed on Jan 3rd, 2026). To access the standard, please link to https://ifacweb.blob.core.windows.net/publicfiles/2025-09/IAASB-2025-Handbook-Volume-1.pdf

International Federation of Accountants (IFAC, 2025) International Standard on Auditing 500 Audit Evidence, *Handbook of the International Quality Management, Auditing, Review, Other Assurance, and Related Services Pronouncements*, p. 363–376, September 24, 2025, https://www.iaasb.org/publications/2025-handbook-international-quality-management-auditing-review-other-assurance-and-related-services, Accessed on Jan 3rd, 2026). To access the standard, please link to https://ifacweb.blob.core.windows.net/publicfiles/2025-09/IAASB-2025-Handbook-Volume-1.pdf

Jain P (n.d.) Audit procedures. Retrieved August 10, 2020 from https://www.wallstreetmojo.com/audit-procedures/.

Johnstone KM, Gramling AA, Rittenberg LE (2014). Auditing: a risk-based approach to conducting a quality audit, Nineth Edition

Karacan S, Uygun R (2016) Denetim ve Raporlama, Umuttepe Yayınları, 2nd edn. Kocaeli

Kaval H (2005) Muhasebe Denetimi, Gazi Kitabevi, 2nd edn. Ankara

Kavut L, Taş O, Şavlı T (2009). Uluslararası Denetim Standartları Kapsamında Bağımsız Denetim, İSMMMO Yayın No. 130. Retrieved from https://ismmmo.org.tr/Yayinlar/E-Kitap/sayi-49/–2212

KGK (n.d.). Retrieved August 8, 2020 from https://www.kgk.gov.tr/Portalv2Uploads/files/Duyurular/v2/sunumlar/sunum.pdf.

KPMG (2018). New auditor's report requirement—communication of key audit matters. Retrieved August 8, 2020 from https://home.kpmg/content/dam/kpmg/in/pdf/2018/03/AAU-March2018-Ch2.pdf.

McConnell Jr DK., & Schweiger CH (2007) Implementing the New ASB Risk Assessment Audit Standards. Retrieved August 20, 2020 from http://archives.cpajournal.com/2007/607/essentials/p20.htm

Procedure (n.d.) Cambridge Dictionary. Retrieved August 20, 2020 from https://dictionary.cambridge.org/dictionary/english/procedure

Procedure (n.d.) Oxford Learners Dictioanary. Retrieved August 20, 2020 from https://www.oxfordlearnersdictionaries.com/definition/academic/procedure

Prosedür (n.d.) Türk Dil Kurumu Sözlükleri. Retrieved August 20, 2020 from https://sozluk.gov.tr/

Ryen V (2018). What is a critical audit matter? Retrieved August 20, 2020 from https://www.cfo.com/auditing/2018/07/whats-critical-audit-matter/

Sağlam N, Yolcu M (2014) Türkiye Denetim Standartlarına Göre Finansal Tabloların Bağımsız Denetimi ve Raporlanması. Yaklaşım Yayıncılık, Ankara

Soltani B (2007) Auditing: an international approach. Trans-Atlantic Publications

Stamford L, Murray Z (2016) KAM: the matters that matter—embracing the spirit of The New Requırements, 1-20. Retrieved August 20, 2020 from https://www.charteredaccountantsanz.com/tools-and-resources/client-service-essentials/audit-and-assurance/key-audit-matters-the-matters-that-matter

Uyar S. (n.d.). Denetim Kanıtları.Sakarya Üniversitesi Sürekli Eğitim Uygulama ve Araştırma Merkezi Ders Notları

Yanık S, Ve Karataş M (2017) Denetim raporlarının geleceği: yeni düzenlemeler ve ülke uygulamaları. Muhasebe Ve Finansman Dergisi 73:1–26. https://doi.org/10.25095/mufad.396739

Chapter 4
The Role of Materiality in Independent Audit Sample Selection

Özgür Teraman and Fatma Temelli

Abstract This study examines the role of materiality in determining audit sample selection within the framework of International Standards on Auditing (ISA), particularly (IAASB, International Standards on Auditing (ISA) 320 Materiality in Planning and Performing an Audit, pages 321–326) and (IAASB, International Standard on Auditing (ISA) 530: Audit Sampling, pages 407–417). It explores how auditors apply professional judgment in setting materiality thresholds and how these thresholds influence audit planning, sampling, and the evaluation of audit evidence. The paper distinguishes between accounting and auditing materiality, emphasizing their conceptual and practical interdependence. A numerical application demonstrates how variations in materiality levels affect sample size, detection risk, and overall audit assurance. The findings show that appropriately determined materiality thresholds contribute to efficient audit sampling, reduced audit risk, and enhanced reliability of financial statements. The study concludes that the integration of materiality assessment and audit sampling decisions is critical for achieving audit effectiveness and maintaining users' confidence in financial reporting.

Keywords Materiality · Audit sampling · Audit risk · International Standards on Auditing (ISAs) · Professional judgment

This chapter was previously published in Turkish by Gazi Kitabevi with the ISBN: 978–975-7727-16-7.

Ö. Teraman (✉)
Solihull, UK
e-mail: teramanozgur@gmail.com

F. Temelli
Department of Business Administration, Agri Ibrahim Cecen University, Ağrı, Türkiye
e-mail: ftemelli@agri.edu.tr

G. Kurt, Ö. Sarısoy (eds.), *Recent Advancements in Auditing*, Accounting, Finance, Sustainability, Governance & Fraud: Theory and Application,
https://doi.org/10.1007/978-981-95-5811-7_4

4.1 Introduction

With globalization, the rise in international corporate mergers and the redirection of foreign investment toward developing countries have compelled businesses—the driving forces of economic activity—to adapt to dynamic and evolving conditions. To enhance their competitive advantage and facilitate access to emerging capital markets, firms must strengthen their existing accounting systems and produce transparent, comparable, and accurate financial statements. These statements must be subjected to independent auditing to enhance their credibility and reliability.

In Turkey, the practice of independent auditing initially emerged under pressure from the private sector. Over time, legal regulations have shaped and institutionalized its development. An examination of the regulatory framework reveals a system grounded in institutional regulatory authorities, such as the Capital Markets Board and the Banking Regulation and Supervision Agency (BRSA). Within this system, Law No. 3568 establishes a foundational framework that informs both regulatory institutions and the formulation of independent auditing standards aligned with the provisions of the new Turkish Commercial Code.

Auditors are required to comply with two principal sets of standards during the audit process: accounting standards and auditing standards. In Turkey, under the framework of the Turkish Commercial Code (TCC) No. 6102, auditing is governed by the Independent Auditing Standards (Türkiye Auditing Standards), which are harmonized with the International Standards on Auditing (ISA). These standards, issued by the Public Oversight, Accounting and Auditing Standards Authority (POA), are tailored to suit varying business scales, sectors, and non-profit organizations.

The overarching objective of auditing is to enhance the confidence of users in the information presented within financial statements. This confidence is fostered when the auditor issues an opinion on whether the financial statements conform to the applicable financial reporting framework, taking all material aspects into account (İnaltong and Taş 2015: 74). Typically, the fundamental aim of independent audits is to obtain a professional judgment that the financial statements provide a true and fair view of the entity's financial position, performance, and cash flows, in all material respects, in accordance with financial reporting standards (Güredin 2007: 213).

In practice, auditors apply audit procedures by selecting samples from accounting records and transactions to provide reasonable assurance regarding management's assertions at the financial statement level. Where auditors opt to employ sampling techniques, the provisions of IAASB (2025b) are applicable. This standard regulates the auditor's use of both statistical and non-statistical sampling methods in the design and selection of samples, the application of tests of controls and substantive procedures, and the evaluation of sample results (IAASB 2025b, Par. 1–2). Additionally, IAASB (2025a) provides a critical framework for determining materiality—one of the most significant elements of the audit process. The assessment of materiality in financial statement audits relies on the auditor's professional judgment and scepticism, exercised within the general framework established by the ISAs. As such, the determination of materiality is inherently subjective. A contextually appropriate materiality threshold aligned with the financial characteristics of the entity yields more effective and meaningful audit outcomes for auditors, entities, and financial statement users alike (İnaltong and Taş 2015: 88).

This study includes a numerical application to illustrate the role of materiality in the auditor's sample selection during the audit process. The discussion begins by defining the concept of materiality in accounting, followed by an examination of its treatment under the Independent Auditing Standards (ISA). The paper then explores how materiality is determined in practice, the process of audit sampling, and the specific role of materiality in sample selection, culminating in a practical example. The study concludes with a synthesis of findings and a general evaluation.

4.2 The Concept of Materiality

The concept of *materiality* is employed in both accounting and auditing disciplines. Within the *Fundamental Concepts of Accounting*, materiality is defined as follows: if the omission of information from financial statements, or the inaccuracy of disclosed information, would influence the decisions of users relying on those financial statements, such information is deemed material (https://vergidosyasi.com, 2019). More broadly, materiality encompasses matters of sufficient magnitude that their omission or misstatement could alter the decisions of reasonable users who rely on financial information (Güredin 2007: 216). Accordingly, material account items, financial events, and other significant elements must be disclosed in financial statements (Yükçü 2014: 181; Karesioğlu 2016: 30).

In auditing, materiality is a key concept in planning the audit scope and directly influences the nature, extent, and timing of audit procedures necessary to obtain reasonable assurance (Raman and Van Daniker 1994: 74). Notably, a distinction exists between accounting materiality and audit materiality, which is both conceptually significant and underdeveloped in the literature. Despite their conceptual linkage, these terms have not been consistently or clearly differentiated in audit literature or widely accessible sources. Accounting materiality supports decision-making related to known, identified, or anticipated misstatements. In contrast, audit materiality provides a threshold to guide the auditor in determining the level of misstatement that warrants detection. While interconnected, the notions of "material" and "materiality" in accounting and auditing diverge in scope and application (Jacoby and Levy 2016: 17).

Materiality is inherently relative and influenced by the auditor's professional experience and judgment. It refers to the relative importance of a specific item within the overall financial statements. If the exclusion or misstatement of a particular element significantly affects the decisions of users relying on the auditor's report, that item is considered material. In practice, materiality varies depending on factors such as the audit environment, the characteristics of the entity under audit, the subject matter of the audit, and the auditor's professional competence (Socol 2008: 209; Şamiloğlu and Akgün 2015: 35).

The issue of materiality is addressed in both the International Standards on Auditing (ISA)—issued by the International Auditing and Assurance Standards Board (IAASB) under the International Federation of Accountants (IFAC)—and the Independent Auditing Standards issued by the Public Oversight Authority (POA) in Turkey.

4.2.1 The Concept of Materiality From the Perspective of Independent Auditing Standards (ISA)

According to auditing standards, materiality must be considered by the auditor when determining the nature, timing, and extent of audit procedures, evaluating the impact of misstatements, and forming the audit opinion (Akdoğan and Muluk 2019: 704).

International Auditing and Assurance Standards Board (IAASB) (2025a), Materiality in Planning and Performing an Audit, addresses the relevance of materiality in the context of financial reporting. As in financial reporting standards, auditing standards recognize the importance of professional judgment. According to POA's translation, IAASB (2025a) states: "The auditor's determination of materiality is a matter that requires the use of professional judgment . . . " (IAASB 2025a, Par. 4).

Financial reporting frameworks generally incorporate the concept of materiality in the preparation and presentation of financial statements. While different frameworks may approach materiality from distinct perspectives, they generally hold that omissions or misstatements—either individually or in aggregate—are considered material if they could reasonably be expected to influence the decisions of financial statement users (IAASB 2025a, Par. 2).

The auditor's determination of materiality is influenced by an understanding of users' information needs. Auditors assume that users possess reasonable knowledge of business, economic activities, and accounting; understand that financial statements are prepared and audited based on materiality thresholds; accept the presence of uncertainties due to estimation and judgment; and make sound economic decisions based on the provided information (IAASB 2025a, Par. 4).

Materiality plays a key role in the planning and execution of audit procedures, in the evaluation of identified misstatements, and in the assessment of uncorrected misstatements, particularly regarding their impact on the financial statements and the auditor's opinion (IAASB 2025a, Par. 5).

In the audit planning phase, the auditor makes informed judgments about the magnitude of misstatements that would be considered material. These judgments inform decisions regarding the nature, timing, and extent of risk assessment procedures, the identification and assessment of risks of material misstatement, and the design of subsequent audit procedures (IAASB 2025a, Par. 6).

It is important to note that the materiality threshold determined during the planning phase does not serve as a definitive lower bound below which misstatements, individually or in aggregate, are always immaterial. In certain circumstances, the auditor may consider a misstatement to be material due to qualitative factors, even if it falls below the quantitative threshold. However, it is not feasible to design audit procedures capable of detecting all potentially material misstatements, particularly those that are material due solely to their nature (IAASB 2025a, Par. 6).

4.3 Determining Audit Materiality

According to auditing standards, the auditor must apply the concept of materiality when determining the structure, timing, and scope of independent audit procedures, when evaluating the impact of misstatements, and when forming an audit opinion (Cömert 2012: 29). To detect material misstatements in financial statements, the independent auditor establishes an acceptable materiality threshold—quantified in monetary terms—during the planning phase of the audit. Setting this threshold requires the exercise of professional judgment. In determining materiality, both the amount and nature of potential misstatements are considered. A misstatement related to the inadequate or incorrect disclosure of accounting policies, which misleads financial statement users, constitutes a qualitative misstatement. In some circumstances, misstatements that are quantitatively immaterial may nevertheless be deemed material due to their qualitative characteristics. For instance, even a small unlawful payment may be considered material if it results in significant income loss or the emergence of a contingent liability. Additionally, the auditor must recognize that multiple individually immaterial misstatements may, in aggregate, have a material impact on the financial statements. Therefore, the auditor must assess materiality both at the financial statement level and at the level of specific classes of transactions, account balances, and disclosures (Güredin 2007: 216–217). In practice, the auditor's responsibility is not to detect and correct every misstatement, but rather to identify and ensure the correction of material misstatements that could reasonably affect users' economic decisions (Kardeş Selimoğlu et al. 2017: 154).

The section titled Main Provisions of IAASB (2025a) includes Paragraphs 10 and 11 under the subheading "Determining Materiality and Performance Materiality When Planning the Audit."

4.3.1 Overall Materiality

In establishing the overall audit strategy, the auditor must determine materiality for the financial statements as a whole. Depending on the specific circumstances of the entity, the auditor may also establish separate materiality thresholds for particular classes of transactions, account balances, or disclosures that are likely to influence users' economic decisions (IAASB 2025a, Par. 10).

4.3.2 Performance Materiality

While IAASB (2025a) requires the use of the materiality concept throughout the planning, execution, and completion stages of the audit, it also introduces the related concept of performance materiality. This concept plays a critical role in risk assessment and in determining the nature, timing, and extent of further audit procedures (Kardeş Selimoğlu et al. 2017: 186). Performance materiality is defined as the amount (or amounts) set below the materiality level for the financial statements as a whole (IAASB 2025a, Par. 9). The purpose of setting this lower threshold is to reduce to an appropriately low level the probability that the aggregate of uncorrected and undetected misstatements exceeds the materiality for the financial statements as a whole. The determination of performance materiality is guided by professional judgment and takes into account various influencing factors. These include the auditor's familiarity with the entity, insights from prior audit engagements, the nature and frequency of material misstatements identified in previous audits, expectations regarding the current period, and the outcome of risk assessments. In practice, performance materiality is typically set as a percentage of the overall materiality threshold for the financial statements (Akdoğan and Muluk 2019: 707).

4.4 Audit Sampling

Audit sampling refers to the application of audit procedures to less than 100% of the units that comprise a class of transactions or account balances, with the aim of forming a conclusion about the entire population (Lessambo 2018: 163).

According to international standards on auditing, sampling is defined as the process of selecting less than the entire population in a manner that ensures each sampling unit has an equal chance of selection. The auditor applies specific audit procedures to the selected items to obtain sufficient and appropriate audit evidence to support conclusions about the population as a whole (IAASB 2025b, Par. 5).

The core principles of audit sampling apply to both tests of controls and substantive procedures for account balances. In audits of small entities, the auditor may be able to examine all journal entries and transactions. However, for larger entities with extensive accounting data and complex transactions, it is typically impractical to audit all records. Therefore, auditors rely on sampling methods to obtain reasonable assurance regarding management's assertions in the financial statements (Messier et al. 2016: 264). In many instances, particularly for control tests, automation is not feasible, prompting auditors to select representative samples from the population. It is crucial that the selected samples reflect the control activities under review and provide reliable audit evidence. Consequently, recent auditing practices emphasize the representativeness of the sample, especially in evaluating the effectiveness of internal controls.

Auditors apply control tests to transactions and activities sampled from across the audit period. This approach allows them to generalize findings from the sample to the entire population and audit period. When control testing is conducted at an interim date, the auditor may need to obtain additional evidence for the remaining period. However, reliance on prior-period audit evidence or assumptions about unchanged circumstances in the current audit period should be approached cautiously. In annual audits, auditors should not presume that prior evidence alone sufficiently supports the continuing effectiveness of controls in reducing the risk of material misstatement (Louwers et al. 2018: 200).

Auditors perform tests of controls and substantive procedures for the following purposes (Arens et al. 2016: 565):

- To determine whether the rate of misstatements in the population is acceptably low,
- To reduce the assessed level of control risk and, consequently, the extent of detailed substantive testing,
- To evaluate whether internal controls over financial reporting are functioning effectively, especially in large entities.

4.4.1 Sample Design and Sample Selection

The audit sampling process begins with the design of the sample, which must align with the auditor's overall audit strategy and the specific objectives of the procedures being performed. Proper sample design enables the auditor to generalize audit evidence from the sample to the broader population and to assess the likely presence of deviations or misstatements IAASB (2025b).

In designing the audit sample, the auditor considers the following elements, as part of the overall audit strategy (Lessambo 2018: 205):

- The relationship between the audit objective and the sample being selected,
- A preliminary assessment of materiality thresholds,
- The auditor's acceptable level of sampling risk (i.e., the risk that the sample does not represent the population),
- The characteristics and variability of the population.

Sample items must be selected in a manner that allows the entire population an equal opportunity of being chosen. Random selection is often used to achieve this objective. Ultimately, the auditor exercises professional judgment to select an appropriate sampling method that reflects the characteristics of the audit population and the risk profile of the engagement.

The development of the auditor's professional judgment is shaped by experience and factors requiring critical assessment, such as (Hay 2020: 59):

- The application of professional scepticism,
- The design and use of audit sampling,
- The choice of analytical procedures,
- The level of reliance placed on the internal audit function (where applicable),
- The findings and evaluations of prior period audit reports.

4.4.2 Sample Selection Methods

While numerous factors influence the determination of an appropriate sample size, maintaining sampling risk at an acceptable level is among the most critical considerations. As the auditor reduces the acceptable level of sampling risk, the required sample size correspondingly increases. Determining sample size through statistical methods is generally more advantageous, as it provides a quantifiable basis for evaluating risk and sample reliability.

Increasing the size of the sample reduces sampling risk. In fact, if the auditor were to examine the entire population, sampling risk would be eliminated. However, testing the full population or using excessively large samples can be highly time-consuming and costly. In practice, auditors are constrained by time and resource limitations, which necessitate the use of sampling methods to gather sufficient and appropriate audit evidence.

With the increasing volume and complexity of data in contemporary audits, auditors face additional challenges. Developments such as intricate supply chain systems, multi-layered organizational structures, and tight audit deadlines demand efficient and effective sampling techniques (Ridley 2017: 130).

Audit sampling methods generally fall into two categories: *statistical* and *non-statistical* approaches.

According to International Standard on Auditing IAASB (2025b), the statistical sampling method possesses two key characteristics:

- Random (chance-based) selection of sample units,
- Use of probability theory to evaluate sampling risk and interpret results.

Statistical sampling methods yield more accurate and reliable outcomes and offer an objective basis for sample selection.

Importantly, using statistical sampling does not eliminate the need for the auditor's professional judgment. On the contrary, statistical methods enable the auditor to quantify and manage sampling risk, allowing for the calculation of a sample size that maintains risk within acceptable limits (Whittington and Pany 2016: 337–338).

IAASB (2025b) also defines non-statistical sampling as an approach that does not exhibit the defining characteristics of statistical sampling. Under this method, the auditor relies on professional judgment—rather than probability theory—to assess sampling risk. The use of non-statistical sampling does not imply a careless or arbitrary selection process. Instead, it reflects the auditor's informed judgment regarding risk and representativeness (Whittington and Pany 2016: 337).

A common misconception is that random sample selection is synonymous with statistical sampling. In reality, random selection refers solely to the method of choosing sample items and may be employed in both statistical and non-statistical approaches. In random sampling, each unit in the population must have an equal chance of being selected. While random selection reduces selection bias, it does not guarantee that the sample will adequately represent the population. Sampling risk still arises if the selected sample lacks the characteristics of the population, even when chosen randomly.

In designing the sample, the auditor decides—based on professional experience and judgment—whether to adopt a statistical or non-statistical approach. IAASB (2025b) makes it clear that sample size alone is not sufficient to determine whether a sampling method is statistical.

Because a sample represents only a portion of the total population, it will not perfectly mirror all population characteristics. As a result, conclusions drawn from a sample will inevitably differ, at least slightly, from those that would be derived from examining the entire population. This discrepancy is referred to as sampling error, and the probability of its occurrence is known as sampling risk.

Sampling risk arises when conclusions drawn from a control or substantive test applied to a sample differ from those that would result if the same test were applied to the full population (Lessambo 2018: 204).

Additionally, auditors may encounter non-sampling errors, which result from human or procedural issues such as data entry mistakes or insufficient expertise in analysis. These errors can lead to incorrect audit conclusions and are classified as non-sampling risk.

Unlike sampling risk, non-sampling risk is avoidable. It can be mitigated through proper training, experienced personnel, and the exercise of sound professional judgment during both sample selection and evaluation. However, sampling risk is inherent to the audit process. Auditors can only minimize, not eliminate, this risk—primarily through thoughtful selection of sampling methods and by increasing sample size as appropriate.

The audit model itself is based on the assumption that a residual risk—a level of uncertainty that cannot be entirely eliminated—will always remain. Therefore, some degree of audit risk concerning material misstatements is inevitable. Recognizing that it is impossible to reduce this residual risk to zero, the auditor must evaluate the possibility of audit failure despite their best efforts, contrary to the expectations of users of the audit report (Hay 2020: 18).

Consequently, in selecting samples for control and substantive testing, the auditor must always consider materiality in conjunction with audit risk to ensure that audit procedures are appropriately focused and proportionate to the identified risks.

4.5 The Role of Materiality Determined in Sample Selection and an Application Example

The auditor conducts control testing and substantive testing of financial transactions in three fundamental stages. These stages consist of several sub-processes, outlined as follows (Arens et al. 2016: 489–490):

- Sample Planning
  - Defining audit objectives,
  - Deciding whether audit sampling is appropriate,
  - Identifying special circumstances or exceptional conditions,
  - Determining the population,
  - Defining the sample units,
  - Establishing the acceptable error rate,
  - Determining the sample size.
- Sample Selection and Application of Audit Procedures
  - Selecting the sample,
  - Applying audit procedures to selected items.
- Evaluation of Results
  - Generalizing the results from the sample to the entire population,
  - Analysing identified anomalies,
  - Assessing the reliability and acceptability of the population.

To illustrate this process, consider a practical application involving a company's domestic sales account. During the audit period, this account comprises 24,172 journal entries, with a total value of 95,928,596 Turkish Lira (TRL).

In line with International Auditing and Assurance Standards Board (IAASB) (2025a), the auditor begins by determining the overall materiality threshold for the financial statements. Subsequently, lower materiality levels are established for individual sub-accounts, particularly those that could influence the economic decisions of users relying on the financial statements (IAASB 2025a, Par. 10).

Failing to allow for a margin of undetected misstatements increases the risk that material misstatements may remain in the financial statements. To mitigate this, auditors establish a performance materiality level, which is designed to reduce to an acceptably low level the probability that the aggregate of uncorrected and undetected misstatements will exceed the overall materiality set for the financial statements (IAASB 2025a, Par. A13).

In this example, the auditor assumes that an appropriate overall materiality rate lies between 0.5% and 1% of the total sales amount. Based on professional judgment, the auditor determines that:

- Performance materiality should be set at 80% of the overall materiality, and
- The acceptable misstatement threshold (or tolerable misstatement) should be set at 5% of the overall materiality.

Thus, overall materiality and performance materiality have been calculated as follows:

		Amount	Performance materiality (80%)	Threshold for misstatements (5%)
Overall materiality	0.5%	479,643	383,714	23,982
Overall materiality	1%	959,286	767,429	47,964

The auditor has set the target audit risk at 5%, indicating that the audit is planned to be conducted with 95% confidence.

In accordance with audit standards, the auditor must assess the risk of material misstatement (RMM) in the financial statements of the audited entity by obtaining sufficient and appropriate audit evidence about the entity's operations, environment, and internal control system (Arens et al. 2016: 262). The RMM consists of two components: inherent risk and control risk (Lessambo 2018: 184):

- *Inherent Risk* (IR): The risk that material misstatements may exist in the financial statements—either individually or in aggregate—before the application of internal controls. This type of risk arises from the nature of the business, transactions, or financial reporting itself.
- *Control Risk* (CR): The risk that the entity's internal controls will fail to prevent or detect material misstatements, either individually or collectively. This risk stems from the design, implementation, and operating effectiveness of the internal control system.

In this case, the auditor has assessed inherent risk at 25% and control risk at 30%, resulting in a risk of material misstatement calculated as:

$$\text{RMM} = \text{IR} \times \text{CR} = 0.25 \times 0.30 = 0.075 = 7.5\% \approx 8\%$$

To meet the target *audit risk* (AR) of 5%, the auditor must manage the detection risk (DR)—that is, the risk that audit procedures will fail to detect material misstatements—such that:

$$AR = RMM \times DR \Rightarrow DR = AR/RMM = 5\%/7.5\% \approx 67\%$$

This implies that audit procedures must be designed to operate with at least 33% assurance (i.e., 1–67%) that any remaining misstatements not addressed by internal controls will be detected.

Alternatively, when presented inversely (as in the original version), if detection risk is 33%, it suggests that audit procedures are expected to eliminate 67% of the risk of material misstatement.

Based on this evaluation, when determining overall materiality, initially considered within the range of 0.5% to 1% of a relevant benchmark (e.g., sales or assets), the auditor may adjust the figure to reflect the strength of the internal control system. In this example, materiality is recalibrated using the lower threshold and the internal control assurance factor:

$$\text{Adjusted Materiality} = 0.5\% + (0.5\% \times 67\%) = 0.5\% + 0.335\% = 0.835\%$$

Thus, it may be deemed appropriate to adopt an overall materiality threshold of approximately 0.83%, acknowledging the mitigating effect of the internal control system on audit risk.

		Amount	Performance materiality (80%)	Threshold for misstatements (5%)
Overall Materiality	0.83%	799,405	639,524	39,970

The auditor has determined overall materiality as 800,000 TL, performance materiality as 640,000 TL, and acceptable misstatement amount as 40,000 TL, respectively.

As demonstrated, to maintain audit risk at the targeted level, the auditor's detection risk—calculated in relation to the assessed risk of material misstatement—has a direct impact on the determination of overall materiality. Consequently, this influences the setting of both performance materiality and the tolerable (acceptable) misstatement threshold.

Following this assessment, the auditor proceeded to apply substantive audit procedures to the selected sample, relying on professional judgment to guide the scope, timing, and nature of the procedures.

Sample size	Total amount of selected samples	Detected misstatements	Total misstatement amount
250	22,055,580 TRL	12	187,500 TRL

Population size	Total amount of population	Total amount of selected samples	The rate of representation of the population (%)
24,172	95,928,596 TRL	22,055,580 TRL	23%

The auditor projects the results of identified misstatements in the selected sample units to the entire population. According to IAASB (2025b), if the extrapolated misstatement—obtained by generalizing detected errors—exceeds the tolerable misstatement (i.e., the acceptable misstatement level), the auditor is required to extend the audit procedures by selecting and testing additional sample units.

In this application, the auditor initially selected 250 sample units, representing 23% of the total population. A misstatement of 187,500 TRL was identified within this sample. When extrapolated to the entire population using proportional estimation:

$$\frac{187{,}500\,\text{TRL}}{23\%} = 815{,}217\,\text{TRL}$$

The projected misstatement of 815,217 TRL exceeds both the auditor's predetermined performance materiality of 640,000 TRL and the overall materiality of 800,000 TRL.

In response, the auditor selected an additional 100 sample units and applied substantive audit procedures to this expanded sample, in accordance with professional standards and judgment.

Sample size	Total amount of selected samples	Detected misstatements	Total misstatement amount
250	22,055,580 TRL	12	187,500 TRL
100	9,512,100 TRL	3	13,250 TRL
350	**31,567,680 TRL**	**15**	**200,750 TRL**

Population size	Total amount of population	Total amount of selected samples	The rate of representation of the population (%)
24,172	95,928,596 TRL	31,567,680 TRL	32.9%

Following the selection of an additional 100 sample units, the auditor's total sample size increased to 350 units, representing 32.9% of the population. The total misstatement identified within this expanded sample amounted to 200,750 TRL.

When this figure is extrapolated to the entire population, the projected misstatement is calculated as follows:

$$\frac{200{,}750 \text{ TRL}}{32.9\%} = 610{,}044 \text{ TRL}$$

The projected misstatement of 610,044 TRL falls below the previously determined performance materiality threshold of 640,000 TRL. As a result, the auditor can form a more robust and reliable audit opinion, supported by a greater degree of assurance that the financial statements are free from material misstatement.

In addition, because the individual misstatements detected during sampling exceed the auditor's established correction threshold, the auditor is obligated to initiate discussions with the entity's management to address and correct the identified misstatements.

By expanding the sample and re-projecting misstatements across the population, the auditor enhances the overall confidence level in the audit results. Given that the revised extrapolated misstatement remains below the acceptable misstatement limit, the auditor is positioned to issue a well-supported opinion regarding the accuracy of the reported sales.

4.6 Conclusion

The concept of materiality refers to deficiencies or misstatements in financial statements that, individually or collectively, are significant enough to influence the decisions of financial statement users. To ensure that users of financial information are not misled in their decision-making, material errors or fraud in the financial statements must be identified and evaluated by independent auditors.

Although materiality in auditing shares similarities with the definition provided by accounting and financial reporting standards, it differs in essential ways. Under financial reporting standards, information is considered material if its omission or misstatement could influence the economic decisions of users, thereby necessitating its inclusion in the financial statements in accordance with the principles of fair presentation and relevance. From an audit perspective, materiality is interpreted as a threshold that guides the auditor in planning and conducting audit procedures, specifically considering the potential of misstatements—individually or in aggregate—to influence user decisions.

The auditor relies on the established materiality levels when obtaining audit evidence that will support the audit opinion. IAASB (2025a) provides guidance on setting both overall materiality and performance materiality during the planning and execution phases of the audit.

Given the volume of accounting data and the increasing complexity of transactions underlying financial statements, it is often impractical—in terms of both time and cost—for auditors to examine all records. Therefore, auditors frequently apply audit procedures to a representative sample of the population rather than performing procedures on every item. IAASB (2025b) offers direction on how to design audit samples, apply procedures to selected items, evaluate results, and ultimately form an audit opinion.

In line with the concept of materiality in auditing, the materiality thresholds determined during the planning phase significantly influence the auditor's sample selection strategy. These thresholds help the auditor ensure that the audit opinion reflects whether the financial statements are free from material misstatement.

Generally, as materiality levels increase, the auditor may select fewer sample units, whereas lower materiality levels—often resulting from a lower acceptable audit risk—require larger samples to obtain sufficient evidence. An auditor aiming to conduct an audit with a low level of audit risk will set lower materiality thresholds, thereby adopting a more cautious and evidence-intensive approach to sampling.

In the application example, the relationship between overall materiality, performance materiality, and acceptable misstatement, as determined through the auditor's professional judgment, was examined in the context of a company's net sales account. For a target audit risk of 5%, and an assessed risk of material misstatement of 8%, the auditor calculated a detection risk of 33%. Based on these risk levels, the auditor selected a sample of 250 transactions from a total of 24,172 sales entries.

However, once the 12 identified misstatements from the sample were extrapolated to the full population, the total projected misstatement exceeded the auditor's overall materiality threshold. In response, the auditor increased the sample size by selecting additional units and re-applied the audit procedures. This was done to determine whether, after extrapolation, the total misstatements would fall below the materiality threshold, thereby allowing the auditor to form a reliable audit opinion.

References

Akdoğan N, Muluk FZ (2019) Bağımsız denetim standartları kapsamında grup şirketlerinin önemlilik düzeylerinin belirlenmesi, kullanılan yöntemlerin incelenmesi ve Bayesian modeli uygulamasının değerlendirilmesi. Muhasebe Bilim Dünyası Dergisi 21(3):704–732. http://dx.doi.org/10.31460/mbdd.562373

Arens AA, Elder RJ, Beasley MS, Hogan CE (2016) Auditing and assurance services: an integrated approach. Pearson. United Kingdom.

Cömert N (2012) Uluslararası denetim standartları kapsamında önemlilik düzeyinin belirlenmesinde kullanılabilecek yöntemler. Mali Çözüm 109:29–50.

Güredin E (2007) Denetim ve güvence hizmetleri (SMMM ve YMM'lere yönelik ilkeler ve teknikler). Arıkan Basım Yayın Dağıtım. Istanbul

Hay D (2020) The future of auditing. Routledge, New York

Inaltong C, Taş O (2015) Bağımsız denetim sürecinde önemlilik düzeyinin belirlenmesi ve bir uygulama. Vergi Dünyası, 401:73–89.

International Auditing and Assurance Standards Board (IAASB) (2025a) International Standards on Auditing (ISA) 320 Materiality in Planning and Performing an Audit. Pages 321–326,

International Federation of Accountants (IFAC), September 24, 2025, New York, https://ifacweb.blob.core.windows.net/publicfiles/2025-09/IAASB-2025-Handbook-Volume-1.pdf, (Accessed on Jan 3rd, 2026)
International Auditing and Assurance Standards Board (IAASB) (2025b) International Standard on Auditing (ISA) 530: Audit Sampling, pages 407–417, International Federation of Accountants (IFAC), September 24, 2025, New York, https://ifacweb.blob.core.windows.net/publicfiles/2025-09/IAASB-2025-Handbook-Volume-1.pdf, (Accessed on Jan 3rd, 2026)
Jacoby J, Levy HB (2016) The materiality mystery—The gap in GAAS. CPA J 14–18
Kardeş Selimoğlu, S, Özbirecikli M, Uzay Ş (2017) Bağımsız denetim (Türkiye Denetim Standartlarıyla uyumlaştırılmış). Nobel Akademik Yayıncılık, Ankara
Karesioğlu F (2016) Finansal muhasebe (Dönem sonu işlemleri TMS/TFRS uygulamalı). Nobel Akademik Yayıncılık, Ankara
Lessambo FI (2018) Auditing, assurance services, and forensics: a comprehensive approach. Palgrave Macmillan, Cham
Louwers T, Blay A, Sinason D, Strawser J, Thibodeau J (2018) Auditing and assurance services. McGraw-Hill Education
Messier W, Glover S, Prawitt D (2016) Auditing and assurance services: a systematic approach. McGraw-Hill Education
Raman KK, Van Daniker R (1994) Materiality in government auditing. J Account 177(2):71–76
Ridley J (2017) Creative and innovative auditing. Routledge, New York
Socol A (2008) Materiality in the context of an audit: between professional judgment and subjectivism. Ann Univ Petroşani, Economics 8(2):209–216
Şamiloğlu F, Akgün Aİ (2015) Finansal tablolar analizi. Ekin Yayınevi, Bursa
Vergi D (2019) Bağımsız denetimde önemlilik nedir? Retrieved July 10, 2020, from https://vergidosyasi.com/2019/12/13/bagimsiz-denetimde-onemlilik-nedir/
Whittington OR, Pany K (2016) Principles of auditing & other assurance services. McGraw-Hill Education
Yükçü S (2014) Yeni TTK uyumlu TMS ve UFRS örnekli genel muhasebe. Altın Nokta Yayınevi, İzmir

Part III
Audit Practices Through the Eyes of MUDEP Academics

Chapter 5
Evaluating Going Concern Assumption in Auditing: A Case in the Renewable Wind Energy Sector

Gizem Çopur Vardar and Zafer Anadolu

Abstract The going concern assumption is a fundamental principle in accounting and auditing, emphasizing an entity's ability to continue its operations in the foreseeable future. This study examines how the going concern assumption is evaluated in the renewable energy sector, specifically within a wind energy entity. Using a case study approach, it explores the stages of the audit process—risk assessment, responding to risk, and reporting—according to International Standards on Auditing (ISA 570). Despite the entity's negative equity due to significant financing expenses from foreign currency-denominated loans, the study demonstrates that understanding sector-specific factors and legal frameworks is critical. After a thorough assessment, the auditor concluded that the use of going concern assumption is appropriate and issued an unqualified opinion, with relevant disclosures highlighted as key audit matters. This paper underscores the importance of professional judgment, analytical procedures, and sector knowledge in forming a reliable going concern evaluation in auditing practices.

Keywords Going concern · Renewable energy · Wind power plant · Auditing · ISA 570 · Material uncertainty

---

This chapter was previously published in Turkish by Gazi Kitabevi with the ISBN: 978-975-7727-16-7.

G. Çopur Vardar (✉)
Faculty of Economics and Administrative Sciences, Mersin University, Mersin, Türkiye
e-mail: gcvardar@mersin.edu.tr

Z. Anadolu
Istanbul, Türkiye
e-mail: zaferanadolu@gmail.com

G. Kurt, Ö. Sarısoy (eds.), *Recent Advancements in Auditing*, Accounting, Finance, Sustainability, Governance & Fraud: Theory and Application,
https://doi.org/10.1007/978-981-95-5811-7_5

5.1 Introduction

Although some basic principles of accounting have changed in the historical process, one of the basic principles that has not changed is the going concern assumption (Shvyreva and Kruglyak 2016, p. 1). Going concern, an essential concept in accounting and auditing, is the basis of accounting in preparing financial statements, as explained in the Conceptual Framework (CF). The going concern assumption is that the entity can and intends to continue its activities for the foreseeable future and does not intend or need to enter liquidation or cease operations.

Along with financial scandals and crises, auditors' lack of early warnings regarding bankruptcies has drawn the attention of financial statement users and the public to audit reports and auditors. An expectation has arisen for auditors to disclose matters that may raise doubts on an entity's ability to continue operations. Regulatory bodies have made various arrangements for auditors to assess whether the entity is able to continue its operations and present the results of their assessment in the audit report. The International Auditing and Assurance Standards Board (IAASB) revised the existing standard on going concern, ISA 570 "Going Concern", and increased the responsibilities of auditors in this regard (Türel and Türel 2016, p. 105). ISA 570 addressed the auditors' and entities' responsibilities of separately and increased the auditors' responsibilities related to going concern, inquiry, performing audit procedures, forecasting, reporting, and communication (KPMG 2019). The positive aspects of the regulation are explained as reducing the expectations gap (Raghunandan and Rama 1995, p. 50) and increasing the quality of the audit with increased communication (reporting) (Knechel and Vanstraelen 2007; Robinson 2008; Chi and Chin 2011).

Auditors' responsibility under ISA 570 is to gather evidence to assess whether the entity has used the going concern assumption correctly while preparing the financial statements, determine if there is a material uncertainty regarding going concern, and report these assessments. In other words, this involves evaluating the entity's claims about using the going concern assumption and reporting appropriately to stakeholders.

Auditors consider the assessment and judgment of going concern one of the most difficult and complex issues (Louwers 1998, p. 144). While going concern is a much-studied topic, academic studies have not focused much on implementing the standard.

This study discusses the audit process of an entity generating electricity with wind energy in the renewable energy sector in Türkiye for the accounting period ending on December 31st. When the events and conditions lead the auditor to question the going concern, evaluating whether these events and conditions create material uncertainty and how this evaluation is reflected in the report is illustrated with an example event.

The renewable energy sector was selected because it distinguishes itself from other sectors regarding its operational processes. Wind power plants (WPPs) are prominent among renewable energy generation facilities because they rapidly grow their share of the total installed capacity worldwide. Wind power is one of the fastest-growing, most established, and cost-effective renewable energy sources, playing a vital role in energy and climate initiatives. It accounts for a significant share of electricity generation, representing 14% in the EU, 20% in Germany and the UK, 57% in Denmark, and 10% in the USA (McKenna et al. 2025, p. 2). Utilizing renewable energy potential to lessen Türkiye's reliance on foreign energy is a crucial long-term goal for the country (Kılınç Savrul 2016, p. 110). In Türkiye, the contribution of wind energy to the total installed power has increased from 0.07% to 10.64% over the past 23 years (2000–2023). Its share of renewable energy has expanded from 0.17% to 18.69% (TEİAŞ 2023). Moreover, wind power plants were chosen due to their substantial initial investment requirements, low operating expenses, and the potential for quick revenue generation. Since an entity operating in Türkiye was considered a case, the study also referenced the legal regulations in Türkiye.

The second part addresses specific issues related to investing in and operating Wind Power Plants (WPPs). The third section outlines the auditor's approach to evaluating the entity's going concern assumption during the audit process according to International Standards on Auditing (ISAs). The fourth section discusses indicators and circumstances that significantly raise concerns about going concern and the procedures for assessing these indicators. Finally, the fifth section presents a case study.

In the case study, negative equity was acknowledged as an event and a condition that could raise significant doubts during the planning phase. However, due to the specific circumstances of the sector and the applicable legal regulations, the auditor does not consider the loss of capital in the financial statements to be a material uncertainty. Therefore, the financial statements are deemed appropriate to be prepared under the going concern assumption. The auditor's report remains unqualified since the entity has supplied the necessary disclosures in the footnotes. The fact that a critical financial indicator, such as capital loss, does not weaken the going concern assumption highlights the importance of understanding the sector's structure and thoroughly analyzing the implications of legal regulations during the audit.

5.2 Investment and Operational Aspects Specific to Wind Power Plants

Wind power plants transitioning from the investment to operation phases differ from other sectors. Site selection, wind measurement, turbine selection and placement, obtaining a license, and post-license procedures lead to the operation phase. In the site selection phase, wind measurements at the site where the facility will be installed should be collected for a year. The land structure should be assessed, road conditions and land ownership should be investigated, and the high voltage lines necessary for transferring energy to the national grid should be examined. During the wind measurement phase, it is essential to determine the wind speed that will impact energy production, the wind direction for turbine placement, and the design of the windmills based on variations in wind conditions. After completing all these stages, a license for sales and distribution activities must be acquired from the Republic of Türkiye Energy Market Regulatory Authority (EPDK) following Law No. 4628. Licenses can be issued for a minimum of 10 years and a maximum of 49 years. Post-licensing procedures include project approval, engineering work, leasing of government lands, commencement of construction, procurement of necessary tools and equipment, and the completion of construction and commissioning (Bozkurt and Karataş 2011, pp. 88–89). According to Law No. 4628, the facility must become operational within three years of obtaining the license, although this period can be extended under specific conditions.

The investment cost of wind power plants is relatively high, with wind turbines comprising the most significant portion of the initial investment (including investment and license fees, wind analysis, project design, wind turbine, and installation). The expense associated with wind turbines accounts for approximately 64–75% of the total cost of wind power plants. Factors influencing turbine costs include components such as the tower, propeller, gearbox, control system, and alternator, all of which significantly contribute to the overall expenditure. Costs fluctuate depending on whether the tower material is steel or concrete and the tower's height (Yılmaz 2014: 74).

Unlike other power plants, one of the most significant benefits of wind power plants is that the unit cost of generated electricity remains unaffected by fuel prices and fluctuations. Operation, maintenance, and repair costs account for approximately 20–25% of the cost per kWh (kilowatt-hour) of electricity produced by a wind turbine. These costs include insurance, periodic maintenance, repairs, and spare parts (Özcan 2009, p. 25). Wind energy is a source of power that demands significant capital investment per kWh with current production technologies, but has the lowest fuel and operating costs. Like any capital-intensive investment, the profitability of wind power plants is highly sensitive to the cost of capital, specifically the conditions surrounding equity and loan financing for the facilities. For example, factors such as the interest rate, repayment schedule, and maturity determine the cost of loan financing, while the period of plant wear allowance and the repayment period affect the cost of equity financing. (Yılmaz 2014, p.75).

Once the operation begins, the wind turbine requires regular maintenance to ensure it continues to function effectively. Maintenance costs encompass expenses associated with the upkeep of turbine components, including propellers, alternators, gearboxes, blades, transformers, power poles, and transmission lines utilized for energy transmission. The government determines the sales revenue of WPP in foreign currency (USD cents per kWh), enabling all generated energy to be sold (Law No. 5346, Annex I).

5.3 Going Concern Assumption in the Audit Process and Responsibilities of the Parties

Financial statements are prepared assuming that the entity will continue as a going concern and will be able to do so for the foreseeable future, unless the entity intends to liquidate or cease operations. (Conceptual Framework, par. 9; IAS 1, par. 25). The valuation methods for the components of the basic financial statements (assets, resources, revenues, expenses) in the Accounting/Financial Reporting Standards, periodicity, and accrual basis can be utilized under the going concern assumption. Therefore, if the entity's management intends to go into liquidation or cease operations, it should prepare its financial statements with a different justification and disclose this in the main financial statements (Conceptual Framework, par. 3.9). While a specific time frame is not defined for the foreseeable future, the entity's management is responsible for conducting a going concern assessment that covers at least 12 months from the financial reporting date (IAS 1, par. 26).

The auditors are responsible for gathering evidence to determine whether the financial statements prepared by management meet specific criteria and for communicating their opinion on those statements to interested parties. Their responsibility includes assessing the appropriateness of using the going concern assumption when preparing the financial statements. If the auditor concludes that the going concern assumption is not appropriate, the basis for preparing the financial statements and, consequently, the auditor's basis for performing the audit will change. However, if the auditor finds that the going concern assumption is appropriate but material uncertainties exist, they must perform additional audit procedures. In both scenarios, further disclosures will be needed in the audit report.

According to auditing standards, it is the responsibility of the entity's management to conduct going concern assessments and, if necessary, to provide appropriate disclosures in the notes to the financial statements. The auditor questions the appropriateness of management's assessments and estimates and, if necessary, evaluates the disclosures' adequacy. Although the auditing standards do not set an upper limit for the period for such an assessment, the auditor should be required to complete the assessments made by the management for a future period of less than 12 months (ISA 570, par.13).

As a result of the assessment, management may become aware of material uncertainties regarding events or conditions that raise substantial doubts about the entity's ability to continue as a going concern. In this case, management is more responsible for disclosing the uncertainty in the financial statements. Such uncertainty may render the use of the going concern assumption inappropriate. In these situations, management is required to explain the basis on which it is preparing the financial statements and why the going concern assumption is not applicable (IAS 1, par. 25).

The auditor's responsibility for the going concern assessment, which primarily falls to the entity's management, is limited. As explained in ISA 200, "Overall Objective of the Independent Auditor, and the Conduct of an Audit in Accordance with International Standards on Auditing," there may be structural constraints on the auditor's ability to detect material misstatements. In cases of future events or conditions that could jeopardize the entity's ability to continue as a going concern, the potential effects of these inherent limitations will be more significant and will impact the audit process. The auditor may not be able to predict such future events or conditions. Thus, when the auditor's report does not reference any material uncertainty regarding the entity's capability to operate as a going concern, it does not assure such capability.

As noted in ISA 570, the auditor must gather enough relevant evidence to assess the appropriateness of the going concern assumption of management when preparing the financial statements. They also need to determine whether there is a material uncertainty regarding the entity's ability to operate as a going concern. Figure 5.1 summarizes the auditor's responsibilities during the risk assessment, risk response, and reporting phases of the risk-focused audit process.

Table 5.1 outlines the auditor's responsibilities regarding going concern assumption of ISA 570 and other relevant standards. The handling of the going

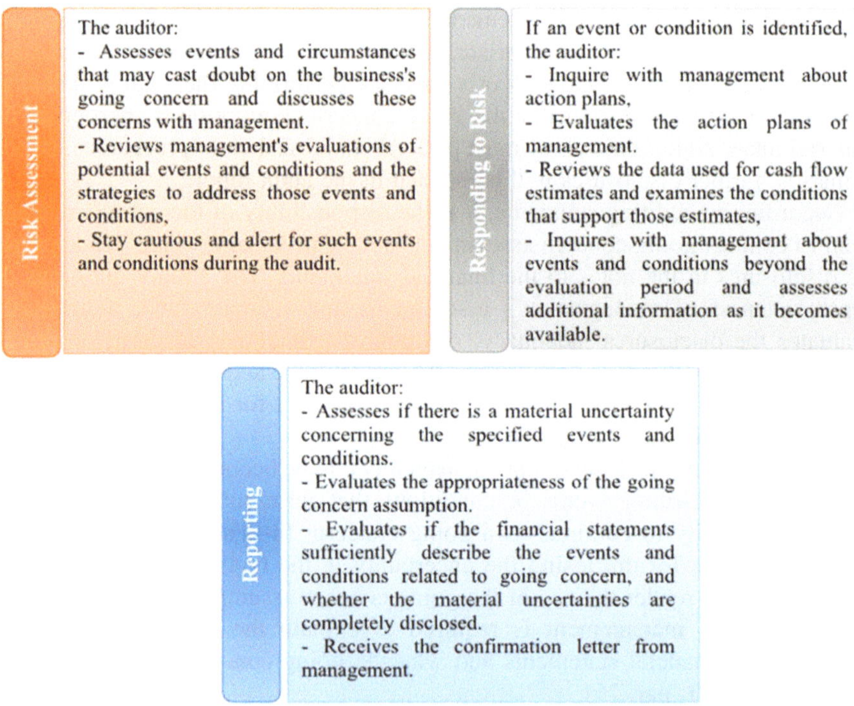

Fig. 5.1 Auditor responsibilities related to going concern in risk-focused auditing. "Guide to using ISAs in the audits of small and medium-sized entities, Vol 2- practical guidance". Fourth Edition, IFAC, 2018, p.133

Table 5.1 Auditors' responsibilities for continuity

More Inquiries	Thoroughly evaluate the adequacy of the auditor's supporting evidence for management's assessment of going concern. Assess the risk of management bias and utilize going concern reports more extensively where available.
More Procedures	It introduced detailed regulations on audit documentation related to the entity and its environment, as well as the key indicators necessary for recognizing the internal control system. Internal control is crucial to the entity's ability to continue as a going concern. Indicators of potential bias regarding the entity's going concern include the auditor's assessment of the audit procedures (ISA 315).
More Insight	Withdraw and review all evidence, whether corroborative or contradictory, that supports or undermines the entity's going concern inferences, and draw conclusions regarding going concern (ISA 570 and ISA 560).
More Reporting	Regardless of whether management's assessment of going concern is appropriate, the auditor's reporting responsibilities have expanded to ensure clarity and a unqualified opinion in their reports. The auditor should disclose their work in forming their judgments, including any key observations (ISA 570, ISA 700, ISA 701, ISA 705, ISA 706).
More Contacts	The auditor has a responsibility to report to an appropriate external authority on going concern matters when the auditor considers it necessary to include in the auditor's report the paragraph "a material uncertainty about going concern" or to express a qualified, adverse, or disclaimer of opinion (ISA 570, ISA 700, ISA 705, ISA 706).

Note Adapted from https://assets.kpmg.com/content/dam/kpmgsites/uk/pdf/2019/10/blc-revisions-to-going-concern-uk-auditing-standard.pdf Copyright KPMG (2019)

concern assumption within the framework of these standards is detailed, including the stages of the audit process.

(a) Going Concern in the Planning Phase (Risk Assessment): After client acceptance, the auditor must prepare the audit plan and determine the nature, scope, and timing of the audit. At this stage, to appropriately prepare the audit plan, the auditor should identify the risks of material misstatement due to fraud and error (ISA 315, par.1). Therefore, the auditor's assessment of going concern starts with getting to know the entity, its environment, and its internal control system by applying risk assessment procedures during the planning stage. The auditor must also assess the risks arising from significant conditions, events, circumstances, and actions, or inactions that could negatively impact the entity's ability to achieve its objectives and implement its strategies, or from setting inappropriate objectives and strategies (ISA 315, par. 11).

Most business risks have financial consequences that impact the financial statements. The entity's business risks can influence the auditor's opinion in two ways. They may directly impact the auditor's judgment when assessing the risk of material misstatement or alter the evaluation of the appropriateness of the going concern assumption in a down economy (ISA 315; A.39, A.41).

Understanding the entity, environment, and internal control system is a dynamic and ongoing process throughout the audit. This process includes gathering, updating, and analyzing information, which serves as a reference for the auditor in planning and exercising professional judgment during the audit (ISA 570, A.1). Consequently, the auditor evaluates relevant references to going concern using professional judgment, aided by updated information and analysis, throughout the audit process. In other words, the auditor's assessment of the use of the going concern assumption begins at the planning stage and continues throughout the audit.

(b) Performing the Audit (Responding to Risk): According to ISA 570, if events or conditions are identified that may raise significant doubts about the entity's ability to continue as a going concern, the auditor reviews management's assessment and plans for future actions to determine whether a material uncertainty exists concerning those events or conditions. The auditor evaluates whether these plans are feasible and whether there is a chance that the current situation will improve due to their implementation (ISA 570, A.20).

The auditor uses considerable professional judgment in making going concern assessments. Going concern is an assessment of the future and inherently involves uncertainty. For this reason, the assessment to be made by entity management includes the judgment of entity management about future estimates and the possible results of these estimates. Therefore, this assessment relies heavily on professional skepticism. The auditor should consider the timing of events, conditions or their consequences, the size and complexity of the entity, the nature and state of its operations, the degree to which it is influenced by external factors, and data acquired after the reporting date that was unavailable before it, as these will impact the judgment made (ISA 315, par. 5).

The auditor should also examine each issue where he applies his professional judgment from the viewpoint of the financial statement users. Going concern refers to the notion that the entity can operate as a going concern for these users. In other words, the entity can utilize its assets and meet its obligations in the normal course of business.

Academic studies on business continuity have indicated that current management, particularly in financially distressed businesses, may produce overly optimistic forecasts to avoid management change (Frost 1997; Koch 2002). Additionally, management plans may be utilized to manage risks to continuity. Behn et al. (2001) identified that two elements in the business plan—issuing shares and raising additional funds—are negatively correlated with going concern disclosure. Consequently, auditors face risks when assessing the forecasts and plans established by the entity. It can be stated that auditors employ their professional skepticism to counter the risk of management's optimism when appraising the forecasts outlined in the plans of businesses with uncertainty about going concern (Feng and Li 2014).

During the execution of the audit plan, the auditor will perform control tests and substantive procedures. The accuracy of the data that will inform the final decision on going concern will directly relate to the appropriateness and sufficiency of the evidence collected during the audit. Therefore, while specific audit procedures tailored to each account are used during the audit, obtaining sufficient and appropriate audit evidence may be more crucial for certain accounts due to industry-specific circumstances than for others.

When evaluating the important issues that affect the auditor's going concern assessment regarding the accounting practices specific to wind power plants in light of the information provided in section 2, it can be concluded that some accounts stand out.

(c) Going Concern (Reporting): In assessing going concern, the auditor must conclude on the appropriateness of management's use of the going concern assumption and, based on the audit evidence obtained, whether a material uncertainty exists regarding events or conditions that may cast significant doubt on the entity's ability to continue as a going concern. If the going concern basis is inappropriate or the auditor concludes that a material uncertainty exists about going concern, the auditor shall determine the appropriate type of opinion following the standards, considering any required disclosures. For users of the auditor's report, forming and presenting the opinion is essential to achieving the IAASB's objectives.

To close the expectations gap for audit report users, the sections of the report that outline the responsibilities of the auditor and those charged with governance should incorporate a statement detailing each party's responsibilities regarding going concern (ISA 570; ISA 700).

The auditor's conclusions are based on the audit evidence obtained up to the date of the auditor's report. However, future events or conditions may lead the entity to cease to continue as a going concern (ISA 700, par. 39. b.iv). Therefore, after the audit, the going concern should be reassessed for events occurring after the reporting date (ISA 560, A.9). If, in the auditor's judgment, the magnitude of the possible effect of the uncertainty regarding going concern and the likelihood of its occurrence are deemed to be a material uncertainty, the auditor shall form an audit opinion based on the existence of certain disclosures in the financial statements (Table 5.2).

In forming the opinion, the auditor will assess the sufficiency of the disclosures and the appropriateness of the going concern assumption based on the evidence gathered (Table 5.2). Table 5.2 outlines the circumstances under which the auditor may issue an unqualified opinion, which will also affect the structure of the audit report. If there is an adequate explanation for the material uncertainty in the financial statements, the auditor shall express an unqualified opinion. The auditor shall create a separate section in the auditor's report under the heading "Material Uncertainty Related to Going Concern" (ISA 570, par. 22). If the explanations are insufficient, the auditor shall provide the appropriate limited unqualified or qualified opinion (ISA 705) and shall disclose the basis for the opinion (ISA 570, par. 23). If the use of the going concern assumption is inappropriate and the entity has prepared its financial statements on another basis, the auditor shall express an

Table 5.2 Adequacy of management's disclosures regarding going concern

Auditor's Assessment	Explanation Expected from Management in the Financial Statements
The entity can appropriately apply the going concern assumption, although there is material uncertainty.	• Adequate disclosure of the key events or conditions that may raise significant doubt about the entity's ability to continue as a going concern, along with management's plans to address those events or conditions. Disclosure of a material uncertainty regarding events or conditions that could considerably impact the entity's ability to continue as a going concern; and • Explanation that it may not be possible for the entity to leverage its assets and meet its obligations in the ordinary course of business
Events or conditions that may cast significant doubts about the entity's ability to continue as a going concern, though there are no material uncertainties.	Adequate disclosures regarding the events or conditions in the financial statements must be provided, considering the provisions of the applicable financial reporting framework.

Note Adapted from ISA 570, A.24-A.25

unqualified opinion, provided the entity has disclosed the basis used and the reasons for using that basis. Additionally, the auditor may include a statement in the audit report to emphasize the footnotes disclosed by the entity under the heading of matters drawing attention to ISA 706 "Emphasis of Matter Paragraphs and Other Matter Paragraphs in the Independent Auditor's Report" (ISA 570, A.27) (Table 5.3).

The auditor is also required to assess events occurring after the balance sheet date for going concern following ISA 560 "Subsequent Events". However, the auditor shall inform the users of the financial statements that the effect of transactions and events that have occurred up to the date of the audit report, and of which he is aware, has been taken into account (ISA 700, A.66).

5.4 Indicators and Procedures Used to Assess Going Concern

The entity's financial data, along with other non-financial factors related to its operations and events, can serve as a benchmark for evaluating its going concern. There has been extensive discussion and many publications concerning the going concern assumption in academic research. Carson et al (2013) and Gissel et al. (2010) offer a thorough literature review. Upon reviewing these studies, it seems that the majority of academic research emphasizes the analysis of financial statements, particularly financial indicators and ratios. Additionally, a few studies focus on non-financial aspects, including market data, strategic initiatives, management structure, the industry in which the entity operates, and ownership structure.

Table 5.3 Forming opinions on going concern

Auditor Assessment	The Use of the Going Concern Assumption in Financial Statements	Financial Explanation in Tables	Auditor's Opinion
Going Concern Assumption: NOT APPLICABLE	Management has prepared the financial statements using the going concern assumption.	It does not matter if there is an explanation in the financial statements indicating that it is inappropriate for management to use this basis.	Qualified Opinion
	Management has concluded that preparing the financial statements on a going concern assumption is inappropriate; therefore, an alternative basis has been used.	The auditor assesses the appropriateness of the basis used and verifies whether there is a sufficient explanation of the basis on which the financial statements are prepared.	Unqualified Opinion (If the substance is appropriate and the disclosure is sufficient)
The Going Concern Assumption is appropriate, but material uncertainties exist.	The financial statements are prepared on the going concern assumption.	There is a sufficient explanation for the uncertainty.	Unqualified Opinion
		Inadequate explanation for the uncertainty	Qualified Opinion or Adverse Opinion
	The financial statements are prepared on the going concern assumption.	In situations where multiple material uncertainties pertain to the financial statements as a whole, the auditor should	Disclaimer of opinion
The auditor will issue either an unqualified or qualified opinion if management requests the auditor to assess or expand the scope of the assessment. However, management does not comply with this request.			

Note Adapted from ISA 570, ISA 700

Furthermore, some research also examines auditor characteristics, such as the number of audit engagements, non-audit services, remuneration, and gender, as additional factors not outlined in the standards (Trana and Alfiero 2019, p. 9).

5.4.1 Indicators

In ISA 570, events or conditions that may significantly doubt an entity's ability to continue as a going concern are classified into three categories: financial, operational, and other indicators. Each category provides examples, including but not limited to the types of events or conditions that may raise serious doubt. The listed

Table 5.4 Indicators that raise serious doubts about going concern

Financial Indicators
• Net liability or short-term net liability status. • Overreliance on short-term debt to finance long-term assets. • Negative cash flows from operating activities are reflected in the historical financial statements. • Substantial operating losses or considerable declines in the value of cash-generating assets, • Negative key financial ratios. • Delays or interruptions in dividend payments. • Failure to pay creditors by the due date. • Failure to adhere to the terms of their contracts. • Transition from deferred payments to advance payments in transactions with suppliers. • Inability to secure funding for new product development or other major investments. • Unrealistic expectations that fixed-maturity debt will be repaid or refinanced at maturity. • Indications that lenders will withdraw financial support. • Negative cash flows from operating activities appear in prospective financial statements.
Operation Indicators
• Management's intention to liquidate the business or cease operations. • Vacancies exist in key management positions without replacements. • Loss of a major market, important customer or customers, concession, license, or essential supplier or suppliers. • Labor shortages. • Significant raw materials bottleneck. • The rise of a highly successful competitor.
Other Indicators
• Non-compliance with capital adequacy requirements or other legal obligations, including solvency or liquidity requirements for financial institutions. • Lawsuits filed against the entity that have not been finalized might lead to claims suggesting that the entity cannot meet its obligations if finalized against it. • Changes in legislation or government policies are anticipated to have a negative impact on the business. • Disasters that are either uncovered or underinsured when they happen.

Note Adapted from ISA 570, A.3

events or conditions, along with these examples, are intended to guide the auditor and are presented in Table 5.4.

In ISA 570, the indicators are not ranked hierarchically; instead, the individually or collectively listed indicators may cast significant doubt on the entity's ability to continue as a going concern. Furthermore, there is no clarification regarding the extent or rate of decline in the financial indicators and the fundamental financial ratios to be employed. The IAASB established the indicators in this standard based on events identified as influencing going concern during the global financial crisis (Bava & Trana, 2018, p. 112).

The auditor must apply professional judgment and consider specific conditions of the entity to assess if events and circumstances suggest that it may not be a going concern. Due to the strong connection between going concern and financial distress, financial indicators are widely used in the assessment. Financial ratios play a key role in evaluating the entity's current status and trends in the analytical review process. Liquidity and financial structure ratios are commonly used to evaluate the capacity to meet short-term obligations. Research indicates that defaults on debt contracts and debt restructuring are critical indicators of going concern (Chen and Church 1992).

While cash and liquidity shortages may lead to bankruptcy, profitability ratios are also important indicators. Current year and/or recurring losses are recognized as financial indicators pertinent to assessing going concern (Lee et al. 2005).

In their study in Italy, Bava and Trana (2013) found that very few entities that made going concern disclosures in the previous year were able to resolve their problems. Another factor that auditors consider is whether the entity disclosed a going concern in the prior year's audit report. Research has shown that if there is a disclosure in the previous year, auditors are more likely to disclose in the current period (Lennox 2000; Vanstraelen 2003; Chan et al. 2006).

5.4.2 Procedures

The nature of an audit procedure refers to its objective (test of control or substantive procedures) and type (audit, observation, inquiry, confirmation, recalculation, reapplication, or analytical procedure). The nature of audit procedures is the most crucial element in addressing matters identified as risks. (ISA, 330, A.6).

If the auditor identifies events or conditions that may cast significant doubt about the going concern, the auditor shall perform additional procedures. Additional procedures aim to determine whether a material uncertainty exists related to those events or conditions. The additional procedures to be performed are described in ISA 570. If management has not assessed the entity's ability to continue as a going concern, the auditor should request management to make that assessment, and assess whether management's plans for future steps related to its assessment of the entity's ability to continue as a going concern are practicable in the circumstances and, even if they are practicable, whether there is a possibility that the current situation will not improve as a result (ISA 570, A.16). If management has prepared a cash flow forecast and the analysis of the forecast is significant in terms of future results that could affect management's plan, management should assess the reliability of the underlying data used to prepare the forecast and determine whether there is sufficient basis (support) for the forecast. An additional procedure is to assess whether any additional information or circumstances have arisen since the date of management's assessment and to request a written statement from management about their plans for future steps and the feasibility of those plans (ISA 570, A.20).

These procedures outline how the auditor operates to reach a decision. During the going concern assessment, auditors primarily apply procedures like requesting and examining necessary documents from the entity's management, along with

Table 5.5 Audit evidence to gather and procedures to implement for the indicators

Indicators	Audit evidence	Procedure
Indicators Related to Contractual Obligations		
Borrowings with an impending maturity and no real prospect of repayment or extension, or loan repayment renewal. Unjustified use of short-term borrowing to finance long-term assets. Difficulties in complying with the loan agreement	Loan agreements, additional agreements, payment orders, entity plans (budgets and forecasts), correspondence with credit institutions (lenders)	Requests, analytical procedures
Changing the payment schedule to suppliers based on maturity or installments, compared to payment by delivery of goods (Economically unsustainable debt)	Contracts with suppliers and customers for supplies, purchases, sales, leases, etc. Additional contracts, plans (budgets, forecasts), correspondence with debtors and creditors	Requests, analytical procedures
Indicators on Financing Sources		
Failure to secure financing for development activity and other significant investments	Accounting (financial) statement, plans (budgets and forecasts) of the audited organization	Analytical procedures
Significant operating loss	Financial Statements	Analytical Procedure
Indicators Related to the Entity's Own Resources		
The sale of a significant volume of raw materials comparable to or exceeding the revenue from manufactured goods or services sales. Lack of primary means of production	Analytical and synthetic accounting records on accounting (financial) statements, financial and final accounts, and asset accounting	Investigation Analytical Procedure
Personnel issues: dismissal of key production and management staff without adequate replacement	Personnel documents (personal files, employment orders, dismissal, etc.)	Investigation
Judicial and Political Indicators		
Lawsuits against the audited entity that are under review and, if the plaintiff is successful, could lead to a court decision that is inappropriate for that entity	Information about cases from the media, correspondence with partners, and evaluation of the case by an independent expert	Demand Investigation Leveraging the Expert
Changes in legislation or changes in the political situation	Information from the media, entity plans (budget and forecasts)	Demand

Note Adapted from Shvyreva, O.I., & Kruglyak, Z.I. (2016), pp. 5–8

inquiries and analytical procedures. Table 5.5. illustrates which procedures are applied in various situations.

Regardless of the applicability of the going concern assumption in the audit process, substantive procedures and control tests are conducted during the audit of the financial statements. When going concern is considered as a separate risk assessment procedure in addition to these, among the risk assessment procedures in ISA 315 (inquiry, analytical procedures, observation and audit), analytical procedures used in the assessment of financial information are mainly used to determine the risks by questioning other persons within the entity who have the necessary information and analyzing the meaningful relationships between financial and non-financial data (Table 5.5.).

When assessing, the auditor should act with professional skepticism, considering risks such as the entity's intentional concealment of information, misrepresentation of plans and estimates, use of cash and cash equivalents, and intentional distortion of financial statement data. The auditor should also ignore the possible adverse outcome of litigation in the entity's assessment (Shvyreva and Kruglyak 2016, pp. 5–8).

5.5 Overview of the Case Study Enterprise

Based on the data of an enterprise producing wind energy, an attempt was made to create a framework within the scope of auditing standards on going concern throughout the entire audit process.

After completing the investment phase, the entity started to generate electricity from wind energy and sold the electricity it generated. The entity prepares its financial statements following IAS/IFRS. It is subject to an independent audit, and its audit is carried out within the scope of ISA.

5.5.1 *Activities Conducted During the Planning (Risk Assessment) Phase*

As part of the planning stage, the auditor assesses the risks related to the entity, its environment, and its internal control system. In addition to other risks, the auditor also assesses whether events and conditions cast significant doubt on the entity's ability to continue as a going concern. The evidence obtained by the auditor at this stage is as follows:

- Due to the nature of the sector, in the early years of operation, certain assets (tangible fixed assets) and resources (financial liabilities, especially long-term ones) constitute a proportionally significant part of the statement of financial position. Similarly, in the income statement, revenue and cost of sales related to operating activities and financing expenses related to loans are the most important account groups. The sector's operating expenses are pretty low compared to the sales-related account groups. In his risk assessment, the auditor has identified the long-term foreign currency denominated financial loans and the possibility of loss and negative capitalization due to the high amount of financing expenses that may arise from the exchange rate risk related to these loans as one of the events and conditions that may raise serious doubts about going concern.

- The enterprise's revenue is indexed to foreign currency, and the collection period does not exceed one month. Therefore, the entity does not have many trade receivables. Hence, whether the entity will be in a cash shortage to fulfill its obligations is highly correlated with the income from net sales and the cost of sales. Therefore, the auditor has selected net sales[1] as the benchmark for determining the materiality level. However, since the risk assessment is high, the auditor determined the rate applied to the general materiality level to be 50%[2] and planned to reduce the audit risk by lowering the materiality level.
- Based on the evidence obtained during the planning stage, the auditor concluded that the uncertainty about going concern is not at a level that would preclude using the going concern assumption. However, it may change during the audit. The auditor has prepared the audit plan and program based on events and conditions that raise concerns about the appropriateness of the going concern assumption.

5.5.2 Activities During the Audit Plan Implementation (Responding to Risk) Phase

The audit plan directed the auditor's focus toward significant economic transactions relevant to the sector. Additionally, additional procedures were undertaken due to material uncertainty regarding the going concern.

5.5.2.1 Sector-Specific Accounting Practices and Audit

Research and Development activities during the establishment phase of wind power plants are more costly than those of other power plants. According to par. 43 (a) IAS 38 Intangible Assets, expenses incurred during the research phase should not be capitalized and must be recognized as an expense in the financial

[1] The amounts that can be considered benchmarks for determining the materiality level will be influenced by the entity's nature. For instance, profit before tax for a profitable business, net sales for a loss-making business or a business at the break-even point, total assets for a business in the investment period, and equity for a non-profit organization can be selected as benchmarks (Şavlı 2019, p.184).

[2] When determining performance materiality, the auditor applies a ratio between 75% and 50% of the general materiality level (İnaltong and Taş 2015, p. 82). Since the entity assesses the risk as high, the auditor has expanded the audit scope by using the low 50% ratio.

statements because the outcome is not yet certain (the potential for future benefit is not certain). On the other hand, expenses incurred in the development phase are studies on applying the information obtained in the research phase to the project being worked on and should be capitalized since the result is certain (potential to provide future benefit) (ISA 38, par. 43 (c)). In cases where research and development expenses cannot be separated, the expenses incurred cannot be capitalized (Kaval 2008). During the establishment process of wind power plants, site selection and wind measurements are the research carried out to obtain information on whether the project is feasible, and the expenses incurred in this process should be recognized directly as expenses. Engineering studies carried out after determining the project's feasibility and the tribunes' structure can be capitalized within the scope of development expenses.

Another important issue is the capitalization of the license. Since the license received is a right, it should be capitalized as an intangible asset and amortized over the license period following IAS 38 (par. 90).

In wind power plants, the turbines, which provide cash flow and constitute a large part of the investment amount, should be capitalized according to IAS 16 Property, Plant and Equipment (par. 6). However, borrowing costs, one of the factors that will constitute the cost of the turbines, are also important. Grandstands are acquired with foreign currency-denominated and long-term borrowings. According to the IAS 23 Borrowing Costs standard, if the asset is a qualifying asset (meaning its production or construction takes more than one year), borrowing costs can be included in the asset's cost (par 8). Therefore, foreign exchange differences and interest on the loans used for the tribunes purchased should be recognized as finance costs without adding them to the cost of the asset. However, for a power plant with a long establishment phase, the foreign exchange difference and interest of the loan used during the establishment phase can be capitalized. Another issue related to wind turbines is their depreciation.

Tribunes consist of various parts (tower, wing, generator, gear, etc.). If their costs are determined separately following IAS 16, each part should be depreciated over its economic life.

Therefore, the auditor shall pay particular attention to the material accuracy and correct classification and presentation of capitalized amounts (property, plant, equipment, intangible assets) and their depreciation and amortization. Another important issue is the calculation of interest and exchange rate differences for power plants with credit-intensive financing and the accurate recognition and presentation of these differences in the period they relate to. Due to the structure of the sector, the correct calculation of the value of assets and periodic depreciation is important for the correct determination of the cost of sales. Since the operating expenses of the enterprise are not very high and the sales, which are the determinant of revenue, are directly related to production and the amount of production does not fluctuate much depending on the installed power and the sales price is determined according to the law, the auditor is more important in determining the gross profit/loss and operating profit/loss and cash flow from operating activities than the sales revenue. Another characteristic of the sector is that it is financed with high amounts of long-term loans in foreign currency. Therefore, the correct presentation of financing expenses is an important issue affecting the auditor's assessment of the going concern.

For the cost and depreciation of property, plant, equipment, and intangible assets, we performed document review (invoices, license agreements, accounting records) and recalculation (economic life assessment and determination of depreciation and amortization amounts) procedures. Reconciliation was performed for loans, and loan agreements were reviewed. Interest and foreign exchange differences were recalculated using the effective interest method. In particular, for the going concern assessment, the entity's short-term, medium-term, and long-term liabilities related to loans were calculated separately.

Sales contracts providing cash flow to the entity, maintenance and repair contracts ensuring uninterrupted production in the sector, and insurance contracts for the tribunes with high investment amounts were analyzed. Recalculation was made in the cost of sales audit.

5.5.2.2 Additional Procedures Due to Material Uncertainty

Following ISA 570, the auditor has requested management's evaluation of going concern due to events or conditions that raise significant doubt about the entity's ability to continue as a going concern. Management has evaluated the going concern for 12 months from the financial reporting date. The entity's assessment and plans include the following matters.

- 80% of the entity's current borrowings consist of foreign currency-denominated loans maturing by 2030.
- The entity has conducted a sensitivity analysis for each of its borrowings based on the fluctuations in foreign exchange rates for the relevant currency.
- Estimates of the enterprise's annual production amounts were made. Due to the sector's structure, the electricity generated is immediately converted into sales; therefore, sales forecasts are also presented alongside production forecasts.
- According to the contract, the entity's sales are calculated in foreign currency indexed terms, and collections occur in approximately one month. Cash flow forecasts have been planned based on production and sales forecasts, considering various scenarios, similar to those for loans.
- An 8-year maintenance contract will begin this year to ensure routine maintenance does not disrupt production.
- The means of production are insured against extraordinary circumstances, including natural disasters.
- In the current situation, the enterprise has no cash shortage for making its loan payments. In the 12-month projection, it is estimated to face no liquidity shortage. Therefore, there are no plans to restructure its loans.

The capital has turned negative due to the foreign exchange differences (related to principal and interest) included in the financial expenses. This situation indicates a material uncertainty regarding the entity's ability to continue as a going concern and requires measures to replenish the deficient capital following Article 376 of the Turkish Commercial Code (TCC). On September 15, 2018, according to the Provisional Article 1 of the "Communiqué on Procedures and Principles Regarding the Implementation of Article 376 of the TCC No. 6102" regarding Article 376 of the TCC, "Until 01.01.2023, foreign exchange losses arising from foreign currency denominated liabilities that have not yet been fulfilled may not be taken into account in the calculations made regarding capital loss or insolvency within the scope of Article 376 of the Law". According to the aforementioned article, the entity does not experience capital loss when foreign exchange losses arising from foreign currency liabilities that have not yet been redeemed are not considered. Therefore, the management has no legal concerns, such as the direct termination or bankruptcy of the entity. Therefore, the entity's management has concluded that there is no need to take any additional measures since the mentioned regulation is appropriate for the entity's situation.

- In discussing the assessment with management, the auditor performed the following work to determine whether it is appropriate for management to use the going concern assumption in preparing the financial statements.
- Requested the entity's loan agreements and reconciled them with the banks. In light of the information contained in the loan agreements, a separate recalculation has been made for each loan agreement. Approximately 88% of the loans consist of long-term loans, with one-half being fixed-rate and the other half floating-rate. Fixed-rate loans have maturities extending until 2025, while floating-rate loans mature until 2030. Possible cash outflows from the loans have been calculated by classifying the liabilities according to the maturity of 0–3, 3–12, 23–36, 37–60, and more than 60 months.
- The entity's estimates of the annual production volume can be easily assessed due to the nature of the sector. For wind power plants, the production potential is evaluated starting from the feasibility studies that commence before the investment phase. Except in extraordinary circumstances, although the production capacity varies seasonally, it does not show significant deviations over the years. For this reason, the auditor assessed the entity by considering its estimates of the average production in the years after the entity began operating the facility and found them reasonable.
- Sales contracts were analyzed. The generated electricity is sold directly and collected within a short period (less than one month) and indexed in foreign currencies. Collections also have a sector-specific structure. Since production forecasts directly affect sales, and collections occur within one month, the potential cash inflows were evaluated based on production forecasts.
- The details of insurance contracts are analyzed.
- It examined whether the enterprise benefits from the incentives applicable to its field and whether the applications for renewal of these incentives are submitted on time. The enterprise benefits from incentives.
- The paid-in capital, which consists of fully paid-in capital, is examined.

- Investigated if there had been a change in key personnel. There has been no change in key personnel.

By the relevant TCC regulation, the auditor has assessed whether the entity has experienced a capital loss by considering the foreign exchange losses from outstanding foreign currency liabilities that have not yet been fulfilled. The auditor has determined that the entity has no capital loss if the associated foreign exchange losses are not considered. The auditor concluded that preparing the financial statements under the going concern assumption is appropriate, considering the risk assessment, analytical reviews, contractual obligations, and rights. The evidence gathered during the audit did not alter the auditor's conclusion regarding the use of the going concern assumption, and the auditor did not view the negative capitalization as a material uncertainty concerning going concern.

5.5.2.3 Activities Related to Going Concern During the Reporting Phase

Events after the balance sheet date: To complete the audit, the auditor utilized investigative procedures and document reviews to assess events occurring after the balance sheet date and did not identify any events that require adjustment or disclosure.

Final financial statement analysis and going concern assessment: After completing the audits for other classes of transactions and accounts, the auditor utilized some of the data gathered from the analysis of the final financial statements within the framework of analytical procedures to reassess his opinion on the use of the going concern assumption in the financial statements compared to data from previous years. The liquidity, operating, profitability, and financial structure ratios were analyzed to achieve this.

The financial ratios the auditor examines to evaluate the going concern assumption are as follows in Table 5.6.

All of the entity's liquidity ratios are greater than one (1) for the previous and current years. There has been an increase in all liquidity ratios this year compared

Table 5.6 Financial ratios analyzed by the auditor

Liquidity Ratios	Current Ratio, Cash Ratio, Acid-Test Ratio
Activity Ratios	Receivables Turnover, Asset Turnover Inventory turnover cannot be calculated because the enterprise does not store energy products.
Profitability Ratios	Gross Profit Margin, Operating Profit Margin, Profit Margin Before Tax, Effective Tax Rate, Profit Margin After Tax, Return on Equity, Return on Assets, Return on Capital, and Operating Expenses/Sales
Financial Structure Ratios	Total Financial Debt to Shareholders' Equity; Total Financial Debt to Total Assets

Note Adapted from the auditor's audit documentation

to last year. This indicates that the entity's net working capital is positive. Since the electricity produced is not stored but delivered directly to the lines, the business has no inventory; therefore, the liquidity ratio is identical to the current ratio. The cash ratio, the most sensitive ratio for meeting short-term liabilities, is also bigger than one (1). The plan achieved the targeted production-sales capacity this year, and this year's receivable turnover rate increased compared to last year.

A comparison of the entity's gross and operating profit margins between the current year and the previous year shows an increase in the current year's profit margins. The entity has no cash shortage in meeting its short-term obligations and conducting its activities. The financial structure ratios are negative due to the negative equity amount Table 5.7.

The auditor's assessment is as follows:

- Although the current operating profit of the enterprise is higher than its capital, it has incurred financing expenses that are approximately twice as high as the capital.
- The long-term, foreign currency-denominated investment loan led to substantial financial expenses due to elevated exchange rate differences.
- As a result, the entity finished the period with a loss.
- The entity has achieved a high gross profit margin. Operating expenses have decreased as a percentage of sales compared to the previous year, and operating profit this year is also higher than last year. However, the entity closed the period with a loss due to financing expenses, which caused the shareholders' equity to turn negative.

The auditor concludes that the long-term return on investment and production-sales forecasts will not create issues regarding the entity's financial balance. Therefore, the auditor has determined that the going concern assumption is appropriate.

Table 5.7 Fundamental Ratios Considered by the Auditor in Forming Their Opinion

	For the Period Ended December 31st of the Current Year	Prior Period Ended December 31
Gross Profit Margin	% 71	%65
Operating Profit Margin	% 62,70	% 55,88
Current ratio	1,3	1,22
Liquidity Ratio	1,3	1,22
Acid-Test (Cash Ratio)	1,1	1,05
Operating Expenses/Sales	% 6,82	% 8,11
Total Financial Debt/ Shareholders' Equity	% −1046	% −37.240
Capital/Equity	% −134	% −5.326

Note Adapted from the auditor's audit documentation

Opinion Formation and Reporting: In cases where the use of going concern assumption is appropriate but uncertainties exist, the auditor should evaluate the adequacy of the explanations provided by the entity's management regarding these uncertainties and form his or her opinion accordingly. The entity management has presented the circumstances causing uncertainty regarding the going concern assumption in its financial statements to the auditor's assessment. This includes its evaluations, risks, plans, and the reasons for relying on the going concern assumption, which are disclosed in the notes to the financial statements. The auditor evaluated the reasons presented by management and found the basis for the assessment reasonable. The auditor expressed an unqualified opinion on the financial statements because management provided sufficient explanations in the notes. However, the auditor directs users' attention to the relevant footnotes under the matters requiring attention section of the audit report, concerning a situation that raises serious doubts about the entity's ability to continue as a going concern, yet is not regarded as a material uncertainty. Additionally, the auditor identified going concern as a key audit matter due to its significance in the current period. In the audit report, under the key audit matter heading, the auditor explained to users why going concern was deemed a key audit matter and described the work performed during the audit process related to going concern.

5.6 Conclusion

An entity prepares its general-purpose financial statements based on the going concern assumption, unless management intends to liquidate or cease operations, or has no other realistic alternative solution. ISA 570 is an auditing standard focused on assessing an entity's ability and intention to continue as a going concern for the foreseeable future.

In the sample entity's statement of financial position as of December 31, equity has become negative due to the significant net loss for the period. This situation suggests material uncertainty regarding the entity's ability to continue as a going concern. Consequently, the auditor established the materiality level based on net sales as the benchmark and applied a 50% rate to the general materiality level to broaden the audit's scope while determining the performance materiality.

The auditor discussed this matter with those charged with governance. Management presented its assessment of the future to the auditor and evaluated the preparation of the financial statements based on the going concern assumption. The auditor reviewed the measures and decisions made by management in light of their assessment of the operating process.

The auditor has established the cause and extent of negative equity. This negative equity results from high financing costs, encompassing unrealized foreign exchange losses and interest expenses on loans denominated in foreign currency used by the entity. When evaluating the legal regulations related to this issue, it is possible, under Article 376 of the TCC, that foreign exchange losses arising from unfulfilled foreign currency liabilities may not be included in calculations regarding capital loss. Therefore, studies have been conducted on the differences in unfulfilled foreign exchanges. The auditor has separated the foreign exchange differences for the period from those of the unpaid loans. Considering the financial expenses arising from these unpaid foreign exchange differences, it has been determined that the entity has no capital loss.

Additionally, when evaluating the liquidity position, gross and operating profitability, foreign currency-denominated collections, and the high turnover rate of receivables in the sector, the auditor believes that the entity will not encounter liquidity problems in the foreseeable future and will be able to meet its obligations. Although an uncertainty related to a condition or event that raises serious doubt has been identified during the planning stage, the auditor finds it appropriate to use the going concern assumption since this uncertainty is not deemed material.

The entity prepared the financial statements using the going concern assumption and provided the necessary disclosures in the footnotes. The auditor highlighted this issue in his report by expressing an unqualified opinion. Furthermore, the auditor recognized the going concern assumption as the most critical issue in the current audit period and highlighted it as a key audit matter in the report. Therefore, the auditor explained to the users why going concern was selected as the key audit matter and the procedures followed during the current period.

The study presents a case where an important financial indicator, such as capital loss, does not negate the going concern assumption. It reveals once again that the impact of economic events (like exchange rate changes) on financial statements through accounting practices should be thoroughly analyzed. In the audit process, in addition to analyzing the structure of the sector and business activities, the significance of legal regulations in risk assessment emerged as another point of interest.

References

Bava F, Trana GM (2013) Going-concern assumption and disclaimer opinion: the Italian case. GSTF J Bus Rev 2(4):6–11

Behn BK, Kaplan SE, Krumwiede KR (2001) Further evidence on the auditor's going-concern report: the influence of management plans. Audit J Pract Theory 20(1):13–28. https://doi.org/10.2308/aud.2001.20.1.13

Bozkurt İ, Karataş M (2011) Türkiye'deki Yenilenebilir Enerji Sektörünün Muhasebe Sorunları. Mali Çözüm 107:85–111

Carson E, Fargher NL, Geiger MA, Lennox CS, Raghunandan K, Willekens M (2013) Audit reporting for going-concern uncertainty: a research synthesis. Audit J Pract Theory 32 (Supplement 1):353–384. https://doi.org/10.2308/ajpt-50324

Chan KH, Lin KZ, Mo P (2006) A political-economic analysis of auditor reporting and auditor switches. Rev Account Stud 11(1):21–48. https://doi.org/10.1007/s11142-006-6394-z

Chen KW, Church BK (1992) Default on debt obligations and the issuance of going-concern opinions. Audit J Pract Theory 11:30–49

Chi HY, Chin CL (2011) Firm versus partner measures of auditor industry expertise and effects on auditor quality. Audit J Pract Theory 30(2):201–229. https://doi.org/10.2308/ajpt-50004

Conceptual Framework. Retrieved from https://www.kgk.gov.tr/DynamicContentDetail/11809/TFRS-2025-Seti-Mavi-Kitap on 06.05.2023

Feng M, Li C (2014) Are auditors professionally skeptical? evidence from auditors' going-concern opinions and management earnings forecasts. J Account Res 52(5):1061–1085. https://doi.org/10.1111/1475-679X.12064

Frost C (1997) Disclosure policy choices of UK firms receiving modified audit reports. J Account Econ 23(July):163–187. https://doi.org/10.1016/S0165-4101(97)00006-2

Gissel J, Robertson J, Stefaniak CM (2010) Formation and consequences of going-concern opinions: a review of the literature. J Account Lit 29:59–141. https://epublications.marquette.edu/account_fac/37

IAS 1. Presentation of Financial Statements, Retrieved from https://www.kgk.gov.tr/DynamicContentDetail/11809/TFRS-2025-Seti-Mavi-Kitap on 06.05.2023

IAS 16. Property, Plant and Equipment, Retrieved from https://www.kgk.gov.tr/DynamicContentDetail/11809/TFRS-2025-Seti-Mavi-Kitap on 06.05.2023

IAS 23. Borrowing Costs, Retrieved from https://www.kgk.gov.tr/DynamicContentDetail/11809/TFRS-2025-Seti-Mavi-Kitap on 06.05.2023

IAS 38. Intangible Assets, Retrieved from https://www.kgk.gov.tr/DynamicContentDetail/11809/TFRS-2025-Seti-Mavi-Kitap on 06.05.2023

IFAC. (2018). Guide to Using ISAs in the Audits of Small and Medium Sized Entities, Vol 2-Practical Guidance, Fourth Edition. Retrieved from https://www.ifac.org/knowledge-gateway/audit-assurance/publications/guide-using-international-standards-auditing-audits-small-and-medium-sized-entities on 08.10.2020

İnaltong C, Taş O (2015) Bağımsız Denetim Sürecinde Önemlilik Düzeyinin Belirlenmesi ve Bir Uygulama. Vergi Dünyası 401(Ocak 2015):73–89

ISA 200. Overall objectives of the independent auditor and the conduct of an audit in accordance with international standards on auditing. Retrieved from https://www.kgk.gov.tr/DynamicContentDetail/11821/TDS-2025-Seti on 08.10.2022

ISA 315. Identifying and assessing the risks of material misstatement. Retrieved from https://www.kgk.gov.tr/DynamicContentDetail/11821/TDS-2025-Seti on 08.10.2022

ISA 330. The auditor's responses to assessed risks. Retrieved from https://www.kgk.gov.tr/DynamicContentDetail/11821/TDS-2025-Seti on 08.10.2022

ISA 560. Subsequent Events. Retrieved from https://www.kgk.gov.tr/DynamicContentDetail/11821/TDS-2025-Seti on 08.10.2022

ISA 570. Going Concern. Retrieved from https://www.kgk.gov.tr/DynamicContentDetail/11821/TDS-2025-Seti on 08.10.2022

ISA 700. Forming an opinion and reporting on financial statements. Retrieved from https://www.kgk.gov.tr/DynamicContentDetail/11821/TDS-2025-Seti on 08.10.2022

ISA 701. Communicating key audit matters in the independent auditor's report. Retrieved from https://www.kgk.gov.tr/DynamicContentDetail/11821/TDS-2025-Seti on 08.10.2022

ISA 705. Modifications to the Opinion in the Independent Auditor's Report. Retrieved from https://www.kgk.gov.tr/DynamicContentDetail/11821/TDS-2025-Seti on 08.10.2022

ISA 706. Emphasis of matter paragraphs and other matter paragraphs in the independent auditor's report. Retrieved from https://www.kgk.gov.tr/DynamicContentDetail/11821/TDS-2025-Seti on 08.10.2022

Kaval H (2008) Muhasebe Denetimi. Gazi Kitabevi, vol 3. Baskı, Ankara

Kılınç Savrul B (2016) Enerji Ekonomisi: Türkiye'nin Enerji Sektörü ve Alternatif Enerji Kaynakları. Dora Basım Dağıtım, Çanakkale

Knechel R, Vanstraelen A (2007) The relationship between auditor tenure and audit quality implied by going concern opinions. Audit J Pract Theory 26(1):113–131. https://doi.org/10.2308/aud.2007.26.1.113

Koch AS (2002). Financial distress and the credibility of management earnings forecasts. GSIA Working Paper No. 2000-10, Available at SSRN: https://ssrn.com/abstract=415580 or https://doi.org/10.2139/ssrn.415580
KPMG. (2019). Revisions to the going concern UK auditing standard. Retrieved from https://assets.kpmg.com/content/dam/kpmgsites/uk/pdf/2019/10/blc-revisions-to-going-concern-uk-auditing-standard.pdf on 10.09.2020
Law N. 4628 Elektrik Piyasası Kanunu. Retrieved from https://www.resmigazete.gov.tr/eskiler/2013/03/20130330-14.htm on 09.10.2020
Law N. 5346 Yenilenebilir Enerji Kaynaklarının Elektrik Enerjisi Üretimi Amaçlı Kullanımına İlişkin Kanun. Retrieved from https://mevzuat.gov.tr/mevzuat?MevzuatNo=5346&MevzuatTur=1&MevzuatTertip=5 on 10.10.2020
Lee P, Jiang W, Anandarajan A (2005) Going concern report modeling: a study of factors influencing the auditor's decision. J Forensic Account 6(1):55–76
Lennox C (2000) Do companies successfully engage in opinion shopping? evidence from the UK. J Account Econ 29(3):321–337. https://doi.org/10.1016/S0165-4101(00)00025-2
Louwers TJ (1998) The relation between going-concern opinions and the auditor's loss function. J Account Res 36(1):143–156. https://doi.org/10.2307/2491325
McKenna R, Lilliestam J, Heinrichs HU, Weinand J, Schmidt J, Staffell I, Hahmann AN, Burgherr P, Burdack A, Bucha M, Chen R, Klingler M, Lehmann P, Lowitzsch J, Novo R, Price J, Sacchi R, Scherhaufer P, Schöll EM, Ramirez Camargo L, et al (2025)System impacts of wind energy developments: key research challenges and opportunities. Joule 9 (1) 101799 https://doi.org/10.1016/j.joule.2024.11.016
Özcan HH (2009). Rüzgar Enerjisi Yatırımları ve Isparta İlinde Kurulabilecek Rüzgar Enerjisi Santrallerinin Ekonomik Analizi. Süleyman Demirel University, Institute of Social Sciences, Department of Business Administration, Unpublished Master's Thesis.
Raghunandan K, Rama DV (1995) Audit reports for companies in financial distress: before and after SAS No. 59. Auditing 14(1):50
Robinson D (2008) Auditor independence and auditor-provided tax service: evidence from going-concern audit opinions prior to bankruptcy filings. Audit J Pract Theory 27(2):31–54. https://doi.org/10.2308/aud.2008.27.2.31
Şavlı T (2019) Uluslararası/Türkiye Denetim Standartları Kapsamında Bağımsız Denetim Sürecinin Tüm Aşamalarınının Ele Alındığı Uygulmaya Yönelik Bağımsız Denetim Rehberi. Huz Akademi Yayıncılık, vol 1. Baskı, İstanbul
Shvyreva OI, Kruglyak ZI (2016) Problems of professional judgment application in evaluating the company's going concern. Indian J Sci Technol 9(14):1–11. https://doi.org/10.17485/ijst/2016/v9i14/91520
TEİAŞ. (2023). Türkiye Elektrik Üretim İletim İstatistikleri, Retrieved from https://www.teias.gov.tr/turkiye-elektrik-uretim-iletim-istatistikleri on 06.05.2025
Trana GM, Alfiero S (2019) The role of the ISA 570 "Adverse Key Financial Ratios" in Going concern assessment in Italy. Corp Own Control 16(4):8–18. https://doi.org/10.22495/cocv16i4art1
Türel A, Türel A (2016) Yeni Denetim Raporlarının Finansal İletişime EtkileriIn Seçmeler 2016 içinde (Editor: göksel Yücel), Muhasebe Enstitüsü Yayın No:75. Baskı, İstanbul, pp 1
Turkish Commercial Code (TCC). https://www.mevzuat.gov.tr/mevzuat?MevzuatNo=6102&MevzuatTur=1&MevzuatTertip=5
Vanstraelen A (2003) Going-concern opinions, auditor switching, and the self-fulfilling prophecy effect examined in the regulatory context of Belgium. J Account Audit Finance 18:231–253. https://doi.org/10.1177/0148558X0301800204
Yılmaz B (2014). Yenilenebilir Enerji (Rüzgâr Enerjisi) Üreten İşletmelerin Türkiye Muhasebe Standartları Açısından Değerlendirilmesi, Gazi University Institute of Social Sciences, Department of Accounting and Finance, Unpublished Doctoral Thesis

Chapter 6
Examining the Effect of Related Party Transactions on the Value of the Enterprise Within the Scope of ISA 550: The Case of ISBANK

Ömer Faruk Demirkol and Abdulrezzak İkvan

Abstract Related party transactions refer to the commercial transactions of a financial nature that economic institutions conduct with institutions or organizations that they are directly or indirectly affiliated with, such as partnerships, management, shareholders or in other ways. Such transactions are likely to produce results that do not reflect the truth in the financial reports of the enterprises. This situation increases the concerns of the stakeholders and may affect their decisions regarding the enterprise. In this study, the effects of related party transactions on the market value of the enterprise within the scope of International Standard on Auditing 550 (ISA 550) were analyzed using the event study method. In the study, the related party transactions carried out by ISBANK, the leading financial institution of Turkey, in the 2019 period and reported to the Public Disclosure Platform (KAP) were evaluated. The enterprise reported a total of seven related party transactions in the 2019 period and all of the transactions were carried out with ISGYO. ISBANK has a 50.51% share in İŞGYO and the transactions to be carried out between the enterprises are qualified as related party transactions. In the evaluated period, loans and leasing transactions were generally carried out between the parties. According to the findings, it has been determined that ISBANK, which

This chapter was previously published in Turkish by Gazi Kitabevi with the ISBN: 978-975-7727-16-7.

Ö. F. Demirkol
Faculty of Economics and Administrative Sciences, Department of Business Administration, Harran University, Şanlıurfa, Türkiye
e-mail: ofdemirkol@harran.edu.tr

A. İkvan (✉)
Department of Finance, Banking and Insurance, Adıyaman University, Kahta Vocational School, Adıyaman, Türkiye
e-mail: aikvan@adiyaman.edu.tr

G. Kurt, Ö. Sarısoy (eds.), *Recent Advancements in Auditing*, Accounting, Finance, Sustainability, Governance & Fraud: Theory and Application,
https://doi.org/10.1007/978-981-95-5811-7_6

is the creditor or tenant company in non-cash loan and leasing transactions, negatively affects the market value of the company; on the other hand, cash loan transactions produce positive results in the market value of the company. The relevant transactions have produced different results for ISGYO. Accordingly, it has been determined that leasing transactions increase the market value of the company, while cash and non-cash loan transactions affect it in the opposite direction. The direction in which transactions between related parties affect the decisions of stakeholders varies depending on whether the company is the provider of the relevant transaction or not. The study has revealed that related party transactions have a strategic importance on the decisions of stakeholders. The results of the study are similar to the findings of the literature, and it is seen that related party transactions affect the market value of the companies. In this context, it is important for companies to act by taking into account the direction and level of the impact of related party transactions on the decisions of stakeholders. Finally, although the number of events analyzed and evaluated is sufficient, the fact that all of the events belong to a company and a certain period constitutes the limitations of the study.

Keywords Related party transactions · ISA 550 · Market value · Stakeholder decisions · Case study method

6.1 Introduction

Enterprises are in relationships with many individuals, institutions and organizations due to their activities. While some of the elements that the enterprises are in relationships with are considered as related parties, some are not subject to such a qualification. The related party qualification is expressed in the ISA 550 Related Parties Standard as having control or significant influence over the enterprise or the enterprise having control or significant influence over other enterprises (ISA 550, m10/a).

Businesses and transactions conducted with related party elements affect stakeholders and shape their decisions. Since the risk potential of transactions conducted with related parties is high, it can especially affect investors' preferences regarding the enterprise. Considering the impact of investor decisions on business value, businesses need to meet the information needs of their stakeholders and especially their investors. In this respect, management should be willing and make great efforts to ensure transparency regarding related party transactions.

Depending on the complexity of the business partnership structure, the risk of fraud and forgery in related party transactions and transactions increases. At the same time, transactions carried out with related parties generally give the impression of a secret agreement between the parties. For these and similar reasons, in order to ensure the comprehensibility of financial statements and stakeholders' access to accurate information, it is necessary to determine the quality and quantity of transactions carried out by businesses with related parties. Within the scope of independent audit, auditing the transactions carried out by businesses with related parties and identifying the risks of material misstatement arising from these transactions, if any, is important in terms of audit quality and ensuring reasonable assurance. In this context, partners who hold the majority of the capital can benefit from independent auditors who provide high-quality service in information disclosure in order to alleviate the concerns of minority partners regarding related party transactions (Fan and Wong 2005).

ISA 550 Related Party Standard is a standard that regulates the scope of related party relationships and transactions, the procedures to be applied in their determination, and the responsibilities of independent auditors regarding the evaluation of issues such as whether they carry a risk of material misstatement. The conceptual framework of the study consists of general evaluations regarding the scope, purpose, related party distinction of ISA 550 Related Party Standard and the importance of the transactions and transactions arising from this relationship in terms of independent audit. The literature section covers how related party transactions are evaluated in domestic and foreign studies and the findings obtained from these studies. In the application section of the study, the impact of related party transactions on the value of the enterprise is discussed in line with the literature studies. In this context, the related party transactions carried out by ISBANK in the 2019 period and reported to the Public Disclosure Platform (PDP) were analyzed within the framework of the event study method and the findings obtained were evaluated. In the conclusion section, the findings of the study were compared with the literature findings and various suggestions were included. Although the number of events analyzed and evaluated is sufficient, the fact that all of the events belong to a single business and a certain period constitutes the limitations of the study.

6.2 Assessment of Related Party and Transactions Within the Scope of Isa 550 Standard

In addition to the facts presented to stakeholders in businesses, there may also be related party transactions that include risks related to the enrichment of one party despite the other parties. By taking advantage of these relationships and transactions, the annexation of minority shares, providing benefits to active partners and managers, and credit or purchase-sale agreements with characteristics different from market conditions can be realized (La Porta et al. 2003).

Determination of related party relationships and transactions is important due to issues such as protecting minority shareholders, transparency, providing confidence to investors and creditors, preventing unfair competition, reducing representation costs, and ensuring the continuity of businesses. Independent audit reports generally constitute the reliable source of information for stakeholders regarding the specified issues. Independent auditors evaluate the claims of the business management within the framework of audit standards and strive to provide a reasonable level of assurance to stakeholders. In this context, related parties and transactions are also important issues that should be evaluated in detail by independent auditors. If the characteristics of related parties and transactions differ from similar parties and transactions, it is likely that they will also contain risks of material misstatement. In order for these possibilities not to have negative consequences on the quality of the audit, independent auditors should evaluate related parties and transactions within the scope of ISA 550 standard.

6.2.1 *Scope and Purpose of ISA 550 Related Parties Standard*

ISA 550 standard covers the responsibilities of auditors regarding related party relationships and transactions in independent audits and detailed information on the applications of other relevant standards if these relationships and transactions are at a material misstatement risk level. The auditor's responsibility within the scope of the standard is primarily to determine whether any related parties and transactions exist and whether they are presented in accordance with the management's reporting framework criteria. Determining the adequacy level of records and explanations regarding related party relationships and transactions reported in accordance with the reporting framework criteria, and the existence and size of the risk of material misstatement arising from these relationships and transactions are also among the auditor's responsibilities. The failure of the management of the company to provide information on related party relationships and transactions, intentionally or unintentionally, does not eliminate the auditor's responsibility in this regard. In this case, the auditor must determine the existing related party relationships and transactions related to the company by applying audit procedures and question the relevant parties who caused this situation.

There are two main objectives in the target of the related party standard ISA 550 (ISA 550, m9). These are;

- Independent of the financial reporting frameworks, the auditor should determine the risk factors related to related party relationships and transactions that pose a risk of material misstatement, especially due to fraud, and reach a conclusion on the compliance of these factors with the principles of truth and appropriateness in the financial statements based on the evidence.
- If the financial reporting frameworks specify criteria related to related parties, the auditor should obtain sufficient and appropriate audit evidence that these are determined, recorded and disclosed in accordance with the frameworks.

Failure to sufficiently and appropriately determine or disclose related party relationships and transactions may lead to misleading results in the evaluation of the financial statements. In order to avoid such consequences, auditors must identify related party transactions based on the relevant standard and their professional judgment and disclose sufficient and appropriate information regarding these matters.

6.2.2 Distinction Between Related and Non-Related Parties

The awareness of the elements that the enterprises are in relationship with in their activities and the dimensions and characteristics of the relationships maintained with these elements are important for the decisions of the stakeholders. The fact that the characteristics of the activities carried out with some elements differ from the market conditions may damage the reality and accuracy of the information claimed by the enterprise in its financial reports and may victimize many stakeholders. In this respect, it is necessary to present transparently who the related and non-related parties are and the nature, numerical amounts and characteristics of the transactions and transactions carried out with related parties.

ISA 550 Standard (ISA 550, m10) has expressed the framework of related parties as follows. Accordingly;

- Those specified as related parties in financial reporting frameworks,
- If related party provisions are not specified in financial reporting frameworks, those with the following characteristics are considered as related parties.
- Persons or businesses that have direct or indirect control or significant influence over the entity through intermediary(s),
- Other businesses that the entity has direct or indirect control or significant influence over through intermediary(s),
- In other businesses under common control with the entity; the partners with control are the same, the partners are close family members or the key managers are the same.

Within the scope of the framework established by the standard regarding related parties; elements such as parent organization and its subsidiaries, companies whose partners are close family members, affiliates, subsidiaries, key managers can be given as examples of related parties.

In the framework drawn for unrelated parties in TAS 24 Related Party Disclosures Standard (TAS 24, m11);

- Two businesses with a common manager or key manager or two businesses where a key manager in one business has significant influence over the other business,
- Joint controls shared by the partners in a business partnership,
- Financiers, unions, public service companies, government authorities and authorities
- It is stated that the business and transactions carried out with a customer, supplier, agent, distributor or general representative with whom the business has significant transactions will not be considered as related parties.

In addition to the issues mentioned above regarding unrelated parties in the TAS 24 standard, it is stated in the ISA 550 standard (ISA 550, m10) *that businesses under the joint control of the public will not be considered as related parties unless they carry out significant transactions or share significant resources with each other.*

In terms of related parties, the principles of control and significant influence are prominent. In this context, it can be said that the persons who veto some important decisions taken by the management of the company, who are the final approval authority, and whose transactions cannot be canceled or questioned by the management are the parties with control and significant influence.

The independent auditor must determine the related parties and the nature, purpose and quantitative magnitude of the transactions they conduct with the company during the period they audit. For this purpose, the auditor must first check the identity information of the related parties recorded in the continuous audit file and updated every year and the transactions they conduct with the company. In addition, the management and potential employees related to the subject should be questioned in order to determine the related party relationships and transactions. In this context, in addition to the management level, internal auditors, legal advisors, and persons who initiate, maintain and record important transactions are also persons from whom information can be obtained regarding the subject.

In order to understand the related party relationships and transactions, the auditor must investigate the management and the relevant persons, and determine the control environment and purpose level of the company. Understanding the control environment will make significant contributions to the auditor in determining the level of risk of material misstatement due to the transactions the company conducts with related parties. In the absence or inadequacy of a control environment, the auditor must obtain sufficient and appropriate audit evidence regarding related party relationships and transactions. If it is not possible to obtain sufficient and appropriate evidence in such an environment, the auditor must take this into account when forming an opinion.

6.2.3 Importance of Related Party Relationships and Transactions in Terms of Independent Audit

Businesses carry out relationships and transactions with many related and unrelated parties within the scope of their activities. When it comes to related party transactions, the internal control system is insufficient and there are no legal procedures regarding how businesses will disclose these relationships and transactions (Gordon et al. 2006). International standards, stock market supervisors and regulators or relevant legislation aim to increase the quality of information provided to target audiences and to publish this information in as wide areas as possible (Nekhili and Cherif 2011). In line with this purpose, in order to provide reasonable assurance in independent audits, both related party transactions and unrelated party transactions should be evaluated by auditors within the framework of the principle of professional skepticism. The reason for opening a special area in accounting (TAS 24 Related Party Disclosures) and auditing (ISA 550 Related Parties) standards for related party transactions is that the complexity, fraud and forgery risk potential is higher in transactions arising from these relationships. Depending on the complexity of the related party relationship and transactions, additional audit procedures are applied and more effort is spent to provide reasonable assurance in the audit (Kohlbeck and Mayhew 2014). The fact that related party transactions are not in accordance with market conditions, the characteristics of the transactions conducted, their pricing, and the possibility of a high level of confidentiality regarding the manipulation of their purpose between the parties make cross-examinations of the auditor difficult (Raval 2018). In the ISA 550 standard, transactions conducted under market conditions have been determined as a criterion as a measure of the risk of material misstatement in transactions conducted with related parties. Accordingly, the standard (ISA 550, m10/b) defines "transactions conducted under market conditions as transactions conducted between a willing buyer and a willing seller who are not related to each other, act independently of each other and look after their own interests". In this context, if the characteristics of transactions conducted between related parties differ from the characteristics of transactions conducted under market conditions, it is likely that there are risks of material misstatement in these transactions. Within the framework of the stated possibilities, it is important to define related party relationships and transactions and determine their effects in independent audits.

Related party relationships and transactions are a fundamental problem in financial statement audits (Gordon et al. 2007). The auditor must determine the reflections of the risks of material misstatement related to related party relationships and transactions in the financial statements and evaluate whether these transactions are explained with accurate and realistic data. The procedures that guide the definition of related party relationships and transactions and the determination of the risks of material misstatement related to them are specified in the relevant articles of the ISA 550 standard (ISA 550, m12-17).

The main objective in an independent audit is to provide a reasonable level of assurance. For this purpose, the auditor must evaluate the statements of the business management within the framework of audit objectives such as accuracy, truthfulness and completeness. In general, auditing standards provide auditors with some examples of issues that may be potential risk factors in businesses. In this context, related party relationships and transactions are evaluated as potential risk factors in auditing standards. In order to provide reasonable assurance, the auditor should approach related party transactions from this perspective and form his opinion accordingly.

The auditor should consider related party relationships and transactions as an important element in the audit, regardless of whether the management of the business reports them or not. It should not be forgotten that concealing important relationships and transactions is a structural problem when there is interest, including businesses reporting related party transactions. Within this framework, the auditor must evaluate the following relationships and transactions with sufficient and appropriate evidence and professional judgment by taking into account the possibility of material misstatement:

- Loans with unclear characteristics and maturity structure,
- Loan transactions made without interest or at rates that are not comparable to market interest rates,
- Leases with conditions different from market conditions,
- Real estate purchases and sales that differ significantly from market value,
- High fees paid to key managers,
- Transactions carried out free of charge,
- Abnormal guarantees provided to some individuals and institutions,
- Dispositions of family members on business resources in family businesses,
- The existence of products, suppliers or customers on which the business is heavily dependent may be indicators that the business is conducting related party relationships and transactions.

These issues can be evaluated as possible risk elements for fraud and forgery. Although the existence of these elements is not evidence that fraud and forgery has been committed, it is anticipated that the relevant elements will provide auditors with warning signals regarding the risks of material misstatement. If relevant factors exist in the entity, the auditor may adjust the scope of audit procedures appropriately, taking into account the possibility that the risk level of material misstatement is high.

6.2.4 Effects of Related Party Relationships and Transactions on the Risk of Material Misstatement

If there are related party relationships and transactions in the company, the company management must present them transparently. In this context, the independent auditor must examine the information provided by the management in the financial reports; whether the identities of the related parties are presented, whether there were transactions based on the relationship in the audited period, whether the transactions carried out are properly accounted for. The independent auditor can also track related party relationships and transactions by examining previous audit reports, management and committee meeting minutes, loan agreements, investment decisions, unusual movements at the end of the period, deviations from the sector and previous periods in production and sales transactions.

In independent audits, the audit team must negotiate both the information reported by the management and the issues revealed by professional skepticism regarding related party relationships and transactions. The audit team must evaluate the related party transactions reported in the previous period audit reports and the situations reported by the management or revealed by the audit team in the current period in terms of fraud and forgery. In this context, the audit team should determine whether the company's assets are misused due to related party relationships and transactions. In independent audits, in addition to determining related party and transactions, it is important to determine whether they carry a risk of material misstatement. Determining the risk dimension will directly affect the approach to the subject. Because in general, academic studies have intensive evaluations that related party transactions are used for the purposes of income management and asset transfer. However, it should not be forgotten that related party transactions are a natural part of business activities. Businesses that do not intend to cheat and forgery also conduct transactions with related parties, and at the same time, it is not seen that these transactions are completely prohibited in any country (Djankov et al. 2008). In fact, in some cases, related party transactions are used to ensure efficiency and reduce costs (Jian and Wong 2010), support the allocation of financial resources (Khanna and Palepu 1997), or are a supportive element in achieving the economic and financial goals of businesses (Gordon et al. 2007). If related party relationships and transactions have characteristics different from the normal flow of activities, they should be evaluated as a risk of material misstatement. The auditor should aim to obtain sufficient and appropriate evidence against transactions in this situation. In this context, audit procedures such as examining the consistency of the characteristics of the relevant transactions with the management's claims, the contract terms, if any, whether they are recorded in accordance with the financial reporting criteria, and the appropriateness of authorizations related to the transactions may be applied.

Related party transactions will not carry the risk of material misstatement if they are carried out in accordance with the workflow logic in market conditions. However, the fact that transactions carried out with related parties differ from market conditions, are not defined or reported by management, are recorded in inappropriate ways, and have negative effects on the continuity of the business strengthens the possibility of material misstatement risks.

When auditing related party relationships and transactions, it is among the responsibilities of auditors towards stakeholders to act with a detailed understanding and to evaluate traces of fraud or forgery in the relevant transactions, if any. Considering the benefits that related party relationships and transactions will provide to some stakeholders of the business, it can be said that the risk of detection is higher than other management claims. Audits should be carried out with a risk-based perspective, considering the high probability of material misstatements in related party relationships and transactions. It is important for the quality of the audit to further deepen the professional skepticism applied in audits in general while auditing these issues.

6.3 Literature Review

Carolina Bona-Sánchez et al. (2017) examined the effects of related party transactions on the market value of companies in Spain. They found that related party transactions were present in the vast majority of companies in the analyzed period, and that these transactions negatively affected the financial, operating and investment dimensions, and therefore had a negative effect on the value of the company.

Fang et al. (2018), examined the potential risks of related party transactions (RPT), which are intensively carried out in the Chinese market, and their effects on the auditor's opinion in the independent audit. According to the findings, they determined that auditors caused the audit opinion to be changed (Modified Audit Opinion-RPTMAO) of companies reporting high levels of sales and lending transactions with related parties. They determined that auditors warned the relevant companies about the profits and assets obtained by the companies due to the transactions related to purchases, borrowing and asset/equity ratios made with related parties, rather than changing their audit opinions. They stated that the positive relationship between sales to related parties and change of audit opinion due to related party transactions (RPTMAO) is due to pricing policies that are far from market conditions and difficult to express and sales that are realized at a higher level than the sector averages. They stated that changed audit opinions due to related party transactions will have a strong predictive power in the detection and evaluation of possible related party transactions in the future periods.

Ge et al. (2010), determined in their study that the reported earnings of companies that sell goods or assets to related parties in China exhibit a lower valuation coefficient than companies that do not have such transactions. It was stated that until the legal regulations of the Chinese Ministry of Finance regarding related party transactions at the end of 2001, the earnings levels of companies that carry out related party transactions were lower than other companies. They determined that there was no significant difference between the value coefficients regarding the earnings of companies that carry out related party transactions and those that do not after the legal regulation. As a result, they emphasized that the legal regulations made by the public regarding related party transactions are effective in reducing the misuse of related party relationships and transactions by businesses for earnings management purposes.

Gordon et al. (2007), examined related party transactions in their studies within the framework of confidentiality, trust, business management claims, material misstatement risks, materiality, fraud and forgery or corporate governance effects. They stated that the identification, examination and disclosure of related party transactions in particular pose difficulties for auditors. They stated that considering the literature studies and the accounting scandals experienced in recent times, the evaluations of the Public Company Accounting Oversight Board (PCAOB) regarding the audit of related party transactions are important.

Jian and Wong (2010), determined in their study that businesses in China that held high levels of partnership shares between 1998 and 2002 provided profits to their owners through sales that differed from market conditions. They stated that the profit support provided to business owners through this method was more common in public enterprises and companies in regions with poor economic conditions. They emphasized that the risk of fraud and dishonesty was higher, especially in cash-based sales made with related parties, and that there were high levels of cash transfers in the form of refunds to business owners after audits in companies traded on the stock exchange. Kassem (2019) measured the perceptions of experienced, international and big four audit firms in Egypt and examined the practices, confidentiality, prevalence of financial reporting fraud in the country and those who committed financial reporting fraud or were negatively affected by these attempts. The study offered various suggestions to stakeholders on issues such as how financial reporting fraud schemes are processed or concealed, how auditors can design effective audit tests to assess fraud risk, or how management can implement techniques to detect and prevent related risks.

Lee et al. (2014), examined the connection between related party transactions and accounting information comparability in South Korea. They stated that the management's discretion in related party transactions is high, which reduces comparability. Similarly, in the study, it was emphasized that in the comparison of accounting information aimed at detecting illegal practices by supervisory and regulatory institutions, the comparability of this information is lower in businesses with related party transactions. According to the findings obtained in the study covering South Korea, they stated that the increases experienced due to the size, flexibility and non-cash characteristics of related party transactions negatively affect the comparability of financial statements.

Nekhili and Cherif (2011), examined the effects of related party transactions on the market value of the business in French companies. They stated that the quantitative size of the board of directors increases the intensity of related party transactions. In addition, independent directors stated that the existence of an audit committee and effective independent external audit are factors that reduce the frequency of related party transactions. They emphasized that the audit committee should include at least one expert in accounting and finance, depending on the complexity of related party transactions.

6.4 Analysis of the Impact of Related Party Transactions on Enterprise Value Using the Event Study Method

Although there are many studies in the foreign literature on related party transactions, it is seen that there are not enough studies on this issue in our country. As can be seen in the literature research section, the risk dimensions of related party transactions and their effects on the values, financial structures or performances of enterprises are generally examined in the studies conducted. In our study, the event study method was used to determine the impact of related party transactions on the value of the enterprise. Within the scope of the study, related party transactions carried out by ISBANK in 2019 and reported to PDP were analyzed. Information on the related party transactions carried out by the company in 2019 is presented in Table 6.1.

ISBANK carried out a total of 7 related transactions on different dates during the 2019 period. All of the transactions were made with the same related party and generally occurred in the form of the use of credit. When the notification hours to the Public Disclosure Platform are taken into consideration, it is seen that the transactions are reported intensively in a time period close to the closing hours of the sessions. It is thought that the management acts in this way by taking into account the possible effects of the related transactions on the stock values of the company.

Table 6.1 ISBANK 2019 period related party transactions

No	Related party	Related transaction	Transaction date	Transaction time	Duration/ Maturity	Transaction detail
1	İŞ Real estate investment partnership INC.	About the lease transaction	12.06.2019	16:13	Not specified	Lease of 1008 m2 office space in İş Tower 2
2	İŞ real estate investment partnership INC.	About the use of cash loan	17.06.2019	09:45	1 year	120 million TL cash loan usage
3	İŞ real estate investment partnership INC.	About the use of non-cash loan	09.08.2019	12:09	Not specified	2,800,594 TL non-cash loan usage
4	İŞ real estate investment partnership INC.	About the lease transaction	26.08.2019	16:50	Not specified	Lease of 68.7 m2 area in Maslak Office Building, Istanbul
5	İŞ real estate investment partnership INC.	About the use of cash loan	11.11.2019	15:51	2 years	150 million TL cash loan usage
6	İŞ real estate investment partnership INC.	About the use of cash loan	25.11.2019	16:30	1 year	100 million TL cash loan usage
7	İŞ real estate investment partnership INC.	About the use of cash loan	04.12.2019	16:44	1 year	70 million TL cash loan usage

In order to determine the effects of related party transactions on the stock value of the company, the event day and the event window should be determined within the framework of the event study method. In our study, the day on which the related transaction was notified to the Public Disclosure Platform as the event day, and the 3 business days before the event, the event day and the 3 business days after the event were evaluated as the event window.

6.4.1 Event Study Method

The event study method can be expressed as the investigation of whether there is an abnormal change in the subject as a result of the evaluations made based on the data of the event window period in order to measure the effect of any event or situation on a determined subject. In the study, related party transactions represent the event and the stock value of the company represents the subject.

The event study method has a long history, but over time, some revisions have been made to its methodology and it has taken its current form. The first studies on the new application have been used intensively in studies conducted in the field of finance since the second half of the twentieth century.

The event study method is used for evaluations in different fields. This method is especially used intensively in studies conducted to examine the impact of any event on the stock value of a company. According to the findings obtained in the examinations conducted within the scope of the event study method, the impact level of the event on the subject should be significant. If the impact level remains at low levels, it makes it difficult to determine the impact level of the event and may give the impression that other events are effective on the subject. For this reason, in studies conducted on the impact of events on stock values, an abnormal return level is generally expected according to the value of the stock value on the day of the event during the event window period.

Abnormal return is evaluated as the difference between the average market return of the stock value between the presentation and non-presentation of information about the company to stakeholders. In order to more clearly measure the impact of the event on the stock value, the value change of the relevant stock during the event window period should be compared with the value changes of all other stocks traded on the stock exchange. If a value of the stock that differs from the values of other stocks is detected in the comparison, it can be said that there is an abnormal return and this abnormal return is caused by the relevant event. In the study, in order to measure the effect of related party transactions on the stock value, related party transactions and stock value of ISBANK in 2019 were analyzed. In order to determine abnormal returns, ISBANK Class C (ISCTR) stock returns and average returns of stocks traded in Istanbul Stock Exchange (BIST) National All (XUTUM) index were compared within the scope of the event window period.

The calculation of abnormal returns is made with the formula below (Tuomınen 2005, 50).

Abnormal Return = Return rate of the relevant stock − Market return rate (ARit = Rit − Rmt)

ARit = Abnormal return of İ stock in period t

Rit = Return of İ stock in period t and its calculation is made with the formula Rit = (D + Pit−Pit−1)/Pit−1.

D represents the dividend payment for the stock on day t, Pit represents the closing price of the stock on day t, and Pit-1 represents the closing price of the stock on day t−1.

Rmt = Indicates the average return of the market on day t and is calculated with the equation Rmt = (It−It−1)/It−1.

It represents the closing price of BIST National All (XUTUM) index on day t,

It−1 represents the closing price of BIST National All (XUTUM) index on day t−1.

Table 6.2 Event, event day and event windows

S. no	Event description	Event day	Event window
1	Related party transaction (Leasing transaction)	12.06.2019	07–17.06.2019
2	Related party transaction (Usage of cash loan)	17.06.2019	12–20.06.2019
3	Related party transaction (Usage of non-cash loan)	09.08.2019	06–19.08.2019
4	Related party transaction (Leasing transaction)	26.08.2019	21–29.08.2019
5	Related party transaction (Usage of cash loan)	11.11.2019	06–14.11.2019
6	Related party transaction (Usage of cash loan)	25.11.2019	20–28.11.2019
7	Related party transaction (Usage of cash loan)	04.12.2019	29.11–09.12.2019

The main purpose of the event study method is to determine the cumulative abnormal return (Cumulative Abnormal Return—CAR) for the periods evaluated before and after the event in order to determine the effects of the relevant event (Serra 2002, 5). Cumulative abnormal returns are the cumulative collection of the parts of the stock return evaluated during the event window that differ from the average market return.

The process of applying the event study method can be summarized in four stages.

Stage 1: Determining the relevant stock and market returns for the event window period

Stage 2: Calculating abnormal returns

Stage 3: Determining cumulative abnormal returns by collecting abnormal returns depending on the historical process

Stage 4: Evaluating the event effect based on cumulative abnormal returns (Table 6.2).

6.4.2 Analysis and Evaluations

In order to more clearly determine the effects of related party transactions on the stock value of the company, data belonging to both parties performing the transaction were analyzed. Within the scope of the event study method, the stock values of the counterparties of the related transaction were analyzed within the framework of the event window and the findings obtained are presented below in the order of the event date.

6.4.2.1 12.06.2019 Leasing Event

ISBANK rented 1,008 m2 of office space in İş Tower 2 from its subsidiary İş Real Estate Investment Partnership within the scope of the expert rental fee. The

Table 6.3 Abnormal and cumulative abnormal returns of related party shares on leasing transactions

Event window	ISCTR Rit (%)	ISGYO Rit (%)	National index Rmt (%)	ARit (İSCTR) (%)	ARit (İSGYO) (%)	CARit (İSCRT) (%)	CARit (İSGYO) (%)
t − 3	5,68	1,05	3,66	2,02	−2,61	2,02	−2,61
t − 2	1,34	0,00	0,39	0,95	−0,39	2,97	−3,00
t − 1	−2,46	1,04	−1,29	−1,17	2,33	1,80	−0,67
t	−0,97	1,03	−0,20	−0,77	1,23	1,03	0,56
t + 1	−2,55	−1,02	−2,18	−0,37	1,16	0,66	1,72
t + 2	2,41	0,00	0,29	2,12	−0,29	2,78	1,43
t + 3	3,14	1,03	1,56	1,58	−0,53	4,36	0,90

findings regarding the effects of the leasing event between related parties on the stock values of the parties and their situation against the average market return are presented in Table 6.3, and the visualization of the findings regarding cumulative abnormal returns is presented in Graph 6.1.

The leasing transaction caused opposite movements in the stock values of the parties during the event window period. While the abnormal return of ISGYO shares, which was the lessor in the pre-event period,

was negative, it is observed that there was a positive movement on the event day and the following days. This situation was evaluated as a positive development by the investors of the relevant company regarding the leasing transaction and increased the demand level for its shares. ISBANK, which was the lessor, provided positive returns in the period before the event day due to the same event, but experienced decreases in its returns as the event day approached and recovered again in a short time after the event day and kept the return level high. It is thought that the investors of the relevant company shaped their investment decisions by

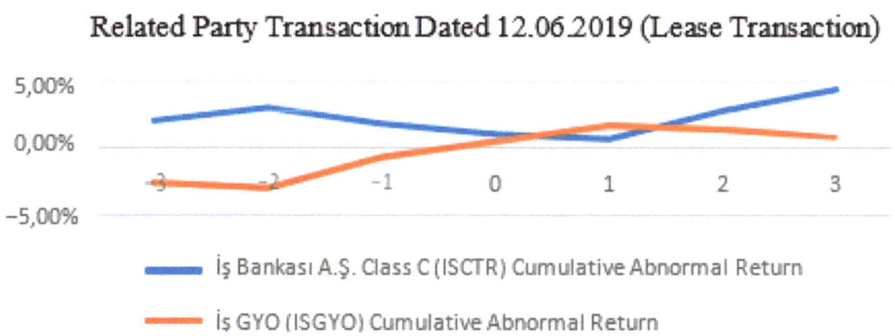

Graph 6.1 Cumulative abnormal returns generated on related parties' shares by the lease transaction that took place on 12.06.2019

evaluating the leasing transaction as a negatively related transaction between the parties at first, but later as a performance-enhancing initiative.

As can be seen in the cumulative abnormal return graph, the leasing transaction between related parties caused a significant loss in value in ISBANK shares until the day of the incident and the following day. Afterwards, it is seen that there was a rapid recovery in the share value of the company. In the same transaction, it is seen that the cumulative abnormal return graph of ISGYO, which was the lessor, moved in the opposite direction and there were significant increases in value in its shares throughout the event window period.

6.4.2.2 17.06.2019 Cash Loan Incident

ISGYO company used a 1-year term 120 Million TL cash loan from ISBANK on 12.06.2019. The findings regarding the cash loan transaction reported to the Public Disclosure Platform as a related party transaction and its effects on the share values of the parties are presented in Table 6.4.

Accordingly, the credit provider ISBANK had a negative abnormal return level before the incident day, but it gained a positive abnormal return on the incident day and afterwards. This situation shows that investors increased their investment decisions in favor of the company, considering the possible positive impacts of the credit transaction on the company's income. It can be said that ISGYO investors narrowed their investment decisions because they considered that the credit drawn would cause a loss of profit due to interest payments and would also negatively affect the liquidity of the company due to being a short-term foreign source.

As seen in Graph 6.2, the cumulative abnormal returns of the companies that are parties to the cash credit transaction move in opposite directions. In the credit provider company, the cumulative abnormal returns followed a negative axis line in the pre-event period and a positive axis line on the day and after the event. In the

Table 6.4 Abnormal and cumulative abnormal returns of related party shares regarding the cash loan transaction

Event window	ISCTR Rit (%)	ISGYO Rit (%)	National index Rmt (%)	ARit (İSCTR) (%)	ARit (İSGYO) (%)	CARit (İSCRT) (%)	CARit (İSGYO) (%)
t − 3	−0,97	1,03	−0,20	−0,77	1,23	−0,77	1,23
t − 2	−2,55	−1,02	−2,18	−0,37	1,16	−1,14	2,39
t − 1	2,41	0,00	0,29	2,12	−0,29	0,98	2,10
t	3,14	1,03	1,56	1,58	−0,53	2,56	1,57
t + 1	4,57	1,02	2,05	2,52	−1,03	5,08	0,54
t + 2	0,55	−1,01	−0,01	0,56	−1,00	5,64	−0,46
t + 3	0,36	1,02	−0,04	0,40	1,06	6,04	0,60

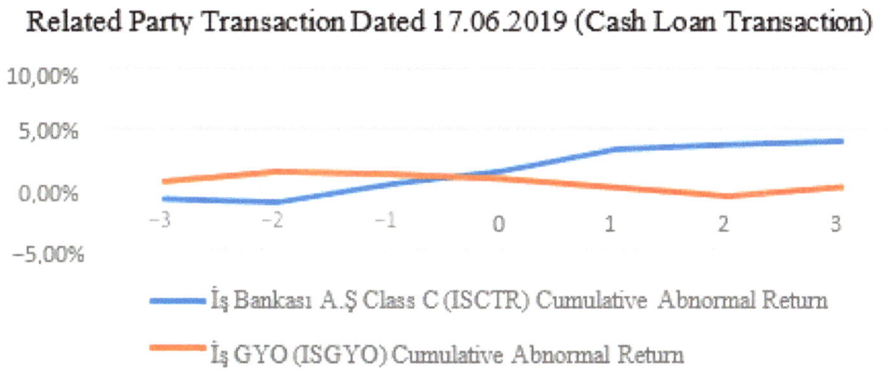

Graph 6.2 Cumulative abnormal returns generated on related parties' shares by the cash loan transaction that took place on 17.06.2019

credit customer company, the cumulative abnormal return level was positive in the pre-event period, but it decreased on the day and after the event, and finally completed the process at an ineffective level. The fact that the cash credit transaction was evaluated positively by investors in the creditor company stock values and negatively in the credit customer company stocks indicates that the transaction was seen as a natural credit transaction. Therefore, if the transaction was evaluated as a fraudulent related party transaction, it should have been reflected negatively in the creditor company stocks.

6.4.2.3 09.08.2019 Non-Cash Credit Incident

ISBANK provided a non-cash credit of TL 2,800,594 in favor of ISGYO on the relevant date (Table 6.5).

On the day of the incident, there was a significant decrease in the share value of the creditor company, while there was an increase in the shares of the credit

Table 6.5 Abnormal and cumulative abnormal returns of related party shares on non-cash loan transaction

Event window	ISCTR Rit (%)	ISGYO Rit (%)	National index Rmt (%)	ARit (İSCTR) (%)	ARit (İSGYO) (%)	CARit (İSCRT) (%)	CARit (İSGYO) (%)
t − 3	−0,17	1,08	0,87	−1,04	0,21	−1,04	0,21
t − 2	−1,17	−3,19	−1,50	0,33	−1,69	−0,71	−1,48
t − 1	−0,17	0,00	1,12	−1,29	−1,12	−2,00	−2,60
t	−2,21	1,10	0,18	−2,39	0,92	−4,39	−1,68
t + 1	−6,25	−3,26	−2,66	−3,59	−0,60	−7,98	−2,28
t + 2	−0,93	−1,12	−0,81	−0,12	−0,31	−8,10	−2,59
t + 3	0,75	0,00	−0,40	1,15	0,40	−6,95	−2,19

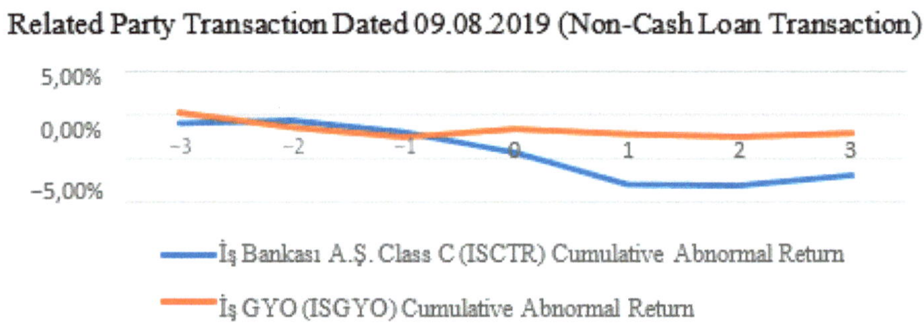

Graph 6.3 Cumulative abnormal returns generated on related parties' shares by the non-cash loan transaction that took place on 09.08.2019

customer company. A similar situation is observed in the abnormal returns reflecting the situation of the relevant companies against the average market returns. While the average market return on the day of the incident was positive, the negative return of ISBANK increased the level of negativity in the abnormal return. It shows that the fluctuations in the share returns of the credit customer company during the event window were in parallel with the average market returns. Therefore, the abnormal return level was in an ineffective range (Graph 6.3).

It is seen that the non-cash credit transaction between related parties has a negative impact on the party company stock values. As seen in the cumulative abnormal returns graph, the negative level of the relevant transaction on the credit customer company stock remained at a lower level than the creditor company. Accordingly, it is seen that creditor company investors evaluate the non-cash credit transaction between related parties as a negative when shaping their investment decisions regarding this process. Because even if the transaction is a non-cash credit transaction, it will ultimately be an income-generating activity for the company and will contribute positively to the profitability of the company. It can be said that investors narrowing down their investment decisions in response to this transaction, and that they evaluate the transaction as the creditor company using its reputation in a way that is not in accordance with market conditions for the customer company it is related to.

6.4.2.4 26.08.2019 Leasing Incident

ISBANK stated in its notification to the Public Disclosure Platform on 26.08.2019 that it rented 68.7 m2 of space in the Maslak Office building in Istanbul from ISGYO, which is a related party. The findings showing the impact of the leasing transaction between related parties on the relevant date on investor decisions are presented in Table 6.6.

Table 6.6 Abnormal and cumulative abnormal returns of related party shares on leasing transactions

Event Window	ISCTR Rit (%)	ISGYO Rit (%)	National Index Rmt (%)	ARit (İSCTR) (%)	ARit (İSGYO) (%)	CARit (İSCRT) (%)	CARit (İSGYO) (%)
t − 3	0,38	0,00	−0,51	0,89	0,51	0,89	0,51
t − 2	0,00	−2,27	−0,12	0,12	−2,15	1,01	−1,64
t − 1	2,62	0,00	1,76	0,86	−1,76	1,87	−3,40
t	0,55	0,00	0,02	0,53	−0,02	2,40	−3,42
t + 1	−1,09	1,16	−0,96	−0,13	2,12	2,27	−1,30
t + 2	0,73	1,15	−0,08	0,81	1,23	3,08	−0,07
t + 3	0,18	0,00	0,82	−0,64	−0,82	2,44	−0,89

Accordingly, ISBANK investors, who are in the position of tenants, have responded positively by evaluating the leasing transaction as an indicator of expansion of a field of activity and volumetric growth, and have increased their demand for the company's shares, albeit to a limited extent. It is observed that the company's shares have performed better, especially against the average market yield level. ISGYO, which is in the position of lessor, has shown a continuous downward trend in its share value before the incident day, but has caught an upward trend on the day of the incident and afterwards. This situation shows that investors expect the leasing transaction to have positive reflections on the income and therefore profitability of the relevant company (Graph 6.4).

The leasing transaction did not save the abnormal return image of the lessor from being negative, but it significantly brought its level closer to positive. In particular, the increase in the cumulative return level related to ISGYO stock on the day of the incident and afterwards indicates that the stock performed better than

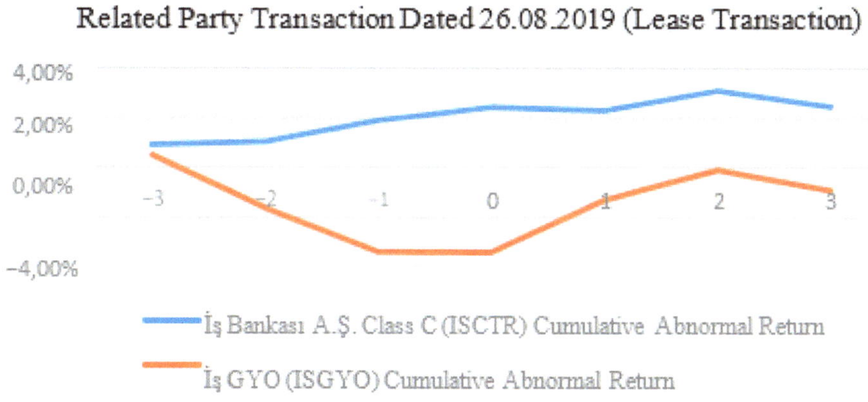

Graph 6.4 Cumulative abnormal returns on shares of related parties generated by the leasing transaction that took place on 26.08.2019

the average market return, and therefore the related transaction was evaluated positively by investors.

6.4.2.5 11.11.2019 Cash Loan Incident

ISBANK provided a 2-year term 150 Million TL cash loan to ISGYO, of which it was a related party, on 11.11.2019 (Table 6.7).

In general, cash credit transactions create positive reflections on the stock value depending on the income expectations of creditor company investors. However, this situation narrows the demand for the relevant stock by evaluating the company as having cash, liquidity and payment problems in the credit customer company investors. It is observed that the cash credit event analyzed within the scope of the study causes an increase in demand on the day of the event and a decrease in demand in the following days in credit customer company investors. It can be said that the long-term nature of the relevant credit contributes to the positive expectations of credit customer company investors. Creditor company investors, on the other hand, increased their demand for the relevant stock by taking into account the credit income within the framework of the general rule (Graph 6.5).

The cash credit transaction has created different results in the cumulative abnormal returns of the companies against the average market return. The cash credit transaction, which did not cause a significant change in the cumulative abnormal returns of the creditor company, has caused increases in the cumulative abnormal returns of the credit customer company compared to the period before the incident day. In the period after the incident day, the cumulative abnormal returns of the credit customer company have experienced significant decreases as in the period before the incident. This situation shows that the incident created short-term optimism in the credit customer company investors, but this optimism did not last long.

Table 6.7 Abnormal and cumulative abnormal returns of related party shares related to the cash loan transaction

Event Window	ISCTR Rit (%)	ISGYO Rit (%)	National Index Rmt (%)	ARit (İSCTR) (%)	ARit (İSGYO) (%)	CARit (İSCRT) (%)	CARit (İSGYO) (%)
t − 3	1,68	1,03	0,66	1,02	0,37	1,02	0,37
t − 2	2,31	0,00	2,26	0,05	−2,26	1,07	−1,89
t − 1	−0,97	−1,02	−0,31	−0,66	−0,71	0,41	−2,60
t	0,00	2,06	0,05	−0,05	2,01	0,36	−0,59
t + 1	1,46	0,00	0,78	0,68	−0,78	1,04	−1,37
t + 2	0,64	−1,01	0,74	−0,10	−1,75	0,94	−3,12
t + 3	−1,75	0,00	−0,87	−0,88	0,87	0,06	−2,25

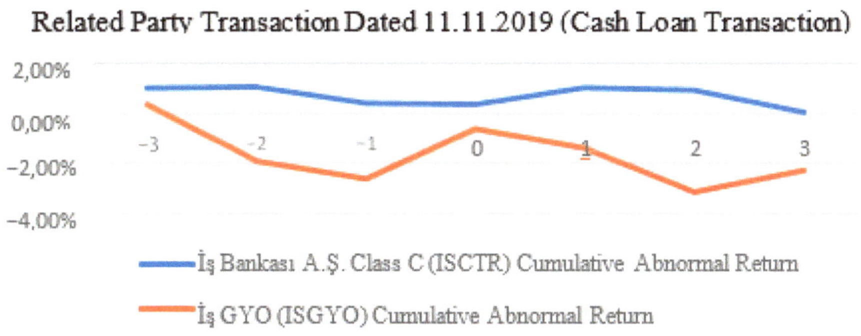

Graph 6.5 Cumulative abnormal returns generated on related parties' shares by the cash loan transaction that took place on 11.11.2019

6.4.2.6 25.11.2019 Cash Credit Incident

ISBANK provided a 1-year term cash loan of 100 Million TL to ISGYO company on 25.11.2019 (Table 6.8).

When the cash credit transaction is evaluated in terms of its effect on the stock values of related party companies, it has produced different results during the event window period. While the credit event caused negative returns in the creditor company shares on the event day, it generally provided positive returns after the event day. It is seen that the return level in the related company shares on the event day and the following days is lower than the average market returns. This situation shows that the cash credit provided by the company to the related party is not welcomed by investors. On the other hand, the same event provided positive returns in the stock value of the credit customer company on the event day, and then a return lower than the average market return and negative returns. When abnormal returns are taken into consideration, it can be said that the return level of the credit customer

Table 6.8 Abnormal and cumulative abnormal returns of related party shares on cash credit transaction

Event window	ISCTR Rit (%)	ISGYO Rit (%)	National index Rmt (%)	ARit (İSCTR) (%)	ARit (İSGYO) (%)	CARit (İSCRT) (%)	CARit (İSGYO) (%)
t − 3	−2,03	−1,85	−0,62	−1,41	−1,23	−1,41	−1,23
t − 2	0,00	1,89	0,17	−0,17	1,72	−1,58	0,49
t − 1	−0,80	3,70	−0,08	−0,72	3,78	−2,30	4,27
t	−2,57	1,79	−1,03	−1,54	2,82	−3,84	7,09
t + 1	1,48	0,00	0,60	0,88	−0,60	−2,96	6,49
t + 2	−0,49	−1,75	−0,04	−0,45	−1,71	−3,41	4,78
t + 3	0,98	1,79	1,23	−0,25	0,56	−3,66	5,34

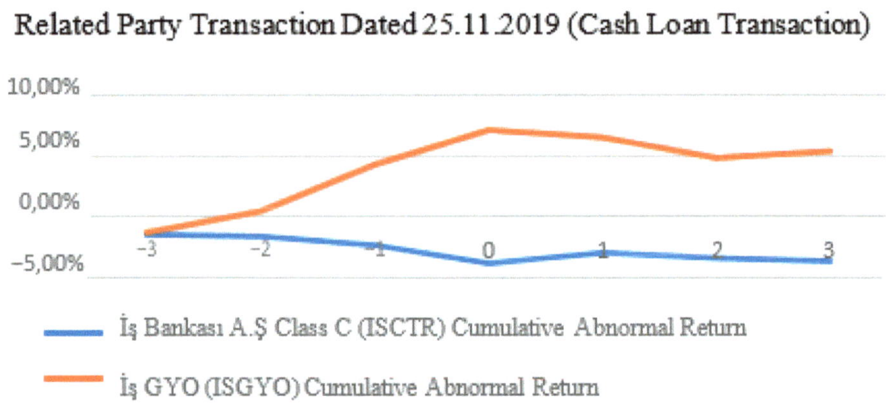

Graph 6.6 Cumulative abnormal returns generated on related parties' shares by the cash loan transaction that occurred on 25.11.2019

company is generally at a better level than the creditor company during the event window period (Graph 6.6).

The cash credit transaction between related parties significantly affected the cumulative abnormal returns of the credit customer company during the event window process. It is observed that there were no significant changes in the cumulative abnormal returns of the creditor company throughout the process. This situation shows that the creditor company investors were indifferent to the fact that the relevant loan was made with the related party and did not make any significant changes in their investment decisions. On the other hand, it is seen that the credit customer company investors made their investment decisions in favor of the company based on the credit event and increased their share demands. The fact that companies use cash credit at short intervals actually negatively affects investor decisions. However, depending on the future perspectives of the areas or projects where the provided credit will be used, it can positively affect the decisions of investors. Similarly, the provision of the credit shows that the company's credit rating is at a reassuring level and this situation can positively affect investors.

6.4.2.7 04.12.2019 Cash Credit Incident

A cash credit agreement of 70 Million TL with a maturity of 1 year was made between the related parties on 04.12.2019. In the credit transaction, ISBANK represents the creditor company, and ISGYO represents the credit customer company (Table 6.9).

The share value of ISGYO has experienced significant positive developments on the day of the incident and the period following the cash loan transaction. It is observed that the loan provided by İş Bankası has positively affected the investor decisions and thus increased the demand for the share. While the share value of the company generally followed a negative course in the period before the incident, it has experienced a course of significant value increases on the day of the incident

Table 6.9 Abnormal and cumulative abnormal returns of related party shares regarding the cash credit transaction

Event window	ISCTR Rit (%)	ISGYO Rit (%)	National index Rmt (%)	ARit (İSCTR) (%)	ARit (İSGYO) (%)	CARit (İSCRT) (%)	CARit (İSGYO) (%)
t − 3	−0,65	−0,88	−0,11	−0,54	−0,77	−0,54	−0,77
t − 2	0,16	2,65	1,16	−1,00	1,49	−1,54	0,72
t − 1	−1,62	−0,86	−0,88	−0,74	0,02	−2,28	0,74
t	1,82	1,74	1,03	0,79	0,71	−1,49	1,45
t + 1	1,30	4,27	0,93	0,37	3,34	−1,12	4,79
t + 2	−0,80	1,64	0,11	−0,91	1,53	−2,03	6,32
t + 3	−1,13	6,45	0,06	−1,19	6,39	−3,22	12,71

and after. Similarly, the high level of abnormal returns in the company's share on the day of the incident and after the incident clarifies the effect of the event on the share value. The situation is a little different for the creditor company. There were low-level increases in the share of the creditor company on the day of the incident and the day after, but there were decreases afterwards. In the evaluations to be made within the scope of abnormal returns, it can be said that the relevant event negatively affected the share value of the creditor company.

It is possible to clearly see the effect of the cash credit transaction between related parties during the event window process on the cumulative abnormal returns of the related companies in Graph 6.7. Accordingly, it is seen that there are steady increases in the cumulative abnormal returns of the credit customer ISGYO company. This also shows that the related company provided a return of approximately 13% more than the average market return during the event window process. It is seen that there are continuous decreases in the cumulative abnormal returns of the credit provider İş

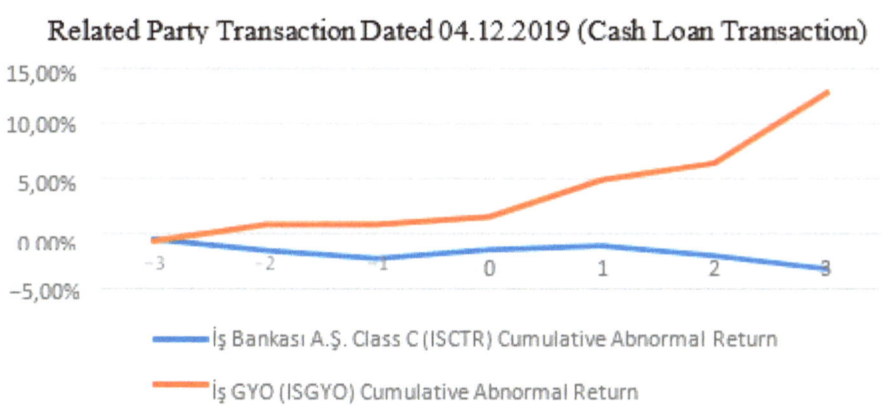

Graph 6.7 Cumulative abnormal returns generated on related parties' shares by the cash loan transaction that occurred on 04.12.2019

Bankası company during the event window process and that it has suffered a total loss of more than 3% compared to the average market return. As a result, the cash credit transaction affected the shares of the related party companies, reflected negatively on the creditor company shares and positively on the credit customer company shares.

6.5 Conclusion

It is normal for businesses to establish relationships with related parties and carry out transactions related to them in economic activity processes. What is unusual in related party relationships and transactions is the intentions of the parties behind these relationships or transactions. While these relationships are generally suitable for market conditions, it is seen that some relationships are not suitable for these conditions. Relationships that are not suitable for market conditions have a high potential for risks such as fraud and forgery. This situation can cause many stakeholders to have negative results in their decisions. Related party transactions are considered important by public authorities in order to prevent such risks and negative results from occurring and various measures are taken to ensure transparency of the issue. In this context, the PDP (Public Disclosure Platform) has published standards regarding information that can guide the recording and auditing of the issue. Similarly, the Capital Markets Board shares the requirements related to the issue with the public.

In the study, the ISA 550 Related Party Standard regarding related party transactions has been evaluated in general and some examples of relationships that can be defined as related parties have been included in particular. In the literature studies on the subject, the effects of related party transactions on the value, performance or financial elements of the enterprise have been examined in general. The study was shaped within this framework and in the application section, the notifications submitted to the PDP by ISBANK as related party transactions in 2019 were evaluated within the scope of the event study method and their effects on the company's stock return were analyzed. The company reported a total of seven related party transactions to the PDP in 2019 and all of the transactions were carried out with ISGYO. ISBANK owns a 50.51% share of ISGYO and the transactions to be carried out between the companies are qualified as related party transactions. It is seen that the notifications submitted in the evaluated period generally took place in the form of relational transactions related to loans and leasing. The findings obtained show that ISBANK, which is a creditor or tenant company in non-cash loan and leasing transactions, experienced decreases in its share value both before the incident and on the day and after the incident. These transactions carried out by the relevant company with the related party created a negative impression on its investors and therefore negatively affected their investment decisions. In the cash loan transactions of the same company, there were decreases in the period before the incident and increases on the day and after the incident.

The related transactions made within the scope of cash credit did not negatively affect the decisions of the investors, therefore, these transactions between the related parties were not evaluated as risky by the investors. On the other hand, the related transactions in ISGYO, the other business of the related party, produced different results in the share value. Accordingly, in the leasing, cash and non-cash credit transactions, the share value of the related company decreased in the period before the incident. Leasing transactions caused increases in the share value of the company, while credit transactions caused decreases on the day of the incident and after. This situation caused the credit transactions to be evaluated negatively by the investors and therefore decreased their demands for the shares of the related company. However, in the leasing transactions, the demand for ISGYO shares increased and their values increased. As a result, the direction in which the transactions between the related parties affect the decisions of the investors varies depending on whether the company is the provider of the relevant transaction. Accordingly, while ISBANK investors, who are the creditors in the credit transactions, do not evaluate the issue as risky, ISGYO investors, who are the credit customers, evaluated it as risky. Similarly, in the leasing transaction, the subject was evaluated as risky by the ISGYO investors, who are the lessor party; however, the same transaction was evaluated as a risky related transaction by the İş Bank investors, who are the tenant party.

It has been determined that the findings of the study and the literature are similar and that related party transactions affect the market value of the companies. In this context, it is seen that it is important for companies to act by taking into account the direction and level of the impact of related party transactions on the decisions of the stakeholders. In order to change the prejudices of the stakeholders towards related party transactions, the managements should give more importance to transparency and increase their efforts in this regard. In this context, the companies should be willing to share the contracts and terms related to related party transactions with their stakeholders. The management should convince its stakeholders that the transactions are made in accordance with the market conditions and do not have the characteristics of providing benefit to any party or persons. Finally, what distinguishes the study from literature studies is that the companies that play a role in the related party transaction are evaluated together. This situation has provided the determinations as to whether the related transaction has different results on the share values of the related companies. Evaluating the subject from a different perspective aims to contribute to the literature or new studies.

References

Bona-Sánchez C, Fernández-Senra CL, Pérez-Alemán J (2017 January–March) Related- party transactions, dominant owners and firm value. BRQ Bus Res Q 20(1):pp4–17

Djankov S, La Porta R, Lopez-de-Silanes F, Shleifer A (2008) The law and economics of self-dealing. J Financ Econ 88(3):430–465

Fan JP, Wong TJ (2005) Do external auditors perform a corporate governance role in emerging markets? Evidence from East Asia. J Account Res 43(1):35–72
Fang J, Lobo GJ, Zhang Y, Zhao Y (2018) Auditing related party transactions: evidence from audit opinions and restatements. Audit J Pract Theory 37(2):73–106
Ge W, Drury DH, Fortin S, Liu F, Tsang D (2010) Value relevance of disclosed related party transactions. Adv Account 26(1):134–141
Gordon EA, Henry E, Palia D (2006) Related party transactions: corporate governance and relationships to firm value, working paper, Rutgers University, New Brunswick, NJ
Gordon EA, Henry E, Louwers TJ, Reed BJ (2007) Auditing related party transactions: a literature overview and research synthesis. J Account Horiz 21:81–102
Internatıonal Standard on Audıtıng 550 (ISA 550) Related Parties, Official Gazette dated 29/01/2014 and numbered 28897
Jian M, Wong TJ (2010) Propping through related party transactions. Rev Acc Stud 15(1):70–105
Kassem R (2019) Understanding financial reporting fraud in Egypt: evidence from the audit field. Third World Quarterly ISSN: 0143–6597 (Print) 1360–2241 (Online) Journal homepage. https://www.tandfonline.com/loi/ctwq20
Khanna T, Palepu K (1997) Why focused strategies may be wrong for emerging markets. Harv Bus Rev 41–51
Kohlbeck M, Mayhew BW (2014) Are related party transactions red flags? SSRN Electron J. https://doi.org/10.2139/ssrn.2427439
La Porta R, Lopez-de-Silanes F, Zamarripa G (2003) Related lending. Q J Econ 118(1):231–268
Lee M, Kang M, Lee H, Park JC (2014) Related-party transactions and financial statement comparability: evidence from South Korea. Asia Pac J Account Econ 23(2):224–252
Nekhili M, Cherif M (2011) Related parties transactions and firm's market value: the French case. Rev Account Finance 10(3):291–315
Raval V (2018) A disposition-based fraud model: theoretical integration and research agenda. J Bus Ethics 150(2). https://doi.org/10.1007/s10551-016-3199-2
Serra AP (2002) Event study tests – a brief survey: working Papers Da FEP 117. https://www.fep.up.pt
Turkish Accounting Standard 24 (TAS 24). Related party disclosures. Official gazette dated 13/08/2008 and numbered 26966
Tuomınen T (2005) Corporate layoff announcements and shareholder value: empirical evidence from Finland, Master's Thesis, Department of Business administration, Kuala Lumpur, Lappeenranta University of Technology

Chapter 7
ISA 560 Subsequent Events: An Application in Borsa Istanbul

Hayrettin Uzunoğlu

Abstract This study aims to evaluate the extent to which companies listed on Borsa Istanbul comply with the disclosure requirements related to subsequent events under International Standard on Auditing (ISA) 560. ISA 560 outlines the auditor's responsibilities regarding events occurring between the balance sheet date and the date of the auditor's report that may require adjustment or disclosure in the financial statements. In this context, the annual and interim financial statements of 333 companies traded on Borsa Istanbul between 2017 and 2019 were analyzed using content analysis. A total of 3996 financial statements were examined. The findings reveal that while 1454 financial statements disclosed subsequent events and 2134 statements declared that no such events occurred, 408 statements lacked any disclosure in this regard—despite ISA 560 requiring at least a note. All 408 non-compliant statements were interim reports. Furthermore, 2146 events were classified into 40 categories, with capital increases, bond issuances, and subsidiary transactions being the most frequently disclosed. The results underline the need for enhanced compliance, especially in interim reporting, and suggest the adoption of an ISA 560-specific audit checklist to improve audit quality and consistency.

Keywords Subsequent events · ISA 560 · Audit · Borsa istanbul · Financial reports

This chapter was previously published in Turkish by Gazi Kitabevi with the ISBN: 978-975-7727-16-7.

H. Uzunoğlu (✉)
Faculty of Applied Sciences, Kayseri University, Kayseri, Türkiye
e-mail: hayrettinuzunoglu@kayseri.edu.tr

G. Kurt, Ö. Sarısoy (eds.), *Recent Advancements in Auditing*, Accounting, Finance, Sustainability, Governance & Fraud: Theory and Application,
https://doi.org/10.1007/978-981-95-5811-7_7

7.1 Introductıon

Financial statements are indicate the financial position and performance of the firm during the relevant accounting period. Pursuant to the provisions of the Turkish Commercial Code and Tax Procedure Law, each company in Türkiye is required to prepare financial statements at least once a year (as of the end of the accounting period) and submit these financial statements to the relevant authorities. Pursuant to Article 4 of the Communiqué on Amendment to the Communiqué on Principles Regarding Financial Reporting in Capital Markets; (a) Companies whose capital market instruments are traded on a stock exchange and/or other organized marketplaces, (b) Investment institutions, (c) Investment trusts, (d) Portfolio management companies, d) Mortgage financing institutions are required to prepare interim financial statements for 3, 6 and 9-month periods in addition to their annual financial statements (Official Gazette 2017).

In accordance with the provisions of the Tax Procedure Law, the accounting period in Türkiye refers to a year between January 1 and December 31. Therefore, the balance sheet date for annual financial statements is accepted as December 31. However, as mentioned above, companies in the capital markets in Türkiye are required to prepare 3, 6 and 9-month interim financial statements in addition to their annual financial statements. The balance sheet date is March 31 for 3-month interim financial statements, June 30 for 6-month interim financial statements and September 30 for 9-month interim financial statements. Subsequent events are considered to be events that occur between the balance sheet date (the last day of the accounting period) and the approval of the financial statements by the company's managers.

International Standard on Auditing (ISA) 560 was issued to "set out the auditor's responsibilities in relation to subsequent events in an audit of financial statements". In accordance with this standard, "the auditor is expected to perform audit procedures designed to obtain sufficient appropriate audit evidence regarding the identification of all events occurring between the balance sheet date and the date of the auditor's report that require adjustment or disclosure in the financial statements" (POA, p.1–4).

The purpose of this study is to determine the status of disclosures of subsequent events within the scope of ISA 560 for firms whose shares are traded on Borsa Istanbul (BIST). Accordingly, in the second part of the study, International Standard on Auditing 560 is mentioned, and in the third part, a literature review is provided. The fourth part of the study is the research part, in which the financial statements of the relevant companies are examined using the content analysis technique, which involves categorizing data into themes to identify patterns, in order to realize the purpose of the study. In the fifth section, which is the last section of the study, the results of the study are mentioned.

7.2 ISA 560 Subsequent Events

Among the basic concepts of accounting are the concepts of going concern and periodicity. In accordance with the concept of going concern, the enterprise is assumed to continue indefinitely; in accordance with the concept of periodicity, the life of the enterprise, which is considered to be unlimited, should be divided into certain periods and financial statements for the relevant period should be prepared in order to determine the operating results of each period independently from other parts. The last day of the period to which the financial statements belong is called the balance sheet day or reporting day. However, there is a difference between the balance sheet date, which is the last day of the period covered by the financial statements of an entity, and the publication date of the audited and approved version of these financial statements. Events occurring between the balance sheet date and the date of approval of the financial statements are referred to as subsequent events.

After the balance sheet date, various events may occur in favor of or against the entity. These favorable or unfavorable events may affect the financial statements of the company and may change the opinions of various internal and external stakeholders interested in the financial position of the company. For example, the collection of a large amount of receivables or the conclusion of a lawsuit filed on behalf of a company will change the views of users of the financial statements about the company. Therefore, subsequent events should be included in the financial statements of the related firm. As a result of the need for a standard on this issue, "International Accounting Standard (IAS) 10" was adopted in December, 2003. "Turkish Accounting Standard (TAS) 10: Subsequent Events" was adopted for the accounting periods beginning after January 1, 2006 in order to apply the same standard to the companies in Türkiye. Following these standards, it has become necessary to introduce a new standard in order to regulate the responsibilities of independent auditors, who audit the financial statements of companies, in relation to subsequent events. As a result, "Independent Standard on Auditing 560: Subsequent Events" has been issued and put into practice.

The first version of ISA 560 Subsequent Events was published in the Official Gazette dated 01/22/2014 and numbered 28,890 to be applied in the audit of accounting periods beginning on or after 01/01/2013 and the latest version was published in the Official Gazette dated 12/13/2017 and numbered 30,269 to be applied in the audit of accounting periods beginning on or after 01/01/2017. In accordance with this standard (POA, p. 5):

- Balance sheet date: "The last day of the most recent period to which the financial statements relate",
- Date of approval of the financial statements: "The date on which the financial statements, including their notes, are authorized for issuance and the entity's authorized personnel assume responsibility for them",
- Date of the auditor's report: The date on which the auditor obtains sufficient appropriate audit evidence to provide a basis for his or her opinion on the

financial statements and issues the auditor's report on the financial statements, provided that it is subsequent to the date of approval of the financial statements; and

- Subsequent events: "Events occurring between the balance sheet date and the date of the auditor's report, and events of which the auditor becomes aware after the date of the auditor's report".

In accordance with the main provisions of ISA 560, the following three situations can be mentioned in the audit of subsequent events (Ertaş and Güngör 2017):

1. Events of which the auditor becomes aware between the balance sheet date and the date of the auditor's report,
   a. Events requiring adjustments in financial statements,
   b. Events to be disclosed in financial statements.
2. Events of which the auditor becomes aware after the date of the auditor's report but before the date of issuance of the financial statements; and
3. Events of which the auditor becomes aware after the issuance of the financial statements.

7.2.1 Events of Which the Auditor Became Aware Between the Balance Sheet Date and the Auditor's Report Date

Events that occur after the balance sheet date and of which the auditor becomes aware between the balance sheet date and the date of the auditor's report are divided into two categories: events that require adjustments to the financial statements and events that require disclosure in the financial statements. Events that require adjustments to the financial statements are events that directly affect the financial statements of the company. If there is an event that requires an adjustment in the financial statements of the company after the balance sheet date, the companies are responsible for adjusting their financial statements according to this new situation. Examples of such events are the conclusion of a lawsuit against the company before the date of the auditor's report and the discovery of errors in the company's financial statements. Events that should be declared in financial statements are events that occur after the balance sheet date and do not require adjustments to the financial statements of the period (Ertaş and Güngör 2017). However, in accordance with the concept of materiality, which is among the basic concepts of accounting, such events should be disclosed in the footnotes in the company's financial statements (Karacan and Uygun 2016). Examples of events that occur between the balance sheet date and the date of the auditor's report and that need to be disclosed in the company's financial statements are; a significant change in the exchange rate and the emergence of disputes such as strikes and lockouts (Ertaş and Güngör 2017).

Under ISA 560, the auditor is expected to "perform audit procedures designed to obtain sufficient appropriate audit evidence that all events have been identified" in order to identify an event occurring after the balance sheet date that requires adjustment or disclosure in the company's financial statements. These audit procedures are performed separately from routine audit procedures that may be applied to specific transactions occurring after the balance sheet date to obtain audit evidence about the account balances at the balance sheet date (Kishalı et al. 2013). Audit procedures within the scope of ISA 560 in clude the following (POA, p. 7):

- Understand the procedures established by management to enable the identification of subsequent events,
- Inquiring of management and those charged with governance about any subsequent events that may affect the financial statements after the balance sheet date that may affect the financial statements,
- Reading the minutes of the meetings of shareholders, management and those charged with governance held after the date of the financial statements, if any, and questioning them about matters discussed at those meetings but for which minutes have not yet been prepared; and
- Reading the most recent interim financial statements of the entity after the balance sheet date, if any.

The audit procedures listed above are required under ISA 560. However, in addition to the mandatory audit procedures, the auditor may perform the following additional audit procedures (POA, p. A8):

- Reading the entity's latest available budget, cash flow forecasts and other relevant management statements for periods subsequent to the date of the financial statements,
- Questioning the entity's legal advisors in relation to lawsuits and claims, or following up on prior written or oral inquiries,
- Considering whether written representations covering specific subsequent events would be necessary to supplement the other audit evidence and thereby obtain sufficient appropriate audit evidence.

The auditor may prepare the auditor's report after performing the mandatory and additional audit procedures described above for subsequent events.

7.2.2 *Events of Which the Auditor Becomes Aware After the Date of the Auditor's Report but Before the Date of Issuance of the Financial Statements*

The auditor is not required to perform any audit procedures on events that the auditor becomes aware of after the date of the auditor's report but before the date of issuance of the financial statements. However, in accordance with ISA 210, “Management has a responsibility to communicate to the auditor any matters of which it becomes aware between the date of the auditor’s report and the date of issuance of the financial statements that may affect the financial statements” (Tüm 2018). Therefore, in the event of such a situation, the company management is required to inform the auditor. The auditor is expected to do the following if there is a situation after the date of the auditor’s report that the auditor became aware of before the date of issuance of the financial statements and that would cause the auditor to change its report if it had become aware of it on the date of the auditor’s report (POA, p. 10):

- Discuss the matter with management and—where appropriate—those responsible for senior management,
- Deciding whether amendments to the financial statements are necessary,
- If it is necessary to amend the financial statements, inquire about how management intends to address the matter in the financial statements.

If it is necessary to make changes to the financial statements, the auditor shall prepare a new auditor’s report on the restated financial statements by applying the necessary audit procedures. In such a case, the audit opinion need not be modified (Kaval et al. 2015). If the management does not make the changes in the company’s financial statements as stated by the auditor, the auditor is expected to; “(a) if the auditor’s report has not yet been issued to the entity, express an opinion other than an unmodified opinion as required by ISA 705 and then issue its report; or (b) if the auditor’s report has been issued to the entity, notify management and those charged with governance not to issue the financial statements without the required modifications, and take appropriate steps to prevent reliance on the auditor’s report if the financial statements are issued without the required modifications despite this notification” (POA, p. 13).

7.2.3 Events of Which the Auditor Becomes Aware After the Issuance of the Financial Statements

The auditor is not required to perform any audit procedures for events of which the auditor becomes aware after the issuance of the financial statements. However, if there is a circumstance that occurred after the issuance of the financial statements that may cause the auditor to modify his or her report if he or she becomes aware of it at the date of the auditor’s report, the auditor is required to discuss the matter with management and those charged with governance, determine whether changes to the financial statements are necessary, and if changes to the financial statements are necessary, make inquiries about how management plans to address the matter in the financial statements (POA, p. 14). If management reviews and makes changes to the financial statements, the auditor should apply audit procedures appropriate in the circumstances, review the actions taken by management to disclose how previously issued financial statements and the auditor's report are affected, and prepare a new auditor's report on the modified financial statements (Ertaş and Güngör 2017).

In summary, International Standard on Auditing 560 emphasizes the auditor's responsibilities for events occurring after the balance sheet date. In this context, it divides the subsequent events into three categories: (a) Events that the auditor becomes aware of between the balance sheet date and the date of the auditor's report, (b) Events that the auditor becomes aware of after the date of the auditor's report but before the date of issuance of the financial statements, and (c) Events that the auditor becomes aware of after the issuance of the financial statements. In the next section of the study, the researches that have been conducted so far on ISA 560 are discussed.

7.3 Literature Review

When the studies on subsequent events are examined, it is seen that most of the studies are conducted within the scope of "Turkish Accounting Standard (TAS) 10: Events After the Reporting Period" instead of "International Standard on Auditing 560 Subsequent Events ". Especially the scarcity of studies conducted in Türkiye within the scope of ISA 560 increases the importance of this study.

Janvrin and Jeffrey (2007) conducted a survey of independent auditors working in the four largest audit firms in the United States to investigate the process of obtaining audit evidence for subsequent events and the factors affecting this process. The study concluded that approximately 75% of the auditors surveyed generally follow the audit procedures recommended by auditing standards to obtain audit evidence. They also stated that as a result of the US Securities Exchange Commission (SEC) bringing forward the public disclosure date of the financial statements of listed companies, the time for independent auditors to obtain audit evidence for subsequent events has shortened and this situation has negatively affected the independent auditors.

In their study, Chung et al. (2013) reported that one-third of the American Public Company Accounting Oversight Board (PCAOB) inspection reports and most of the American Stock Exchange (SEC) bulletins mention the deficiencies of audit work on events occurring after the balance sheet date. In order to overcome this deficiency, the authors aimed to develop a new model that includes the factors that affect the effectiveness of audit procedures for subsequent events, taking into account the behavioral accounting and psychology literature. According to the developed model, the main factors affecting the effectiveness of audit procedures for subsequent events are the auditor's environment, individual perception and task-specific factors.

In their study, Herda and Lavelle (2014) conducted a survey with open-ended questions to 76 independent auditors working in the United States in order to develop processes that will benefit the audit of subsequent events within the scope of ISA 560. According to the study, it was concluded that audit firms preparing training materials on subsequent events and establishing a strong bond based on mutual trust between the audit firm and the client can help auditors to identify and evaluate subsequent events.

In their study, Nawaiseh and Javel (2015) surveyed 62 auditors working in an audit firm to examine the extent to which auditors in Jordan try to comply with the requirements of ISA 560. In the study, it was concluded that auditors act in accordance with the scope of ISA 560 in the period between the balance sheet date and the date of the auditor's report, but they do not apply the requirements of ISA 560 in the events that occur after the date of the auditor's report. In addition, another result of the study is that there is no significant relationship between the demographic structure of independent auditors and compliance with ISA 560.

Özdemir and Ataman Gökçen (2016) surveyed 108 independent auditors registered with the Public Oversight, Accounting and Auditing Standards Authority of Türkiye and living in Istanbul in order to examine the audit experience and the process of obtaining audit evidence on subsequent events and to measure the use of ISA 560. According to the study, it was concluded that auditors rated the disclosures about subsidiaries, affiliates and other related parties, disclosures about capital structure and disclosures about securities in the financial report disclosures (footnotes) related to subsequent events as very important, while they rated the disclosures about corporate governance, regulatory disclosures and disclosures about the decisions of the general assembly meeting minutes as less important. In addition, it has been declared that the auditors stated that the subsequent events are significant enough to affect the independent audit opinion. Finally, we concluded that the independent auditors used the procedures in ISA 560 in obtaining evidence about subsequent events.

Ertaş and Güngör (2017) surveyed 50 independent auditors registered with the Public Oversight, Accounting and Auditing Standards Authority of Türkiye in order to determine the extent to which independent auditors in Türkiye meet the requirements of ISA 560 in the audit process. According to the results obtained from the analysis, it was determined that independent auditors comply with the provisions of ISA 560 in the audit of events between the date of issuance of the financial statements and the date of issuance of the independent audit report.

Tüm (2018) examined subsequent events within the scope of International Standard on Auditing 560 and the Financial Reporting Standard for Large and Medium-Sized Enterprises (BOBI). In the related study, sample applications were made about the issues that independent auditors should pay attention to during the accounting of subsequent events and as a result, it was declared that the accounting and auditing of subsequent events are very important.

7.4 Research

In this section of the study; the purpose, method, scope and findings of the research will be emphasized.

7.4.1 *Purpose and Method of the Study*

Subsequent events are events that occur between the balance sheet date and the date of issuance of the financial statements. International Standard on Auditing 560 was issued to determine the auditor's responsibilities and the audit procedures to be applied in the process of obtaining audit evidence about events occurring after the balance sheet date and to indicate how the related events should be included in the company's financial statements.

The purpose of this study is to determine the status of disclosures of events occurring after the balance sheet date within the scope of ISA 560 by companies whose shares are traded on Borsa Istanbul. In order to achieve this objective, the annual financial statements and interim financial statements of the relevant companies for the years 2017, 2018, and 2019 were analyzed using the content analysis technique. The main purpose of content analysis is to reach concepts and relationships that will help explain the collected data. The basic process in content analysis is to bring together similar data within the framework of certain concepts and themes (Yıldırım and Şimşek 2008).

7.4.2 *Scope of the Study*

Auditing Standard 560 requires companies to disclose separately in their financial statements "subsequent events". Pursuant to this standard, even if there is no event after the balance sheet date that would require a firm to make a disclosure, "Subsequent Events" or a similar heading should be included in the financial statements of the firm, and under this heading, it should be stated that no event has occurred after the balance sheet date. In this context, the financial statements of firms whose shares were traded on Borsa Istanbul (BIST) between 2017 and 2019 are analyzed. The study starts with 2017 because the latest version of ISA 560 was published in the Official Gazette dated 12/13/2017 and numbered 30,269 to be applied in the audit of the accounting periods starting on and after 1/2017.

As a result of the review, a total of 333 companies whose shares are traded on Borsa Istanbul (BIST) and whose interim and annual financial statements for the three, six and nine months of 2017, 2018 and 2019 were publicly disclosed on Public Disclosure Platform's website "kap.org.tr" were identified. The list of the relevant firms can be found in "Annex-1: List of Firms Included in the Study" at the end of the study. The financial statements of each firm included in the scope of the study were analyzed for 12 different accounting periods, including 3, 6 and 9-month interim and annual financial statements for 2017, 2018 and 2019. Accordingly, the total number of financial statements analyzed and included in the scope of the study is 3996.

7.4.3 Findings of the Study

The financial statements of 333 companies within the scope of the study were examined for the accounting periods of March 2017, June 2017, September 2017, December 2017, March 2018, June 2018, September 2018, December 2018, March 2019, June 2019, September 2019 and December 2019. A total of 3996 financial statements of 333 companies for 12 different accounting periods were analyzed;

- 1454 of which included a notification that an event occurred after the balance sheet date,
- 2134 of which include a statement that no events occurred after the balance sheet date
- 408 did not have a title such as "Subsequent Events" or a similar title.

As stated in the previous section, within the scope of ISA 560, companies are required to disclose in their financial statements even if no event has occurred after the reporting period. However, 408 of the 3996 financial statements included in the scope of the research did not include a heading such as "Subsequent Events" or a similar heading, and no disclosure was made. When this situation is taken into consideration, it can be said that approximately 10% of the company financial statements within the scope of the research do not comply with the provisions of ISA 560 standard. Another point to be noted here is that all of the 408 financial statements are interim financial statements for 3, 6 and 9-month accounting periods.

Of the 3996 financial statements within the scope of the study, 2134 financial statements contain a statement that no event occurred after the balance sheet date and 1454 financial statements contain a statement that an event occurred after the balance sheet date. The total number of events that occurred after the balance sheet date in the 1454 financial statements is 2146. In Table 7.1 on the next page, the disclosures made by 333 companies in the scope of the research regarding the 2146 events that occurred after the balance sheet date in their interim and annual financial statements for the 3, 6 and 9 months of 2017, 2018 and 2019 are shown in 40 different event groups using the content analysis technique.

When the information in Table 7.1 regarding the subsequent events is analyzed:

- Under the heading of subsequent events in the financial statements of the company, it is seen that a total of 15 notifications regarding the collection, postponement, sale or doubtful collection of receivables for each of the years

Table 7.1 Subsequent events

No.	Subsequent Events	Mar/17	Jun/17	Sep/17	Dec/17	2017 Total	Mar/18	Jun/18	Sep/18	Dec/18	2018 Total	Mar/19	Jun/19	Sep/19	Dec/19	2019 Total	SUM TOTAL
1	Notification Regarding Collection, Deferral, Sale, or Impairment of Receivables	2	1	2	10	**15**	1	4	7	3	**15**	3	5	2	9	**19**	**49**
2	Notification Regarding Capital Increase of Parent Company	17	20	11	14	**62**	15	13	10	23	**61**	11	15	12	21	**59**	**182**
3	Notification Regarding Capital Reduction of Parent Company	1	0	2	1	**4**	2	2	1	0	**5**	0	0	0	0	**0**	**9**
4	Notification Regarding Independent Audit Firm Agreement	2	0	0	0	**2**	2	0	0	0	**2**	1	1	0	0	**2**	**6**
5	Notification Regarding Subsidiary Merger	5	8	4	5	**22**	1	3	4	5	**13**	2	6	2	7	**17**	**52**
6	Notification Regarding the Establishment/Acquisition/Sale of Subsidiary	10	15	15	19	**59**	12	13	12	19	**56**	9	10	6	18	**43**	**158**
7	Notification Regarding Capital Increase of Subsidiary	1	2	6	9	**18**	5	9	3	5	**22**	4	1	4	8	**17**	**57**
8	Notification Regarding Capital Decrease of Subsidiary	0	0	0	0	**0**	0	1	0	1	**2**	0	0	0	0	**0**	**2**
9	Notification Regarding BIST Market Change	0	0	0	1	**1**	1	0	0	0	**1**	0	0	0	0	**0**	**2**
10	Notification of Acquisition/Payment/Deferment/Restructuring of Debts	12	10	8	12	**42**	9	11	9	17	**46**	10	8	4	13	**35**	**123**

(continued)

Table 7.1 (continued)

No.	Subsequent Events	Mar/ 17	Jun/ 17	Sep/ 17	Dec/ 17	2017 Total	Mar/ 18	Jun/ 18	Sep/ 18	Dec/ 18	2018 Total	Mar/ 19	Jun/ 19	Sep/ 19	Dec/ 19	2019 Total	SUM TOTAL
11	Notification Regarding Lawsuits/ Investigations	4	3	2	9	**18**	4	4	5	4	**17**	1	4	2	7	**14**	**49**
12	Notification Regarding Significant Exchange Rate Changes	2	2	1	3	**8**	4	38	7	2	**51**	1	3	0	0	**4**	**61**
13	Notification Regarding Equity in the Financial Statements	0	0	0	1	**1**	1	1	1	1	**4**	1	1	1	1	**4**	**9**
14	Notice Regarding the Approval of the Financial Statements	9	6	6	7	**28**	7	6	6	7	**26**	5	4	3	5	**17**	**71**
15	Notification Regarding the General Assembly Date	2	0	1	1	**4**	3	0	1	2	**6**	2	1	1	0	**4**	**14**
16	Notification Regarding Acquisition/Sale of Subsidiary	5	2	4	11	**22**	3	4	4	3	**14**	2	2	7	6	**17**	**53**
17	Notification Regarding Capital Increase of Subsidiary	1	0	1	2	**4**	0	0	0	3	**3**	0	1	1	1	**3**	**10**
18	Notification Regarding the Change in the Severance Pay Ceiling	5	19	4	15	**43**	3	12	3	15	**33**	3	8	2	10	**23**	**99**
19	Notification of Credit/Other Rating Change	0	1	1	3	**5**	0	1	2	2	**5**	0	2	2	2	**6**	**16**
20	Notification Regarding Acquisition/Sale/Modification of Property, Plant and Equipment/ Real Estate	5	7	6	9	**27**	1	4	8	9	**22**	1	5	5	16	**27**	**76**

(continued)

Table 7.1 (continued)

No.	Subsequent Events	Mar/17	Jun/17	Sep/17	Dec/17	2017 Total	Mar/18	Jun/18	Sep/18	Dec/18	2018 Total	Mar/19	Jun/19	Sep/19	Dec/19	2019 Total	SUM TOTAL
21	Notification of Change of Headquarters Address	1	1	1	1	**4**	1	4	0	2	**7**	1	0	0	2	**3**	**14**
22	Notification Regarding the Change in Accounting Policy	0	0	2	0	**2**	0	0	4	0	**4**	0	0	0	0	**0**	**6**
23	Notification Regarding Transfer/Receipt of Shares	5	9	5	10	**29**	5	17	10	6	**38**	4	5	6	6	**21**	**88**
24	Notice Regarding the Issuance of Share Certificates	7	1	2	3	**13**	6	2	4	7	**19**	2	1	4	9	**16**	**48**
25	Notification Regarding Change in Capital Structure	13	9	8	11	**41**	10	10	9	7	**36**	5	6	6	6	**23**	**100**
26	Notification of Contract Signing/Termination	8	12	8	12	**40**	9	10	11	17	**47**	15	5	10	13	**43**	**130**
27	Notification Regarding Merger/Division of Companies	1	4	5	2	**12**	1	1	1	0	**3**	1	1	0	3	**5**	**20**
28	Notification Regarding the Amendment of the Company's Articles of Association	5	3	2	6	**16**	4	0	3	4	**11**	1	1	0	7	**9**	**36**
29	Notification Regarding Change of Company Title	3	0	0	0	**7**	0	0	1	0	**1**	2	0	0	1	**3**	**7**
30	Notification of Branch Opening/Closing/Address Change	3	6	2	5	**16**	1	4	2	5	**12**	2	2	2	6	**12**	**40**
31	Notification Regarding Bond/Bill Issuance/Payment	10	15	10	19	**54**	16	18	16	18	**68**	14	17	11	17	**59**	**181**

(continued)

Table 7.1 (continued)

No.	Subsequent Events	Mar/17	Jun/17	Sep/17	Dec/17	2017 Total	Mar/18	Jun/18	Sep/18	Dec/18	2018 Total	Mar/19	Jun/19	Sep/19	Dec/19	2019 Total	SUM TOTAL
32	Notification Regarding Dividend Distribution	24	4	1	6	**35**	21	2	3	3	**29**	18	4	5	2	**29**	**93**
33	Notification of Incentives/ Exemptions	1	4	5	1	**11**	3	0	4	1	**8**	1	2	2	2	**7**	**26**
34	Notice Regarding Collective Labor Agreement	3	1	5	12	**21**	1	0	0	3	**4**	1	0	0	7	**8**	**33**
35	Notification of Production Change	1	4	4	1	**10**	2	3	3	4	**12**	4	1	1	3	**9**	**31**
36	Notification Regarding the Change in Senior Management	4	2	1	2	**7**	3	2	6	4	**15**	6	3	6	4	**19**	**43**
37	Notification Regarding Tax/Other Legislative Changes	2	4	1	24	**31**	4	4	8	2	**18**	0	1	1	2	**4**	**53**
38	Notification of Tax/ Administrative Fine	2	2	0	3	**7**	0	2	0	1	**3**	0	0	1	4	**5**	**15**
39	Notification of Fire/Natural Disasters	2	1	0	0	**3**	0	0	1	0	**1**	0	0	0	0	**0**	**4**
40	Statement on Investment Activities	5	12	8	6	**31**	2	6	3	13	**24**	9	3	5	6	**23**	**78**
TOTAL		**183**	**190**	**144**	**256**	**773**	**163**	**211**	**172**	**218**	**764**	**142**	**129**	**114**	**224**	**609**	**2.146**

2017 and 2018, and a total of 19 notifications in 2019 interim and annual financial statements were shared with the public.

- Regarding the capital increase of the parent company, it is seen that there were a total of 182 notifications in the 12 accounting periods included in the scope of the study, including 62 notifications in 2017 interim and annual financial statements, 61 notifications in 2018 interim and annual financial statements, and 59 notifications in 2019 interim and annual financial statements, making it the most notified event within the scope of the study.
- There are 4 notifications regarding the capital decrease of the parent company in 2017 interim and annual financial statements and 5 notifications in 2018 interim and annual financial statements. In 2019 interim and annual financial statements, there is no notification about this event. In addition, it is understood that capital decreases by parent companies were primarily to offset balance sheet deficits from prior losses. Another noteworthy point is that all firms that reported a capital decrease by the parent firm either simultaneously (in the same period) or in the following period reported a capital increase.
- Regarding the independent audit firm agreement, a total of 2 notifications were made in the interim and annual financial statements for each of the years 2017, 2018 and 2019.
- Regarding subsidiaries of companies (notification regarding subsidiary merger, notification regarding subsidiary establishment/acquisition/sale, notification regarding subsidiary capital increase and notification regarding subsidiary capital decrease) A total of 269 notifications were included in the interim and annual financial statements for 2017, 2018 and 2019. Regarding the subsidiaries of the firms during the relevant accounting periods; the highest number of notifications was related to the establishment/acquisition/sale of subsidiaries (158), while the lowest number of notifications was related to the capital decrease of subsidiaries (2).
- During the relevant 12 accounting periods, a total of 2 disclosures were made in the firm's financial statements under the subsequent events heading, and the Borsa Istanbul (BIST) market change was the least disclosed event together with the disclosure of the capital decrease of the subsidiary.
- Regarding the acquisition, payment, deferral or restructuring of debts, a total of 42 disclosures were made in 2017 interim and annual financial statements, 46 disclosures were made in 2018 interim and annual financial statements, and 35 disclosures were made in 2019 interim and annual financial statements.
- Regarding lawsuits and investigations; a total of 18 disclosures were made in 2017 interim and annual financial statements, 17 disclosures were made in 2018 interim and annual financial statements, and 14 disclosures were made in 2019 interim and annual financial statements. What is meant by the disclosures related to lawsuits and investigations are the disclosures made under the heading of subsequent events, regarding the filing of lawsuits and investigations against the company or by the company against someone else, the continuation or conclusion of lawsuits and investigations.
- During the 12 accounting periods, a total of 63 disclosures were made regarding foreign exchange rates. Of these 63 disclosures, 51 are included in the 2018

financial statements. The main reason for this is the sudden and high-frequency changes in the value of the exchange rate in 2018.

- The total number of disclosures related to the equity item in the statement of financial position is 9. What is meant by the disclosure related to the equity in the statement of financial position is that the balance sheet of the company is prepared to include the brand value of the company in accordance with Article 376 of the Turkish Commercial Code as a result of the negative (−) value of the equity in the statements of financial position of the company and thus the equity appears to be positive (+).
- Regarding the approval of the financial statements, a total of 28 notifications were made in 2017 interim and annual financial statements, 26 in 2018 interim and annual financial statements, and 17 in 2019 interim and annual financial statements.
- During the 12 accounting periods, a total of 14 announcements were made regarding the date of the general shareholders' meeting under the subsequent events heading in the company financial statements.
- In the interim and annual financial statements for 2017, 2018 and 2019, companies made a total of 63 notifications regarding their subsidiaries (notifications regarding the acquisition/sale of subsidiaries and notifications regarding the capital increase of subsidiaries).
- Regarding the change in the severance pay ceiling, a total of 43 notifications were made in 2017 interim and annual financial statements, 33 notifications were made in 2018 interim and annual financial statements, and 23 notifications were made in 2019 interim and annual financial statements.
- In the company financial statements, under the heading of subsequent events, there are a total of 16 notifications regarding credit and other rating changes during the relevant 12 accounting periods. Credit and other rating change notifications refer to the changes in the ratings assigned to the banks in the study by various rating agencies.
- Regarding the acquisition, sale or modification of tangible fixed assets and real estate, a total of 27 disclosures were made in 2017 interim and annual financial statements, 22 disclosures were made in 2018 interim and annual financial statements, and 27 disclosures were made in 2019 interim and annual financial statements.
- During the relevant 12 accounting periods, a total of 14 notifications regarding the change of headquarters address were made under the subsequent events heading in the company financial statements.
- In the financial statements of the company, under the heading of subsequent events, a total of 6 notifications were made regarding the change in accounting policy during the 12 accounting periods. In all of the related notifications, the transition to the "Revaluation Model" method in the valuation of land, land and buildings in the tangible fixed assets section is mentioned.
- Regarding the transfer or repurchase of shares, a total of 13 notifications were made in 2017 interim and annual financial statements, 19 notifications were

made in 2018 interim and annual financial statements, and 16 notifications were made in 2019 interim and annual financial statements.

- Regarding the change in capital structure, a total of 100 disclosures were made during the 12 accounting periods covered by the study. A change in the capital structure refers to a change in the proportion of shares held by the firm's shareholders in the firm.
- A total of 130 notifications regarding the signing or termination of contracts were made during the 12 accounting periods covered by the study, 40 in 2017 interim and annual financial statements, 47 in 2018 interim and annual financial statements, and 43 in 2019 interim and annual financial statements.
- During the relevant 12 accounting periods, a total of 20 disclosures were made under the heading of subsequent events in the company financial statements; a total of 20 disclosures related to mergers or demergers, a total of 36 disclosures related to changes in the articles of association of the company and a total of 7 disclosures related to changes in the title of the company.
- During the relevant 12 accounting periods, a total of 40 notifications were made under the subsequent events heading in the company financial statements regarding the opening, closing or change of address of branches.
- A total of 181 disclosures regarding the issuance or payment of bonds and bills were made during the 12 accounting periods covered by the study, 54 in 2017 interim and annual financial statements, 68 in 2018 interim and annual financial statements, and 59 in 2019 interim and annual financial statements.
- Regarding dividend distribution, a total of 35 notifications were made in 2017 interim and annual financial statements, and 29 notifications were made for each of 2018 and 2019.
- During the 12 accounting periods, a total of 26 notifications regarding incentives and exemptions were made under the subsequent events heading in the company financial statements.
- Regarding the collective labor agreement, a total of 21 disclosures were made in 2017 interim and annual financial statements, 4 disclosures were made in 2018 interim and annual financial statements, and 8 disclosures were made in 2019 interim and annual financial statements.
- A total of 31 production change notifications were made during the 12 accounting periods. Production change notification refers to the increase/decrease in the number of production or the decision of the firm to stop production.
- During the 12 accounting periods, a total of 43 disclosures regarding the change in top management were made under the subsequent events heading in the company financial statements.
- A total of 53 notifications regarding tax and other legislative changes were made during the 12 accounting periods. Of these 53 notifications, 31 were disclosed in the 2017 financial statements. The main reason for this is the change in the corporate tax rate in accordance with the legal articles enacted in the relevant period (Article 91 of the Law No. 7061 on the Amendment of Certain Tax Laws and Some Other Laws and Provisional Article 10 added to the Corporate Tax Law).

- In the company financial statements, under the heading of subsequent events, during the related 12 accounting periods; 15 notifications related to tax and administrative fines, 4 notifications related to fire and natural disasters and 78 notifications related to investment activities were made.

7.5 Conclusıon

International Standard on Auditing 560 was issued to regulate the auditor‘s responsibilities for events occurring after the balance sheet date. According to this standard, “the auditor is expected to perform audit procedures designed to obtain sufficient appropriate audit evidence regarding the identification of all events occurring between the balance sheet date and the date of the auditor’s report that require adjustment or disclosure in the financial statements”. In addition, in accordance with the same standard, there should be a separate heading for subsequent events in the financial statements of the company and this should be declared even if no event has occurred.

The purpose of this study is to determine the situation regarding the disclosures of events occurring after the balance sheet date in the financial statements of companies whose shares are traded in Borsa Istanbul within the scope of International Standard on Auditing 560. In order to achieve this objective, firstly, International Standard on Auditing 560 was briefly mentioned, then the studies on the subject were mentioned, and finally, the financial statements of the companies whose shares were traded in Borsa Istanbul between 2017 and 2019 were examined. As a result of the examination, a total of 333 companies whose shares are traded on Borsa Istanbul (BIST) and whose 3-, 6- and 9-month interim financial statements and annual financial statements for the years 2017, 2018 and 2019 were shared with the public on “kap.org.tr” were identified.

A total of 3996 financial statements of 333 companies for the fiscal periods of March 2017, June 2017, September 2017, December 2017, March 2018, June 2018, September 2018, December 2018, March 2019, June 2019, September 2019 and December 2019 were analyzed. It has been observed that 1454 of the 3996 financial statements included a notification that an event occurred after the balance sheet date, 2134 included a notification that no event occurred after the balance sheet date, and 408 did not have a title such as “Subsequent Events” or a similar title and did not include any notification regarding subsequent events, in violation of ISA 560 requirements. The number of financial statements without any disclosure of subsequent events corresponds to approximately 10% of the total number of financial statements included in the scope of the study. It is also noteworthy that all of the 408 financial statements are interim financial statements of the firms. This may be due to the obligation to submit annual financial report disclosures by the 60th day following the end of the accounting period and interim financial report disclosures by the 30th day following the end of the accounting period (for consolidated financial statements, 70 days for annual financial statements and 40 days for interim financial statements) as per Articles 10 and 11 of the Communiqué on Principles of Financial Reporting in Capital Markets published in the Official Gazette (2017).

In the remainder of the study, 1454 financial statements containing event disclosures after the balance sheet date were analyzed and it was determined that a total of 2146 events were mentioned. These 2146 events were grouped into 40 different event groups using the content analysis technique. As a result of the analysis:

- The five events with the highest number of notifications were: notifications regarding the capital increase of the parent company (182 notifications), notifications regarding the issuance or payment of bonds and bills (181 notifications), notifications regarding the establishment, acquisition or sale of subsidiaries (158 notifications), notifications regarding the signing or termination of contracts (130 notifications) and notifications regarding the acquisition, payment, postponement or restructuring of debts (123 notifications),
- Three of the five events with the highest number of notifications (notification of capital increase of parent company, notification of issuance or payment of bonds and bills, and notification of acquisition, payment, deferral or restructuring of debts) firms' search for new sources of capital,
- The five events with the lowest number of notifications are as follows; notifications regarding BIST market change (2), notifications regarding subsidiary capital decrease (2), notifications regarding fire and natural disasters (4), notifications regarding accounting policy change (6) and notifications regarding independent audit firm agreement (6).

Although there have been both national and international studies on subsequent events, the majority of the studies in the literature have addressed the issue from the perspective of accounting standards rather than auditing. This may be due to the fact that international accounting standards were issued and started to be applied earlier than auditing standards. In the studies conducted within the scope of ISA 560, auditors were generally surveyed and it was concluded that subsequent events have an important role in determining the auditor's audit opinion, but the process of obtaining audit evidence on subsequent events is complex and lengthy. In this study, annual and interim financial statements of 333 companies whose shares are traded on Borsa Istanbul for the years 2017, 2018 and 2019 were analyzed and it was determined that approximately 10% of the relevant financial statements did not comply with the provisions of ISA 560 and all financial statements that did not comply with the provisions were interim financial statements. In the light of this information, the main recommendations of this study are to extend the reporting periods for interim financial statements and to prepare an ISA 560 checklist for auditors.

Appendix: List of Companies Included in the Study

Acıselsan Acıpayam Selüloz	Adel Kalemcilik	Adese Alışveriş Merkezleri
Afyon Çimento	Ak Yatırım	Akbank
Akçansa Çimento	Akdeniz Güvenlik	Akenerji Elektrik
Akfen Gayrimenkul	Akın Tekstil	Akmerkez Gayrimenkul
Aksa Akrilik Kimya	Aksa Enerji	Aksigorta
Aksu Enerji	Aktif Yatırım Bankası	Alarko Carrıer
Alarko Gayrimenkul	Alarko Holding	Albaraka Türk Katılım Bankası
Alcatel Lucent Teletaş Telekomüni.	Alkim Alkali Kimya	Alkim Kağıt
Alternatifbank	Altın Yunus Çeşme Turistik Tesisler	Altınyağ Kombinaları
Anadolu Anonim Türk Sigorta	Anadolu Cam Sanayii	Anadolu Efes Biracılık
Anadolu Hayat Emeklilik	Anadolu Isuzu Otomotiv	Arçelik
Arena Bilgisayar	Armada Bilgisayar Sistemleri	Arsan Tekstil
Artı Yatırım Holding	Aselsan Elektronik	Ata Gayrimenkul
Atakule Gayrimenkul	Atlantis Yatırım	Atlas Menkul Kıymetler
Avivasa Emeklilik	A.V.O.D. Kurutulmuş Gıda	Avrasya Gayrimenkul
Avrasya Petrol	Ayen Enerji	Aygaz
A1 Capıtal Yatırım	Bagfaş Bandırma Gübre	Bak Ambalaj
Bantaş Bandırma Ambalaj	Banvit	Batıçim Batı Anadolu Çimento
Batısöke Söke Çimento	Berkosan Yalıtım	Bilici Yatırım
Bim Birleşik Mağazalar	Birko Birleşik Koyunlulular Mensucat	Birlik Mensucat
Bizim Toptan Satış	Borusan Mannesmann Boru	Borusan Yatırım
Bosch Fren Sistemleri	Bossa Ticaret	Brisa Brıdgestone
Burçelik Bursa Çelik Döküm	Burçelik Vana	Bursa Çimento
Carrefoursa Carrefour	Coca-Cola İçecek	Cosmos Yatırım
Credıtwest Faktoring	Çelebi Hava Servisi	Çelik Halat
Çemaş Döküm	Çemtaş Çelik Makina	Çimbeton Hazırbeton
Çimentaş İzmir Çimento	Çimsa Çimento	Çuhadaroğlu Metal
Dagi Giyim	Dagi Yatırım	Dardanel Önentaş Gıda
Datagate Bilgisayar Malzemeleri	Demisaş Döküm Emaye Mamülleri	Deniz Gayrimenkul
Deniz Yatırım	Denizbank	Denizli Cam Sanayii
Derimod Konfeksiyon	Desa Deri Sanayi	Despec Bilgisayar

(continued)

(continued)

Deva Holding	Diriteks Diriliş Tekstil	Ditaş Doğan Yedek Parça
Doğan Burda Dergi	Doğan Şirketler Grubu	Doğtaş Kelebek Mobilya
Doğuş Gayrimenkul	Doğuş Otomotiv	Duran Doğan Basım
Dyo Boya	Eczacıbaşı Yatırım	Edip Gayrimenkul
Ege Endüstri	Ege Gübre	Ege Profil
Ege Seramik	Egeli & Co Girişim	Egeli & Co Tarım
Egeli & Co Yatırım	Egeplast Ege Plastik	Eis Eczacıbaşı İlaç
Ekiz Kimya	Emek Elektrik	Eminiş Ambalaj
Emlak Konut	Enka İnşaat	Erbosan Erciyas Boru
Ereğli Demir ve Çelik	Ersu Meyve	Escort Teknoloji
Etiler Gıda	Euro Kapital Yatırım	Euro Menkul Kıymet
Euro Trend Yatırım	Euro Yatırım	Federal-Mogul İzmit Piston
Fibabanka	Flap Kongre	Fonet Bilgi Teknolojileri
Ford Otomotiv	Frigo-Pak Gıda	Garanti Faktoring
Garanti Yatırım	Gedik Yatırım Holding	Gedik Yatırım Menkul Değerler
Gediz Ambalaj	Gentaş Genel Metal	Gersan Elektrik
Global Menkul Değerler	Global Yatırım Holding	Goodyear Lastikleri
Göltaş Göller Bölgesi Çimento	Gsd Denizcilik	Gsd Holding
Gübre Fabrikaları	Güler Yatırım Holding	Güneş Sigorta
Hacı Ömer Sabancı Holding	Halk Gayrimenkul Yatırım	Hateks Hatay Tekstil
Hedef Girişim Sermayesi Yatırım	Hektaş Ticaret	Hürriyet Gazetecilik
Icbc Turkey Bank	Işıklar Enerji	İdealist Gayrimenkul Yatırım
İhlas Ev Aletleri	İhlas Gayrimenkul Proje Geliştirme	İhlas Gazetecilik
İhlas Holding	İhlas Yayın Holding	İndeks Bilgisayar Sistemleri
İntema İnşaat	İş Finansal Kiralama	İş Gayrimenkul Yatırım
İş Girişim Sermayesi Yatırım	İş Yatırım Menkul Değerler	İş Yatırım Ortaklığı
İttifak Holding	İzmir Demir Çelik	Jantsa Jant Sanayi
Kaplamin Ambalaj	Kardemir Karabük Demir Çelik	Karel Elektronik
Karsu Tekstil	Kartonsan Karton	Kent Gıda
Kerevitaş Gıda	Kiler Gayrimenkul Yatırım	Klimasan Klima
Koç Holding	Konfrut Gıda	Konya Çimento
Kordsa Teknik Tekstil	Körfez Gayrimenkul Yatırım	Kristal Kola
Kron Telekomünikasyon	Kt Kira Sertifikaları	Kuyumcukent Gayrimenkul

(continued)

(continued)

Kütahya Porselen	Link Bilgisayar	Logo Yazılım
Lokman Hekim Engürüsağ Sağlık	Lüks Kadife	Makina Takım
Marmaris Altınyunus	Marshall Boya	Mavi Giyim
Mazhar Zorlu Holding	Menderes Tekstil	Mepet Metro Petrol
Merko Gıda	Metemtur Otelcilik	Migros
Milpa Ticari	Mistral Gayrimenkul Yatırım	Mmc Sanayi
Mondi Tire Kutsan Kağıt	Net Holding	Netaş Telekomünikasyon
Niğbaş Niğde Beton	Nuh Çimento	Nurol Gayrimenkul Yatırım
Nurol Yatırım Bankası	Odaş Elektrik	Odea Bank
Olmuksan Internatıonal Paper	Orge Enerji Elektrik	Osmanlı Yatırım Menkul Değerler
Ostim Endüstriyel Yatırımlar	Otokar Otomotiv	Oyak Yatırım Menkul Değerler
Oyak Yatırım Ortaklığı	Oylum Sınai	Özak Gayrimenkul Yatırım
Özbal Çelik Boru	Özderici Gayrimenkul Yatırım	Panora Gayrimenkul Yatırım
Park Elektrik Üretim	Parsan Makina Parçaları	Pasha Yatırım Bankası
Pegasus Hava Taşımacılığı	Penguen Gıda	Pera Gayrimenkul Yatırım
Pergamon Status Dış Ticaret	Petkim Petrokimya Holding	Petrokent Turizm
Phillipcapital Menkul Değerler	Pınar Entegre Et ve Un	Pınar Su Sanayi
Pınar Süt Mamulleri	Plastikkart Akıllı Kart İletişim	Polisan Holding
Prizma Pres Matbaacılık	Ray Sigorta	Reysaş Gayrimenkul Yatırım
Rhea Girişim Sermayesi Yatırım	Rta Laboratuvarları	San-El Mühendislik
Sanifoam Sünger	Saray Matbaacılık	Sarkuysan Elektrolitik
Sasa Polyester	Selçuk Ecza Deposu	Selçuk Gıda
Senkron Güvenlik	Serve Kırtasiye	Servet Gayrimenkul Yatırım
Silverline Endüstri	Sinpaş Gayrimenkul Yatırım	Soda Sanayii
Söktaş Tekstil	Sönmez Filament Sentetik İplik	Sönmez Pamuklu
Şeker Faktoring	Şeker Yatırım Menkul Değerler	Şekerbank
Tacirler Yatırım Menkul Değerler	Tat Gıda	Tav Havalimanları
T.C. Ziraat Bankası	Tek-Art İnşaat	Tekfen Holding
Teknosa	Temapol Polimer Plastik	Tera Yatırım Menkul Değerler
Tf Varlık Kiralama	Tgs Dış Ticaret	Tofaş

(continued)

(continued)

Torunlar Gayrimenkul Yatırım	Trakya Cam	Tskb Gayrimenkul Yatırım
Tuğçelik Alüminyum	Tukaş Gıda	Turcas Petrol
Turkcell	Turkısh Bank	Tümosan Motor
Tüpraş-Türkiye Petrol Rafinerileri	Türk Hava Yolları	Türk Prysmian Kablo
Türk Telekomünikasyon	Türk Traktör	Türk Tuborg Bira
Türker Proje Gayrimenkul	Türkiye Garanti Bankası	Türkiye Halk Bankası
Türkiye İhracat Kredi Bankası	Türkiye İş Bankası	Türkiye Kalkınma Bankası
Türkiye Sınai Kalkınma Bankası A	Ufuk Yatırım Yönetim	Ulaşlar Turizm Yatırımları
Ulusoy Elektrik İmalat	Ulusoy Un Sanayi	Uşak Seramik
Utopya Turizm	Ülker Bisküvi	Ünlü Menkul Değerler
Vakıf Finansal Kiralama	Vakıf Gayrimenkul Yatırım	Vakıf Menkul Kıymet Yatırım
Vakko Tekstil	Verusa Holding	Verusaturk Girişim Sermayesi
Vestel Beyaz Eşya	Vestel Elektronik	Viking Kağıt
Yapı Kredi Koray Gayrimenkul Yat.	Yapı Kredi Yatırım Menkul Değerler	Yapı ve Kredi Bankası
Yaprak Süt	Yataş Yatak	Yatırım Finansman Menkul Değerler
Yayla Enerji Üretim	Yeni Gimat Gayrimenkul	Yeşil Gayrimenkul Yatırım
Yeşil Yapı Endüstrisi	Yeşil Yatırım Holding	Yünsa

References

Chung JOY, Cullinan CP, Frank M, Long JH, Mueller-Phillips J, O'Reilly DM (2013) The auditor's approach to subsequent events: insights from the academic literature. Audit J Pract Theory 32(1):167–207. https://doi.org/10.2308/ajpt-50328

Herda DN, Lavelle JJ (2014) Auditing subsequent events: perspectives from the field. Curr Issues Audit 8(2):10–24. https://doi.org/10.2308/ciia-50886

Janvrin DJ, Jeffrey C (2007) An investigation of auditor perceptions about subsequent events and factors that influence this audit task. Account Horiz 21(3):295–312. https://doi.org/10.2308/acch.2007.21.3.295

Karacan S, Uygun R (2016) Denetim ve raporlama, 2 edn. Umuttepe Publishings, İstanbul, Türkiye

Kaval H, Karapınar A, Bayırlı R, Altay A, Torun S (2015) Türkiye denetim standartları uygulama ve yorumları TDS. Gazi Kitabevi, Ankara, Türkiye

Nawaiseh MAL, Jaber J (2015) Auditing subsequent events from the perspective of auditors: study from Jordan. Int J Financ Res 6(3):78–85. https://doi.org/10.5430/ijfr.v6n3p78

Özdemir Z, Ataman Gökçen B (2016) Auditing of subsequent events: a survey of auditors in the city of İstanbul in Turkey. Account Finance Res 5(2):42–53. https://doi.org/10.5430/afr.v5n2p42

Tüm K (2018) Raporlama döneminden sonraki olayların bağımsız denetim standartları (BDS 560) ve büyük ve orta boy işletmeler için finansal raporlama standardı (BOBİ FRS) kapsamında incelenmesi. J Polit Econ Manag 1(1):49–61

Yıldırım A, Şimşek H (2008) Sosyal bilimlerde nitel araştırma yöntemleri, 8th edn. Seçkin Publishings, Ankara, Türkiye

Online References

Ertaş FC, Güngör S (2017) Standard of the events after ISA (ındependent standard on audıtıng) 560 balance sheet date: a research on ındependent auditors. Paper presented at the IV. International Symposıum on Accounting and Finance, Ohrid, Macedonia. Retrieved from https://www.researchgate.net/publication/328127464_STANDARD_OF_THE_EVENTS_AFTER_ISA_INDEPENDENT_STANDARD_ON_AUDITING_560_BALANCE_SHEET_DATE_A_RESEARCH_ON_INDEPENDENT_AUDITORS

Kishalı Y, Güner MF, Pehlivanlı D (2013) Modül I - denetim standartları. Retrieved from https://docplayer.biz.tr/8094110-Denetim-standartlari.html

Official Gazette (2017) Communiqué Amending the Communiqué on Principles Regarding Financial Reporting in the Capital Markets (II-14.1). Retrieved from https://www.resmigazete.gov.tr/eskiler/2017/02/20170203-6.htm

PDP (n.d.) Public Disclosures from Companies Listed on Borsa Istanbul. Retrieved from https://www.kap.org.tr/tr/bildirim-sorgu

POA (n.d.) Retrieved from https://www.kgk.gov.tr/Portalv2Uploads/files/Duyurular/v2/BDS/bdsyeni25.12.2017/BDS%20560-Site.pdf

Chapter 8
ISA 570 Going Concern Standard: Implementations in Audit Reports in the Banking Sector

Beyhan Beller Dikmen and Musa Özçelik

Abstract Independent auditors who have significant doubts about a business's ability to continue as a going concern are required to disclose this uncertainty in their audit reports. The effective implementation of ISA 570 Going Concern Standard in audit reports is important for financial statement users. Due to the complex structures of banks and their roles in the financial system, the ISA 570 Standard is of greater importance in this sector. This study aims to determine whether the audit reports of selected deposit banks operating in Türkiye include disclosures regarding continuity within the scope of the International Standards on Auditing (ISA) 570 Going Concern Standard and to examine the types of opinions given by the auditors. In the study, audit reports between the years 2013–2019 were examined; banks with operating losses were determined and the reports of these banks were evaluated using the content analysis method. The review was carried out within the framework of "significant operating losses or significant decreases in the value of assets generating cash flows" specified in Article A3 of ISA 570. The findings revealed that the ISA 570 standard is not effectively implemented in the banking sector. While this standard was not included in audit reports until 2017, it has been observed that it has started to be implemented, albeit limitedly, since the year it was updated. In addition, it has been determined that auditors did not sufficiently address

This chapter was previously published in Turkish by Gazi Kitabevi with the ISBN: 978–975-7727-16-7.

B. B. Dikmen (✉)
Faculty of Applied Sciences, Department of International Trade and Logistics, Tarsus University, Tarsus, Türkiye
e-mail: b.beyhanbeller@gmail.com.tr

M. Özçelik
Faculty of Applied Sciences, Department of Finance and Banking, Tarsus University, Tarsus, Türkiye
e-mail: musaozcelik@tarsus.edu.tr

G. Kurt, Ö. Sarısoy (eds.), *Recent Advancements in Auditing*, Accounting, Finance, Sustainability, Governance & Fraud: Theory and Application,
https://doi.org/10.1007/978-981-95-5811-7_8

the going concern assumption and the effects of these losses on going concern in the audit reports of banks with significant operating losses.

Keywords Going concern · Independent audit · Banking sector · Audit quality · Auditor independence · Profitability

8.1 Introduction

Independent auditors, who have significant concerns related to the ability to maintain the continuity of business, are required to explain this uncertainty in audit reports (ISA 570). Although there is a requirement to explain the ominous uncertainties in audit reports, there are some claims that the uncertainty evaluation by auditors is not more superior than the evaluation by users (Brown 1989). This constitutes question marks in terms of the effectiveness of the continuity of the business. However, since independent auditors are well informed about the firms' activities and future plans, the auditor's opinion can provide useful information (Mutchler 1985; Menon and Schwartz 1987). Independent auditors' going concern opinions are increasingly valuable in models used to predict firm bankruptcies (Hopwood et al. 1989; McKee 2003; Geiger et al. 2005). For this reason, effective implementation of the International Standards on Auditing (ISA) 570 Going Concern Standard in audit reports is important for financial statement users.

There are many risks that banks struggle to manage and cope with, and banks are described as trust institutions that handle investors' deposits. Due to the complex transactions of banks and their being trusted institutions, ISA 570 Going Concern Standard has more importance in this sector. In this study, the relevant standard is examined in detail and its importance for the banking sector is emphasized. In addition, the reflections of uncertainties that may closely affect the profitability of banks and therefore their sustainability in the audit reports are examined by the content analysis method.

8.2 Concept of "Going Concern" and ISA 570 Going Concern

This section covers the concept of going concern and the general evaluation of the ISA 570 Going Concern Standard.

8.2.1 Concept of "Going Concern"

Businesses established to meet the unlimited needs of people carry out their activities regardless of the life span of their owners or partners. This shows that businesses have an unlimited life unless there is a statement to the contrary in the contract drawn up during the establishment phase of the business. The expression unlimited life here expresses the concept of going concern (Sevilengül 2003: 23).

The concept of going concern was discussed in ARB (Accounting Research Bulletin) No: 43 "Restatement and Revision of Accounting Research Bulletins" published by the American Financial Accounting Standards Board (FASB) in 1953, and the bulletin emphasized the use of this concept during the preparation of financial statements. In 1962, the US SEC (The Securities and Exchange Commission) published an official professional guide to be taken into consideration in the evaluation of the concept by publishing ASR No.: 90 "Accounting Series Release" regarding the going concern concept. In the following years, this concept was included in many international and national regulations (Uzay and Güngör Tanç 2010: 146). In line with the concept of going concern, businesses continue their activities in a predictable future and prepare their financial statements as a result of these activities (Yaşar 2017: 59).

The economic crises experienced in the past have made the assumption of the going concern important for people or organizations that need financial information about businesses. It is because that the continuity of businesses concerns many people or organizations, especially business managers, those who invest in the business or those who plan to invest in the business, auditors who will audit the financial statements, regulatory bodies and employees, in terms of the decisions they will make (Moradi et al. 2012: 38).

When the concept of going concern is examined in terms of independent auditing, it is stated in SAS No.: 2 published by the American Institute of Certified Public Accountants (AICPA) in 1974 that auditors should evaluate the going concern of businesses. In this context, the concept of going concern is an indicator of whether the auditor has faith in whether the business has the ability to continue its activities in the future. While auditing the financial statements, the independent auditor should re-examine and present whether there are significant developments or uncertainties that cast doubt on the going concern assumption before the report (Kaval 2005: 161; Triani et al. 2017: 31).

8.2.2 The Importance of the Concept of Continuity in the Banking Sector

Banks are trust institutions that collect funds and provide loans with the funds they collect. In addition, a wide literature shows that there is a positive relationship between the level of financial development and economic growth (Gregorio and Guidotti 1995; Calderón and Liu 2003; Kenourgious & Samitas 2007; Durusu-Ciftci et al. 2017). For this reason, it is thought that the banking sector, which cannot be maintained, can harm the investors and the country's economy.

The banking sector was negatively affected by the global financial crisis in 2008, and the question of whether banks should be treated differently than other companies in auditor reports regarding the going concern of the business has arisen. The banking sector is faced with many risks due to its structure. According to the Banking Regulation and Supervision Agency (BRSA), these risks are listed as credit risk, market risk, operational risk, liquidity risk, interest rate risk, concentration risk, securitization risk, country and transfer risk, reputation risk and strategic risk (BRSA 2001). These risks that may affect the continuity of banks need to be managed and how they will be managed has been determined by BRSA (2001). Therefore, it is thought that the ISA 570 Going Concern Standard will not be sufficient for banks on its own.

8.2.3 Evaluation of ISA 570 Going Concern Standard

ISA 570 Going Concern Standard was published in the Official Gazette dated 23/01/2014 and numbered 28,891 and entered into force with the decision to apply it in the audit of accounting periods starting on or after 01/01/2013. The standard was updated with the amendment made in the Official Gazette dated 24/03/2017 and numbered 30,017(M) for the purpose of applying it in the audit of accounting periods starting on or after 01/01/2017.

ISA 570 is a standard covering the going concern of the businesses, the effects of going concern on the report to be prepared by the auditors and the responsibilities of the auditor in the audit of the financial statements regarding the audit procedures to be carried out by independent auditors (ISA 570: Article 1). According to this standard; financial statements to be prepared as a result of financial transactions are based on the assumption that the business has an indefinite life and will continue its activities in the future (ISA 570: Article 2). This assumption gives the authority to make an evaluation regarding the continuation of the business's going concern to the business management (ISA 570: Article 3). The management makes an evaluation by taking into account the information for at least the twelve months after the balance sheet date and forms judgments with valid explanations (IAS 1: Article 26; Çil Koçyiğit, Güngör Tanç, & Elitaş 2018: 147). The judgments to be formed by the management may be affected by some situations. These situations can be listed as follows (ISA 570: Article 5):

- The prolongation of the results of events or conditions related to the going concern of the business will increase the uncertainties related to the result.
- The status of the business activities, the complexity of the activities, and the impact of external factors will affect the judgment to be taken regarding the events or conditions.
- Since the judgment to be formed by the management after the evaluation will be in line with the available information, inconsistent results may occur between the events and judgments after the audit.

ISA 570 places the responsibility of evaluating whether the evaluation made by the management of the company is in accordance with the going concern assumption and, if appropriate, ensuring that this situation is maintained, on the independent auditors. At this point, the independent auditors have two different options to decide whether the management should apply the going concern assumption. The first option is to determine whether the management has made an evaluation regarding the ability of the company to continue as a going concern. The second option is to question the management of the company regarding the existence of events and conditions that would negatively affect the ability of the company to continue as a going concern assumption if the management has not made an evaluation (ISA 570: A15; Demirkol 2019: 480).

Among the risk assessment procedures included in ISA 570, there are some events and conditions that may negatively affect the continuity of the business. These events and conditions can be exemplified as in Table 8.1 (ISA 570: A3; Demirkol 2019: 481; Kurnaz and Güner 2020: 129).

As seen in Table 8.1, events and conditions that may negatively affect the continuity of the business may be related to the financial position of the business, business activities, or other issues that can be expressed, but are not limited to the examples in this table. Independent auditors can make their evaluations by obtaining evidence on whether these events or conditions will cause a significant uncertainty by taking into account the examples in this table, as well as additional audit procedures (ISA 570: A16). This standard imposes certain responsibilities on auditors who will perform independent audit activities and make evaluations by obtaining appropriate and sufficient evidence in businesses. These responsibilities can be listed as follows (ISA 570: Article 6):

Table 8.1 Events and conditions that may negatively affect the continuity of the business

Events and Conditions Regarding the Financial Situation of the Business
• Short-term foreign resource status • Clues that financial support provided by creditors to the business will be withdrawn • Negative cash flows • Significant operating losses or significant decreases in the value of assets that generate cash flows • Failure to pay business debts on time • Switching from transactions carried out with supplier businesses in the form of deferred payments to cash payments • Negativity in financial ratios of financial statements prepared by businesses • Problems with financing required for product development or investments to be made
Events and Conditions Regarding Business Activities
• The intention of the business management is to liquidate • The departure of personnel with important duties in business management, and their places being vacant • Difficulties experienced in the process of providing raw materials • The emergence of strong competitor companies • The decrease in the market, customers, privileges, licenses, or suppliers • Problems experienced in the process of providing for employees in the business
Events and Conditions Regarding Other Topics
• Lawsuits filed against the business that include significant compensation elements • Negativities that will be created by changes in legislation or policies • Violations of capital and other legal obligations

Source (ISA 570: A3; Demirkol 2019: 481; Kurnaz and Güner 2020: 129)

- It is necessary to reach a conclusion regarding the availability of sufficient and appropriate audit evidence by evaluating the appropriateness of the use of the going concern assumption by the management in the preparation of the financial statements prepared in relation to the activities of the businesses.
- It is necessary to reach a conclusion regarding whether there is a significant uncertainty regarding the ability of the business to continue its a going concern in line with the audit evidence.

According to the requirements stated above, the information obtained regarding the going concern of the business affects the decisions to be taken by the auditor. In this context, it is possible to show the relationship between the auditor's opinion resulting from the examination of the audit reports of the businesses and the going concern assumption, as in Fig. 8.1 (Provasi and Riva 2014: 437).

As seen in Fig. 8.1, if the management of the company does not prepare the financial statements by taking the going concern assumption into consideration or in accordance with this assumption, the auditors may give different opinions. The auditors give a negative opinion for the tables that are not prepared in accordance with the assumption despite the going concern assumption being taken into consideration during the preparation of the financial statements, a positive opinion if it is in accordance with the assumption and there are no significant uncertainties, a positive opinion with the necessary explanatory information if the explanation

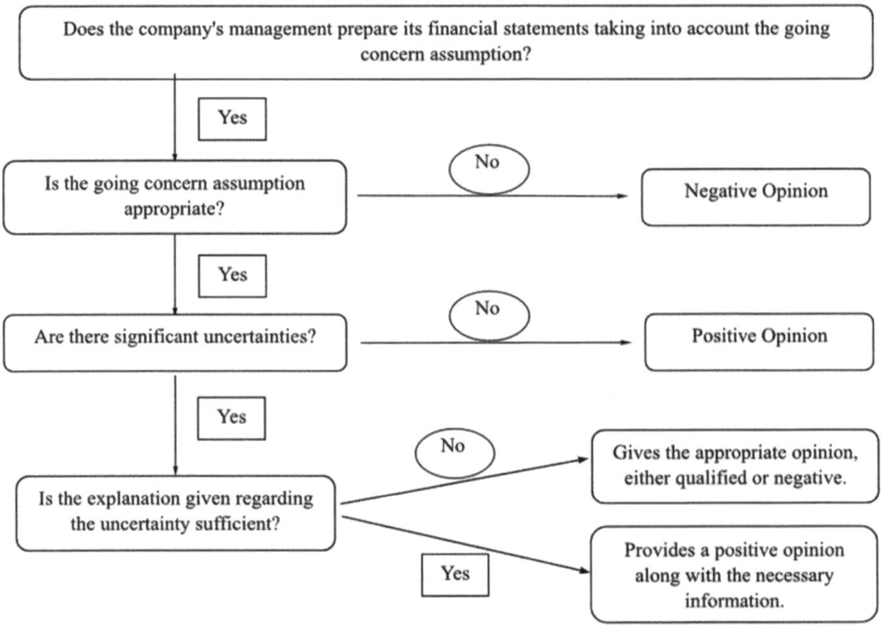

Fig. 8.1 Relationship between going concern assumption and auditor's opinion. *Source* (Provasi and Riva 2014)

made regarding the uncertainty is sufficient, and a qualified or negative opinion if the explanation made is not sufficient, whichever is appropriate.

8.3 Literature Review

There are some quantitative and qualitative studies in the literature regarding the ISA 570 Going Concern Standard, which is among the independent auditing standards. In this context, summary information regarding the literature on the subject of the study is given in Table 8.2.

8.4 Methodology

In this section, the purpose, scope, method, and findings obtained as a result of the analysis and evaluations of the findings are included.

8.4.1 The Aim of the Study

The aim of the study is to determine whether the audit reports of selected deposit banks operating in the banking sector in Türkiye include disclosures regarding the going concern of businesses within the scope of the ISA 570 Going Concern Standard and to examine the types of opinions given by independent auditors.

For this aim, answers to the following questions will be sought.

Research Question 1: Was the ISA 570 Going Concern Standard Effectively Used in Banking Sector Audit Reports?

Research Question 2: Has the auditor's opinion been affected in the audit reports of banks that incurred operating losses within the scope of ISA 570 Going Concern Standard?

8.4.2 Scope and Method of the Study

The study utilized the annual audit reports of selected deposit banks operating in Türkiye as of 2013.[1] The relevant audit reports were evaluated within the scope of

---

[1] ISA 570 Going Concern Standard has been implemented in the audit of accounting periods as of 01/01/2013.

Table 8.2 Studies on including the concept of going concern in independent audit

Authors (Year)	Methodology of the Study	Purpose and Scope of the Study	Results of the Study
Kuruppu (2009)	Cross-tabulation method using independent samples t-test, asymptotic significance, and Somer D statistics	It aims to examine the effectiveness of the enterprise's corporate information failure models and to assist auditors in producing reliable information regarding the enterprise's going concern.	As a result of the study, it was determined that one-third of the respondents were from the Big Four, and the rest were from local or national audit firms. It was found that the use of institutional failure models alleviated the limitations of human information processing and that the financial situation of the clients could reach more appropriate results. The provision of unqualified audit reports to unsuccessful clients was perceived as synonymous with audit failures. Therefore, it was identified that the audit expectations gap could be minimized by routinely applying institutional failure models and providing more appropriate audit opinions.
Uzay & Güngör Tanç (2010)	Content Analysis	The purpose was to examine whether the responsibilities assigned to independent auditors and managers are fulfilled in accordance with the requirements of the going concern standard in terms of auditing by the ISA 570 Going Concern standard. The companies that have independent audit reports in the BIST between the years 2000–2007 and 2008 were examined. The 41 companies consist of those that were traded in the BIST between the years 2000–2007 and whose continuity was in	As a result of the study, it was found that some enterprises whose continuity was at a dangerous level between 2000 and 2007 had independent audit reports with positive opinions. It was seen that the disclosures in the audit reports following the years in which the ISA came into effect, especially for the years 2008 and later, are compatible with the ISA.

(continued)

Table 8.2 (continued)

Authors (Year)	Methodology of the Study	Purpose and Scope of the Study	Results of the Study
		danger, went bankrupt or were in the process of bankruptcy and whose transaction order was closed. The ones in 2008 include 37 companies that referred to the continuity of the business out of 342 companies traded in the BIST.	
Tamas et al. (2012)	Content Analysis	As a result of the global financial crisis, the aim is to determine the deficiencies in the financial statements published by the companies and the auditors who audited these statements, regarding the going concern.	The results showed that indicators that negatively affect the continuity of the business have been identified. These indicators are expressed as; operating losses, transfer from the previous period, increasing stock numbers, equity value, increase in short-term debts, and failure to pay debts exceeding 90 days. In case of a yes answer to these indicators, it was observed that a significant uncertainty regarding the continuity of the business may occur, with comments such as the management intending to liquidate the business, the management intending to stop or reduce operations, the management not having a realistic alternative to continue.
Carson et al. (2013)	Content Analysis	It aims to classify the academic studies that investigate audit opinions that have been changed due to uncertainties regarding the going concern. Previous academic studies in the audit literature in the last forty years have been examined.	As a result of the study, three main research areas were identified regarding audit opinions containing uncertainty regarding the going concern. These areas were classified as; determinants of modified audit opinions regarding customer and auditor relations and other environmental factors; accuracy of

(continued)

Table 8.2 (continued)

Authors (Year)	Methodology of the Study	Purpose and Scope of the Study	Results of the Study
			modified audit opinions and finally, conclusions arising from audit opinions.
Myers et al. (2014)	Content Analysis	The aim is to examine whether the institutional failures experienced after 2001 and the Sarbanes-Oxley Act, which came into force in 2002, affected the behavior of independent auditors in terms of the going concern assumption. In the United States sample, independent audit reports for the periods 2000–2006 were examined.	The study results showed that auditing firms other than the Big Four made more conservative decisions in their audit opinions given within the scope of uncertainty related to continuity after 2001. It was determined that the probability of auditing firms other than the Big Four to give audit opinions to clients who experienced financial failure and did not go bankrupt increased after 2001; however, the probability of giving audit opinions to clients who experienced financial failure and went bankrupt decreased.
Terzi, Atmaca, & Terzi (2016)	Genetic Algorithm	It is aimed to create a reliable model to be used in the evaluation of the going concern in terms of auditing. The variables obtained from the financial statements of the companies continuously listed in the BIST Industrial Index between 2009 and 2014 were examined.	According to the results of the study, the current ratio and the ratio of stocks to total assets were determined as the two most important variables in the evaluations to be made regarding the continuity of the business during the audit phase. The success rates of the models created by using the genetic algorithm were determined as 73%, and the average of Type I errors of the rules created was determined as 20%. In line with these data obtained, it was determined that the models created for the BIST Industrial Index were reliable.

(continued)

Table 8.2 (continued)

Authors (Year)	Methodology of the Study	Purpose and Scope of the Study	Results of the Study
Terzi, Atmaca, & Öktem (2016)	Correlation Analysis, Logistic regression method	The companies traded in the BIST Industrial Index were examined. It was aimed to develop a reliable model in evaluating the going concern of businesses. The data of 119 companies operating continuously in the BIST Industrial Index between 2009 and 2014 were analyzed.	As a result of the study, four models were created in line with the logistic regression method by considering the correlation analysis data. It was determined that whether the companies in the BIST Industrial Index are traded in the primary market or not has no significant effect on the evaluation of the continuity of the companies. In all of the models created, the period between the balance sheet date and the date the auditor's report was signed, the financial success of the companies, the financial leverage ratio and the ratio of the total cash flow from business activities to the total assets were determined to have a significant effect on the continuity of the company. In the evaluation of the continuity of the companies, it was determined that the size of the companies for models 1 and 2, the turnover of the companies for models 3 and 4, and the share of the working capital of the companies in the total assets for models 2 and 4 had a significant effect.
Yaşar (2017)	Univariate analysis and logistic regression method	The aim is to determine the factors that affect audit opinions that include uncertainties regarding the going concern. The annual activity and independent audit reports of 135 companies traded continuously in the BIST	As a result of the study, it was determined that there were some companies that were given a negative audit opinion regarding going concern. It was found that these companies had lower liquidity and profitability ratios, higher debt, and smaller business sizes than the companies that

(continued)

Table 8.2 (continued)

Authors (Year)	Methodology of the Study	Purpose and Scope of the Study	Results of the Study
		Industrial Index for the periods of 2011–2015 were examined.	were given positive audit opinions. The factors that were effective in determining the negative audit opinions that contained significant uncertainty regarding the going concern in independent audit reports were determined as follows: the situation where the previous audit opinion contained uncertainty regarding going concern, the situation where the audit report delay was long, and the situation where the business was small in terms of net sales/total assets.
Taş et al. (2018)	Content Analysis	It is aimed to understand the assumption of going concern, to determine the importance of including information about continuity in independent audit reports of businesses for business management and investors, and to form an opinion on how continuity should be processed in reports. Five-year financial statements and independent audit reports of four companies traded on BIST were examined.	As a result of the study, it was determined that although the going concern assumption was included in the independent audit reports of the companies examined, there was no sufficient explanation on the subject and the auditor's opinion was not included in accordance with the going concern concept.
Yılmaz and Yaşar (2018)	Content Analysis	The aim is to determine the events or conditions that may create doubt regarding the going concern assumption and to determine which audit opinions are given by which auditing institutions. The audit reports of manufacturing industry companies traded on BIST between 2013 and 2016 were examined.	As a result of the study, the events or conditions that create uncertainty regarding the going concern were reported the most in 2013, with a rate of 39% and the least in 201,6 with a rate of 0%. Between 2013 and 2016, 44% positive opinions, 0% negative opinions, and 5% limited positive and disclaimer opinions were given in

(continued)

Table 8.2 (continued)

Authors (Year)	Methodology of the Study	Purpose and Scope of the Study	Results of the Study
			equal rates. It was determined that 50% of the audit opinions containing uncertainty regarding the going concern were given by the Big Four, 44% by international and 6% by national audit firms. Some of the most frequently encountered events and conditions that may create suspicion were identified. These events and conditions include; short-term debts exceeding current assets, significant operating losses or significant decreases in the value of assets generating cash flows, violations related to capital adequacy obligations, failure to comply with the conditions in the credit agreement, significant financial difficulties and raw material bottlenecks, and negative cash flows related to business activities.
Koçyiğit, Güngör Tanç, & Elitaş (2018)	Content Analysis	ISA 570 Going Concern Standard was explained and the aim was to determine the compliance of companies' independent audit reports with the Turkish Independent Audit Standards. The Financial Statements Independent Auditor Reports of 176 companies in the manufacturing sector traded on Borsa Istanbul for the period of 2016 were examined.	As a result of the study, it was found that in the companies where the independent auditor report was obtained, the independent auditor reports were mostly prepared in accordance with the standards within the framework of ISA 570 and ISA 700, while a small portion of them were found to be incompatible with the standards in question.
Senal & Erkan (2019)	Altman Z Score	It was aimed to estimate whether there is any uncertainty regarding continuity in the financial statements of the companies with the help of the model. The relationship between the estimation	As a result of the study, uncertainty related to continuity was estimated in 155 financial reports published between 2009 and 2017. It was determined that 117 of these financial reports had

(continued)

Table 8.2 (continued)

Authors (Year)	Methodology of the Study	Purpose and Scope of the Study	Results of the Study
		results and the audit reports has been examined. It is aimed to reveal whether the uncertainty is included in the audit reports prepared for the financial reports, where the uncertainty regarding continuity is estimated by the model. A total of 351 financial statements published by 39 companies traded in the manufacturing industry on Borsa Istanbul between 2009 and 2017 were examined.	a positive audit opinion, 30 had a qualified audit opinion, 8 had a disclaimer of opinion or a negative opinion. In 30 of the reports with a positive opinion, a statement was made to express uncertainty related to continuity. However, no result was determined that there was uncertainty in 196 financial reports. It was found that 171 of these reports had a positive audit opinion, 24 had a qualified audit opinion, and 1 had a disclaimer of opinion or a negative opinion.
Demirkol (2019)	Content Analysis	The aim is to determine whether the ISA 570 Going Concern Standard has been stated in independent audit reports since its publication and to obtain findings on the predictability levels of financial difficulties experienced in the construction sector in the reports. Independent audit reports of nine companies traded in the BIST Construction and Public Works sector for the periods of 2013–2017 were examined.	As a result of the study, it was found that the independent audit reports did not include statements regarding the application of the standard for going concern. Statements regarding going concern were stated in the audit reports of five companies in 2017, but no events or conditions that would create serious uncertainty were found in these reports. It was identified that positive opinions were given in all companies in the independent audit reports of 2017 and in all companies except one between 2013 and 2016.
Yaşar and Çetin (2020)	Content Analysis	The aim was to evaluate the communication value of auditor reports emphasizing significant uncertainty regarding the going concern within the scope of ISA 570 Going Concern.	As a result of the study, it was determined that six of the companies whose audit reports were examined were given positive opinions and 15 were given qualified opinions. It was found that the most positive audit opinions were given in

(continued)

Table 8.2 (continued)

Authors (Year)	Methodology of the Study	Purpose and Scope of the Study	Results of the Study
		Auditor reports of 21 companies other than financial sector companies traded on Borsa Istanbul in 2018 were examined.	the Restaurants and Hotels sector; and the most qualified opinions were given in the Food, Beverages and Tobacco sector and the Sports, Entertainment and Game activities sector. Results showed that there was no separate section under the title of "Material Uncertainty Regarding Going Concern" in the positive auditor reports, and explanations were made under different sections or headings. In the auditor reports where qualified opinions were given, it was found that the title of "Material Uncertainty Regarding Going Concern" was given under different sections and headings in the other 12 auditor reports, except for 3 audit reports, in different sections and headings than the presentation format of the standard. It was determined that both positive and qualified opinions were given in the audit reports in terms of ensuring transparency and therefore the communication value of the auditor report were not sufficient.

the article "Significant operating losses or significant decreases in the value of assets generating cash flows" under the heading of ISA 570: A3 risk assessment procedures and related activities. The annual operating profits/losses of the banks were examined, and banks incurring operating losses were identified. The auditor's opinions within the scope of ISA 570 Going Concern were examined with the content analysis method in the audit reports of the identified banks.

8.4.3 *Findings of the Study*

In the study, the financial statements of the selected banks between 2013 and 2019 were primarily examined, and their annual operating profits or losses were determined. Then, the independent audit reports of the 15 banks included in the scope of the research, especially these banks, were examined within the scope of the ISA 570 Going Concern Standard, and the independent auditor opinions and analysis results were included.

8.4.4 *Operating Profits of Selected Banks*

The financial statements of selected deposit banks operating in Türkiye between 2013 and 2019 were examined, and the annual operating profits or losses of these banks are shown in Table 8.3. In order not to create a negative perception of the banks, the names of the banks were not included, and the banks were coded with numbers. In the following section, the banks will be mentioned with these codes.

As seen in Table 8.3, banks other than B5 and B8 made operating profits between 2013 and 2019. B5 bank made high operating losses in 2014, 2015, 2016, and B8 bank in 2019. In this context, the independent audit reports of the relevant banks for the specified years were examined within the scope of the ISA 570 Going Concern standard.

8.4.5 *Opinions of Independent Auditors*

The independent audit reports of selected deposit banks operating in Türkiye between 2013 and 2019 were examined within the scope of the ISA 570 Going Concern Standard, and the results obtained are shown in Table 8.4.

As seen in Table 8.4, three different conclusions were reached regarding the going concern assumption in the audit reports examined within the scope of the study. These are;

- The going concern assumption was not included in some audit reports.
- In some audit reports, the responsibility of management regarding the going concern was mentioned, and it was stated that if there was a significant

Table 8.3 Operating profits of selected banks[2] by year (thousand Turkish liras (TL))

	2013	2014	2015	2016	2017	2018	2019
B1	3.853.607	4.037.966	3.827.671	5.676.787	7.151.494	6.670.897	6.180.844
B2	116.370	176.838	175.395	226.426	200.067	335.174	431.676
B3	1.268.530	1.214.681	1.142.911	948.282	1.274.646	851.674	582.438
B4	58.928	95.100	109.465	160.917	200.386	220.714	247.980
B5	65.814	**– (50.790)***	**– (274.680)***	**– (352.367)***	167.835	437.284	774.252
B6	233.193	246.074	167.588	716.611	1.063.818	1.344.827	2.172.886
B7	937.594	1.142.209	902.849	1.483.821	2.048.965	3.058.741	3.106.846
B8	264.339	280.701	85.246	139.615	139.527	1.225.544	**– (391.429)***
B9	699.164	795.055	791.062	1.181.963	1.312.931	1.280.720	1.393.521
B10	4.378.523	5.178.733	6.567.623	8.569.135	10.286.699	10.033.684	6.293.584
B11	3.951.115	4.197.357	3.908.562	5.895.166	7.543.371	7.693.570	7.128.888
B12	3.364.892	2.727.255	2.855.643	3.351.550	4.709.582	2.717.818	1.140.213
B13	3.856.699	4.231.068	3.783.697	5.753.782	6.548.625	4.921.129	2.857.692
B14	1.982.914	2.213.676	2.470.293	3.395.524	4.675.132	5.153.927	2.582.436
B15	2.556.327	2.197.965	2.021.348	3.168.213	3.898.596	5.079.987	4.511.332

Source Independently audited financial statements of the relevant banks (BRSA, 2020)
*Banks reporting an operating loss in their annual financial statements

uncertainty regarding the going concern, this situation would be highlighted in the audit report.

- The going concern assumption was not included in audit reports before 2017.

In the audit reports, under the title of "*Responsibilities of Management and Those Responsible for Senior Governance Regarding the Financial Statements*", the responsibility of the management regarding the continuity of the business is stated as follows.

"*When preparing the financial statements, the management is responsible for evaluating the Bank's ability to continue as a going concern, explaining issues related to continuity when necessary, and using the going concern principle unless there is an intention or obligation to liquidate the Bank or terminate commercial activity.*" (Şekerbank 2019).

In the audit reports, under the title of "*Independent Auditor's Responsibilities Regarding the Independent Audit of Financial Statements*", the auditor's responsibility regarding the going concern is stated as follows.

"*Based on the audit evidence obtained, we conclude whether there is a material uncertainty related to events or conditions that may cast significant doubt on the Bank's ability to continue as a going concern and on the appropriateness of management's use of the going concern principle. If we conclude that there is a*

[2] Deposit banks that have been operating in Türkiye for the last 10 years and have more than 1000 employees.

Table 8.4 Independent Auditor Opinions in Independent Audit Reports of Selected Banks

	2013 O/GC/IAF	2014 O/GC/IAF	2015 O/GC/IAF	2016 O/GC/IAF	2017 O/GC/IAF	2018 O/GC/IAF	2019 O/GC/IAF
B1	QO/N/EY	QO/N/EY	QO/N/EY	QO/N/EY	QO/N/PwC	QO/N/PwC	QO/N/PwC
B2	+/N/KPMG	+/N/KPMG	+/N/KPMG	+/N/KPMG	+/N/KPMG	LP/N/KPMG	LP/N/KPMG
B3	+/N/EY	+/N/EY	+/N/EY	+/N/EY	+/N/EY	+/N/EY	+/N/EY
B4	+/N/DELOITTE	+/N/DELOITTE	+/N/DELOITTE	QO/N/DELOITTE	LP/N/EY	LP/N/EY	LP/N/KPMG
B5	+/N/KPMG	+/N/KPMG	+/N/PwC	+/N/PwC	+/N/PwC	+/N/PwC	+/N/EY
B6	+/N/EY	+/N/EY	+/N/DELOITTE	QO/N/DELOITTE	LP/N/EY	LP/N/KPMG	LP/N/KPMG
B7	+/N/DELOITTE	QO/N/EY	QO/N/EY	QO/N/EY	LP/N/EY	+/N/EY	+/N/EY
B8	+/N/KPMG	+/N/KPMG	+/N/KPMG	+/N/KPMG	+/N/DELOITTE	+/N/DELOITTE	LP/N/DELOITTE
B9	+/N/PwC	+/N/PwC	+/N/PwC	+/N/PwC	+/N/PwC	+/N/PwC	+/N/DELOITTE
B10	QO/N/PwC	QO/N/PwC	QO/N/PwC	QO/N/PwC	LP/N/PwC	LP/N/KPMG	LP/N/KPMG
B11	QO/N/DELOITTE	QO/N/DELOITTE	QO/N/DELOITTE	QO/N/DELOITTE	LP/N/KPMG	LP/N/KPMG	LP/N/KPMG
B12	+/N/KPMG	+/N/KPMG	QO/N/KPMG	+/N/KPMG	+/N/DELOITTE	QO/N/DELOITTE	QO/N/DELOITTE
B13	+/N/KPMG	+/N/KPMG	QO/N/KPMG	+/N/KPMG	+/N/DELOITTE	QO/N/DELOITTE	QO/N/DELOITTE
B14	+/N/KPMG	+/N/PwC	+/N/PwC	+/N/PwC	+/N/PwC	LP/N/PwC	LP/N/PwC
B15	+/N/EY	+/N/EY	+/N/EY	+/N/EY	+/N/PwC	+/N/PwC	+/N/PwC

O: Opinion, GC: Assumption of Going Concern, IAF: Independent Audit Firm
+: Positive Opinion, QO: Qualified Opinion, LP: Limited Positive Opinion, N: None

Table 8.5 Use of Going Concern Assumption Summary

		2013-2019[3]			After 2017[4]			
		Going Concern Assumption				Going Concern Assumption		
Audit Firm	**Total Audit**	**Included**	**Not-included**	%	**Total Audit**	**Included**	**Not-included**	%
EY	27	10	17	37,03	10	10	0	100
KPMG	30	5	25	16,66	11	5	6	45,45
DELOITTE	21	9	12	42,85	10	9	1	90
PwC	27	6	21	22,22	14	6	8	42,85
Total	**105**	**30**	**75**	28,57	**45**	**30**	**15**	66,66

material uncertainty, we are required to draw attention to the relevant disclosures in the financial statements in our report or, if these disclosures are inadequate, to express an opinion other than a positive opinion. Our conclusions are based on the audit evidence obtained up to the date of the independent auditor's report. However, future events or conditions may terminate the Bank's going concern." (Şekerbank 2019).

The inclusion of the going concern assumption in the independent audit reports examined within the scope of the research is summarized in Table 8.5.

Research Question 1: Was ISA 570 Going Concern Standard effectively used in banking sector audit reports? (No)

Within the scope of the research, a total of 105 audit reports of 15 banks between the years 2013 and 2019 were examined. According to the results, it was found that the going concern assumption was included in 28.57% of the relevant audit reports. Another striking result was that the going concern assumption was not used until 2017, but this assumption started to be included in audit reports as of 2017. While Deloitte was the audit company that included the going concern assumption the most in its reports with 42.85% in general until 2017, Ernst & Young was the audit company that included the going concern assumption in all of its audit reports after 2017. No significant uncertainty or negative opinion was stated regarding the going concern assumption in any of the relevant audit reports. The usage graph of the going concern assumption by year is shown in Fig. 8.2.

[3] It was created using data obtained from audit reports between 2013 and 2019.

[4] It was created with data obtained from audit reports for the years 2017–2019. (The standard was updated with the regulation made in the Official Gazette dated 24/03/2017 and numbered 30,017 (M) for the purpose of applying it in the audit of accounting periods starting on or after 01/01/2017. For this reason, 2017 and the years after were evaluated separately.)

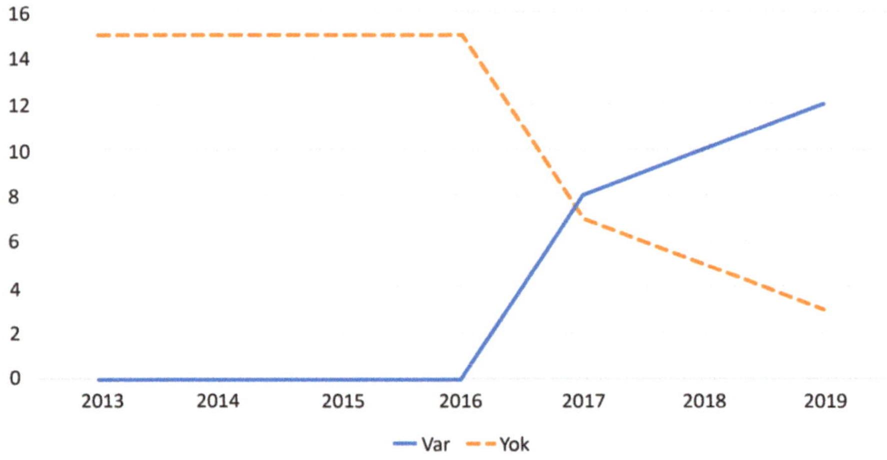

Fig. 8.2 Use of going concern assumption in audit reports by year

As seen in Fig. 8.2, the inclusion of the going concern assumption in audit reports began in 2017 and a proportional increase occurred each year. As of 2019, the going concern assumption was included in 12 of the 15 audit reports.

Research Question 2: Has the auditor's opinion been affected in the audit reports of banks that incurred operating losses within the scope of ISA 570 Going Concern Standard? (No)

The risks banks face and the factors affecting their continuity differ from other businesses. For this reason, a separate assessment was made within the scope of the study "Significant operating losses or significant decreases in the value of assets generating cash flows" under the heading of ISA 570: A3 risk assessment procedures and related activities, which is a common factor for every business. Within the scope of the study, the net operating profits/losses of the relevant banks were examined and the audit reports of the banks that had high operating losses in the relevant year were examined. It was observed that B5 bank had high operating losses in 2014, 2015 and 2016 and B8 bank in 2019. B5 bank declared operating losses due to losses from foreign exchange transactions, while B8 bank declared operating losses due to losses from derivative financial transactions and foreign exchange transactions. As seen in Table 8.4, B5 bank received a positive opinion in the audit report in the relevant years, while B8 bank received a limited positive opinion due to the provisions it set aside. No significant uncertainty regarding the going concern was mentioned in the relevant audit reports and a positive opinion was given.

8.5 Conclusion and Recommendations

As seen in the 2008 global financial crisis, the banking sector closely affects the country's economy due to its structure. In addition, with increasing globalization and digitalization each passing year, the structures of banks become more complex and possible banking sector problems can lead to greater destruction in the economy. Therefore, it is thought that the ISA 570 Going Concern Standard is more important for the banking sector.

The present study, which examined the independent audit reports of 15 banks between 2013, when the ISA 570 Going Concern Standard came into force, and 2019, tried to answer two research questions. As a result of the study, it was found that the ISA 570 Going Concern Standard was not used effectively in the banking sector. The results showed that this standard, which was not applied in any audit report examined until 2017, the year the standard was updated, started to be included in the reports as of 2017. Figure 8.2, created in line with the obtained data, shows that the use of the standard in audit reports increased in the years after 2017. Another result of the study is that the auditors' opinions in the audit reports of banks that incurred significant operating losses were not affected by this situation. Although the B5 bank included in the scope of the study declared significant operating losses in 2014, 2015 and 2016, it is observed that the auditors did not include the going concern assumption in the audit reports of the relevant years and did not explain the reason for the operating loss and whether this situation would affect the going concern.

The structure of the banking sector differs from other businesses and businesses in this sector have a complex structure. In addition, since banks are trust institutions that collect funds and provide loans with the funds they collect, the reputation of banks is important. In addition to the banking sector being subject to strict regulation and inspection by the BRSA, there is also a banking law specific to banks.

The current ISA 570 Going Concern Standard should be reviewed and updated according to the regulations that banks are subject to. With the update to be made, it will be possible for auditors to make objective assessments using quantitative data regarding the continuity of the business. In this direction, it is thought that in order to both present a healthy audit report and to provide convenience to users, the preparation of an audit report draft by the Public Oversight Authority (POA) and the submission of all auditors' audit reports in accordance with this draft will eliminate subjectivity.

References

Banking Regulation and Supervision Agency of Turkey (BRSA) (2001) *Bankaların iç denetim ve risk yönetimi sistemleri hakkında yönetmelik*. Official Gazette of the Republic of Turkey. Retrieved from https://www.resmigazete.gov.tr/eskiler/2001/02/20010208.htm

Banking Regulation and Supervision Agency of Turkey (BRSA) (2020) *Independent audit reports*. Retrieved from https://www.bddk.org.tr/BdrUyg

Brown H (1989) Should 'going concern' be auditor's headache. Account Today 3:6–8
Calderón C, Liu L (2003) The direction of causality between financial development and economic growth. J Dev Econ 72(1):321–334. https://doi.org/10.1016/S0304-3878(03)00079-8
Carson E, Fargher NL, Geiger MA, Lennox CS, Raghunandan K, Willekens M (2013) Audit reporting for going—concern uncertanity: a research synthesis. Audit J Pract Theory 32(1):353–384. https://doi.org/10.2308/ajpt-50324
Demirkol ÖF (2019) BDS 570 işletmenin sürekliliği standardının uygulama süreci ve bağımsız denetim raporlarına etkisi: bist inşaat ve bayındırlık sektöründe uygulama. İşletme Araştırmaları Dergisi 11(1):478–489
Durusu-Ciftci D, Ispir MS, Yetkiner H (2017) Financial development and economic growth: some theory and more evidence. J Policy Model 39(2):290–306. https://doi.org/10.1016/j.jpolmod.2016.08.001
Geiger M, Raghunandan K, Rama DV (2005) Recent changes in the association between bankruptcies and prior audit opinions. Audit J Theory Pract 24(1):21–35. https://doi.org/10.2308/aud.2005.24.1.21
Gregorio J, Guidotti PE (1995) Financial development and economic growth. World Dev 23 (3):433–448. https://doi.org/10.1016/0305-750X(94)00132-I
Hopwood W, McKeown J, Mutchler J (1989) A test of the incremental explanatory power of opinions qualified for consistency and uncertainty. Account Rev 64(1):28–48
International Accounting Standards (IAS) 1: presentation of Financial Statements. Retrieved from https://www.kgk.gov.tr/Portalv2Uploads/files/Duyurular/v2/TMS/TMS_2020/TMS%201.pdf
International Standard on Auditing (ISA) 570: going concern. Public Oversight Accounting and Auditing Standards Authority of Turkey. Retrieved from https://www.kgk.gov.tr/Portalv2Uploads/files/Duyurular/v2/BDS/BDS%20570.pdf
Kaval H (2005) Muhasebe Denetimi. Gazi Kitabevi, Ankara
Kenourgios D, Samitas A (2007) Financial development and economic growth in a transition economy: evidence for Poland. J Financ Decis Mak 3(1):35–48
Koçyiğit SÇ, Güngör Tanç Ş, & Elitaş BL (2018) İşletmenin sürekliliği ve bağımsız denetçi raporlarının türkiye bağımsız denetim standartları (BDS 570 ve BDS 700) açısından incelenmesi. Muhasebe Ve Denetime Bakış Dergisi 17(53):143–162
Kurnaz E, Güner M (2020) BDS 570 İşletmenin Sürekliliği Standardı Kapsamında Bist Spor Endeksinde Yer Alan Şirketlerin Bağımsız Denetim Raporlarının İncelenmesi. In Kurt G, Özbek CY (eds) Denetimde Seçme Konular 3. Gazi Kitabevi, Ankara, pp 121–144
Kuruppu T (2009) Evidence on auditors use of business continuity models as an analytical procedure. Accounting & Taxation 1(1):63–74
McKee T (2003) Rough sets bankruptcy prediction models versus auditor signalling rates. J Forecast 22(8):569–586. https://doi.org/10.1002/for.875
Menon K, Schwartz K (1987) An empirical investigation of audit qualification decisions in the presence of going concern uncertainties. Contemp Account Res 3(2):302–315. https://doi.org/10.1111/j.1911-3846.1987.tb00640.x
Moradi M, Salehi M, Yazdi HS, Gorg.ani ME (2012) Going concern prediction of Iranian companies bu using fuzzy c- means. Open J Account 1:38–46. https://doi.org/10.4236/ojacct.2012.12005
Mutchler J (1985) A multivariate analysis of the auditor's going-concern opinion decision. J Account Res 23(2):668–682. https://doi.org/10.2307/2490832
Myers LA, Schmidt J, Wilkins M (2014) An investigation of recent changes in going concern reporting decisions among Big N and non—big N auditors. Rev Quant Financ Acc 43:155–172. https://doi.org/10.1007/s11156-013-0368-6
Provasi R, Riva P (2014) The Assessing of going concern for the Italian listed companies: relevance and ımplıcations, Global Conference on Business and Finance Proceedings 9 (1):435–439
Şekerbank (2019) Independent audit report. Retrieved from https://sekerbank.com.tr/docs/default-source/yatirimciurunleri/sekerbank31122019konsolide.pdf

Senal S, & Erkan A (2019) Bağımsız Denetim kapsamında işletme sürekliliği: Borsa İstanbul'da imalat sektöründe faaliyet gösteren işletmeler üzerine bir araştırma. Anadolu Üniversitesi Sosyal Bilimler Dergisi 19(4):105–118

Sevilengül O (2003) Genel Muhasebe. Gazi Kitabevi, Ankara

Tamas AS, Joldos AM, Dobra I, & Turta I (2012) The principle of business continuity in terms of financial audit. Annales Universitatis Apulensis: Series Oeconomica 14(2):451

Taş O, Mert H, Güner M, Duyar G (2018) BDS 570 işletmenin sürekliliği standardının denetim raporlarına etkisi. Press Acad Procedia 7(1):339–343. https://doi.org/10.17261/Pressacademia.2018.911

Terzi S, Atmaca M, & Öktem B (2016) İşletmenin sürekliliği varsayımının değerlendirilmesi: Borsa İstanbul (BİST) sinaî endeksi örneği. Öneri Dergisi 12(45):515–535

Terzi R, Atmaca M, & Terzi S (2016) Denetim açısından işletmenin sürekliliğinin değerlendirilmesinde genetik algoritmanın kullanımı: Borsa İstanbul sınaî endeksi örneği. Uluslararası Yönetim İktisat ve İşletme Dergisi 12(12):685–693

Triani NNA, Satyawan MD, Yanthi MD (2017) Determining the effectiveness of going concern audit opinion by Isa 570. Asian J Account Res 2(2):29–35. https://doi.org/10.1108/AJAR-2017-02-02-B004

Uzay Ş, & Tanç ŞG (2010) İMKB'de işlem gören şirketlerin bağımsız denetim raporlarında işletmenin sürekliliği kavramının analizi. Muhasebe Bilim Dünyası Dergisi 12(2):143–179

Yaşar A (2017) İşletmenin sürekliliğinde ortaya çıkan belirsizliğin bağımsız denetim raporlarındaki denetçi görüşleri açısından incelenmesi: Bist'de işlem gören sınai şirketlerine yönelik bir araştırma. Muhasebe Bilim Dünyası Dergisi 19(1):58–86

Yaşar A, Çetin E (2020) BDS 570 kapsamında verilen denetçi raporlarının iletişim değeri açısından incelenmesi. İşletme Araştırmaları Dergisi 12(1):384–391

Yılmaz Z, Yaşar A (2018) Bağımsız denetim raporlarının işletmenin sürekliliği denetim standardı 570 çerçevesinde incelenmesi: bist imalat sanayi şirketleri üzerine bir araştırma. Mali Çözüm 28(145):55–90

Part IV
Artificial Intelligence and Digitalization in Auditing Through the Eyes of MUDEP Academics

Chapter 9
Effects of the Digital Integration Process on the Practice of Independent Auditing

Murat Karahan

Abstract The aim of this study is to examine how the digital integration process driven by Industry 4.0 affects the field of independent auditing. Digital integration has increased audit speed, efficiency and accuracy by enabling businesses to automate data collection and processing. In this study, the concept of auditing, the digital integration process, and the impact of this process on independent auditing, auditors and tax practices are discussed based on a literature review. Technologies such as artificial intelligence, big data analytics, IoT, cloud computing and blockchain have transformed traditional auditing procedures into real-time, technology-driven processes known as Auditing 4.0. These developments have reduced auditing costs and increased transparency, allowing for more comprehensive risk assessment and decision-making processes. This study emphasizes that auditors need to improve their technological competencies to keep up with evolving auditing methodologies and adopt data-driven tools. In addition, the digitalization of tax processes such as e-invoice and e-book in Türkiye has facilitated cross-auditing and strengthened tax security. As a result, digital auditing supports better governance, minimizes human error, and increases stakeholder confidence in financial reporting.

Keywords Digital integration · Audit · Industry 4.0 · Audit 4.0

This chapter was previously published in Turkish by Gazi Kitabevi with the ISBN: 978-975-7727-16-7.

M. Karahan (✉)
Faculty of Economics and Administrative Sciences, Department of Business Administration, Department of Accounting and Finance, Gaziantep University, Gaziantep, Türkiye
e-mail: karahan@gantep.edu.tr

G. Kurt, Ö. Sarısoy (eds.), *Recent Advancements in Auditing*, Accounting, Finance, Sustainability, Governance & Fraud: Theory and Application,
https://doi.org/10.1007/978-981-95-5811-7_9

9.1 Introduction

Physical contactlessness is becoming more prevalent in social life due to the global pandemic, and this contactless environment makes technological advancements even more crucial. Because of this, firms must adjust to technology due to growing competitiveness and shareholder demand. These technical advancements are also crucial for tracking and disclosing business financial and non-financial data. Because of the complexity of the operations and the large number of transactions in the activities, physical monitoring becomes challenging when attempting to determine whether the financial outputs coming from business activities are accurate and dependable. Industry 4.0 and Audit 4.0's components—such as the Internet of Things, robots, artificial intelligence, cyber-physical systems, smart factories, etc.—have made it simpler for companies to cut expenses, boost productivity, and simultaneously gather financial and non-financial data.

The fourth industrial revolution, or Industry 4.0, can be experienced thanks to it (Porter and Heppelmann 2015; Cenamor et al. 2017; Celayir and Celayir 2020). Most industries undergo significant transformation as a result of mechanized technologies (Ejaz et al. 2016). If company processes are streamlined by implementing automation, these technologies offer numerous benefits, including accelerating production, improving efficiency by decreasing production errors, and increasing profitability by lowering production costs (Hasselblatt et al. 2018).

Apart from the previously mentioned benefits, companies that offer digital integration become more resilient in competitive environments and boost productivity by integrating technology into their operations.

In the short, medium, and long term, this adaptation will help firms in numerous ways, including cost, time, speed, and flexibility (Gerpott and May 2016). Businesses that capitalize on these advantages of digital integration will always be one step ahead of their rivals in terms of success, cost, speed, efficiency, and expertise. Businesses will not be able to compete in the market and maintain their existence in the current environment if this modification is not made. As a result, companies need to use smart digital technologies, including the internet, the internet of things (IoT), coding devices, cloud computing, data analytics, and big data in their operations (Lenka et al. 2017).

With the favorable ratings they will receive from credit rating agencies, companies looking to expand their global operations will have access to overseas investment and capital flows.

The progress of globalization has made business financial reports more significant, particularly in the nation where investments will be made. It has also made it necessary for the data in financial reports to be trustworthy and easy for all investors to grasp. International accounting and financial reporting standards are put into practice, and these reports are audited using independent auditing standards to do this (Türker 2006; Türker and Örerler 2004; Türker 2018).

The impact of digital integration on independent auditing is sought to be conceptually addressed in this paper. The study will cover the following topics: the idea of auditing, the process of digital integration, and how these factors affect independent auditing, auditors, and taxation.

In order to deliver higher information volume and quality audit services, digital integration makes it feasible to automate data collection and processing. This makes it simpler to identify potential risks and frauds (Nwankpa 2014; KPMG 2017; Celayir and Celayir 2020). For this reason, the study evaluates the practices and standards in detailed automatic digital audit processes, what the audit field will face in the future, what needs to be done to prepare the infrastructure, and potential outcomes prior to the presentation of the financial statements prepared by institutions on a periodic or annual basis.

9.2 The Concept of Control

According to Beisland et al. (2015) and Hope et al. (2008), auditing is crucial to maintaining openness between management and shareholders in companies. All tasks, including the accounting and auditing procedures, should fall under the purview of managers. Since they are often external to the business, shareholders can only access information that managers transmit to them. According to Jensen and Meckling (1976), the purpose of auditing is to avoid knowledge asymmetry between management and shareholders. Independent auditing helps shareholders make informed decisions by lowering the possibility that inaccurate information will be conveyed to them (Watts and Zimmerman 1986). By offering suggestions for business management to avoid mistakes and irregularities that can arise in the organization, it also improves managerial success (Jensen and Meckling 1976; DeFond and Zhang 2014; Beisland et al. 2015). To put it another way, independent audits ought to strive to satisfy the requirements and demands of all parties involved, not just shareholders.

Accounting audit is defined as *"a systematic process that impartially collects evidence and evaluates this evidence in order to investigate the degree of conformity of claims regarding economic activities and events with predetermined criteria and to report the results to those who are interested"* (Güredin 2008; Bozkurt 2018:29). The fact that accounting incorporates both pragmatic and inductive approaches is crucial to the ongoing evolution and modification of procedures. The likelihood that accounting information is unreliable is increased by the volume and complexity of transactions, the relevant parties' inability to obtain business-specific information, and the proclivities of individuals who provide it (Bozkurt 2018: 25).

For this reason, the data generated by accounting procedures is probably risky. The distribution of audited financial reports to the appropriate parties, the relevant parties auditing the business, and the relevant parties and management taking responsibility for the risk are the strategies to be used in order to reduce the ensuing information risk (Bozkurt 2018: 25–26). Stated differently, presenting financial reports that adhere to international reporting standards, auditing these reports in line with independent auditing standards, and providing them with a solid legal foundation would all help to mitigate these risks.

Like many other professions, auditing is a field that is always evolving due to the rapid advancements in information technologies. The changing audit environment brought about by these technological advancements forces auditors to reevaluate their auditing procedures (Nwankpa and Datta 2012; Celayir and Celayir; 2020). Compared to physical settings, digitalization trends in accounting information systems may facilitate access to and auditing of financial statement source data.

9.3 Digital Integration

A new industrial revolution is represented by the idea of Industry 4.0, which was introduced at the 2011 Hannover Fair under German leadership (Eğilmez 2018:264). The last phase of modern industrialization is known as "Industry 4.0." Industry 4.0 anticipates that digital data, software, and information technologies are used in harmony with one another and that all units that are directly or indirectly related to production will collaborate (Schuh et al. 2014:1). To put it another way, Industry 4.0 is a time when production technology is being used at its peak and all systems are operating in unison. In contrast to earlier industrial revolutions, technology is at the vanguard of this one (Banger 2018:24). Features including speed, system effect, width, and depth are prioritized in Industry 4.0 (Fırat and Fırat 2017:213).

Transferring manually collected data or operations to digital settings is known as digital integration. According to Özen and Gürel (2020), Industry 4.0-driven digitalization is the process of leveraging information technology to turn resources into optimal outcomes. The process of moving available data and resources to digital settings so that computers can process and make them readable is another way to describe digital integration. Businesses can see that better service is being offered and that workflows are continuing in a more creative and current manner when information and documents are moved to digital platforms. Corporate memory can be created by implementing workflows and activities in a more methodical manner and directing the way activities are carried out toward a significant change and improvement (Mckinsey 2017). In activity flows, learning new digital skills and drawing conclusions from data-driven outcomes will be beneficial. It is important to report on the measures made during the digital integration process and compare them to earlier times. Realizing the shift to digitization and process integration in the most effective manner would be feasible in this manner.

The six basic principles in the design and implementation of Industry 4.0 are explained as follows (EBSO 2015; Dai and Vasarhelyi 2016:1; Schwab 2016;

TOBB 2016; Banger 2016; Vladimirovich and Linder 2017; Akdoğan and Akdoğan; 2018; Yıldız and Ağdeniz, 2019; Tutar 2019):

- Interoperability
- Virtualization
- Autonomous administration (Decentralization)
- Real-time capability
- Service Orientation
- Modularity

9.4 Historical Process of Auditing and Digital Auditing

Auditing has been around since 3000 BC, according to numerous artifacts discovered during the historical process (Sharkansky 1991:5). Based on information gleaned from historical relics, it has been discovered that in many Mesopotamian kingdoms, the kingdom employed clerks whose job it was to keep an eye on the workers in the grain warehouses and conduct counting operations. These conclusions serve as the foundation for the regulation of public accounting and state actions (Khan 1995:2). Furthermore, according to Demir (2006), historical documents from the Egyptians, Greeks, Chinese, Persians, and Hebrews all contain applications resembling these systems.

By contrasting the records of officials with those of others, the Ancient Roman Civilization developed an inquiry system. This system gave rise to the term "audit." However, this system and many other financial practices vanished together with the fall of the Roman Empire (Lawrence 1996:221). Due to time and expense restrictions, testing and sample techniques started to be utilized around 1885 as business volume increased throughout the Industrial Revolution (Sakin 2018:2464). After the 1970s, there was a widespread use of various analytical review procedures to decrease the facts, including deviation disparities in auditing, substantial errors produced by error, and fraud, as a result of continuously rising economic activities (Çalış 2011:40).

Even while research on artificial intelligence, which helped shape technology, began in 1943, it wasn't until the 1990s that its industrial applications led to a shift in business practices (Keskenler and Keskenler 2017:16; Erturan and Ergin 2018:827).

The auditing process will be impacted by Industry 4.0's altering business structures and production processes. A new data storage system (data environment) is required as a result of the development of data-intensive technologies like ERP systems, sensors, cloud storage, and remote communication tools, which have made it easier to produce vast volumes of data. Over time, data has begun to move to the computer environment due to the challenges of handling the data generated by businesses using conventional methods.

Industry 4.0 will increase the burden and risk of audits in a number of areas, including new production processes, new activities, smart factories, smart robots, and artificial intelligence. Nonetheless, one of the primary demands on auditors is to use technology to lessen the risk and burden of audits.

The primary characteristic of the current period is speed and the capacity to respond instantly in the least amount of time. In terms of both number and quality, the risks that businesses confront are changing and growing at a rapid pace. It goes without saying that the same pace must be used for both process control and monitoring. "Control 4.0" is the term used to describe the certainty that real-time data control through technology means (Dai and Vasarhelyi 2016). With the Internet of Things, one of the fundamental elements of Industry 4.0, auditors will have access to a wealth of data that may be utilized for auditing both inside and outside the entity. One of the fundamental elements of Industry 4.0 is big data, which is what this particular data is. The term "big data analysis systems" refers to the entirety of methods and tools used to collect, store, move, process, and display vast volumes of both structured and unstructured data. Information technology solutions are primarily used to improve corporate performance and operational management. In addition to improving productivity and company performance, big data analysis technologies also help make better decisions in real time (Verma et al. 2018:803). Big data analysis necessitates the application of technology in both quantity and quality. Artificial intelligence systems now provide auditors with suitable answers.

Beyond continuous auditing, Audit 4.0 leverages big data from the Internet of Things to gather information from both internal and external sources. Artificial intelligence technologies are then used to analyze the data. As a result, the audit offers real-time and increasing certainty. In audit 4.0, the auditor's primary focus shifts to risk, risk management, and consulting activities. Generally speaking, Audit 4.0Tn differs from the typical audit process in terms of the audit methods employed, the audit's scope, duration, and cost. The fundamental elements of Industry 4.0Tn—big data analysis, the Internet of Things, and artificial intelligence—appear as novel auditing methods in audit 4.0Tn.

By using these technologies, the audit's scope is expanded while its duration and expense are greatly decreased. All audit areas inside the company can be audited by auditors thanks to Audit 4.0's technical architecture. In Audit 4.0, the idea of auditing the entire universe is replacing time-to-cost restrictions.

Cloud, blockchain, and cybersecurity technologies must be widely deployed to protect data in order to store it within the parameters of Audit 4.0. Below is a basic explanation of these ideas.

9.4.1 Internet of Things

In 1999, Ashton presented the idea to a private corporation for the first time (Ashton 2009). Through sensors found in real-world items, these technologies allow data to be gathered, exchanged, and arranged from the internet network (Banger 2016:95).

9.4.2 *Processing of Big Data*

Using the appropriate analysis and techniques in big data applications aids businesses in risk analysis, strategic decision-making, and creative endeavors (EBSO 2015:19).

Big data is the term used to describe the gathering, storing, cleaning, visualizing, analyzing, and interpreting of vast amounts of data that are generated by sensors and systems created by the advancement of information and technological infrastructure (Akdoğan and Akdoğan, 2018:4; Yıldız and Ağdeniz, 2019). Big data is the process of rapidly analyzing diverse data kinds gathered from multiple sources by utilizing technology and human resources (Banger 2018:83).

The data used in Audit 4.0 is big data. Audit 4.0 allows for a real-time audit of all corporate transactions, whether they are financial or non-financial. Furthermore, the big data that will be utilized in Audit 4.0 includes both data generated by companies and data that will be acquired from sources outside of them.

9.4.3 *Cloud Technology*

It is a technique that makes shared hardware capable of processing and storing large amounts of data accessible to anyone. Global interest in cloud computing, a quickly evolving information technology, is growing. Computers and other devices may now access information whenever they need it thanks to a technology called cloud computing.

Access to shared data, software, and information is possible at any time and from any location thanks to this internet-based technology.

Businesses' data is being transferred to cloud computing in order for auditing firms to employ cloud computing technology. There are two ways that cloud computing technologies can impact auditing firms. First, auditing information systems is a prerequisite for auditing businesses that use cloud computing. Depending on the chosen service model, risks and controls may vary, and the auditing methodology will also change. Additionally, they move their internal auditing procedures to the cloud. With cloud computing technologies, auditors will have effective and efficient access to materials in any setting with internet connectivity. As a result, auditors can conduct auditing tasks from any location with internet connectivity, improve audit quality, and conduct thorough, real-time auditing. They can thus get a competitive edge as well (Ciğer and Kınay, 2018).

9.4.4 *Blockchain*

One of the biggest inventions of the digital age is blockchain technology, which has garnered a lot of attention lately, is in high demand from both the public and commercial sectors, and is seen to be possibly more potent than the internet (Sultan et al. 2018; Uysal and Kurt 2018). Blockchain is a technology protocol that allows trust-based transactions, including identification and authorization, and data exchange in a distributed, decentralized network environment without requiring central authority approval or control.

Blockchain technology:

- It is described as a distributed architecture and is briefly explained as a feature that allows copies of the data to be kept in thousands of nodes in the network.
- It emerges as a transparency feature that allows control and tracking of all transactions occurring on the network.

The design and immutability of blockchain make it unique. The architecture is viewed as a register where all transactions and numerical data are gathered, and the immutability characteristic forbids any operations on the created data (Uysal and Kurt 2018; Ganne 2018).

All aspects of record keeping, including transaction initiation, processing, recording, authorization, and reporting, are made possible by blockchain technology. Financial reporting activities are impacted by modifications to activity models and activity processes (Uysal and Kurt, 2018).

9.4.4.1 Cyber Security

It can be characterized as a collection of procedures and technologies intended to safeguard data, networks, computers, and programs. Network and host security systems are examples of cybersecurity systems. Firewalls, intrusion detection systems, and antivirus software guard each of these systems.

There are serious risks associated with cybersecurity for companies that perform audits. Therefore, an auditing firm's reputation might suffer severe and permanent harm if it has a weak cybersecurity infrastructure and is subjected to a serious attack, particularly for the companies it works with. As a result, auditing firms should address cyber hazards as a significant component of their risk management process (KPMG 2017).

9.4.4.2 Artificial intelligence

John McCarthy coined the term "artificial intelligence" in 1956. Artificial intelligence, broadly speaking, refers to any technology that attempts to mimic the functioning of the human brain. According to a specified direction, artificial intelligence extracts meanings from data (Canan and Acungil 2018:224). The term “artificial intelligence” refers to systems that possess human-level skills like learning, creativity, and intuition. Technologies that attempt to mimic various facets of intelligence are used in artificial intelligence. These technologies include artificial neural networks, fuzzy logic, expert systems, and hybrid systems that combine these technologies.

The ability to replicate human intelligence one-on-one is the primary objective of artificial intelligence. Human intelligence cannot yet be replaced by artificial intelligence, which is a byproduct of the human brain. The following succinctly describes the advantages of artificial intelligence over natural intelligence (Yıldız 2009:25; Yıldız & Ağdeniz 2019):

- ***Documentability*** Since natural intelligence processes cannot be fully revealed, it is not possible to document a human decision-making process.
- ***Efficiency*** Human nature does not always allow them to work with the same performance. Certain human characteristics, such as fatigue, stress, and insomnia, directly affect the use of human intelligence. However, artificial intelligence technology is independent of these human-specific conditions and can always work with the same efficiency.
- ***Permanence*** Natural intelligence is limited to human life. Natural intelligence dies with death. However, artificial intelligence can be stored, transferred and copied in digital environments.
- ***Objectivity*** Humans can make decisions emotionally by nature. This situation sometimes causes wrong and biased decisions to be made. However, artificial intelligence technology always reaches the same decision in a particular case.

For Audit 4.0, artificial intelligence is a crucial technological instrument. This technology can be used in audits to accomplish the primary goals of Audit 4.0, which are diagnosis and continuous assurance. In the near future, it is anticipated that a large number of routine audit jobs will be completed by machines. In this instance, it is determined that auditors should concentrate on topics like data analysis and risk analysis in the new audit process, which we refer to as Audit 4.0. Subtypes of artificial intelligence, such as machine learning and deep learning algorithms, yield positive outcomes in these problems. As a result, the new procedure calls for auditors to be highly tech-savvy and skilled in computerized auditing methods.

The primary issue with Audit 4.0 is the dearth of qualified staff and inadequate understanding of how to use this large data. For this reason, a new set of tools is needed for the study of massive data. Big data enables businesses to make wise strategic decisions, better manage risks, and generate innovative opportunities when analyzed with sophisticated accounting software (Oracle, Systems Analysis and Program Development (SAP), and financial analysis tools (Banger 2018: 41). Artificial intelligence technologies now appear as a remedy and facilitate management’s job.

9.5 The Impact of the Digital Integration Process on Independent Audit

The 2000s saw the rise of Enron, Tyco, and Worldcom, which damaged public confidence in the accuracy and dependability of corporate data (Yang et al. 2017). The purpose of independent auditing is to provide an assessment of the dependability and correctness of financial accounts. By offering a fair level of certainty that the financial statements are free of material errors, independent auditing helps to eliminate information asymmetry and safeguard the interests of investors and other stakeholders (Hassan and Farouk 2014). But in this procedure, the audit's quality is equally crucial. Investors and other stakeholders continue to prioritize audit quality despite legislation that tighten auditor oversight (Beisland et al. 2015).

The objectives of the audit must be clearly defined, and an auditing system that is accurate, dependable, accountable, and does not lag behind competitors and technological advancements and transformations is necessary to guarantee the efficacy of independent auditing (Bozkurt 2013). To achieve the most accurate findings, data must be examined clearly, accurately, and securely using a quality auditing methodology that is appropriate and compatible with digital integration. Development and change must also be adhered to (Özdemir and Sağıroglu, 2018).

In order to provide their clients with more value in the marketplace, auditing firms are now also adjusting to digital integration, creating internal procedures, and investigating the circumstances for gaining advantages from big data, digital twins, and new digital technologies. As a result, digitization improves audit quality and efficiency while better satisfying the needs of stakeholders and shareholders. Instead of collecting samples, the auditor can analyze all of the inspected company's data using digital tools like big data, digital twins, and robotics. In actuality, the digitization of auditing procedures guarantees that all unknowns are exposed, risk assessments are conducted with recommendations for solutions, and audit quality is raised.

Digital integration has not only had a big impact on company life, but it has also helped to revolutionize how things are done in every aspect of the auditing industry (Dengler and Matthes 2018). Auditing firms must embrace digital integration, integrate cutting-edge technology into their operations, and continuously improve their services in order to remain competitive and deliver higher-quality auditing services (Sahut et al. 2013; Van Den Broek ve Van Veenstra 2018).

In addition to satisfying client needs, digital integration alters how auditors conduct audit operations.

The discipline of auditing and independent auditing benefits from technological advancements and creative thinking abilities brought about by the digital integration process. (Manita et al. 2020) These are:

- Having the opportunity to make an analysis,
- Ability to perform comparative data analysis quickly,
- Obtaining findings that add value,

- Having the opportunity to examine all data,
- To detect risks in a short time and seize the opportunity to intervene immediately,
- Ability to perform financial analyses and due diligence,
- Opportunity to share real-time data,
- Ability to make advanced content and detailed analysis,
- Gaining the opportunity to use the limited time in the audit effectively,
- Ability to apply advanced auditing techniques.

It is feasible to decrease auditing time and expenses while also improving the quality and effectiveness of auditing operations by utilizing digital tools in accounting and auditing. The accounting and auditing industries have recently shown a great deal of interest in artificial intelligence solutions. The application of expert systems methodology in various auditing domains involving expert knowledge and judgment, such as assessing internal control systems, valuing commercial receivables, and determining materiality levels in auditing, has been thoroughly studied by researchers in the auditing field (Marcella and Rauff 1995).

The following is a list of topics in which expert systems can be used for independent auditing (Vasarhelyi and Kogan 1998).

- Conducting preliminary checks during the customer evaluation and acceptance phase,
- Existence of an internal control environment and examination of the internal control system,
- Planning the tactics to be used in the audit,
- Determining an appropriate audit plan,
- Determining the conformity tests between the internal control environment and the accounting system of the client company,
- The internal control system, according to the findings determined as a result of compliance tests,
- Evidence obtained,
- Creation of the audit plan,
- Determination of material accuracy tests,
- Classification, grading and evaluation of audit evidence and other findings obtained,
- Determining an audit opinion on the financial statements reviewed,
- Proper reporting of the audit performed and the audit opinion expressed, and filing of working papers.

According to the report to be created within the scope of big data analytics, financial statement data obtained and collected through digital systems that are harmonized within the country can be beneficial in determining the risk groups of businesses, accelerating audit processes, reducing audit costs, enabling stakeholders to make fast and accurate decisions, increasing the number of audited companies, spreading the concept of auditing in society, increasing the transparency of financial statements, and increasing assurance in financial statement audits.

Thus, with independent auditing becoming a widespread process in all businesses, it will be possible to easily detect tax evasion, false declarations, and tax evasion events of businesses through technological systems.

9.6 The Impact of the Digital Integration Process on the Independent Auditor

Digital activities that have increased with digital developments have also brought about developments in the auditing profession. Unlike traditional methods, much data recorded in an electronic environment necessitates the use of information technologies in the auditing activities carried out for a higher quality and continuous audit. Information Technology (IT) is the application of computer and telecommunication equipment to receive, process, transmit and store data. In other words, it can be expressed as a concept that provides data in a visual format through any multimedia distribution mechanism (Ghasemi et al. 2011). Today, it is possible to process, manage, analyze and produce usable outputs in an acceptable time for the information and data required for auditing in an electronic environment.

For auditing the human factor is of critical importance as the ultimate guarantor of the validity of the audit process. Therefore, in terms of the audit process, the knowledge and skills of auditors should also be developed (Pilos 2020). It is an inevitable fact that information technologies have a significant impact on auditing in all aspects, such as audit planning, audit process and evaluation.

Computer-aided auditing techniques provide the methods required for more effective and efficient auditing of activities carried out in the increasingly growing information technologies environment, and save auditors from dealing with data stacks, allowing them to audit based on results that have been subjected to certain controls (Önce and îşgüden 2012: 134).

High technology enables the auditor to detect the important activities of the business and significant errors originating from fraud (Bierstaker et al. 2001). The digital technology order requires auditors to motivate themselves to better understand and learn advanced information technologies. This issue is expressed in International Standards on Auditing (UDS) 315 as auditors should change their thoughts and gain skills in using information technology and control systems in audit activities (IAASB 2009). High technology emerging as a result of digitalization causes the auditor's audit activity to change significantly and it is foreseen that technology will be used more effectively and efficiently. Digital technology; It will reduce the pressures on timing and workload as it facilitates the audit process in the planning phase, field activities and reporting phase (Bierstaker et al. 2001; Vasarhelyi and Romero 2014). A more digital audit increases the efficiency and accuracy of the audit and, more importantly, facilitates the audit of all of a company's financial data instead of a sample (Serçemeli 2018:381).

9.7 Regulations Made in Tax Laws Regarding the Digital Integration Process in Turkey

In our country, the data obtained through e-documents, e-ledgers and electronic declarations through the Tax Audit Analysis System (VEDAS) of the Tax Audit Board (VDK) are analyzed and sent to audit according to the identified risk groups (Calayoğlu 2019:155). When viewed according to their usage, digital tools have a wide scope in auditing. Auditing has changed with various digital tools and carries elements that will benefit it for each audit.

According to Article 242 of the Tax Procedure Law, electronic documents, electronic books and electronic records are defined. According to this article;

- An electronic ledger is defined as the entirety of electronic records that contain the information that must be included in the ledgers that are required to be kept according to this Law, regardless of the formal provisions.
- Electronic documents are defined as a set of electronic records that contain the information contained in documents that are required to be prepared in accordance with this Law, regardless of the formal provisions.
- Electronic records refer to the smallest information element that is kept in an electronic environment and constitutes electronic books and documents, and that can be accessed and processed by electronic means.

The amendments made to Article 257 of the Tax Procedure Law specify how the information and documents that need to be prepared should be prepared and how they should be notified. According to this article;

- "To remove the obligation to keep and organize the books to be kept and the documents to be prepared in accordance with this Law",
- "To permit or impose obligations for the books, records and documents that must be kept and arranged to be kept on microfilm, microfiche or electronic information and recording tools or to be stored in these recording media",
- "The information requested from those who are required to provide information on a regular basis, as well as declarations, notifications, letters, petitions, minutes, reports and other documents, shall be provided through all kinds of electronic information communication tools and environments, including the internet, by using passwords, electronic signatures or other security tools",
- "To use electrical, electronic, magnetic and similar devices and systems whose qualities it determines and approves in order to ensure tax security, and to impose obligations on the use of special labels and signs such as banderol, stamp, barcode, hologram, clipping, stamp and symbol through these devices and systems",
- "In order to ensure tax security in electronic commerce, commercial services are provided to real or legal person service providers who carry out commercial activities in an electronic environment and/or to real and legal person

intermediary service providers who provide an electronic commerce environment for the economic and commercial activities of others.
- Its activities, to impose an obligation to store and submit information and notifications within the scope of this clause electronically and to determine other procedures and principles regarding implementation",
- "The assessment slips and/or notices issued electronically upon the electronic submission of declarations submitted voluntarily or with a request for repentance after the legal period has expired, and the notices issued electronically upon the submission of notifications, letters, petitions, minutes, reports and other documents that are required to be submitted electronically after the due date, shall be transmitted electronically to the taxpayer, the tax responsible or the real or legal person authorized by them to send declarations, notifications, letters, petitions, minutes, reports and other documents electronically. This communication shall replace the notification of the assessment slip and/or notice to the addressee."

9.8 Conclusion

With digital integration, auditing activity has changed from manual auditing to digital auditing, and digital-based auditing has gained importance today. In line with the opportunities offered by digital technologies and changes in social needs, it has become necessary to bring together components such as people, business processes and technology in order to provide effective and efficient auditing services. The transition to digital auditing requires auditing firms to review their working methods and organization. The objectives of the auditing function, such as accountability, focusing on transparency, and increasing the trust of shareholders and third parties regarding the efficient, effective and economical use of resources, do not change.

It is seen that digital integration has a positive effect on the auditing profession and that this situation is a subject that needs to be developed in line with today's conditions. In today's conditions, new digital technologies such as analytics, big data, blockchain, cloud technology, artificial intelligence, cyber technology, robots and mobile etc. are emerging. Such digital technologies are reshaping existing products, leading to the emergence of new products and services and transforming in-house digital resources into a new revenue stream. These emerging digital technologies bring the auditing processes, controls and implemented auditing procedures of auditors to the forefront and their development. The rapid change and development in digital technologies to their activities and audit quality. However, in this process, auditors should also change their audit processes from traditional audit procedures to digital change procedures. As businesses turn to digital integration, auditors will be able to focus more on access controls and material misstatement risk areas and accelerate their audit work. Therefore, in order for audit firms to benefit from the digitalization process, auditors' capacity to use digital tools and new technology products in practice should be developed and they should be directed towards concepts with educational content such as the training required for this. In addition, audit companies should develop software and technology that is completely adapted to the needs and company structure by blending the flexibility of in-house software, hardware and all audit teams with the needs and process standards or external support should be obtained. This will provide an advantage to audit firms in terms of increasing the quality of audit work and reputation and respect in the sector.

Digital technology will enable auditing to evolve towards better control of client data and improvement of audit relevance and quality. New digital tools and coverage of all client data will allow for more relevant analysis of the client's various processes and data, and will identify most errors and anomalies in the financial statements. This will allow auditing to fully fulfill its role as a governance mechanism and become a resource for limiting the discretion of managers, as well as a tool for informing them in decision-making processes. In addition, the evolution of auditing towards real-time auditing and verification of projected data will further limit the risk of misuse and opportunistic behavior of managers. The development of auditing through digitization will also increase the transparency of financial statements and enable the board to make the right decisions.

- The advantages of digital transformation in independent auditing can be expressed as follows;
- Increased audit quality in terms of audit evidence,
- Decrease in control risks as a result of increasing sample sizes,
- Reduction of structural risks of the business as a result of digitalization,
- In line with these, it will reduce the risk of failure to detect, which is inversely proportional to the risk of material misstatement, and thus reduce the audit risks of businesses. It will increase the level of reasonable assurance, which is an important element of auditing.
- Since cross-checking is done, the reliability level of the financial statements can be increased and the results can be evaluated more effectively.
- With the spread of digitalization applications in accounting, such as e-Invoice, higher auditing rates can be achieved and public revenues can increase, which will have positive effects on the economies of countries.
- If e-Ledger applications can be made widespread by the Ministry of Finance, cross-auditing in accounting transactions between companies will be facilitated and the error possibilities of CPAs in this regard will be minimized.
- Among the independent auditing standards, (BDS) 315 Risks of material misstatement, BDS 320 Audit planning, BDS 500 Audit evidence, BDS 530 Sampling in auditing, BDS 540 Accounting estimates standards, Auditing 4.0 and the digitalization process must be evaluated within this scope and must be in compliance with the Turkish Commercial Code.

Audit 4.0 will be able to minimize human-based accounting errors and fraud. It is possible to obtain and audit data in audit processes in a way that does not leave room for material errors. In addition, in terms of compliance audit, it will allow the data of thousands of businesses to be checked more quickly and effectively, especially by public authorities. With the increase in trust in financial statements thanks to Audit 4.0, investors will be able to enter the capital markets more as companies become more transparent.

With artificial intelligence applications, incorrect data entry inside and outside the business can be prevented. For example, stock control can become very simple and effective. Other contributions of digitalization are; more reliable cross-checking of balance sheets of businesses in the same sector, application of analytical procedures, reduction of audit costs and saving time, and the possibility of reducing the number of personnel to be assigned to the audit team are among the positive effects.

References

Akdoğan N, Ve Akdoğan MU (2018) Büyük veri-bilişim teknolojisindeki gelişmelerin muhasebe uygulamalarına ve muhasebe mesleğine etkisi. Muhasebe ve Denetime Bakış 55:1–14

Ashton K (2009) That “Internet Of Things” Thing. RFID J. https://www.rfidjournal.com/articles/view74986, Accessed 27 Jan 2017

Banger G (2016) Endüstri 4.0 ve akıllı işletme. Dorlion Yayıncılık, Ankara

Banger G (2018) Endüstri 4.0. Ekstra. 2. Baskı Dorlion Yayınları, Eskişehir

Beisland LA, Mersland R, Strom RO (2015) Audit quality and corporate governance: evidence from the microfinance industry. Int J Audit 19(3):218–237

Bierstaker JL, Burnaby P, Thibodeau J (2001) The impact of information technology on the audit process: an assessment of the State of the art and implications for the future. Manag Audit J 16(3):159–164

Bozkurt N (2018) Muhasebe Denetimi. 8. Baskı. Alfa Basını Yayını Dağıtım, İstanbul

Bozkurt P (2013) Denetim kavramı ve denetim anlayışındaki gelişmeler. Denetişim Dergisi 12:56–62

Calayoğlu İ (2019) Elektronik vergi denetimindeki teknolojik gelişmeler ve tam denetime geçiş adımları. Muhasebe ve Finansman Dergisi 81:143–162

Canan S, Ve Acungil M (2018) Dijital gelecekte insan kalmak. Tuti Kitap

Celayir D, Ve Celayir Ç (2020) Dijitalleşmenin denetim mesleğine yansımaları. Avrasya Sosyal ve Ekonomi Araştırmaları Dergisi (ASEAD) 7(6):128–148

Cenamor J, Sjödin DR, Parida V (2017) Adopting a platform approach in servitization: leveraging the value of digitalization. Int J Prod Econ 192:54–65

Ciğer A, Ve Kınay B (2018) Bağımsız denetim firmalarının bulut bilişim uygulamalarını benimseme düzeylerine yönelik nitel bir araştırma: antalya ili örneği. Muhasebe Bilim Dünyası Dergisi 20(3):629–649

Çalış YE (2011) Bağımsız denetim sürecinde analitik inceleme prosedürleri. Denetişim 8:31–40

Dai J, Vasarhelyi MA (2016) Imagineering audit 4.0. J Emerg Technol Account 13(1):1–15

DeFond M, Zhang J (2014) A review of archival auditing research. J Account Econ 58(2/3):275–326

Demir Ö (2006) İç Kontrol Kavram ve Modelleri”, içinde 5018 Sayılı Kamu Mali Yönetimi ve Kontrol Kanunu kapsamında güncel mali sorunlar. Muhasebat Kontrolörleri Derneği Yayınları, Ankara

Dengler K, Matthes B (2018) The impacts of digital transformation on the labour market: substitution potentials of occupations in Germany. Technol Forecast Soc Change 137:304–316

EBSO (2015) Sanayi 4.0 Uyum Sağlamayan Kaybedecek. Ege Bölgesi Sanayi Odası, http://www.ebso.org.tr/ebsomedia/documents/sanayi-40_88510761.pdf. Accessed 17 July 2020.

Eğilmez M (2018) Endüstri 4.0. Accounting and Financial History. Res J 15:264–271

Ejaz W, Anpalagan A, Imran MA, Jo M, Naeem M, Qaisar SB, Wang W (2016) Internet of Things (IoT) in 5G wireless communications. IEEE 4:10310–10314

Erturan İE, Ve Ergin E (2018) Dijital denetim ve dijital ikiz yöntemi. Muhasebe Bilim Dünyası Dergisi 20(4):810–830

Fırat OZ, Ve Fırat SÜ (2017) Endüstri 4.0 yolculuğunda trendler ve robotlar. İstanbul Üniversitesi İşletme Fakültesi Dergisi 46(2):211223

Ganne E (2018) Can blockchain revolutionize international trade? World Trade Organization Accessed 18 July 2020. https://www.wto.org/english/res_e/booksp_e/blockchainrev18_e.pdf

Gerpott TJ, May S (2016) Integration of internet of things components into a firm's offering portfolio. Info *18*(2):53–63

Ghasemi M, Shafeiepour V, Aslani M, Barvayeh E (2011) The impact of information technology (it) on modern accounting systems. Procedia Soc Behav Sci 28:112–116

Güredin E (2008) Denetim ve güvence hizmetleri, SMMM ve YMM'lere yönelik ilkeler ve teknikler. 12 Baskı. Arıkan Basım Yayım Dağıtım Ltd. Şti, İstanbul

Hassan SU, Farouk A (2014) Audit quality and financial performance of quoted cement firms in Nigeria. Eur J Bus Manag 6(28):73–82

Hasselblatt M, Huikkola T, Kohtamâki M, Nickell D (2018) Modelling manufacturer's capabilities for the internet of things. J Bus Ind Mark 33:822–836

Hope OK, Kang T, Thomas W, Yoo YK (2008) Culture and auditor choice: a test of the secrecy hypothesis. J Acc Pub Pol 27(5):357–373

https://www.kgk.gov.tr/Portalv2Uploads/files/Duyurular/v2/TDS/Standartlar_Tablosu.pdf. Accessed 20 July 2020

https://www.mevzuat.gov.tr/MevzuatMetin/1.4.213.pdf. Accessed 20 July 2020

https://www.kgk.gov.tr/DynamicContentDetail/10240/TDS-2020-Seti. Accessed 20 July 2020

IASSB (2009) International Standard On Auditing 315 Identifying And Assessing The Risks Of Material Misstatement Through Understanding The Entity And Its Environment. https://www.ifac.org/system/files/downloads/aO17-2010-iaasb-handbook-isa-315.pdf

Jensen MC, Meckling WH (1976) Theory of the Firm: managerial Behaviour, Agency Costs and Ownership Structure. J Financ Econ 3(4):305–360

Keskenler MF, Ve Keskenler EF (2017) Geçmişten günümüze yapay sinir ağları ve tarihçesi. Takvim-i Vekayi 5(2):8–18

Khan MA (1995) Yeni Başlayanlar. In: Eroğlu F Sayıştay Dergisi 19: 15

KPMG (2017a) Beyaz yakanın yerini yapay zeka alacak. https://kpmg.com/tr/tr/home/medya/press-releases/2017/03/beyaz-yakanin-yerini-yapay-zeka-alacak.html, Accessed 17 July 2020.

KPMG (2017b) Clarity On Dynamic Audit. https://assets.kpmg/content/dam/kpmg/ch/pdf/clarity-on-dynamic-audit-en.pdf, Accessed 17 July 2020.

Lawrence S (1996) Sawyer's internal auditing. The Institute of Internal Auditors, Florida

Lenka S, Parida V, Wincent J (2017) Digitalization capabilities as enablers of value co-creation in servitizing firms. Psychol Mark 34(1):92–100

Manita R, Elommal N, Baudier P, Hikkerova L (2020) The digital transformation of external audit and its ımpact on corporate governance. Technol Forecast Soc Change 150:1–10

Marcella A, Rauff JV (1995) Utilizing expert systems to evaluate disaster recovery planning. J Appl Bus Res 11(1):30–38

Mckinsey (2017) Introducing the next-generation operating model. McKinsey & Company. https://www.mckinsey.com/~/media/mckinsey/business%20functions/mckinsey%20digital/our%20insights/introducing%20the%20next-generation%20operating%20model/introducing-the-next-gen-operating-model.pdf. Accessed 17 July 2020

Nwankpa J (2014) Digital business environment and audit quality. Int J Account Res 2(1)

Nwankpa J, Datta P (2012) Perceived audit quality from ERP implementations. Inf Resour Manag J 25(1):61–80

Önce S, İşgüden B (2012) Bilgi teknolojilerindeki değişimlerin ön plana çıkardığı sürekli denetim yaklaşımının ve güvence ve danışmanlık hizmetlerinin değerlendirilmesi: İMKB-100 işletmelerinde bir araştırma. MÖDAV 1:127–155

Özdemir İ, Ve Sağıroğlu Ş (2018) Denetimlerde büyük veri kullanımı ve üzerine bir değerlendirme. Gazi Üniversitesi Fen Bilimleri Dergisi Part C: Tasarım ve Teknoloji 6(2):470–480

Özen A, Ve Gürel F (2020) Kamu denetiminde dijital dönüşüm: dijital ikiz yöntemi. İzmir Sosyal Bilimler Dergisi 2(1):16–23

Pilos S (2020). Auditing the digital reality.https://www.eca.europa.eu/Lists/ECADocuments/JOURNAL20_01/JOURNAL20_01.pdf. Accessed 20 July 2020

Porter ME, Heppelmann JE (2015) How smart, connected products are transforming companies. Harv Bus Rev 93:96–114

Sahut JM, Hikkerova L, Khalfallah M (2013) Business model and performance of firms. Int Bus Res 6(2):64–76

Sakin T (2018) Bağımsız denetim ve denetimin ekonomik etkileri. Hitit Üniversitesi Sosyal Bilimler Enstitüsü Dergisi 11(3):2455–2466

Schuh G, Potente T, Wesch-Potente C, Weber AR, Prote JP (2014) Collaboration mechanisms to increase productivity in the content of industrie 4.0: robust manufacturing conference. Procedia CIRP 19:51–56

Schwab K (2016) Dördüncü endüstri devrimi. Çev: Zülfü Dicleli, 1. Baskı. Optimist Kitap, İstanbul

Serçemeli M (2018) Muhasebe ve denetim mesleklerinin dijital dönüşümünde yapay zekâ. Electron Turk Stud 13(30):369386

Sharkansky I (1991) The development of state audit. State Audit and Accountability, State of Israel Comptroller's Office, Jerusalem

Sultan K, Ruhi U, Lakhani R (2018) Conceptualizing blockchains: characteristics and applications. IADIS Int Conf Inf Syst 49–57

TOBB (2016) Sanayi 4.0'a hazır mıyız? TOBB Ekonomik Forum Dergisi. (259). 16–27. http://haber.tobb.org.tr/ekonomikforum/2016/259/016_027.pdf. Accessed 17 July 2020

Tutar S (2019) Endüstri 4.0'ın muhasebe mesleğine olası etkileri. Uluslararası Ekonomi, İşletme ve Politika Dergisi 3(2):323–344

Türker M (2006) Uluslararası denetim standartlarına yakınsama ve Türkiye Denetim Standartları'nın oluşturulması. Muhasebe ve Denetime Bakış Dergisi 6(9):87–97

Türker M (2018) Dijitalleşme sürecinde küresel muhasebe mesleğinin yeniden şekillenmesine bakış. Muhasebe Bilim Dünyası Dergisi 20(1):202–235

Türker M, Ve Örerler EO (2004) Türk işletmelerinin küresel işletme haline getirilme yolları. İstanbul Ticaret Odası, Yayın No: 2004-60, İstanbul

Uysal TU, Ve Kurt G (2018) Muhasebede ve denetimde blok zinciri teknolojisi. Süleyman Demirel Üniversitesi İktisadi ve İdari Bilimler Fakültesi Dergisi 23(2):467–481

Van Den Broek T, Van Veenstra AF (2018) Governance of big data collaborations: how to balance regulatory compliance and disruptive innovation. Technol Forecast Soc Change 129:330–338

Vasarhelyi MA, Kogan A (1998) Artifıcal intelligence in accounting and auditing: towards new paradigms. Wiener Publishers, Princeton

Vasarhelyi MA, Romero S (2014) Technology in audit engagement: a case study. Manag Audit J 29(4):350–365

Verma S, Bhattacharyya SS, Ve Kumar S (2018) An extension of the techology acceptance model in the big data analytics system implementation environment. Inf Process Manag 54(5):791–806

Vladimirovich AT, Linder NV (2017) Innovation and productivity: an empirical investigation of factors preventing growth by the longitudinal analysis method. Adm Sci 7(3):43–58

Watts R, Zimmerman J (1986) Positive accounting theory. Prentice-Hall. Englewood Cliffs, New Jersey

Yang D, Jiao H, Buckland R (2017) The determinants of financial fraud in Chinese firms: does corporate governance as an institutional innovation matter? Technol Forecast Soc Change 125:309–320

Yıldız B (2009) Finansal analizde yapay zekâ. Beta, İstanbul

Yıldız B, Ve Ağdeniz Ş (2019) Denetim 4.0'ın teknolojik altyapısı. Muhasebe ve Denetime Bakış 58:83–102

Chapter 10
The Internet of Things in Audit Processes: A New Dimension of Digital Transformation

İlkay Ejder Erturan

Abstract The rapid advancement of digital technologies has led to significant transformations across all business functions, including auditing. Among these technologies, the Internet of Things (IoT) stands out as a game-changer, enabling real-time data collection, communication between devices, and automation of numerous operational processes. This paper explores how IoT is reshaping traditional audit practices by enhancing data accuracy, reducing human error, and enabling continuous auditing. Through the integration of smart sensors, interconnected devices, and real-time analytics, auditors can now obtain more timely, relevant, and comprehensive insights. The study highlights the potential of IoT to improve audit quality, efficiency, and cost-effectiveness, while also discussing the challenges and structural changes required for successful adoption. This new dimension of digital transformation in auditing not only enhances operational efficiency but also provides a strategic advantage in an increasingly data-driven business environment.

Keywords Internet of things · Auditing · Digital transformation · Automation · Continuous auditing · Smart technology

---

This chapter was previously published in Turkish by Gazi Kitabevi with the ISBN: 978-975-7727-16-7.

İ. E. Erturan (✉)
Düzce University, Düzce, Turkey
e-mail: ilkayerturan@duzce.edu.tr

G. Kurt, Ö. Sarısoy (eds.), *Recent Advancements in Auditing*, Accounting, Finance, Sustainability, Governance & Fraud: Theory and Application,
https://doi.org/10.1007/978-981-95-5811-7_10

10.1 Introduction

Peter F. Drucker once said, *"The most important thing in communication is hearing what isn't said."* In today's world, what we call digital technology—driven by the Internet of Things (IoT)—has brought about intense new competition and transformation. Sensors, drones, smart shelves, intelligent machines, and other interconnected, human-free smart devices have found their place in the business world. These technologies are now helping us by "hearing" and "learning" the unspoken. The use of high-tech machines has become one of the essential tools that make life easier.

Today, digitalization and automation have become key factors offering the potential to enhance the efficiency of business processes. In this context, digital transformation is rapidly expanding into nearly every field. At the heart of this transformation lies the Internet of Things (IoT), which enables physical objects to communicate with one another and exchange data. IoT systems continuously collect data through devices and sensors, providing businesses with real-time information. This data supports decision-making processes and enables various benefits, such as optimized operations, improved energy efficiency, and cost savings.

Objects that are becoming more intelligent and increasingly integrated into daily life have also begun to influence accounting systems and auditing processes, just as they have in many other areas. In this era of advanced technology, where traditional auditing techniques may no longer be sufficient, auditing must undergo a structural transformation. The Internet of Things (IoT) offers significant benefits, including the elimination of human-related errors, enhanced audit quality, more efficient use of time, cost savings, and the potential to gain a competitive advantage.

10.2 THE Internet of Things

The concept of the Internet of Things (IoT) was first introduced by Kevin Ashton in 1999 during a presentation at Procter & Gamble (P&G), where he described the benefits of Radio Frequency Identification (RFID) technology (Ashton 2009). The Internet of Things refers to the extension of existing internet services to encompass every physical object that currently exists or may exist in the future. It involves the use of smart interfaces by social and environmental users to connect and communicate. IoT can also be defined as a network of objects with virtual identities and roles, interacting within intelligent environments. Another definition describes the Internet of Things as a concept in which everyday objects are connected through various types of sensors—such as RFID—and actuators, working together to perceive, collect, and transmit relevant information from their surroundings (Sun 2012). Our world is now filled with smart objects and numerous service providers collectively known as the Internet. The ultimate goal of IoT architecture is to visualize each service provider as an intelligent recorder within a globally interconnected system.

The **Internet of Things (IoT)**: technology is based on the principle that physical objects connect to the internet, collect data from their environment, analyze it, and, when necessary, perform actions automatically (Atzori et al. 2010). The operational mechanism of the IoT can be summarized as follows:

Object + Sensor: Sensors embedded in a physical object collect data from the environment. For example, a refrigerator measures the internal temperature.

Internet Connectivity: The collected data is transmitted to the internet—typically to cloud platforms—using communication protocols such as Wi–Fi, Bluetooth, or LTE (Gubbi et al. 2013).

Data Processing: Once the data reaches the cloud, it is analyzed. If an anomaly is detected (e.g., excessive temperature), the system generates an alert or initiates a response.

User Interface or Autonomous Action: A notification is sent to the user via a mobile app, or the device takes autonomous action (e.g., activating the air conditioning system or shutting down a machine) (Xu et al. 2014).

Examples of application areas of the Internet of Things are presented in Fig. 10.1.

Machines that exist independently in our daily lives form an intelligent communication ecosystem capable of interacting with each other through the Internet of Things (IoT) technology (Akkuş 2016). This emerging system is defined as the Internet of Things. Additionally, the IoT concept has been described as systems where objects connected to the internet share data through the internet without face-to-face interaction with humans (Arslan and Kırbaş 2016). IoT encompasses not only computers connected to the internet but also all smart devices. The main idea behind the Internet of Things is to acquire information in order to understand, control, and measure the environment, expand our ability to act, and detect and prevent errors occurring within the system in advance.

The concept of the Internet of Things (IoT) introduced the idea of the internet communicating not only with humans but also with objects (machines). This

Field	Example of Application
Home	Smart thermostats, lighting systems, security cameras
Agriculture	Soil moisture sensors, automated irrigation systems
Healthcare	Patient monitoring via wearable devices, medication reminders
Industry	Predictive maintenance in machines, production automation
Transportation	Smart traffic signal systems, GPS-based vehicle tracking

Fig. 10.1 Application Areas of the Internet of Things (IoT). *Source* Adapted from Borgia (2014)

interaction is expected to bring about a significant transformation (Ashton 2009). According to Ashton, for this major change to occur and yield results, the data input by humans into computers is crucial. However, this process is limited and dependent on the time, knowledge, and accuracy of human data entry dedicated to the internet. The internet's knowledge about physical objects (things) in the world relies heavily on data input. Therefore, it is emphasized that relying solely on information provided by humans is insufficient to meet the data intensity of the internet; data collection from objects themselves is also necessary. This approach reduces human-related errors, damages, and costs. Furthermore, by gathering information from objects, the internet can provide timely insights on when items need to be replaced, maintained, or recalled (Erturan and Ergin 2017).

In another study, Miorandi, Sicari, De Pellegrini, and Chlamtac (2012) defined the Internet of Things as a system that connects large-scale networks formed by the convergence of necessary supporting technologies and applications using extended internet technology (Miorandi 2012). Similarly, the Internet of Things has also been referred to as the "Internet of Everything" or the "Industrial Internet," emphasizing that it is a network of machines and devices capable of communicating with each other (Lee and Lee 2015). Furthermore, the IoT has been described as a comprehensive and open network of smart objects with the capacity for autonomous regulation, sharing of data, information, and resources, responding to changes, and acting accordingly (Madakam 2015). The Internet of Things involves connecting objects for purposes such as sensing various information (identity, communication data, etc.) and data collection (Metallo 2018). In their 2018 study, Thibaud, Chi, Zhou, and Piramuthu defined IoT as a network of physical objects (such as vehicles, machines, household appliances) and highlighted that, through the network, communication between objects can occur without human intervention (Thibaud 2018).

From the perspective of the Internet of Things, defining the concept of an object is quite challenging due to its broad meaning. In IoT, an object can be defined as a monitoring device, a sensor, a biochip, or an access mechanism. Objects represent the flow of large volumes of sensor data from physical environments, which, after evaluation, are transmitted as information to operators or relevant personnel, or processed by systems to initiate an action (https://tr.wikipedia.org/wiki/Nesnelerin_interneti).

Machine-to-machine communication enables machines to communicate with each other without human intervention. This concept forms the fundamental basis of the Internet of Things.

10.2.1 Evolution Stages of the Internet of Things

ARPANET (Advanced Research Projects Agency Network), which emerged in 1969, was a large-scale network system that enabled communication between a limited number of devices and laid the foundation for the modern internet. It is estimated that by 2020, this network would connect approximately 50 billion objects (Cisco). Between 2020 and 2025, many objects such as furniture, paper documents, food products, and electronic devices are expected to be connected to the internet and communicate with us (Giusto 2010).

The internet has gone through numerous stages and developments to become an integral part of our lives.

Stage 1: Research Phase; ARPANET (Advanced Research Projects Agency Network) is an experimental computer network considered the precursor to the internet. The Advanced Research Projects Agency (ARPA), a branch of the U.S. Department of Defense, funded the development of ARPANET in the late 1960s. The project aimed to connect computers at research institutions funded by the Pentagon via telephone lines (https://www.britannica.com/topic/ARPANET, 2020). The digitization of information and digital access to data began between 1990 and 1995.

Stage 2: Business Awareness Period; This phase can be defined as the period when businesses started to inform the public. Each business obtained a domain name related to its line of work and communicated what they do and how they do it, delivering one-way information to a broader audience. The collaborative use of digitized information resources and the initiation of e-commerce activities began in the late 1990s.

Stage 3: Active Use of Web Pages; Web pages began to be used more actively. The infrastructure that enabled real-time purchasing of products and services offered interactively became widespread and accessible to large audiences. E-commerce experienced significant growth, with platforms such as eBay and Amazon.com multiplying. The early 2000s saw accelerated adoption of social media, mobile media usage, cloud computing, and the digitization of interactions such as video streaming.

Stage No	Period	Description
0	1960-1990	Research and Infrastructure Development –ARPANET, TCP/IP, microprocessors
1	1990'lar	Conceptual Development – Emergence of RFID and the term "IoT"
2	2000-2010	M2M Communication – First IoT applications, mobile networks
3	2010-2015	Expansion – Smart devices, user-level adoption
4	2015-2020	Big Data & Cloud – Emphasis on data analysis and cybersecurity
5	2020-2024	AI + IoT – Intelligent systems, 5G integration
6	2024 ve sonrasi	Autonomous and Sustainable IoT – Advanced integration, focus on ethics and efficiency

Fig. 10.2 Evolution Stages of the Internet of Things. *Source* McKinsey Global Institute **(2015)** The Internet of Things: Mapping the Value Beyond the Hype

Stage 4: The Era of Social Media and the Semantic Web; This period marks the emergence of concepts such as social media and the semantic web. Platforms that enable users to share text, photos, and videos—such as YouTube, Facebook, and Twitter—gained popularity and became profitable. Additionally, the digital connection of objects to the internet began during this era and continues to the present day. In this stage, it is possible to talk about the online interactions of objects.

Each stage has a deeper impact on humanity compared to the previous one. As a technology-driven society, we are currently at the final stage of the internet: the Internet of Things. To better understand these stages, the figure we created based on the timeline is shown Fig. 10.2.

10.2.2 The Smart World and Application Areas of the Internet of Things

The **Internet of Things (IoT)**, which has fundamentally transformed our world, has forced businesses to adopt this disruptive technology due to the intense competitive pressure it creates. Disruptive technology is defined as a form of innovation that changes the basis of competition and significantly affects inter-organizational dynamics (Danneels 2004). As the Internet of Things (IoT) increasingly integrates into every aspect of daily life, businesses are compelled to adapt to this technological shift. Figure 10.3 illustrates the growth trend and the increasing usage of IoT between 2015 and 2025.

On October 10, 2011, PR Newswire, one of the world's largest online press release distribution networks, published the results of a joint research study conducted by GSMA in collaboration with Machina Research, and supported by AT&T, Deutsche Bank, KT, Telenor Connexion, and Vodafone, in San Diego. According to the findings, the total number of mobile-connected devices, which was approximately 9 billion in 2011, was expected to exceed 24 billion by 2020. This projection indicated more than a 100% increase in mobile-connected devices. The study also emphasized that the proliferation of connected devices would create a $1.2 trillion revenue opportunity for the mobile industry (PR Newswire, 2011).

Today, the Internet of Things (IoT) has become far more widespread than initially anticipated, creating a **smart world**. With this smart world, the **age of privacy** has come to an end, giving rise to an **age of transparency**. Jeremy Rifkin, in his book *The Internet of Things*, states: *"When you connect everyone and everything on a global neural network, you take the human race out of the era of privacy and push it into an era of transparency."* (Rifkin 2015). An explanation of the smart world is provided in the following Fig. 10.4.

As can be seen from the figure, the Internet of Things is used in many areas. Applications can be found in a variety of fields, including smart wearable devices, smart cities, smart homes, and smart environments.

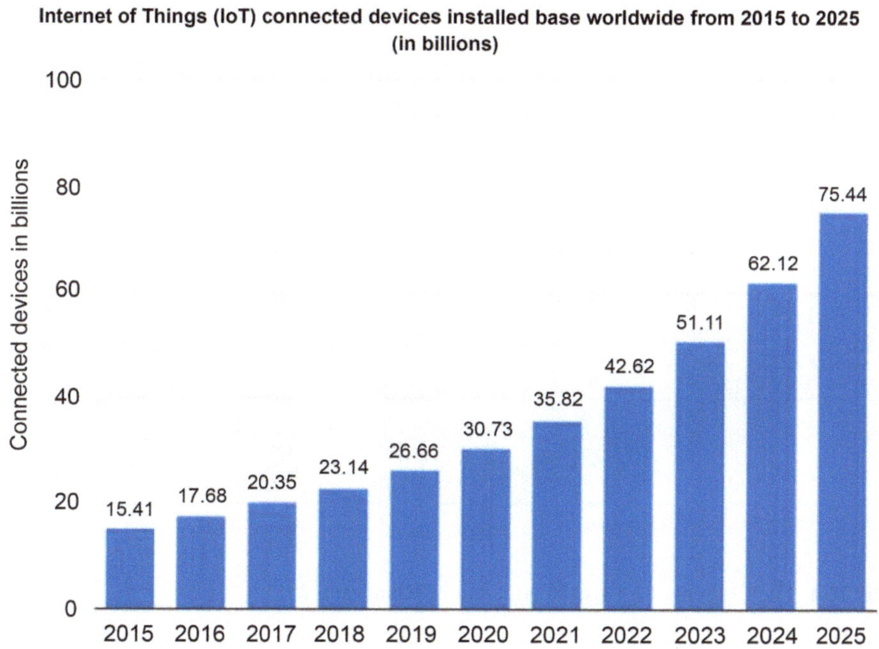

Fig. 10.3 Growth Trend of the Internet of Things. *Source* Statista (2023)

The Internet of Things (IoT) can be utilized in many different fields. Some of the main areas of application are as follows (Kesayak, 2017):

Home and building applications: Smart lighting systems that easily adapt to different environments; wireless and internet-connected lights that can be operated via web or mobile applications; surveillance, security, and alarm systems; and safety systems based on smoke and gas detection.

Industrial applications: Real-time monitoring of production processes and process control; smart machines; smart sensors; intelligent controllers; and high-precision automation systems with advanced control and security mechanisms.

Applications in the energy sector: Advanced metering infrastructure (AMI), SCADA (Supervisory Control and Data Acquisition) systems, smart inverters, remote control of energy-consuming devices, and the use of digital twin technology.

Applications in the healthcare system: IoT is widely used in various healthcare services, including remote patient monitoring, emergency alert systems, wearable IoT devices, and real-time infant monitoring. Monitoring individuals' health data and storing health-related information is made possible through the Internet of Things. These capabilities are implemented using sensors, microchips, and RFID-based devices (Agarwal 2011). In the management of chronic diseases—such as diabetes, coronary heart disease, cancer, stroke, and Alzheimer's—continuous health monitoring and the storage of

Fig. 10.4 The Concept of a Smart World. *Source* Rijmenam, 2013

medical records are expected to make a significant difference by enabling early detection and real-time observation of potential emergencies(Bandyopadhyay 2011).

Applications in the field of transportation: Examples include smart traffic lights, autonomous vehicles, inter- and intra-vehicle communication, automatic transmission for emergency rescue, safety and roadside assistance, and smart parking systems.

Applications in environmental analysis: These include cloud-based air monitoring, noise and air pollution tracking, fire detection systems, early warning systems for earthquakes and tsunamis, and soil condition monitoring applications (Türkiye'nin Endüstri 4.0 Platformu 2025)

The "Smarter Planet" initiative, developed by IBM Research Laboratory, aims to minimize carbon emissions. Additionally, in Japan, another study conducted by Ibaraki University and Fukuyama Consulting involves monitoring the Earth's surface through wireless sensors and tags, allowing for the real-time collection of various data. This information is then used with the goal of preventing potential disasters (Dlodlo 2012).

In summary, the use of the Internet of Things (IoT) offers significant capabilities in various fields, including the collection, processing, and storage of environmental data such as temperature, pollution, heating, humidity, noise, and radiation. In addition, numerous sensors will be used to monitor volcanoes, seismic activity, and glaciers, enabling the system to issue automatic alerts in the event of an emergency

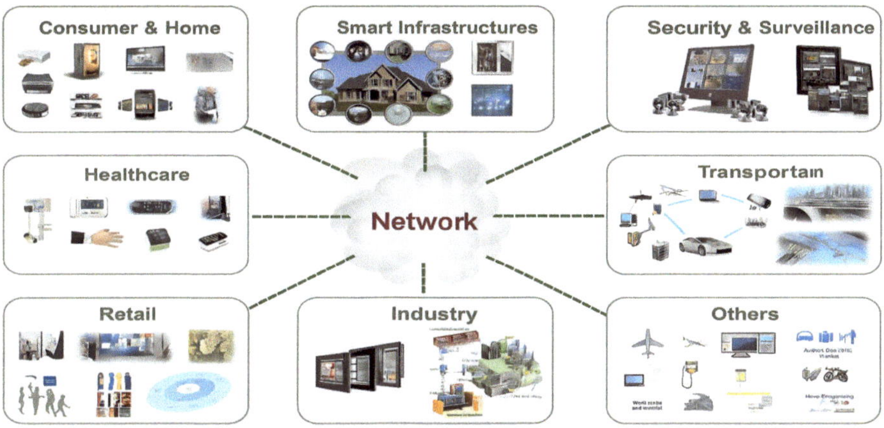

Fig. 10.5 Application Areas of the Internet of Things

(Cheng 2014). The various application areas of the Internet of Things are collectively illustrated in Fig. 10.5.

10.3 THE Role of the Internet of Things in Auditing

The Internet of Things (IoT) has also been described as the Internet of the future and defined as a network consisting of physical and virtual entities that are self-configuring, identifiable, and intelligent (Erturan and Ergin 2017). With IoT, self-managing and self-learning machines, along with real-time data-recording smart systems, are becoming part of our lives—developments that are expected to have a significant impact on the accounting system as well.

IoT-based devices and intelligent software allow for the continuous monitoring of financial transactions, automated detection of anomalies, and remote auditing capabilities, significantly transforming traditional accounting practices into a dynamic, data-driven environment. The evolution of smart businesses and intelligent systems has been summarized in Fig. 10.6 based on the data from our study.

As illustrated in the figure, the integration of interoperable and virtualized real-time systems introduces a new perspective in auditing practices.

10.3.1 Intelligent Auditing and the Use of Digital Twin Technology

The new process, which can be referred to as Audit 4.0, consists of components such as the Internet of Things (IoT), the Internet of Services, cyber-physical

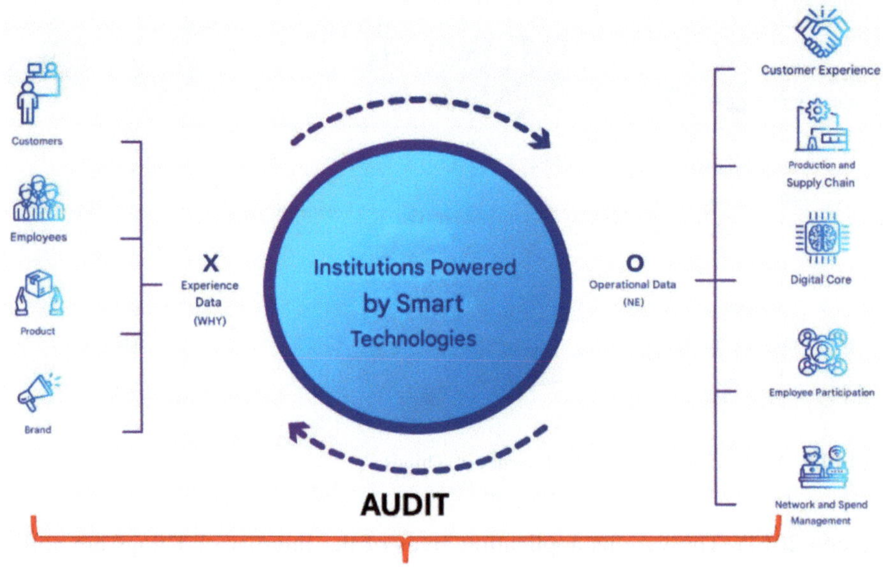

Fig. 10.6 Smart Businesses, Smart Systems

systems, and smart factories. In traditional accounting systems, it is relatively easier to process records and shape the audit process based on physical documents, compared to detecting potential issues within complex, technology-driven infrastructures. In such traditional systems, auditors can more directly trace and analyze irregularities through tangible records.

However, in digital environments, the auditor has no direct influence over processes, transactions, or outputs. As a result, the auditor's ability to leave audit trails is significantly hindered, making it more difficult to ensure transparency and accountability in highly automated and virtualized systems.

In this new dimension of auditing, there arises a need to redefine the role of the auditor.The definition of the auditor is provided in the studies on Digital Auditing and Digital Twin by Erturan and Ergin (2018) as follows (Erturan and Ergin 2018):

> *"Independent Auditor: Refers to an expert individual—or an audit firm composed of such individuals—who is unrelated to the company being audited, both in appearance and in fact independent, proficient in the use of technology, and capable of producing solutions in the face of increasing data volumes and complexity levels within enterprises.This auditor possesses the knowledge and ability to utilize technological tools throughout the audit process, employs virtual reality and other smart applications to understand the multi-dimensional nature of events that occur prior to financial statement preparation, and instead of relying on sampling during evidence collection, makes use of technological advancements that allow for observing the entirety of transactions.Such an auditor is able to obtain deeper and higher-quality insights through intelligent algorithms, and operates with zero-error precision, embodying all the necessary competencies of a modern, digital-age auditor."*

As can be understood from the definition, the auditor must possess the technical knowledge necessary to define the scope of the audit, determine its boundaries, reduce its duration, and access accurate and reliable information using a strong technological infrastructure. The auditor must firmly establish their role within this disruptive business model, as the auditing of such new systems will differ significantly from traditional approaches.

The journey of auditing, which once began with manual tools such as a basic calculator and paper-based methods, has now evolved into a process carried out using learning intelligent machines, sensors, and other smart technologies. Today's advanced systems have transformed Audit 1.0, which relied on pen, paper, and simple calculation tools, into an era of self-learning and self-designing intelligent machines. This evolutionary journey of auditing is summarized in Fig. 10.7 (Demirkol 2020).

In our world, which is transforming into a global neuro-network, everyone and everything will be connected through virtual links. The cloud technology currently in use (Singh, 2016) can be considered the beginning of this process. As we move toward smart planets, smart cities, and smart factories, accounting processes in businesses—from raw material procurement onwards—will be recorded at every stage with the help of intelligent systems, and errors will be easily detected by smart and learning systems. In intelligent systems, machine-to-machine (M2M) communication can occur, and within this technology, machine-to-human communication is also possible. Faced with these developments, the question of how auditing should be conducted and designed becomes inevitable.

The audit conducted with virtual assistants, using data accessed by the auditor in the office environment and uploaded by smart enterprises, can transform into smart auditing with a digital twin model, as shown in Fig. 10.7. Information collected from machines through sensors for every daily operation performed by businesses

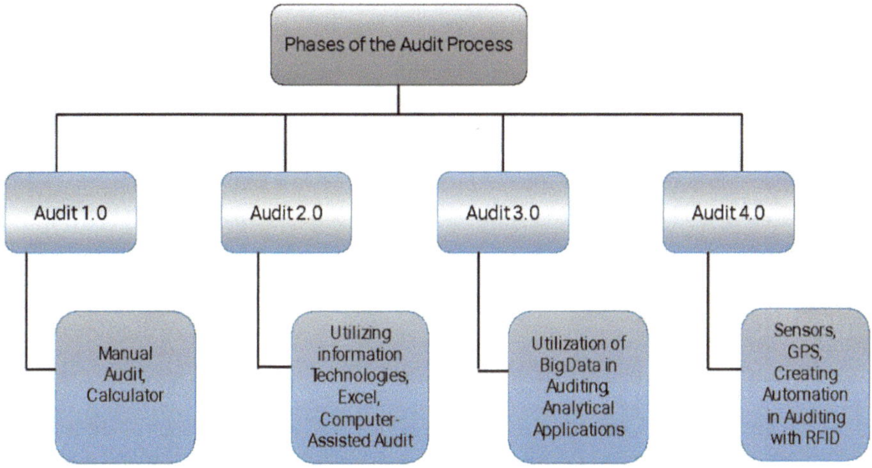

Fig. 10.7 Phases of the Audit Process. *Source* Demirkol, Ö.F., İkvan, A. (2020)

will be stored and prepared for processing. The collected data will be transformed into knowledge with the help of artificial intelligence and presented to the decision-maker. The auditor will have access to all the information needed during the audit process to form their judgment while in the office environment.

Smart Auditing will operate in real-time to achieve effective and efficient results, and to access accounting data uploaded to the system, it will perform data analysis, modeling, and visualization within big data containing yottabytes (YB)—$1{,}024^8$ or 81,208,925,819,614,629,174,706,176 bytes—to extract the correct information.

The smart enterprises and smart auditing processes are shaped in the model shown in Fig. 10.8, based on the work of Erturan and Ergin. The digital twin created by Erturan and Ergin (2018) can be described as the virtual representation or digital image of a smart enterprise in a virtual environment. Thanks to this representation, auditing the enterprise's digital twin in the virtual environment will require auditors who are more specialized and proficient in using technology.

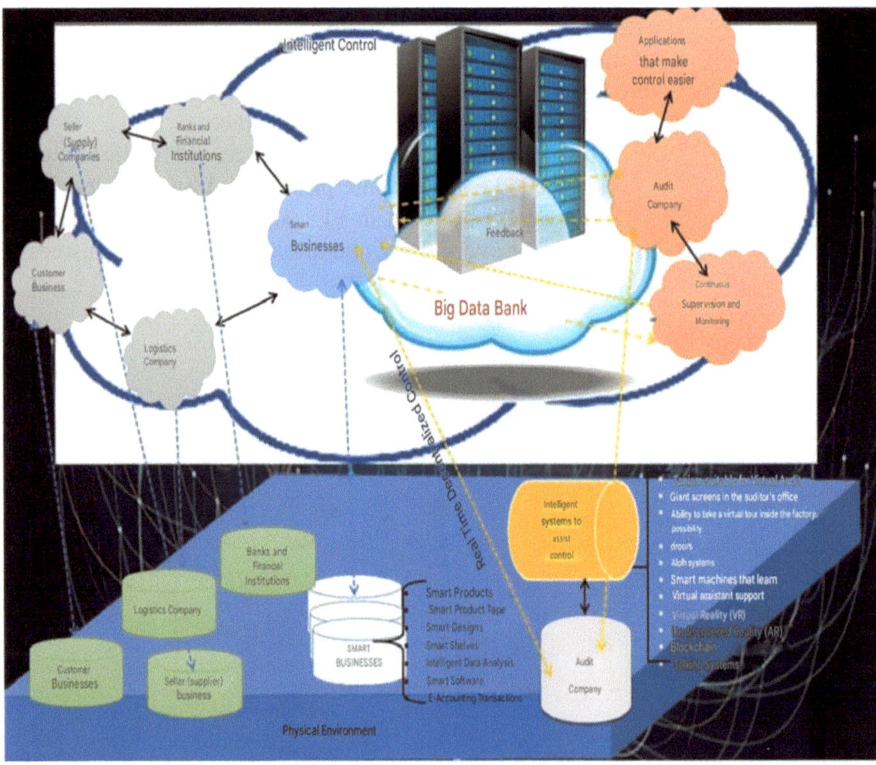

Fig. 10.8 Digital audit and digital twin application. *Source* Erturan, İ. Ve Ergin, E. (2018) by (Dai and Vasarhelyi 2017)

The digital auditing system uses data collection tools such as sensors, embedded computer systems (fiber optic systems), and software to gather data. Through the digital twin, every transaction occurring within the enterprise is uploaded to the cloud in real-time. In the cloud, there is diverse information uploaded from smart machines, enterprise ERP systems, customers, suppliers, public institutions, and banks.

If the customers, suppliers, logistics companies, and financial institutions that the enterprise communicates with also use smart systems, all data is collected in the big data repository (Erturan and Ergin 2018).

Continuous auditing will be possible through the information collected. In case of any issues in the system, these problems will be detected and easily resolved through intelligent systems. Preventive measures can be taken without incurring costs for information users, allowing problems to be solved proactively. One of the main challenges in this structure could be the absence of a standardized method for the uploaded data, which may cause difficulties for the auditor. To ensure healthy auditing, it is necessary to adapt international accounting and auditing standards to new technological developments, aiming to make the uploaded data reliable, consistent, and comparable (Erturan and Ergin 2018).

All transactions occurring in the physical environment will be uploaded in real time to the data cloud shown in Fig. 10.8. The physical environment and the digital twin will be integrated and operate in harmony. Internal and external auditors will access real-time data related to the audited enterprise in the big data pool through access codes and will be able to correct any errors in real time.

The integration of smart auditing systems into business processes offers significant advancements in efficiency, accuracy, and cost-effectiveness. As highlighted by Erturan and Ergin (2018), such systems reduce audit costs, alleviate the workload on auditors, and enhance the overall quality of the auditing process. By leveraging the enterprise's digital twin, smart auditing ensures secure data management and enables real-time monitoring and verification of transactions. This is achieved through interconnected technologies such as sensors, intelligent software, smart shelves, and automated product lines. Ultimately, smart auditing paves the way for a transformative approach to assurance services, aligning audit practices with the demands of Industry 4.0 and beyond.

This system will help reduce audit costs, reduce workload, and increase audit quality (Erturan and Ergin 2018). As a result, Smart audit will provide data security with the help of the business's digital twin application and will find a real-time data collection and auditing area with the help of systems such as sensors, smart computer software, smart shelves, smart product lines.

10.4 Conclusion

With the development of information technologies in our country, accounting applications have started to be done in an electronic environment and e-invoice, e-ledger, e-declaration, and e-reconciliation have started to be implemented by the Ministry of Finance (Tektüfekçi 2012). It would be appropriate to perform digital (virtual) auditing with the digital twin method for the accounting system that has started to be transferred to the virtual environment through these applications.

Some difficulties experienced during traditional auditing activities, transportation and labor costs to the company to be audited, auditing activities being carried out long after the company has completed its registration process, the time spent for verifications received from third parties, etc. (Erturan and Ergin 2018) can be solved with the digitalization of the auditing process and the digital twin model. The digital twin method will cause radical changes in the auditing field.

The digital twin method will prevent audit errors and fraud, as well as prevent tax evasion and the informal economy. In this system, the auditor will be able to instantly access the data in the digital environment and instantly determine the errors and fraud that occur. The auditor will be able to reach the company management very quickly, objectively, and reliably about the errors that occur. The dynamic structure of the audit process will create value for all information users.

This extraordinary and rapid transformation will change the perception of privacy and confidentiality that has entered our lives with the concept of ownership, and both society and businesses will begin to become more transparent. In the face of this impressive change, security measures other than those applied and a new perspective will be required. In this new transformation created by smart systems, the supervisor and the auditor should also take their place.

References

Agarwal RD (2011) Internet of things—A paradigm shift of future internet applications. In Eng (Nuicone) 1–7. https://doi.org/10.1109/NUiConE.2011.6153246

Akkuş S (2016) Nesnelerin interneti teknolojisinde güvenli veri iletişimi- programlanabilir fiziksel platformlararasında WEP algoritması ile kriptolu veri haberleşmesi uygulaması. Marmara Fen Bilimleri Dergisi 100–111. https://doi.org/10.7240/mufbed.73633

Arslan K, Kırbaş M (2016) Nesnelerin İnterneti Uygulamaları İçin Algılayıcı/Eyleyici Kablosuz Düğüm İlkörneği. Mehmet Akif Ersoy Üniversitesi Fen Bilimleri Enstitüsü Dergisi. 35–43. https://dergipark.org.tr/tr/download/article-file/227296

Ashton K (2009) That 'internet of things' thing. RFID J. https://www.rfidjournal.com/expert-views/that-internet-of-things-thing/73881/. Accessed 15 June 2025

Atzori L, Iera A, Morabito G (2010) The internet of things: a survey. Comput Netw 54(15):2787–2805. https://doi.org/10.1016/j.comnet.2010.05.010

Bandyopadhyay DV (2011) Internet of things: applications and challenges in technology and standardization. Wirel Pers Commun. 49–69

Borgia E (2014) The internet of things vision: key features, applications and open issues. Comput Commun 54:1–31. https://doi.org/10.1016/j.comcom.2014.09.008
Cheng YM (2014) Exploring the intention to use mobile learning: the moderating role of personal innovativeness. J Syst Inf Technol 40–61
Cisco. https://www.cisco.com/c/dam/en_us/about/ac79/docs/innov/IoT_IBSG_0411FINAL.pdf
Dai J, Vasarhelyi MA (2017) Toward blockchain-based accounting and assurance. J Inf Syst 31(3):5–21. https://doi.org/10.2308/isys-51804
Danneels E (2004) Disruptive technology reconsidered: a critique and research agenda. J Prod Innov Manag 246–258. https://doi.org/10.1111/j.0737-6782.2004.00076.x
Demirkol Öİ (2020) Denetimin Geleceği: Endüstri 4.0'ın Etkisinde Denetimin Yeniden Dizaynı. Muhasebe Ve Finans Araştırmaları Dergisi 55–72
Dlodlo NF (2012) The state of affairs in internet of things research
Erturan İE, Ergin E (2018) Dijital Denetim ve Dijital İkiz. Muhasebe Bilim Dünyası 810–820
Erturan İ, Ergin E (2017) Muhasebe Denetiminde Nesnelerin İnterneti: Stok Döngüsü. Muhasebe Ve Finansman Dergisi p. 15
Giusto D, Iera A (2010) The internet of things: 20th tyrrhenian workshop digit. p. 442
Gubbi J, Buyya R, Marusic S, Palaniswami M (2013) Internet of things (IoT): a vision, architectural elements, and future directions. Future Gener Comput Syst 29(7):1645–1660. https://doi.org/10.1016/j.future.2013.01.010
https://doi.org/10.1016/j.future.2013.01.010
https://tr.wikipedia.org/wiki/Nesnelerin_interneti
https://www.britannica.com/topic/ARPANET. https://www.britannica.com
https://www.prnewswire.com/news-releases/gsma-announces-that-the-proliferation-of-connected-devices-will-create-a-us12-trillion-revenue-opportunity-for-mobile
Kesayak, B. (2017). Nesnelerin İnterneti ve Endüstriyel Uygulamaları, http://www.endustri40.com/ nesnelerininterneti-ve-endustriyel-uygulamalari/ Accessed 24 December 2025
Lee I, Lee K (2015) The internet of things (IoT): applications, investments, and challenges for enterprises. Bus Horiz 431–440. https://doi.org/10.1016/j.bushor.2015.03.008
Madakam SR (2015) Internet of Things (IoT): a literature review.
Metallo CA (2018) Understanding business models in the internet of things industry. Technol Forecast Soc Change
Miorandi DS (2012) Internet of things: vision, applications and research challenges. Ad Hoc Netw 1497–1516. https://doi.org/10.1016/j.adhoc.2012.02.016
Rifkin J (2015) Nesnelerin İnterneti ve İşbirliği Çağı. Optimist, İstanbul
Rijmenam M, How the internet of things creates a smart world – infographic, Published: August 20, 2013. https://datafloq.com/read/internet-create-smart-world-infographic/. Accessed 15 Jun 2024
Singh J, Pasquier T, Bacon J, Ko H, Eyers D (2016) Twenty security considerations for cloud-supported internet of things. IEEE Internet Things J 3(3):269–284. June. https://doi.org/10.1109/JIOT.2015.2460333
Sun C (2012) Nesnelerin İnternetinde Lojistik için RFID teknolojisinin uygulanması. AASRI Prosedürü 106-111. https://doi.org/10.31590/ejosat.1004953
Tektüfekçi F (2012) Bilgi Teknolojilerinin Muhasebe Uygulamalarına Entegresyonu ve Bütünleşik Sistemlerle Olan Etkileşim. Organizasyon ve Yönetim Bilimleri pp. 51–59–4
Thibaud MC (2018) Internet of things (IoT) in high-risk environment, health and safety (EHS) industries. Decis Support Syst 79–95. https://doi.org/10.1016/j.dss.2018.02.005
Türkiye'nin Endüstri 4.0 Platformu (2025) Nesnelerin İnterneti ve Endüstriyel Uygulamaları. Accessed on 22 June 2025
Xu LD, He W, Li S (2014) Internet of things in industries: a survey. IEEE Trans Ind Inform 10(4):2233–2243. https://doi.org/10.1109/TII.2014.230075

Chapter 11
Application of Artificial Intelligence in the Independent Audit Process

Selçuk Gülten

Abstract Developments in the fields of computing, the internet, and software—such as Industry 4.0, big data, the Internet of Things, robotic technologies, cloud computing, machine learning, and artificial intelligence—have begun to demonstrate their effects on daily human life. This study is fundamentally based on the considerations regarding how technology may transform the auditing profession, alter the auditor's role, and influence the execution of audit activities as well as the application of audit techniques. Artificial intelligence can be addressed by auditors in two ways. The first is the audit of artificial intelligence, and the second is the use of artificial intelligence in the audit field. Artificial intelligence auditing is important in terms of who will be responsible for the mistakes made by the artificial intelligence software and the negative consequences it will cause. Considering that artificial intelligence is created by humans, the control of AI algorithms in terms of fraud, corruption, and abuse constitutes the core subject of auditing artificial intelligence. In the context of auditing with artificial intelligence, it is expected that many routine controls performed during independent audit engagements will be conducted by AI systems. It is anticipated that with the increase in the use of artificial intelligence agents, it will be possible for routine, boring tasks in independent audit studies to be performed by artificial intelligence, while independent auditors will be able to focus on other areas with audit risk. As a result, the aim of this study is to draw attention to the advantages as well as disadvantages that may arise from the increased use of artificial intelligence in independent audit studies.

This chapter was previously published in Turkish by Gazi Kitabevi with the ISBN: 978-975-7727-16-7.

S. Gülten (✉)
Project Independent Audit Joint Stock Company, Ankara, Türkiye
e-mail: selcukgulten2@hotmail.com

G. Kurt, Ö. Sarısoy (eds.), *Recent Advancements in Auditing*, Accounting, Finance, Sustainability, Governance & Fraud: Theory and Application,
https://doi.org/10.1007/978-981-95-5811-7_11

Keywords Artificial intelligence · External auditors · External auditors' perceptions · Audit quality

11.1 Introduction

Developments in the fields of computing, the internet, and software—such as Industry 4.0, big data, the Internet of Things, robotic technologies, cloud computing, machine learning, and artificial intelligence—have begun to demonstrate their effects on daily human life. Similarly, these technological advances also have both positive and negative impacts on various professions. While some professions are becoming obsolete due to technological progress, new occupations are also emerging. Even if not as striking as the emergence or disappearance of certain professions, the nature of some professions has undergone significant transformations. While robotic technologies are expected to replace human physical strength, artificial intelligence is anticipated to substitute human cognitive power. This study is fundamentally based on the considerations regarding how technology may transform the auditing profession, alter the auditor's role, and influence the execution of audit activities, as well as the application of audit techniques. Although the use of technology in independent auditing is not a new phenomenon, current technological advancements have reached a level that may lead to a paradigm shift.

Independent auditors have long been utilizing the opportunities brought by technology and various technological devices during the audit process. Technological tools such as computers, calculators, and independent audit software assist both audit institutions and independent auditors throughout the conduct of audit activities. In the use of these tools and software, the dominant factor continues to be the "human" and their professional knowledge. Regardless of the tools employed, the auditor's professional experience and educational background remain crucial for ensuring the quality of the independent audit. With the integration of artificial intelligence into independent auditing, the role of the "human" component in the audit process will shift, and the dominant element will become "artificial intelligence."

This paradigm shift results in a transformation of the focus of independent auditing. The independent auditor will assume the role of an individual who applies audit techniques, supervises the process, prepares the audit report, and monitors the functioning of artificial intelligence.

Can a computer software, even one equipped with artificial intelligence, perform all the tasks carried out by an independent auditor? Could audit processes be conducted entirely by artificial intelligence to an extent that may lead to the unemployment of auditors? Or will audit procedures that previously required considerable time be completed in a significantly shorter period through the use of artificial intelligence? Will the utilization of artificial intelligence enable auditors to dedicate more time to detecting errors and fraud, as well as conducting analytical review procedures? Undoubtedly, such questions can be further multiplied.

In audit processes, auditors should utilize the latest technological advancements in data analytics, machine learning, and artificial intelligence to conduct their audit work more rapidly and innovatively (Parida et al. 2017:55). There are certain critical issues that independent auditors must consider when it comes to the use of artificial intelligence technologies in independent audits. Artificial intelligence should be addressed by auditors in two distinct ways (Yildiz and Agdeniz 2019:98):

- Audit of artificial intelligence,
- Audit with artificial intelligence.

In the context of auditing artificial intelligence, it is important to consider who will be held responsible for the errors made by AI-powered software and the potential negative consequences it may cause. The risks associated with the use of artificial intelligence must also be evaluated during the audit process. Currently, there are no specific provisions regarding the audit of artificial intelligence within the independent auditing standards. Considering that artificial intelligence is created by humans, the control of AI algorithms in terms of fraud, corruption, and abuse constitutes the core subject of auditing artificial intelligence.

In the context of auditing with artificial intelligence, it is expected that many routine controls performed during independent audit engagements will be conducted by AI systems. The focus of artificial intelligence capabilities in auditing lies in the automation of labor-intensive tasks (Rapoport 2016). In this way, independent auditors will be able to concentrate on matters such as audit risks, audit evidence, and the analysis of data obtained during the audit process. While the human brain is subject to fatigue, forgetfulness, error, and confusion, the use of artificial intelligence in independent auditing introduces a significant cognitive aid to the auditor. Since records and documentation are maintained in digital environments and algorithms operate within the system, it becomes possible to conduct an audit with an enhanced level of assurance by utilizing support from artificial intelligence (Tas and Mert 2019:66).

11.2 Conceptual Framework Regardıng Artıfıcıal Intellıgence Technology

The structure of the human brain is complex, and claiming that all of its mysteries have been unraveled would be a highly ambitious assertion. While the human brain may take a few minutes to perform numerical calculations, it is capable of comprehending events intended for perception in a very short amount of time (Elmas 2018:25). The public perception of artificial intelligence can be summarized by the following statement: “Computers, machines, and/or robots will reach and even surpass human intelligence" (Doğan 2020:52). Artificial intelligence has become a commonly used term in our daily lives, even in contexts such as cinema and theatre. However, there is no universally accepted definition of artificial intelligence. This is due to the fact that artificial intelligence encompasses a broad range of disciplinary fields and maintains interactions with them (Allahverdi 2002:2). The discipline of artificial intelligence is an official discipline founded in 1956, based on the foundations of philosophy, mathematics, psychology, linguistics and computer science (McCorduck 1977:953).

Artificial intelligence has emerged as a result of humanity's efforts to understand its own intelligence and to model a similar form on electronic machines (Aydın 2013:3). Artificial intelligence refers to the ability to endow a computer or a machine with human-like capabilities such as reasoning, inference, generalization, and learning from past experiences, in order to replicate human intelligence (Yilmaz 2019:1). In these definitions, the process of enabling a machine to think constitutes the foundation of artificial intelligence. If one were to formulate artificial intelligence, it could be expressed as: "Thinking Machine = Artificial Intelligence."

Artificial intelligence is the general term for the technology that involves the development of machines capable of exhibiting human-like behaviors and actions, created entirely through artificial means without the use of any living organism (Aydın and Değirmenci 2018:19). In short, artificial intelligence is intelligence that exists within non-organic systems (Avuclu 2019:32). These definitions emphasize the "artificial" nature of artificial intelligence by highlighting that it is non-living and non-organic.

One of the cornerstones in the history of computers and artificial intelligence is the article titled *"Computing Machinery and Intelligence,"* written by the renowned British mathematician Alan M. Turing in 1950 and published in the journal *Mind*. This article is considered one of the earliest and most famous publications in the field of artificial intelligence (Yilmaz 2009:21). The "Turing Test," introduced in this article, holds significance in terms of measuring artificial intelligence. The test can be described as follows: Two closed (visually opaque) rooms or booths are used—one contains a human, and the other contains a computer equipped with artificial intelligence software. The critical component is the set of questions posed by a third party who does not know which room contains the machine and which contains the human. If this individual, despite being allowed to ask any questions freely, cannot determine from the responses which room contains the human, the computer is said to possess artificial intelligence. In other words, if the machine with artificial intelligence is able to provide responses that closely resemble those of a human and can convince the interrogator, it is considered to have achieved the goal of creating artificial intelligence. If, as a result of the test, the interrogator is unable to conclusively identify the human based on the responses, the machine is deemed to have passed the Turing Test (Kurkcu 2019:89). In such a case, according to Turing, the machine should be regarded as having acquired the ability to think and to imitate human intelligence.

11.3 Objections to the Concept of Artificial Intelligence

There are various objections raised concerning the concept of artificial intelligence. When artificial intelligence is briefly defined as a thinking machine, a counter-argument emerges claiming that machines cannot think, and therefore artificial intelligence can never truly exist. Turing not only envisioned that computers could imitate all human cognitive activities but also foresaw that people would find it difficult to accept that computers are capable of thinking (Say 2019:83). A second notable feature of Turing's article was its engagement with arguments that could be posed against the possibility of achieving intelligent computers (Nilsson 2019:67–68). These objections include:

- **Religious Objections**: Since God gave a soul to humans, only humans can think. Machines, having no soul, cannot think.
- **Head-in-the-Sand Objection**: Artificial intelligence will bring about the end of humanity; therefore, AI research should be halted.
- **Mathematical Objections**: Due to logical and probabilistic limitations, the capacity of machines will always remain constrained.
- **Objection from Consciousness**: Machines cannot possess emotions and thus cannot possess thoughts.
- **Objections Based on Various Inadequacies**: Since humans themselves cannot have complete knowledge in all fields, progress with AI will be limited to specific and narrow domains.
- **Lady Lovelace's Objection**: Machines do not act independently; rather, they operate within the boundaries set by humans and in accordance with their programming.
- **Biological Objections**: Since machines lack nervous systems and sensory organs, they cannot perform the act of thinking.
- **Objection Based on the Randomness of Behavior**: Even humans can hold different thoughts on the same issue; therefore, a universal and consistent model of thought cannot exist.
- **Extrasensory Perception Objections**: Humans sometimes act based on unexplained extrasensory perceptions such as intuition, premonition, or gut feeling—abilities that machines cannot possess.

John Searle put forward a well-known and influential argument in this area known as the **"Chinese Room Argument."** In this thought experiment, it is assumed that there is a person inside a room who does not know the Chinese language. Questions written in Chinese are submitted through a slot in the door. This person follows instructions, procedures, and catalogues available in the room to produce appropriate responses, finding the best answer in a very short time. The answer is then passed out through another slot. Searle argues that although this person provides correct answers to every Chinese question, he still does not understand Chinese. Likewise, even if computers—equipped with artificial intelligence—are able to provide correct responses, they must operate within a framework of programming and code. This leads to the objection that, rather than truly thinking, computers are simply producing outputs that conform to predetermined algorithms.

11.4 Fields of Application and Operation of Artificial Intelligence

Artificial intelligence is currently being used in numerous fields such as banking, insurance, healthcare, retail shopping, military, security, voice recognition, natural language processing, and image processing, and its usage continues to expand day by day (Aydemir 2018:29). Particularly in recent years, it is an undeniable fact that artificial intelligence has been increasingly used in financial analyses and decision-making processes due to many of its prominent features (Cavdar 2018:19).

The fields of operation and the types of problems artificial intelligence addresses can be classified into the following major categories (Nabiyev 2016:61–62):

- Problem solving
- Game modeling
- Knowledge representation
- Theorem proving
- Expert systems
- Natural language processing
- Visual and auditory object (pattern) recognition
- Robotics (reasoning and motion)
- Fuzzy logic
- Genetic algorithms

Artificial intelligence has made significant progress in areas such as image recognition, voice recognition, voice-based responses, chatbot software, and language translation. Furthermore, it is known that AI applications, particularly those categorized as narrow or specific AI, have reached a level where they can defeat expert players in domains like chess and the game of Go. However, applications of what can be termed general artificial intelligence remain quite limited. If general artificial intelligence were to be compared to the developmental stages of a human being, it would still be considered in its infancy.

11.5 Operational Logic of Artificial Intelligence Technology

At the core of artificial intelligence technologies lie two fundamental components: artificial neural networks and the concept of machine learning. Without a full understanding of these two concepts, drawing conclusions or making assessments about artificial intelligence may lead to incorrect outcomes. Artificial neural networks are computer systems developed with the aim of automatically performing, without external assistance, cognitive functions characteristic of the human brain, such as deriving new knowledge through learning, generating new information, and discovering new patterns (Namli 2012:49).

An artificial neural network is a hierarchical organization of numerous interconnected artificial neurons arranged in parallel (Aleksandr and Norton 1995:1). Algorithms form the foundation of software and are analytical frameworks that direct the computer step-by-step on what processes to perform, effectively schematizing the workflow. Instead of executing a predefined step-by-step method as in traditional programming, a neural network generates its own internal associative rules and refines them by comparing outcomes with sample results (Fauset 1994:2). With artificial neural network technology, a departure from classical software algorithms has occurred, and the neural structures, neurons, and synapses of the human brain are now being emulated. The structures formed by artificial cells and their associated layers are linked to the external environment with the purpose of receiving inputs and transmitting outputs (Sahin 2020:9). Artificial neural networks are composed of a layered structure, which includes the following:

(a) **Input Layer:** This is the layer that receives input data from the external environment and transmits it to the hidden layer in artificial neural networks. The information and input values acquired through this layer are transferred to the next layer without being subjected to any processing.
(b) **Hidden Layer:** In this layer, the input values are processed and weighted according to the defined network structure, and correct answers or accurate results are determined. It is possible for the network to include multiple hidden layers.
(c) **Output Layer:** This layer presents the output that corresponds to the result processed and identified in the hidden layer, originally received from the input layer.
(d) The operation of these layers described above can also be illustrated through a diagram:

It is also possible to express the figure above in mathematical terms. In this case, it is necessary to define the meaning of the symbols used:

- **Xi**, (i = 0, 1, 2, ... n): Represents the input values
- **Wi**: Denotes the i–th weight. As shown in Fig. 11.1, there are four input values.
- **Wi**: Represents the i–th weight; it can be evaluated in conjunction with the concept of learning in artificial neural networks.
- **Yi**: Represents the output value.
- **g(.)**: Denotes the summation function.
- **Wij**: Represents the connection weights.
- **Qij**: Refers to the threshold value for the i–th neuron.

McCulloch and Pitts expressed a simple mathematical model of the artificial neural network in 1943 as follows:

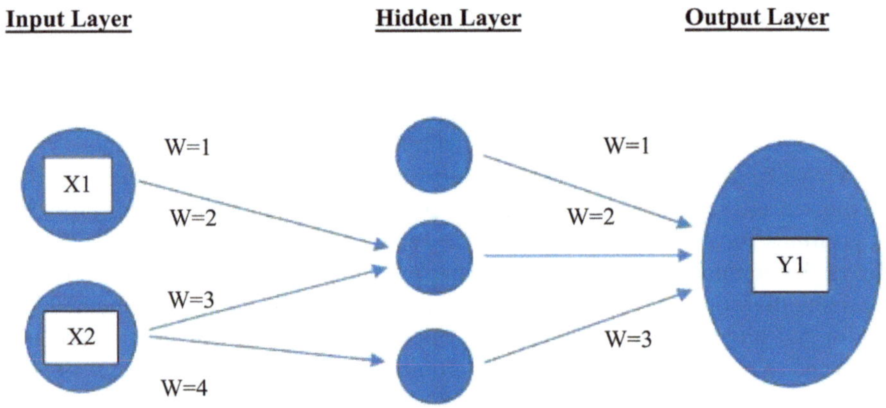

Fig. 11.1 A simple artificial neural network Model. *Source* Adapted from *the above-mentioned work Sahin* (2020:10)

$$Yi. = \psi(\mathrm{g}(\chi)) = \Psi(\Sigma\ WijXi - \mathrm{Qi})$$
$$\psi(.) = 1; \mathrm{g}(.) > 0$$
$$0; \mathrm{g}(.) < 0$$
$$\mathrm{g}(.) = \Sigma\ WijXj - \mathrm{Q}_1$$

In the McCulloch-Pitts model, only the unit step function is used as the transfer function, and a linear function is used as the summation function. However, with the advancements in artificial neural networks today, various other functions can also be utilized (Yurtoglu 2005:17). The increase in the number of layers in the neural network model has resulted from the growth in data sets as well as in the computing power and memory capacity available to process such data (Isik 2019:16). In current applications, a distinction is frequently made between feedforward and feedback (recurrent) artificial neural networks. Although the mathematical modeling in all these neural network types remains fundamentally the same, they do exhibit certain differences.

Today, artificial neural networks—widely applied across numerous fields—possess several important characteristics, which can be listed as follows (Oztemel 2012:31–33):

(a) In artificial neural network technology, machine learning can be achieved through the use of previous examples.
(b) The operational principles of programs implementing artificial neural networks differ significantly from those of conventional software.
(c) For artificial neural networks to operate reliably, they must first be trained and their performance must be tested.

(d) Artificial neural networks can generate information about previously unseen examples.
(e) Artificial neural networks can be used in perception-related tasks; they are capable of pattern association and classification.
(f) Artificial neural networks possess the ability to self-organize and to learn autonomously.
(g) Artificial neural networks are fault-tolerant and can process uncertain or incomplete information.
(h) In artificial neural networks, information is stored within the connections (links) between units.
(i) Additionally, artificial neural networks exhibit graceful degradation, operate with distributed memory, and can only process numerical data.

The significant increase in the volume of data has made analyses conducted manually by humans both costly and time-consuming. In such analyses, the use of computers results in cost reduction and time savings. In order to make predictions about the future using historical data, new methods have been developed, leading to the emergence of the concept of machine learning. Machine learning is a scientific discipline that aims to equip computers with the ability to learn without relying on a program specifically designed for a particular situation, and it primarily draws upon statistics and information technologies (Samuel 2000:206).

The concept of deep learning, when generalized based on definitions in the literature, can be described as machine learning algorithms that possess capabilities similar to those of the human brain—such as analyzing, examining, learning, and decision-making in the face of complex problems—and that can perform feature extraction and classification, either in a supervised or unsupervised manner, by utilizing large volumes of data (Ari 2019:49).

Based on the training methodology and the characteristic structure of the dataset, machine learning is divided into three main categories (Canepa 2016:4):

Supervised Learning: In supervised learning, the machine is trained using selected datasets. In this way, the machine learns and understands the relationships between inputs and outputs that have been predefined and can be considered as examples. The objective in this category is to make predictions or reach classification decisions based on pre-labeled datasets (Russell and Norvig 2003:650).

Unsupervised Learning: In unsupervised learning, the machine is trained using random, non-selected datasets. Through this learning method, the machine autonomously groups the data and organizes them into various clusters. The accuracy of the results is evaluated based on how well each unit resembles the group to which it has been assigned and how distinct it is from other groups (Berry and Linoff 2004:57).

Reinforcement Learning: In reinforcement learning, the machine is trained using random, non-selected datasets. Unlike unsupervised learning, this method operates on a reward-punishment principle. During the learning process, if the outcome of a selected action is positive, that choice is marked with a high score; conversely, if the outcome is negative, the choice is assigned a low score (Kaelbling et al. 1996:238–240).

Applied research in the use of artificial intelligence technologies to address individual auditing tasks necessitates the development of a new scientific research process. In the near future, there may be a need for artificial intelligence systems to function as machine instructors in the field of independent auditing, while also maintaining a continued demand for the expertise of independent auditors.

11.6 The Concept of Independent Auditing

Also known as external auditing, independent auditing is defined as the evaluation of a company's financial statements and other financial information—prepared as a result of its economic activities—with respect to their accuracy and compliance with predetermined criteria, by applying the necessary independent auditing techniques specified in independent auditing standards and by obtaining sufficient and appropriate audit evidence through the examination of books, records, and documents, with the results ultimately compiled into an audit report (Selimoglu 2008:4).

In this context, auditing is a systematic process of objectively collecting and evaluating evidence to determine whether assertions related to economic activities and events comply with predefined criteria, and to communicate the results to interested parties (Yakar 2015:252).

The following are some fundamental elements included in the definition of independent auditing (Saglam and others 2020:14–16):

(a) Auditing is a process.
(b) It examines assertions related to economic activities and events.
(c) Audit activities are conducted for a specific entity or time period.
(d) The audited information is compared with predetermined criteria.
(e) The degree of compliance is assessed.
(f) Evidence related to the subject matter of the audit is collected and evaluated.
(g) Audit work is carried out by qualified, impartial, and experienced professionals.
(h) The opinion resulting from the audit process is presented in the form of a report.

Independent auditing aims to increase the reliability of financial information by examining the impact of such events on financial data and business operations (Kavut 2001:2).

11.7 The Effects of Artıfıcıal Intellıgence on the Fıeld of Independent Audıtıng

Operationally, artificial intelligence can be defined as a hybrid set of technologies that complements and transforms the audit process (Issa et al. 2016:14). Organizations in the independent auditing sector have begun to consider whether they need artificial intelligence in their services, how they can integrate it, and what it might mean for the future of their profession. The potential benefits of using artificial intelligence in the field of independent auditing can be listed as follows:

(a) Enhancing overall success and quality in independent auditing,
(b) Increasing the effectiveness, speed, and efficiency of audit procedures,
(c) Enabling the application of advanced auditing techniques and statistical methods,
(d) Providing convenience in conducting logical and mathematical analyses,
(e) Reducing errors during the implementation of auditing techniques,
(f) Easily carrying out routine tasks and calculations performed by independent auditors,
(g) Facilitating procedures such as the collection of audit evidence and recalculations,
(h) Performing time-consuming tasks rapidly, thereby allowing independent auditors to focus on other responsibilities during the audit process (in other words, enabling professional auditor skills to be concentrated on higher value-added audit tasks),
(i) Facilitating the coordination of independent audit processes,
(j) Since artificial intelligence technologies will be designed to enhance the level of trust in the independent auditor's report, they will also contribute to improving the auditor's professional reputation.

While the applications and benefits of artificial intelligence continue to emerge within the auditing profession, there is also a gradual realization that undesirable consequences may arise (Munuko et al. 2020:2). Just as artificial intelligence has its advantages, it also comes with disadvantages. These can be listed as follows:

(a) The maintenance and repair of artificial intelligence software are costly. Additionally, AI algorithms may require periodic updates, which in turn incur extra expenses.
(b) In independent auditing, there is no guarantee that artificial intelligence will act in accordance with ethical principles and moral values. In cases of malicious interventions—such as those by hackers—issues of responsibility become particularly significant.
(c) Independent auditors gain experience over time based on the events they encounter during their work. Artificial intelligence, however, cannot acquire experience in the same way.
(d) Independent auditors may act with emotions such as dedication, commitment to their profession, and a sense of belonging. By contrast, as noted in various objections to AI, such emotions will not exist in AI-based audit software.
(e) The difficulty in ensuring transparency and interpretability of AI algorithms may create an environment susceptible to manipulation of the results obtained.

(f) It is also suggested that artificial intelligence will not demonstrate flexibility in auditing and may exhibit "overly perfect" behavior, which in itself could have negative implications when dealing with complex or nuanced audit situations.
(g) Blindly accepting the calculations or reports generated by artificial intelligence could undermine trust in independent auditors, especially in cases involving AI malfunctions or incorrect training.

As with any emerging technology, time will reveal what artificial intelligence applications will bring to the field of independent auditing. In addition to the advantages and disadvantages listed above, new developments may also emerge. The answer to the question, *"Can artificial intelligence be used in independent auditing?"*, lies in the Turing Test. If an AI-powered software can perform independent audit processes as effectively as a human expert in the field, then artificial intelligence can be considered as being used in independent auditing.

Among independent audit practitioners, discussions continue regarding how to establish trust in the opinion of an AI auditor performing the functions of a human auditor, what changes might be needed in auditors' professional qualifications and auditing standards, and how AI auditors will adapt to such changes.

Since independent auditing is a process based on data, information, and evidence, the transfer of certain routine audit processes, audit tasks, and audit techniques to computer environments is relatively easy. This inherent nature of auditing provides a positive motivation for the integration of artificial intelligence into the process (Baldwin et al. 2006: 79)

Some of these tasks and the artificial intelligence technologies used are listed below (Baldwin et al. 2006: 80–81; Koskivaara 2003:18; Ramamoorti et al. 1999:159):

(a) Detection of material misstatements (Artificial Neural Networks).
(b) Detection of management fraud (Artificial Neural Networks, Genetic Algorithms, Fuzzy Logic).
(c) Assessment of internal control risk (Artificial Neural Networks, Expert Systems).
(d) Determination of audit fees (Artificial Neural Networks).
(e) Detection of financial problems (Artificial Neural Networks).
(f) Analytical review procedures (Artificial Neural Networks).
(g) Bankruptcy prediction (Artificial Neural Networks).
(h) Collection of audit evidence (Artificial Neural Networks, Expert Systems).
(i) Classification processes (Genetic Algorithms).
(j) Materiality assessments (Expert Systems).
(k) Internal auditing (Artificial Neural Networks, Expert Systems, Fuzzy Logic).

With ongoing developments in software and information technologies, and the advances in artificial intelligence, it is possible to further expand the scope of the areas listed above.

11.8 Areas of Application of Artificial Intelligence in Independent Auditing

Compared to other industries, the auditing sector has the potential to adopt artificial intelligence at an earlier stage. The use of computers to perform accounting operations has made the use of computers in independent auditing widespread, and to some extent, even essential. Since the beginning of 2020, artificial intelligence and digitalization practices have also come to be seen as tools in supporting the fight against the global Covid-19 pandemic. At the same time, the audit industry is recognizing the benefits of using artificial intelligence to process large volumes of data and to identify patterns and anomalies within them. In auditing, artificial intelligence utilizes advanced techniques from the fields of mathematics, statistics, and software engineering to analyze data found in accounting ledgers, trial balances, and financial statements, to detect inconsistencies, if any, and to identify audit risks.

Since it has previously been stated that independent auditing provides reasonable assurance, this concept can also be evaluated in terms of artificial intelligence. Artificial intelligence automates many tasks previously carried out manually by independent auditors—such as data entry and recalculation—and can analyze 100% of the data that constitutes the audit universe during audit testing. What distinguishes the "audit of the future" from classical independent auditing is the capacity of artificial intelligence to redefine the notion of reasonable assurance. AI can comprehend the entirety of data, accounting records, financial transactions, and all account items that constitute financial statements, and it can identify all anomalies beyond the prescribed rules. It can be argued that risk-based programming of artificial intelligence applications is easier to implement. However, it is also possible to train artificial intelligence to audit all transactions and detect red flags accordingly.

Data collection and the gathering of audit evidence lie at the core of the auditing process. By using artificial intelligence, the processes of data acquisition and data processing can be automated and simplified. This can relieve independent auditors from time-consuming tasks such as locating necessary data, extracting information from large volumes of documents, and converting that data into analyzable formats. With the integration of artificial intelligence technologies, the evolution of auditing is gradually moving toward the verification of 100% of the entire data set rather than relying on sampling. Therefore, it can be stated that artificial intelligence will have a significant impact on the shift from sample-based auditing to full-population auditing in independent audit practices.

During the audit planning phase, activities are carried out such as client acceptance and planning of the initial audit, obtaining information about the client and its industry, assessing client risk, applying preliminary analytical review procedures, forming materiality judgments, determining and evaluating the level of audit risk, gathering information related to fraud risk, understanding internal control and assessing control risk, designing the audit programs, creating the audit schedule and timing, and planning workforce requirements, among others (Guredin 2010:

184–197). It is evident that artificial intelligence can be highly beneficial in the calculation of independent audit risk and in the creation of audit plans. The risk level assigned to each account in the financial statements, based on its materiality, directly influences the nature, timing, and extent of audit procedures. The sum of the individual risks associated with each account item determines the overall audit risk (Bozkurt 2010: 105).An incorrect opinion issued as a result of independent auditing may lead to both financial and reputational losses for the audit firm (Millichamp and Taylor 2008: 12). Artificial intelligence can be effectively utilized in managing audit risks and in developing appropriate responses to those risks.

One of the most important characteristics of an independent auditor is professional skepticism. In all audit engagements, the independent auditor operates with professional skepticism under the assumption that the financial statements, documents, information, and records may contain misstatements or may not reflect the truth. The independent auditor may further scrutinize any documents, information, records, or account items that raise suspicion. As stated in the objections to artificial intelligence, since AI does not possess human emotions such as "skepticism," the concept of "professional skepticism" must be approached from a different perspective when applied to artificial intelligence. Through professional skepticism, an independent auditor examines specific portions of the dataset composed of documents, information, records, and account balances in greater detail. However, artificial intelligence is capable of analyzing 100% of this dataset in the same detailed manner, but more rapidly and without the risk of error. AI can apply independent auditing techniques, analytical procedures, and statistical methods uniformly to the entire dataset, without distinguishing between any of the data elements. In certain situations, an independent auditor may not be able to fully apply professional skepticism as required (Arslan 2018:125.).

(a) The presence of incentives and pressures inherent in the audit environment,
(b) Time constraints,
(c) Workload intensity,
(d) Excessive reliance on the management of the audited company.

The negative factors mentioned above—such as reward and punishment expectations, time constraints, heavy workloads, and excessive trust—which may hinder the application of professional skepticism, do not have any effect on artificial intelligence. Since AI is not subject to such human weaknesses, it can be argued that artificial intelligence may, in a sense, apply professional skepticism more effectively. The main types of threats to auditor independence, as outlined in the IFAC Code of Ethics for Professional Accountants, are as follows (Uzay 2004:3):

(a) Self-interest threat
(b) Self-review threat
(c) Advocacy threat
(d) Familiarity and trust threat
(e) Intimidation threat

Since 2018, in line with international developments, a "key audit matters" section has been added to independent audit reports in Turkiye. The inclusion of key audit matters was introduced with the expectation by relevant authorities that "more and significant information regarding the audit" would be disclosed (Sarisoy 2018:67). During independent audit engagements, artificial intelligence may identify areas with the highest volume of calculations or the greatest deviations in audit evidence—based on materiality thresholds—and include these as key audit matters in the independent auditor's report. Moreover, the "key audit matters" section found in independent audit reports prepared in Turkiye could be drafted by artificial intelligence using machine learning techniques, potentially with the same level of proficiency as a human independent auditor.

Artificial intelligence will assist independent auditors in moving away from traditional audit processes and toward visualizing and assessing a complete picture of the entity, allowing them to focus on audit risks and critical audit evidence. Datasets are the raw material for artificial intelligence algorithms used to make decisions, identify audit risks, and detect anomalies. As independent auditors examine the foundation of future AI systems, they will also need to focus specifically on data-related issues, particularly data anomalies.

Rapid access to information enables independent auditors to make strategic decisions regarding the audit process, which makes accurate and reliable data processing critically important. Audit firms are attempting to adapt to this new field of information technology by utilizing artificial intelligence in auditing, thereby aiming to gain competitive advantages in both global and local service markets. From planning to the formation of an opinion in the auditor's report, artificial intelligence technologies can be used to execute cognitive processes and support decision-making throughout all stages of the audit. Furthermore, AI can generate judgment-based hypotheses, collect diverse data—including from unstructured information sources—analyze large volumes of data, visualize the results of such analyses, and evaluate the audit evidence collected.

11.9 The Connection Between Artificial Intelligence and Audit Techniques

Audit techniques refer to the comprehensive set of methods, techniques, and audit work programs that demonstrate the detailed steps to be followed during the audit in order to collect and evaluate audit evidence (Fido 2016:58). The techniques that an auditor may use to gather audit evidence include (Aksoy 2006:377):

a. Physical inspection and inventory counting techniques,
b. Confirmation technique,
c. Recalculation technique,
d. Scanning technique,
e. Inquiry technique,

f. Document inspection technique,
g. Re-examination of the record-keeping system,
h. In-depth investigation of unusual transactions,
i. Correlation and comparison between related accounts,
j. Revision technique,
k. Analytical review technique.

Artificial intelligence can make use of physical inspection and inventory techniques. Its ability to analyze various types of data from images to audio may lead to the emergence of new audit evidence collection methods. Rather than focusing solely on the limited information provided by financial statements, auditors will be able to utilize data from social networks, video recordings, captured images, sensor data (e.g., GPS location information), and text sources, and can integrate extracted features (Issa et al. 2016:15).

Within the scope of visual recognition technologies, artificial intelligence can detect objects and locations, assign them to user-defined categories, perform inventory tracking and stock counting, and identify fraud related to asset misuse. The visual recognition capabilities of AI—through surveillance footage, drone images, facial recognition, and sensor detection—assist independent auditors in interpreting content based on a wide range of visual inputs.

Artificial intelligence is capable of performing tasks related to audit techniques such as preparing confirmation letters, executing account reconciliations, analyzing responses, generating comparison tables, and evaluating discrepancies based on materiality levels during the confirmation procedures.

Within seconds, AI can apply the recalculation technique to reprocess payroll calculations, depreciation expenses, provisions, and legal reserves—this functionality is considered a routine feature. Furthermore, artificial intelligence can compare the recalculated figures with the data obtained from the entity subject to independent audit and analyze the differences that arise from this comparison.

The scanning technique is not among the methods that artificial intelligence is required to use. Rather than examining a limited sample selected through statistical or judgmental methods, AI analyzes the entire dataset. Therefore, artificial intelligence does not need to scan portions of the audit universe to select specific sections for review.

The inquiry technique, however, can be applied by artificial intelligence. By utilizing image processing technologies, AI can detect from facial and eye movements whether the respondent's answer is truthful. It can also apply techniques such as natural language processing and cross-examination to obtain critical audit evidence. As with the Turing Test, the interviewee may not even realize that they are interacting with an artificial intelligence system.

Artificial intelligence can examine all documents of the audited entity by using image and document processing techniques. Moreover, it is not limited to reviewing documents such as invoices or delivery notes; it can also analyze related materials such as email correspondence, fax messages, contracts, purchase orders, internal communications, and board resolutions. By comparing the information it extracts, AI can identify inconsistencies between data sources, analyze these discrepancies, and report the results.

Artificial intelligence can review all entries in accounting ledgers, from the first to the final transaction. In doing so, it can test the consistency between various ledgers and verify whether the accounts presented in the trial balances and financial statements align with the underlying ledger entries. In cases where physical ledgers are used, they must be scanned and uploaded into the AI software; for electronic ledgers, the data must be provided to the system in digital format.

Artificial intelligence–based audit procedures are grounded not in the in-depth examination of only extraordinary transactions, but rather in the thorough analysis of all transactions. AI is capable of completing transaction reviews and analyses in a significantly shorter period of time. Artificial intelligence can also visualize the audit procedures it conducts, the conclusions it reaches, and the data extracted from records and ledgers by applying the technique of establishing relationships and performing comparisons between relevant accounts.

Analytical procedures based on artificial intelligence technologies can provide rapid (almost instantaneous) identification of individual transaction sets that include prices deviating from the average or values significantly diverging from a specific threshold. Artificial intelligence is also capable of identifying relationships among the indicators of audited entities, based on similarities in their nature and scope of operations.

11.10 Comparison Between Artificial Intelligence and the Independent Auditor

Based on various studies comparing computers with humans and natural intelligence with artificial intelligence, it is possible to compare artificial intelligence and the independent auditor across several key characteristics:

(a) An independent auditor acquires the knowledge and skills required for professional expertise through formal university education, followed by stages such as internships and exams—achieved only after years of effort and dedication. In contrast, for artificial intelligence, a few minutes of data transfer in a magnetic medium and/or a brief machine learning process may be sufficient to acquire the same level of expertise.

(b) Artificial intelligence does not get tired, sick, distracted, or affected by personal problems during its operations; it does not act out of emotions such as jealousy or anger. Compared to an independent auditor, AI works continuously and consistently. An independent auditor may resign, transfer to another audit firm, or go on strike. However, artificial intelligence does not resign, transfer, or strike.

(c) Artificial intelligence can explain in detail the audit techniques it applies, the audit evidence it gathers, and the statistical methods it uses throughout the audit process. In contrast, even documenting such elements adequately in working papers may sometimes pose challenges for independent auditors.
(d) In critical and/or emergency situations, artificial intelligence can make the most accurate decisions without being influenced by the circumstances. An independent auditor, on the other hand, may fail to make sound judgments due to stress or other external factors. The absence of emotional influence, stress, or inefficiency in artificial intelligence reduces the likelihood of errors and enables the generation of more accurate results.
(e) Artificial intelligence can produce more consistent and reproducible results than an independent auditor, in other words, a human expert. It has been observed that an independent auditor may sometimes make different decisions for similar situations due to emotional factors or various other reasons.
(f) Artificial intelligence, as a system, can share all the knowledge it possesses regarding the solution to a problem completely and transparently, much like an intellectual instructor. In contrast, an independent auditor may, for various reasons, demonstrate reluctance to share information.
(g) In certain specialized areas, the limited number of independent auditors may lead to an increase in audit fees, sometimes to excessively high levels. However, an artificial intelligence system capable of performing multiple functions simultaneously can quickly recoup its cost, delivering a return on investment in a short period of time.
(h) Compared to an independent auditor, artificial intelligence can reach solutions more quickly, with greater clarity, flexibility, and accuracy. It can also provide detailed explanations accurately and without omission that an independent auditor may not always be able to deliver.
(i) Artificial intelligence possesses continuous and consistent knowledge and expertise. In contrast, the expertise and performance of an independent auditor may decline over time. To maintain their proficiency in their area of specialization, independent auditors must engage in ongoing professional education and continuous practice.
(j) Moreover, with today's technology, the expert knowledge possessed by artificial intelligence can be reused in other tasks and transferred to different domains.
(k) During independent audit engagements, artificial intelligence is not required to perform sampling like a human auditor. It is capable of examining the entire audit dataset in a short period of time.
(l) Artificial intelligence obtains independent audit evidence objectively, without bias or any personal or emotional reaction toward the audited entity.

The comparisons outlined above are generally sufficient; however, it is possible to expand them by adding new aspects.

11.11 The Impact of Artificial Intelligence on the Quality of Independent Auditing

The audit profession is undergoing a significant transformation due to the continuous rise in expectations regarding audit quality and the rapid advancement of information technologies (Ayhan 2019:76). In the context of independent auditing, the concept of quality refers to the accuracy and reliability of the audit opinion formed at the conclusion of the audit engagement (Oktay 2013:46). The quality element in independent auditing encompasses the preparation of financial statements in accordance with applicable rules and regulations, and ensuring their reliability at an appropriate level (Yazar et al. 2018:48).

Since services are inherently intangible, service quality also possesses an abstract structure, and assessments related to service quality are often based on perceptions (Bozdogan 2014:28). With the integration of artificial intelligence applications into independent auditing, errors will be reduced, audit processes will become more efficient, advanced and modern audit techniques will be employed, and the entire dataset of the audited entity will be examined—thereby enhancing the overall quality of the audit.

The benefits of providing a high-quality independent audit service can be listed as follows (Alpaslan and Haksever 2013: 50–51):

- When the audit report is prepared through a high-quality independent audit service, the responsibility toward the relevant parties who rely on the information presented in the report is fulfilled.
- Independent auditors have a duty to act honorably, honestly, and with integrity toward society, their clients, and their colleagues—even when doing so may conflict with their personal interests. The main reason for such high standards of professional conduct is to gain public trust through the provision of quality service.
- The quality of independent audit services enhances the credibility of the audit firm and helps preserve and increase the reputation established in the market.
- A high-quality independent audit service increases the audit firm's competitive strength, which in turn contributes to greater market share and profitability.
- Existing clients of the audit firm, unless faced with significant reasons, are unlikely to seek alternative providers if they are satisfied with the quality of the service delivered.
- High-quality independent auditing contributes to the success of capital markets.

The benefits resulting from the improvement in audit quality through the use of artificial intelligence in independent auditing can be listed as follows:

- As the quality of independent auditing increases with artificial intelligence, users of the audit report will be provided with a level of assurance that exceeds reasonable assurance.

- Since artificial intelligence does not act based on emotions such as personal interest, hatred, or anger, there will be no behavior in violation of ethical principles.
- Because audit firms and independent auditors using artificial intelligence will be less likely to make errors, their reputations will be protected and may even be enhanced.
- The competitive strength of audit firms and independent auditors utilizing artificial intelligence will increase, potentially resulting in greater market share and profitability.
- Clients of audit firms that employ artificial intelligence in auditing will have little need to change their auditor, except where mandatory audit rotation is required.
- Conducting independent audits with artificial intelligence will also contribute to the national economy, and to the development and deepening of capital markets.

In recent years, the artificial intelligence techniques used in quality improvement efforts have included artificial neural networks, expert systems, genetic algorithms, and fuzzy logic methods (Kaya and Engin 2005:103). Through the use of artificial intelligence, the structure of data used in independent auditing can be analyzed, data can be collected, classified, and data management can be enhanced. In the field of independent auditing, which is inherently data-driven, the use of artificial intelligence in this manner will contribute to improving audit quality.

11.12 Conclusion and Discussion

The rapid advancement of communication, transportation, computing, software, and internet technologies in today's world has affected daily life, economic activities, and businesses, initiating a digital transformation. Emerging concepts such as artificial intelligence, blockchain technology, the Internet of Things (IoT), big data, and Industry 4.0 have arisen as a result of this transformation.

The increasing use of technology in business has altered production, service, and commercial structures, and led to a rise in the volume of transactions in accounting and finance departments. In such expanding and evolving organizations, auditing millions or thousands of accounting records and financial transactions has become a significant challenge.

The migration of financial operations and business processes into digital environments, along with the globalization of enterprise activities, has made independent auditing more complex. Consequently, many new audit approaches have emerged—from comprehensive audits of all activities to risk-based audit models.

As a result, the idea of incorporating artificial intelligence into independent auditing has started to gain broad acceptance. Independent auditors must now be prepared for the integration of AI in auditing, as part of the broader digital transformation.

Artificial intelligence will reshape both the role definitions of independent auditors and the fundamental understanding of audit itself. AI and machine learning technologies will soon take over many of the routine tasks currently carried out by auditors. Therefore, a new generation of auditors will be needed to implement these technologies, interpret their outcomes, and optimize their performance.

Independent auditors must first assess the opportunities and risks associated with the application of artificial intelligence in auditing. Nonetheless, the digitization of routine audit processes and the adoption of AI tools will undoubtedly make artificial intelligence an indispensable assistant to independent auditors in the near future.

Studies on artificial intelligence and independent auditing such as books, doctoral and master's theses, and academic articles have been increasing, and a previously limited body of literature is now beginning to expand. Understanding artificial intelligence also requires a foundational grasp of disciplines such as computer science, mathematics, and statistics. AI encompasses a wide array of specialized subfields, including machine learning, deep learning, genetic algorithms, expert systems, and fuzzy logic. Studies addressing the history of artificial intelligence demonstrate that many milestones have occurred since the 1950s. To determine whether a computer, a piece of software, a robot, or using computer terminology an agent possesses artificial intelligence, the Turing Test is commonly used. If we were to apply this test to the field of independent auditing, an AI system would be considered to have passed the Turing Test if it could perform all audit procedures, apply audit techniques, prepare working papers, and draft an independent audit report in such a way that it would be indistinguishable from the work of a qualified human auditor one who has completed the required education, examinations, and internship. In other words, if an audit conducted by artificial intelligence reaches the same level as an audit conducted by a certified independent auditor, then the software performing the audit can be regarded as possessing artificial intelligence.

One of the challenges that artificial intelligence may encounter during independent audit engagements is the ongoing evolution of auditing standards and the fact that local financial reporting frameworks have not yet been fully established in Turkiye. Due to the dynamic nature of the standards and the predetermined criteria that form the basis of independent auditing, artificial intelligence must remain continuously connected to the subfield of machine learning and complete the necessary training processes accordingly. When applied in independent auditing, artificial intelligence will replace traditional sampling methods by auditing the entire dataset—that is, all documents, accounting records, and transactions of the audited entity—through the use of independent auditing techniques in combination with additional statistical methods. AI is capable of processing large volumes of data within short timeframes.

As a result of various accounting and auditing scandals, trust in independent auditing has been, to some extent, undermined. The integration of artificial intelligence into independent auditing may help restore and strengthen this trust. AI can play a critical role in enhancing confidence in both the professional judgment exercised by independent auditors and the reasonable assurance provided in audit reports, particularly by encouraging auditors to focus more on audit risks and key audit matters. Artificial intelligence helps prevent errors during audit procedures and has a high capacity for detecting errors and fraud within datasets. Independent auditors follow a systematic and structured approach when auditing financial statements. In the audit process, auditors must obtain processed audit data in order to apply audit techniques and assess the data for completeness and accuracy. Data is collected from various sources, including invoices, accounting vouchers, purchase orders, collection and payment slips, bank statements, and payrolls. The audit process requires the verification of both the completeness and accuracy of this information. For artificial intelligence to be effectively used in independent auditing, computer programmers and machine learning specialists must systematically understand the structure of these datasets. Additionally, auditors must clearly define the auditing requirements, and collaboration must be established among data scientists, software developers, and AI engineers to ensure those requirements are met.

References

Aleksander I, Morton I (1995) An introduction to neural computing. International Thomson Computer Press

Allahverdi N (2002) Expert systems: an artificial intelligence application, 1st edn. Atlas Publishing, Istanbul

Alpaslan HG, Haksever O (2013) Practices of quality assurance systems in the Turkish independent auditing sector. J Life Sci Batman Univ 3(1):45–69

Ari A (2019) Detection and classification of brain tumors from MRI images based on deep learning (Unpublished Doctoral Dissertation). Inonu University, Institute of Science, Malatya

Arslan O (2018) The importance of internal audit system in detecting accounting frauds and the responsibility of independent auditors against fraud in terms of auditing standards: a field study in independent audit firms (Unpublished Doctoral Dissertation). Cumhuriyet University, Institute of Social Sciences, Sivas

Aydemir E (2018) Artificial intelligence with Weka, 1st edn. Seckin Publishing, Ankara

Aydın AO (2013) Artificial intelligence: towards integrated cognition. Istanbul Gelişim University Press

Aydın IH, Degirmenci CH (2018) Artificial intelligence, 1st edn. Girdap Publishing, Istanbul

Ayhan S (2019) Data analysis with computer-aided audit techniques and an application on accounting data (Unpublished Master's Thesis). Marmara University, Institute of Social Sciences, Istanbul.

Avuclu E (2019). Determining chronological age from dental X-ray images using artificial intelligence and image processing techniques (Unpublished Doctoral Dissertation). Selcuk University, Institute of Science, Konya

Baldwin AA, Brown CE, Trinkle BS (2006) Opportunities for artificial intelligence development in the accounting domain: the case for auditing. Intell Syst Account Finance Manag 14:77–86

Berry MJA, Linoff GS (2004) Data mining techniques: for marketing, sales and customer relationship management, 2nd edn. Wiley Publishing

Bozdogan T (2014) Quality control in independent auditing: a study on the perceptions and readiness of independent auditors. Detay Publishing, Ankara

Bozkurt N (2010) Auditing, 5th edn. Alfa Publishing, Istanbul

Canepa GA (2016) What you need to know about machine learning. Packt Publishing, Birmingham
Cavdar SC (2018) Artificial intelligence and econometric applications in finance: econometric and hybrid model forecasts, 1st edn. Seckin Publishing, Ankara
Dogan M (2020) Artificial intelligence and the problem of consciousness. Cizgi Bookstore Publishing, Istanbul
Elmas C (2018) Artificial intelligence applications, 44th edn. Seckin Publishing, Ankara
Fausett L (1994) Fundamentals of neural networks: architectures, algorithms, and applications. Prentice Hall, New Jersey
Fido EM (2016) Fraud auditing in financial statements and audit techniques to prevent fraud: a comparative study of practices in Turkey and the EU (Unpublished Master's Thesis). Selcuk University, Institute of Social Sciences, Konya
Guredin E (2010) Audit and assurance services, 13th edn. Turkmen Publishing, Istanbul
Issa H, Sun T, Vasarhelyi MA (2016) Research ideas for artificial intelligence in auditing: the formalization of audit and workforce supplementation. J Emerg Technol Account 13(2):1–20
Isik G (2019) Use of deep learning techniques in the recognition of Turkish dialects (Unpublished Doctoral Dissertation). Hacettepe University, Institute of Science, Ankara
Kaelbling LP, Littman ML, Moore AW (1996) Reinforcement Learning: a Survey. J Artif Intell Res 4:237–285
Kaya I, Engin O (2005) The use of artificial intelligence techniques in quality improvement processes. Pamukkale Univ J Eng Sci 11(1):103–114
Kavut L (2001) Views and attitudes of independent auditors and company managers on audit quality. İMKB Journal 20:2
Koskivaara E (2003) Artificial neural networks in auditing: state of the art. Turku Sch Econ Bus Adm Inf Syst Sci 1–21
Kurkcu S (2019) Genealogy of artificial intelligence: the nature of thought in the processes of scientification and commodification (Unpublished Doctoral Dissertation). Mimar Sinan Fine Arts University, Institute of Social Sciences, Istanbul
McCorduck P (1977) History of artificial intelligence. Ijcai August:951–954
Millchamp AH, Taylor JR (2008) Auditing, 9th edn. Cengage Learning, London
Munuko I, Brown-Liburd HL, Vasarhelyi MA (2020) The ethical implications of using artificial intelligence in auditing. J Bus Ethics 167:3–20
Nabiyev VV (2016) Artificial Intelligence, 5th edn. Seckin Publishing, Ankara
Namli E (2012) A risk-based and AI-supported approach in project management (Unpublished work)
Nilsson JN (2019) The past and future of artificial intelligence, 2nd edn. Bogazici University Press, Istanbul
Oktay S (2013) Quality and quality control in audit services for improving the effectiveness of independent auditing: U.S. regulations. Finance Articles 100:42–94
Oztemel E (2012) Artificial neural networks. Papatya Publishing, Istanbul
Parida V, Cenamor J, Sjodin DR (2017) Adopting a platform approach in servitization: leveraging the value of digitalization. Int J Prod Econ 192:54–65
Ramamoorti S, Bailey AD, Traver RO (1999) Risk assessment in internal auditing: a neural network approach. Intell Syst Account Finance Manag 8:159–180
Rapoport M (2016) Auditors count on tech for backup. Wall St J. March 8
Russell S, Norvig P (2003) Artificial intelligence: a modern approach, 2nd edn. Prentice Hall, USA
Sahin HA (2020) Comparison of artificial neural networks and different optimization methods (Unpublished Doctoral Dissertation). Ondokuz Mayıs University, Graduate School of Engineering, Samsun
Saglam M (n.d.) Cost estimation model (Unpublished Doctoral Dissertation). Istanbul University, Institute of Science, Istanbul

Samuel AL (2000) Some studies in machine learning using the game of checkers. IBM J Res Dev 44(1–2):206–226

Sarisoy O (2018) Inclusion of key audit matters in independent audit reports and expectation gaps (Unpublished Doctoral Dissertation). Istanbul University, Institute of Social Sciences, Istanbul

Say C (2019) Artificial intelligence in 50 questions, 8th edn. Bilim ve Gelecek Publishing, Istanbul

Tas O, Mert H (2019) Application of artificial intelligence in auditing. 5th Glob Bus Res Congr 9:65–68

Uzay S (2004) Auditor Independence in Turkey. The 1st annual international accounting conference, MODAV, Istanbul, Conference Proceedings, pp 435–485

Yakar S (2015) The effectiveness of the audit committee on audit quality. Electron J Soc Sci 14(54):251–263

Yazar BB, Gunes R, Yalcin Z (2018) Effectiveness of quality control systems in independent audit firms: the case of Turkey. Inonu Univ Int J Soc Sci 7(1):48

Yildiz B (2009) Artificial intelligence in financial analysis, 1st edn. Detay Publishing, Ankara

Yildiz B, Agdeniz S (2019) Technological infrastructure of audit 4.0. J Account Audit Rev 58:83–102

Yilmaz A (2019) Artificial intelligence, 5th edn. KODLAB Publishing

Yurtoglu H (2005) Forecast modeling using artificial neural networks methodology: the case of Turkiye for selected macroeconomic variables (Specialist Thesis). General Directorate of Economic Models and Strategic Research, Ankara

Part V
Recent Issues on Internal Auditing and External Auditing Through the Eyes of MUDEP Academics

Chapter 12
Expectation Gaps in Internal Auditing: An Examination of the Perspectives of External and Internal Auditors

Özkan Sarısoy and Yasemin Acar Uğurlu

Abstract This research explores the expectation gaps in internal auditing by examining the perspectives of both internal and independent auditors. While audit expectation gaps have traditionally been discussed in the context of external auditing, similar issues arise within internal audit practices, particularly due to differences in stakeholder expectations and the actual scope of audit responsibilities. Utilizing a qualitative research methodology through in-depth interviews with auditors, the study identifies discrepancies in expectations regarding internal audit's role in transparency, institutionalization, risk management, independence, and report objectivity. Findings reveal that while internal auditors generally express confidence in their compliance with ethical and regulatory standards, independent auditors are more skeptical, especially concerning independence and practical impact. The research concludes that reducing the expectation gap requires not only regulatory improvements and performance enhancements but also managing unrealistic stakeholder expectations through education and transparent communication.

Keywords Internal auditing · Expectation gap · Auditor perceptions · Independence · Transparency

---

This chapter was previously published in Turkish by Gazi Kitabevi with the ISBN: 978-625-8443-79-0.

Ö. Sarısoy (✉)
Tekirdağ Namık Kemal University, Tekirdağ, Türkiye
e-mail: osarisoy@nku.edu.tr

Y. A. Uğurlu
Istanbul Arel University, Istanbul, Türkiye
e-mail: yaseminugurlu@arel.edu.tr

G. Kurt, Ö. Sarısoy (eds.), *Recent Advancements in Auditing*, Accounting, Finance, Sustainability, Governance & Fraud: Theory and Application,
https://doi.org/10.1007/978-981-95-5811-7_12

12.1 Introduction

Expectation gaps related to auditing activities have become a widely discussed topic in the literature, particularly since the second half of the twentieth century. Although audit expectation gaps are generally examined from the perspective of external (independent) auditing, they are also relevant for other assurance services that serve multiple stakeholder groups. Internal audit expectation gaps refer to the discrepancies between the responsibilities assigned to internal auditing and the expectations of various stakeholder groups. These gaps may also stem from the divergence between unrealistic expectations held by parties in the audit environment and the actual outcomes that internal audit activities can deliver. The broad scope of responsibilities undertaken by internal auditors often leads to the formation of expectations that are either unrealistic or fall outside their official mandate. Moreover, expectation gaps may also arise from the differing characteristics of stakeholders involved in the audit environment. Although audit activities are conducted according to established standards and are periodically revised in line with evolving practices, expectation gaps continue to persist and remain a subject of contemporary research. In addition to regulatory deficiencies, the very nature of auditing necessitates the exercise of professional judgment by auditors in certain areas. As a result, performance shortcomings that may arise from such judgment are considered among the contributing factors to expectation gaps. Another source of the expectation gap lies in the audit stakeholders' incomplete understanding of the audit's scope—or, even when the scope is understood, the persistence of expectations beyond that scope.

In the literature, expectation gaps are generally regarded as a negative phenomenon, and various efforts have been made to reduce them. Among these efforts is the alignment of audit regulations with current needs. Regulatory adjustments aimed at addressing gaps that may arise due to deficiencies in audit legislation are considered essential. Improving audit performance is also viewed as a key method for narrowing expectation gaps. Moreover, there is evidence in the literature suggesting that correcting misconceptions about auditing can help mitigate such gaps. Since unreasonable demands often stem from expectations that are inherently incompatible with the nature of auditing, managing these demands is thought to be beneficial.

This study aims to examine expectation gaps in the context of internal auditing, drawing on existing research that has primarily addressed the issue from the perspective of external auditing. The first part of the study discusses the definition of internal audit and its core components: corporate governance, risk management, and internal control. The second part introduces key terms related to audit expectation gaps and provides a general conceptual overview. It then explores the factors contributing to expectation gaps, strategies for reducing them, and relevant studies in the literature. In the final section, the research investigates expectations surrounding internal audit activities by analyzing the perspectives of both external and internal auditors. Based on the findings of the in-depth qualitative research method employed, the study identifies varying expectations between internal auditors and external auditors, as well as among individuals within each group, regarding several aspects of internal audit services.

12.2 Internal Auditing

The origins of auditing can be traced back to ancient times. The earliest known practices related to auditing date to Ancient Rome and are understood to have primarily focused on fraudulent activities (Türedi and Zor 2015, p. 3). The initial applications of internal auditing are thought to have emerged in the form of financial audits and compliance audits. Over time, the role of internal auditing has evolved. By the twentieth century, the growth of businesses and the increasing complexity of transactions had brought to the forefront the need for competent management and the efficient and effective execution of business operations. During this period, managerial functions were incorporated into the scope of internal auditing, and internal audit began to be viewed as a tool to support managerial decision-making (Spraakman 2001, p. 19). In the following years, the significance of internal audit within organizations continued to increase, leading to the emergence of international institutions dedicated to advancing the field. Some of the major institutions in this area can be listed as follows (İSMMMO 2015, p. 50):

- The **Institute of Internal Auditors (IIA)** was established in the United States in 1941. It is a globally recognized organization in the promotion of the internal auditing profession, professional training, and certification of internal auditors.
- The **European Confederation of Institutes of Internal Auditing (ECIIA)** was founded in 1982. Its mission is to promote the adoption of internal audit standards and ethical rules in both the private and public sectors by supporting the globally recognized professional standards and ethical principles of the IIA.
- The **Turkish Institute of Internal Auditing (TİDE)** was founded in 1995. TİDE aims to foster professional development and knowledge sharing in accordance with international standards, and to establish national and international professional networks for the advancement of the internal auditing profession.

Although various approaches exist in defining internal auditing, the definition most frequently cited in the literature is that of the IIA. According to the IIA, "Internal auditing is an independent, objective assurance and consulting activity designed to add value and improve an organization's operations" (IIA, n.d.). The assurance function refers to the internal auditor's objective evaluation of findings within the scope of internal audit activities and the formation of an independent opinion (Aslan 2010, pp. 67–68). The consulting function involves providing management with reliable advice aimed at enhancing business operations (Burton et al. 2012, pp. 151–152). This consulting role may also include participating in decision-making processes, maintaining close cooperation with management, and reporting adverse findings when necessary (Munro and Stewart 2010, p. 372).

In the IIA's original definition of internal auditing, the emphasis was placed on the purpose of internal audit and its role in assisting organizational members in fulfilling their responsibilities effectively. Traditionally, the primary aim of internal auditing has been to ensure effective control (Ima 2015, p. 75). In other words, internal audit has been viewed as a mechanism that ensures the reliability of a company's accounting information and the safeguarding of its assets (Marşap et al. 2012, p. 10). However, when considering the range of services provided by internal audit today, it becomes evident that the IIA's original definition is insufficient. Internal audit continuously adds value to organizational operations by identifying existing risks and preventing potential ones. Through a systematic and disciplined approach, internal auditing supports the achievement of organizational objectives. The main objective of internal auditing is to evaluate risk management, control, and governance processes and to prevent deficiencies in these areas (Ahlawat and Lowe 2004, p. 148).

To serve this objective, organizations undertake various internal audit-related practices. Generally, the internal audit process within organizations can be outlined as follows (Uzun, n.d.):

- **Establishing the Internal Audit Charter**: A charter outlining the purpose, authority, and responsibilities of internal audit is prepared under the guidance of professional standards and is approved by the board of directors.
- **Determining the Internal Audit Function's Position within the Organization**: The internal audit unit's placement in the organizational chart must ensure its independence.
- **Defining Job Descriptions for Internal Audit Personnel**: The roles and responsibilities of the chief audit executive and other internal audit staff are clearly documented.
- **Assessment of Internal Controls**: Current and potential risks, along with control processes, are evaluated and recommendations are provided.
- **Risk Assessment**: Risk-prone areas of the organization are identified and prioritized in audit planning.
- **Annual Internal Audit Plan**: Based on risk assessment results, an annual internal audit plan is developed.

To perform internal auditing effectively, internal auditors must possess specific qualifications. Beyond basic education requirements, several professional certifications are recognized in the field (Güldüler, 2021, p. 352):

- Certified Internal Auditor (CIA)
- Certification in Risk Management Assurance (CRMA)
- Qualification in Internal Audit Leadership (QIAL)
- Internal Audit Practitioner (IAP)

The internal audit unit is typically positioned within an organization's structure to report functionally to the board of directors and the audit committee. In cases

Fig. 12.1 Organizational placement of the internal audit function. *Note* Adapted from İSMMMO (2015, p. 18)

where the units shown in Fig. 12.1 are not present in the organization, or in smaller enterprises, it is recommended that the internal audit function be positioned under senior management.

Proper positioning of the internal audit unit within the organization helps establish the working environment necessary for the efficiency of internal audit activities. This, in turn, supports the effective utilization of the unit's existing capabilities and contributes to generating added value for the organization (Özdoğan and Öncü 2016, p. 31). The placement of the internal audit unit within the organizational structure is crucial for ensuring that internal audit activities are conducted independently. Independence in internal audit activities can be achieved through the auditor's unbiased and objective approach. For internal auditors, independence entails ethical behavior, integrity, honesty, and impartiality. To maintain independence, internal auditors must avoid conflicts of interest and act in accordance with their professional expertise, free from the influence of others' opinions or judgments.

The chief audit executive should report functionally to the audit committee and administratively to senior management (Erasmus and Coetzee 2010, p. 928). Internal audit reports are submitted by the chief audit executive to senior management and the audit committee, serving as support for the units receiving the reports. It is recommended by the IIA that the chair of the audit committee receive support from the chief audit executive. In this context, internal audit activities that are supervised and coordinated by the audit committee are considered the most ideal arrangement for organizations (Mollaoğulları and Öncü 2020, p. 409).

In order for internal audit activities to deliver the intended benefits, they must be carried out independently and objectively. Regarding independence and objectivity, the IIA has published a framework titled *"Independence and Objectivity: A Framework for Internal Auditors."* In this publication, seven factors that may compromise internal auditors' objectivity are discussed: social pressure, economic interest, self-review, personal relationships or familiarity, and biases based on cultural, racial, gender, or mental factors. Research indicates that factors such as management pressure on internal auditors, their consulting role to senior management, the appointment process of internal auditors, their proximity to both the audit committee and management, and the use of outsourcing in internal audit significantly affect auditors' objectivity (Kızılboğa 2013, p. 115).

Different stakeholder groups benefiting from internal audit activities may have varying expectations. Senior management is primarily concerned with whether internal audit activities enhance the organization's overall corporate effectiveness. Another stakeholder group—independent auditors—are more focused on whether internal audit functions effectively as an internal control tool that facilitates tasks related to the financial structure of the company (Kızılboğa 2013, p. 109). Independent auditors gain access to internal audit findings to assess the organization's level of risk. A high-quality internal audit function reduces control risk. Therefore, independent auditors evaluate the quality of internal audit work (Johnstone et al. 2014, p. 759).

Both internal and external audit standards provide guidance on how coordination and cooperation between internal and independent auditors should be established (Oussii and Taktak 2015, p. 96). Additionally, auditing standards, such as those issued by the Public Company Accounting Oversight Board (PCAOB), encourage independent auditors to rely on the work of internal auditors in the course of their engagements (Bierstaker et al. 2013, p. 241). This notion was reinforced by the SAS No. 65 standard, which continued to emphasize trust in the internal auditors' work (Desai et al. 2008, p. 5). Although it is important for independent auditors to place trust in the work conducted by internal auditors, certain evaluations are still required. Accordingly, the work of internal auditors must be assessed by independent auditors in terms of performance, objectivity, and competence (Glover et al. 2008, p. 194).

Internal audit units operate in various areas depending on the organizational structure and approach of the enterprise. In general, internal audit types include financial audit, compliance audit, performance audit, and information technology (IT) audit. Financial audits focus on evaluating whether a company's financial statements comply with legal regulations and generally accepted accounting principles, and whether these statements accurately reflect the financial position and performance of the business (Bozkurt 2012, p. 27). Compliance auditing aims to determine whether an entity's operations comply with the internal regulations set by senior management, as well as external legislation such as tax laws and labor regulations (Kaval 2005, p. 10). Performance auditing assesses the effectiveness, efficiency, and economy in the use of human, physical, and financial resources to carry out organizational duties (İSMMMO 2015, p. 22).

Today, businesses record and store their operations in digital environments. However, the information generated in these environments introduces various risks. IT auditing involves assessing the reliability of information and systems that produce such information in organizations. It also serves to evaluate the accuracy and continuity of stored data (Aslan 2010, p. 76).

According to the International Standards for the Professional Practice of Internal Auditing (Standard 2100—Nature of Work), the scope of internal auditing is defined as follows: "The internal audit activity must evaluate and contribute to the improvement of governance, risk management, and control processes using a systematic and disciplined approach" (IIA International Standards 2017). Accordingly, the scope of internal audit encompasses corporate governance, risk management, and internal control.

Corporate governance is defined as "the combination of structures and processes implemented by the board of directors to report, direct, manage, and monitor the institution's operations in pursuit of its objectives" (TİDE, n.d.). As the definition suggests, corporate governance consists of the entirety of processes implemented to achieve organizational objectives. Internal audit activities must identify issues and provide recommendations regarding the assessment of governance processes and the actions required to ensure their effective functioning.

Risk management is defined as "a process to identify, assess, manage, and control potential events or situations to provide reasonable assurance in the achievement of organizational objectives" (TİDE, n.d.) Internal auditors do not assume responsibility for risk management directly; however, they assess the institution's risk management processes through audit activities and offer recommendations. These recommendations aim to improve existing risk management efforts and contribute to the overall process. Risks that may affect the institution are analyzed within the scope of internal audit activities, taking into account the organization's risk management framework, and appropriate solutions are proposed.

Internal control refers to the entirety of systems designed to safeguard an organization's assets, ensure the reliability of its information systems, guarantee compliance of operations with legal regulations, and enhance the efficiency and effectiveness of business activities. As an integral part of daily operations, internal control encompasses all organizational processes. It serves as a management tool employed to achieve corporate objectives and is evaluated by internal audit in terms of its effectiveness. Internal audit is an independent and objective activity distinct from management. The assessments conducted by internal audit regarding the internal control system are critically important for enhancing the system's effectiveness (Yurtsever 2014, p. 108). Moreover, for an effective internal control system to function within the organization, responsibility lies with all stakeholders—from the board of directors to every employee (Özbek 2012, p. 138).

12.3 Audit Expectation Gaps

According to Turkish Language Society, the concept of "expectation," often understood as "what is anticipated to occur," is frequently used in everyday language (Türk Dil Kurumu, n.d.). It refers to any condition that individuals anticipate regarding the future. Although expectations are inherently future-oriented, they are influenced by past experiences as well as by personal and social characteristics. Whether expectations are rational or not, and whether realized expectations are interpreted differently once fulfilled, also varies. In this sense, when a previously anticipated situation occurs, it is possible for two different individuals to interpret it in divergent ways.

While the concept of expectation bears similarities to the concept of "desire," there are fundamental differences between the two. "Desire" is defined as "an inclination toward something that, when fulfilled, brings satisfaction to the individual" (https://www.tdk.gov.tr). In this respect, desire implies satisfaction when realized, whereas the fulfillment of expectations does not always lead to contentment. Additionally, other related concepts such as aspiration, hope, and demand are also commonly used. Although these terms are often used interchangeably in everyday language, they carry nuanced differences, which are beyond the scope of this study.

In short, the concept of expectation refers to circumstances anticipated to occur in the future, shaped by the differing characteristics of the stakeholders involved, and is frequently used both in daily language and in economic contexts. Terms like financial expectations, sales expectations, profit expectations, and exchange rate expectations are prevalent in business discourse. In auditing terminology, however, the concept of expectation carries a specific meaning, and the notion of "audit expectation gap" occupies a significant space in the literature. The term "AEG" is frequently used as an abbreviation of the English expression "Audit Expectation Gap." In Turkish studies, audit expectation gaps have been described using various terms such as "gap," "interval," or "void." However, in everyday Turkish, one does not refer to a gap or void between expectations but rather describes the expectation as being different. Therefore, the term "fark" (difference) is preferred in this study.

Audit expectation gaps are most commonly discussed in the context of independent auditing, where the perceptions of various stakeholder groups toward the auditing process are analyzed. These perceptions, influenced by differing attributes of stakeholder groups, have been found to differ significantly, giving rise to the concept of audit expectation gaps. Although there is no specific study identifying when these gaps first emerged, it is reasonable to suggest that such gaps—minor or major—have always existed due to the varying characteristics that shape expectations.

The first academic use of the term "expectation gap" is commonly attributed to Liggio (1974), who defined it as the difference in performance expectations between independent auditors (accountants) and users of financial statements (Okafor and Otalor 2013, p. 44). Liggio conceptualized this gap as one existing primarily between the auditor and the users of audit reports (Liggio 1974, p. 23).

However, further studies have examined whether such gaps exist between other stakeholder groups and have provided empirical evidence supporting their existence. Over time, the issue of expectation gaps has been addressed not only by researchers but also by professional organizations. A variety of definitions of expectation gaps from different studies are summarized in Table 12.1.

Although the definitions show general similarities, it is observed that the scope of expectation gaps has expanded over time. The audit environment can be broadly categorized into three main groups: those responsible for preparing and presenting financial information, those who audit the reliability of that information, and those who use the financial information. Based on this approach, some studies have examined expectation gaps between preparers and users of financial statements, while others have focused on the gap between auditors and users of financial information. Among these groups, financial statement users constitute a diverse subpopulation, including investors, the general public, clients, financial institutions, members of the judiciary, and others. Each of these groups utilizes financial information for different purposes, and their specific expectations are shaped by those purposes and the characteristics of each subgroup.

Another dimension of expectation gaps is that many definitions tend to reflect desires or wishes rather than objective expectations. In this context, expectation gaps often point to the dissatisfaction of financial information users with audit outcomes. In this sense, expectation gaps reflect not only stakeholders' predictions about audit results but also their aspirations for what those results should be. Thus, audit expectation gaps can be described as the misalignment between what various audit stakeholders ideally desire and what is practically delivered through audit

Table 12.1 Variety of Definition of Expectation Gap

Author (Year)	Definition of expectation gap
Liggio (1974)	... the difference between expected levels of performance by independent accountants and financial statement users ...
Cohen commission (1978)	... differences between what the public expects or needs and what auditors can reasonably be expected to accomplish ...
Campbell and Michenzi (1987)	... differences between the roles of the auditor as perceived by financial statement users of an audited entity and the independent auditors' report taking on ...
Guy and Sullivan (1988)	... differences between the public's and financial statement users' thoughts on auditors' and accountants' responsibility and auditors' and accountants' own thoughts on their responsibility ...
Monroe and Woodliff (1993)	... differences between messages that auditors convey through audit reports and the meanings that the public assigns to those messages ...
Porter (1993)	... the expectation-performance gap, which is the difference between what society expects from auditors and how auditors' performance is perceived ...
Epstein and Geiger (1994)	... differences particularly related to assurances provided between those who use, prepare, and audit financial information ...

services. Because this misalignment can cause significant problems, efforts have been made in the literature to better understand and resolve it.

As is evident from the literature, expectation gaps are typically examined within the scope of independent auditing. Accordingly, audit expectation gaps have been conceptualized with independent audits in mind, and various solution proposals have been developed within this framework. However, expectation gaps can also be considered within the broader context of assurance services. The nature of expectation itself, being shaped by the type of service and characteristics of the stakeholder group, may differ across different types of assurance services. In internal auditing, expectation gaps—similar to those in external auditing—refer to the differences between stakeholders' expectations from internal audit activities and what internal auditing can realistically deliver. In this regard, expectation gaps are influenced by the distinct characteristics of internal audit stakeholders. Unrealistic expectations about internal audit services and the actual outcomes that can be delivered may lead to expectation gaps. It is believed that the diverse functional areas in which internal auditors operate contribute to the emergence of expectations that are either unrealistic or outside their defined areas of responsibility. In the following sections of the study, expectation gaps—primarily discussed from the perspective of independent auditing—are re-examined in the context of internal audit services.

Expectation gaps related to auditing activities have been widely discussed—particularly in the context of independent auditing—since the 1970s. Although it can be argued that such gaps existed in earlier periods as well, their intensification after this time prompted several institutions to pay closer attention to the issue. In the literature, the causes of expectation gaps have been categorized into different components in various studies, with some offering more detailed classifications than others. One of the earliest and most widely recognized studies examining the components of expectation gaps was conducted by the Canadian Institute of Chartered Accountants (CICA) in 1988. This study analyzed public expectations of independent auditors and presented the components summarized in Fig. 12.2.

An analysis of Fig. 12.2 shows that point A represents the public's **unreasonable expectations**, while point E reflects a **perceived performance deficiency**, which does not necessarily correspond to the actual performance of the audit. Through this schematic, the CICA examined expectation gaps under two main components: **standards** and **performance**. It is suggested that with the efforts of regulatory bodies, the current standards defining the scope of auditing could be improved and brought closer to point B, thereby narrowing the expectation gap in this area. However, some argue that even if the standards are elevated to meet reasonable expectations, **unreasonable expectations** will continue to exist (A–B segment). Similarly, performance-related expectation gaps could be reduced through enhanced audit effort (moving from point C to D), yet due to various factors, there may still be a remaining gap between perceived and actual performance (D–E segment). In addition to the components of expectation gaps, several studies have also examined the underlying elements that constitute these components. The following factors have been frequently cited in the literature as common causes of audit expectation gaps (Shaikh and Talha 2003, p. 517; Lee et al. 2009, p. 10).

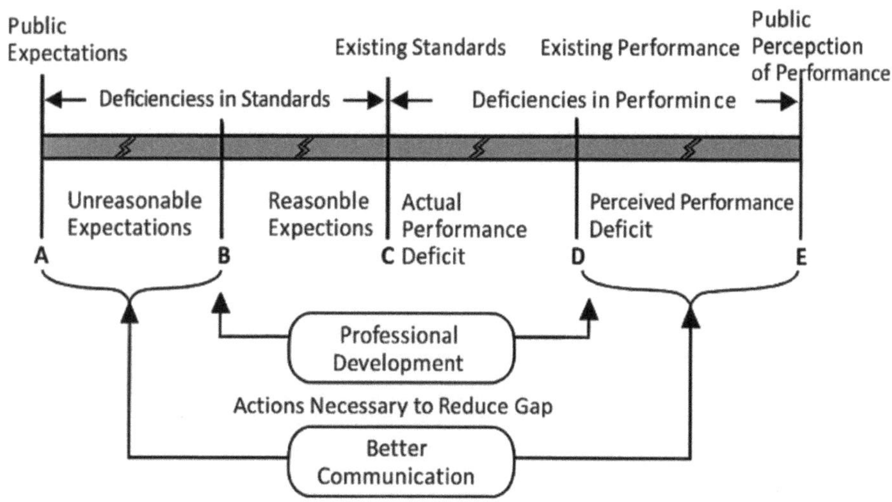

Fig. 12.2 Components of expectation gaps. *Note* Adapted from *CICA Reports* (1988, p. 6)

- The nature of auditing
- The role of auditors
- Misconceptions about auditing
- Misjudgment or inability to assess audit performance
- Delayed or inadequate responses to expectations
- Corporate crises and scandals
- The self-regulatory structure

When examining the factors that lead to expectation gaps, it becomes apparent that there may be interrelationships among the components, and a single factor may influence more than one component. These factors can be categorized under three main components, as presented in Table 12.2. The following sections provide detailed explanations of each of these components.

Table 12.2 Components of expectation gaps

Regulatory deficiency	Performance deficiency	Unreasonable expectations
• Presence of deficiencies in regulations • Failure to respond to expectations	• Nature of auditing • Role of the auditor • Self-regulatory structure of auditing • Auditor's reluctance to take initiative • Lack of effective oversight mechanisms	• Nature of auditing • Role of the auditor • Misconceptions • Misjudgment of performance • Inability to evaluate performance • Prejudices or conditions reinforcing them • Inadequate communication of the audit's purpose

12.3.1 Regulatory Deficiency

Assurance services are carried out in accordance with specific standards. These standards define the framework, objectives, procedures, and completion criteria of the services, as well as the responsibilities of the auditor. Over time, and in line with the evolution of the profession, audit regulations have been revised, expanded, and made more detailed. These revisions are undoubtedly made with the intention of contributing to the fundamental objective of assurance services—namely, increasing the degree of confidence for decision-makers. However, the continued existence of expectation gaps even after these changes suggests that such revisions may not have fully achieved their intended purpose.

Failure to implement timely and effective improvements to audit regulations has also contributed to the persistence of expectation gaps (Humphrey et al. 1992, p. 138). Similar criticisms can be found in earlier works as well (COHEN Report, 1978, p. XII). In many cases, changes in audit regulations have been reactive introduced in response to crises or public pressure rather than grounded in a proactive analysis of stakeholder expectations. This approach has drawn criticism toward the audit profession (Humphrey 2007, p. 10).

Compared to internal auditing, the regulatory framework for independent auditing is more comprehensive and standardized. In most countries today, independent audit activities must be conducted in accordance with International Standards on Auditing (ISAs). Nonetheless, even these globally accepted standards may not fully satisfy all parties within the audit stakeholder environment. In the case of internal auditing, practices often vary from one organization to another. Unlike independent auditing, internal audit functions are not mandatory for all companies, which allows for greater flexibility in the application of standards.

Moreover, structural complexity driven by changes in the business environment has increased the need for updates to internal audit regulations. Therefore, the internal audit framework must be supported by regulatory structures that meet both the reasonable expectations of stakeholders and the evolving demands of the business world.

12.3.2 Performance Deficiency

Performance deficiency refers to an auditor's failure to demonstrate adequate performance. Although audit activities are conducted in accordance with established standards, the principle-based nature of these standards often requires auditors to exercise professional judgment, particularly in significant areas. Concepts such as materiality, risk, and sampling inherently involve subjectivity and are influenced by the auditor's reasoning—hence, their performance. Although the framework for a high-quality audit is defined by standards, as in many other professional fields, practitioners carry out their responsibilities within legal boundaries. However, given the social role of auditing, a broader perspective is often warranted. According to some stakeholder groups, part of the perceived underperformance by auditors may also stem from the nature of their role. The agency relationship, which is one of the key reasons audits are required, can also manifest within the audit process itself. Role conflicts may arise in this relationship, creating ambiguity for the auditor about how to meet the expectations of different parties. While audit standards clearly emphasize that auditors must maintain both actual and perceived independence—free from any connections with the audited entity—it is also recognized that auditors often face pressure regarding audit engagements and fee arrangements (Koo and Sim 1999, p. 207). Moreover, auditors may face additional pressure when they provide other assurance services beyond statutory audits.

Similar to independent audits, internal audit activities are also susceptible to concerns regarding independence, objectivity, and conflicts of interest. For internal auditors to maintain independence, it is expected that management should not interfere with audit planning or request changes to audit reports. Various factors have been found to impact the objectivity of internal auditors, including management pressure, internal auditors' advisory roles to senior management, the processes for assigning audit personnel, auditors' proximity to both the audit committee and management, and the use of outsourcing in internal auditing (Kızılboğa 2013, pp. 113–115). Overall, the positioning of the internal audit function within the organizational structure is a critical issue. To safeguard internal audit from conflicts of interest and bias, and to ensure the independence of internal auditors, it is recommended that the internal audit unit report functionally to the audit committee and administratively to the board of directors (Erasmus and Coetzee 2010, p. 928). In cases where such independence cannot be ensured, the performance expected from internal audit is unlikely to be realized. Furthermore, unlike statutory independent audits, internal audit does not follow a rigid or standardized implementation model, making it more susceptible to the unique characteristics of each organization. Differences in expectations and perspectives on internal audit services across organizations also affect both auditor performance and how that performance is assessed.

12.3.3 Unreasonable Expectations

Another major component of the expectation gap stems from unreasonable expectations, as well as negative prejudices and misperceptions held by those who benefit from audit services. These issues can be broadly grouped into two main causes: first, a lack of understanding of the scope of auditing by audit stakeholders; and second, the existence of expectations that go beyond the defined boundaries of audit responsibilities, even when these boundaries are understood.

Historically, the role of auditing has often been misunderstood by different stakeholder groups. While audit standards (International Auditing and Assurance

Standards Board IAASB, ISA 240) hold auditors accountable for considering fraud in some respects, the primary objective of independent audits is to determine whether financial statements are materially misstated. Nonetheless, there is a common public perception that the auditor's fundamental duty is fraud detection (Sikka et al. 1998, p. 319). A similar misconception applies to internal auditing, where stakeholders may have varied interpretations of the internal auditor's responsibility regarding fraud. In relation to fraud, internal auditors are expected to assist management by assessing the control environment, identifying indicators and red flags of fraud, detecting vulnerabilities that may facilitate fraudulent activity, making recommendations for investigation, maintaining communication with management, and following up on suspected cases (Hillison 1999, pp. 352–353). According to International Internal Auditing Standards, although internal auditors must have sufficient knowledge to evaluate fraud risks and how these risks are managed within the organization, they are not expected to possess the same level of expertise as professional fraud investigators (IIA International Standards, https://www.tide.org.tr/file/documents/pdf/UMUC-2017-updated.pdf). Studies have been conducted to determine whether users of financial statements and investors expect fraud prevention and detection from internal auditors or from external auditors. Some research suggests that expectation gaps may arise when management places full reliance on the internal audit system for the prevention and detection of fraud (El Nashar 2020, p. 2). Moreover, even individuals with a reasonable understanding of auditing may form unrealistic expectations if they perceive the scope defined by auditing standards as insufficient. In other words, despite being aware that fraud detection is not the primary responsibility of auditors, expectations in this direction may still persist.

In addition, the use of inherently subjective concepts in auditing—such as materiality, reasonableness, and risk—makes it more difficult for external parties to fully understand audit practices (Humphrey 2007, p. 4). Furthermore, the inability to present audit findings clearly and accessibly in audit reports is also considered a barrier to public understanding of the audit process (Saladrigues and Grañó 2014, p. 128).

12.4 Reducing the Expectation Gap

Due to the expectation gap hindering the theoretical role of audit activities, various efforts have been made to reduce such discrepancies. Moreover, the expectation gap presents different challenges for different stakeholder groups. The failure of auditors to meet expectations may lead not only to criticism but also to a gradual decline in the profession's reputation. A loss in professional reputation may, in the long term, result in decreased revenue and may undermine stability and accountability within the economic system. These concerns form the rationale behind the efforts to narrow the expectation gap (Lee et al. 2009, p. 10; Sikka et al. 1998, p. 300). It has also been argued that the expectation gap may increase legal liability, lead to higher insurance premiums, and raise the cost of professional responsibility

(Wolf et al. 1999, p. 468; Gramling et al. 1996, p. 132). While some studies in the literature have focused on the measures necessary to reduce the expectation gap, others have questioned whether it is possible to eliminate the gap entirely. Academic research has proposed a variety of suggestions to mitigate the expectation gap. Professional organizations have been held accountable for this issue and have occasionally brought it to public attention through various initiatives (Arrington et al. 1983, p. 249). However, in order to reduce the gap effectively, it is essential to understand which component the discrepancy stems from (Porter 1993, p. 66; Dennis 2010, p. 144). The literature outlines several strategies to reduce the expectation gap, including: enhancing education, expanding the content of audit reports, strengthening auditor accountability, independence and performance, and implementing rigorous quality control and monitoring mechanisms (Koh and Woo 1998, pp. 150–151; Anderson et al. 1993; Salehi 2011, p. 8389).

12.4.1 Aligning Legislation With Stakeholder Needs

Deficiencies in legislation are among the key factors contributing to the expectation gap. If assurance services, as defined by legislative frameworks, fail to meet the reasonable demands of users, this discrepancy is likely to result in an expectation gap. It has been argued that past regulatory changes (e.g., SAS No. 58, 1994) led to a reduction in the expectation gap (Giacomino 1994, p. 35; Miller et al. 1990). Similarly, in periods when expectation gaps were frequently discussed, studies conducted by professional organizations on auditor performance suggested that the gap had narrowed (Porter and Gowthorpe 2004, p. 94). It has also been shown that enhancing auditor responsibility can contribute to reducing the expectation gap (Salehi 2011, p. 8390; Otalor and Okafor 2013, p. 125). In addition to the comprehensiveness of the regulations, clarity in their articulation is also crucial. Ambiguities or vague expressions can lead to misunderstandings and increase the expectation gap (Ojo 2006, p. 10). In an ever-evolving economic system, assurance services must be supported by proactive legislation that enables the optimal fulfillment of their role. Timely and complete responses to reasonable demands for reform can also contribute to the success of such changes.

As in the case of external audit, clearly defining the duties and responsibilities of internal audit in the relevant legislation may help foster rational expectations. Otherwise, internal auditors may be unable to perform their duties correctly or effectively, resulting in expectation gaps related to internal audit services. According to the definition of internal auditing, the internal auditor provides assurance and consulting services aimed at adding value to an organization. However, the scope of internal audit services may vary depending on the structure and expectations of individual organizations. In particular, in organizations lacking fully developed corporate structures, business owners may expect internal audit primarily to protect company assets. Nevertheless, internal audit responsibilities extend beyond management's expectations and include obligations specified in internal audit legislation and international internal auditing standards. These responsibilities are also reflected in the attribute and performance standards that form the foundation of internal auditing.

12.4.2 Enhancing Performance

It is generally acknowledged that stakeholders hold expectations from auditors that go beyond their legally defined responsibilities, or that there is insufficient understanding of the auditors' actual responsibilities. Some of these expectations may be reasonable, while others are unrealistic. From this perspective, improving auditor performance can help address a portion of the reasonable expectations. Although expanding the scope of legal responsibilities may contribute to this goal, auditing by its nature requires professional judgment. Furthermore, the scope and quality of the audit, even when outlined by standards, are heavily influenced by the auditor's effort.

Performance may be negatively affected in the presence of role or interest conflicts (Koo and Sim 1999). The literature suggests that insufficient audit performance contributes to the expectation gap and proposes increased oversight and discipline of auditors as a solution (Dewing and Russell 2002, p. 537). Accordingly, an effective oversight mechanism can help ensure and sustain a certain level of quality in audit engagements. Similarly, when internal auditors experience conflicts of interest, fail to maintain independence and objectivity—core attributes defined in internal auditing standards—or fall short in performance expectations, significant deficiencies may arise.

Internal auditing adopts a risk-based approach focused on organizational activities and informs management on how to enhance operational efficiency and address high-risk areas. It also provides advisory recommendations. However, management retains the discretion to implement or disregard these recommendations. Internal auditors do not possess authority to enforce corrective action. Like external audit, internal audit provides reasonable, not absolute, assurance. Assuming otherwise may also contribute to the expectation gap. In some organizations, internal audit units may lack sufficient or qualified personnel, which could hinder their ability to identify certain risks. Moreover, even when internal auditors identify and report potential risks, these may be ignored by management and still lead to adverse outcomes. Even with qualified and adequately staffed teams, some risks remain inevitable.

Internal audit services must also consider the needs of the current environment. For example, the COVID-19 pandemic has introduced a wide range of risks for organizations, employees, and stakeholders. In such circumstances, internal audit plays a critical role in managing risks effectively (Altuk 2021, pp. 18–19). During the pandemic, remote auditing became more prevalent, and internal audit activities underwent significant transformations. In particular, internal audit departments are increasingly expected to assume a strategic role by offering valuable advisory services to management (Ağdeniz and Çetin 2021, p. 59).

Another potential source of expectation or perception mismatch lies in the relationship between internal and external audit. Due to competitive pressures in the audit market, external auditors may rely more on internal audit work and, as a result, anticipate reduced audit effort and fees. However, some studies have shown the opposite, indicating that audit fees may not necessarily decrease under such circumstances. Audit committee expectations that internal audit should complement external audit efforts may be interpreted as an extension of the overall assurance scope. This perspective frames internal audit as a signal of strong corporate governance, expressed in the notion that "firms with more internal monitoring are also engaged in more independent oversight" (Kyburz 2016, pp. 89–90).

12.4.3 Managing Unreasonable Expectations

Even if the scope of assurance services is broadened and auditor performance reaches an optimal level, expectation gaps may still arise due to the public's lack of awareness, prejudices, or unreasonable demands regarding the audit. Since unreasonable demands consist of expectations that cannot be fulfilled due to the inherent nature of audit services, managing such expectations may be beneficial. Furthermore, misunderstanding the scope of audit services is another cause of expectation gaps. It is therefore suggested that stakeholders with insufficient knowledge about auditing can benefit from educational efforts (McEnroe and Martens 2001, p. 357).

Some studies have shown that individuals with reasonable knowledge of auditing tend to place fewer responsibilities on auditors (Bailey et al. 1983, p. 369). Similarly, research analyzing the opinions of different stakeholder groups has claimed that those who have received audit-related education tend to have more reasonable expectations (Monroe and Woodliff 1993, p. 61; Epstein and Geiger 1994, p. 63; Pierce and Kilcommins 1996, p. 1; Shalimova & Zagiriniak 2020). However, other studies have indicated that even stakeholders with sufficient audit education may still hold expectation gaps (Gramling et al. 1996, p. 149).

In addition to education, effective communication has been proposed as an alternative strategy for managing unreasonable expectations (Salehi et al. 2009, p. 171). Through explanations provided at the end of the audit engagement, as well as through other communication initiatives, it may be possible to reduce prejudice and align expectations to a more reasonable level. Clearly outlining the responsibilities of all parties to the audit stakeholders is another suggestion thought to contribute to the reduction of expectation gaps (COHEN Report 1978, p. XX). Moreover, it is believed that the audit profession's ability to respond quickly to situations that may trigger negative perceptions, while also considering the expectations of stakeholders, may have a mitigating effect on expectation gaps. In internal auditing, if the expectations of management are not reasonable, the internal audit function may be driven to operate outside its intended scope, thereby undermining its actual performance. A lack of understanding by management regarding the purpose and scope of internal auditing may also lead to the emergence of divergent expectations.

Given the different demands of internal audit stakeholders, expectation gaps that influence the scope, workload, and responsibilities of internal audit are inevitable. For instance, differing expectations between the audit committee and the board of directors may lead to such gaps. To reduce the expectation gap in internal auditing, it is essential to establish healthy communication and information sharing between the internal audit function, the board of directors, and senior management (Kyburz 2016, pp. 90–91).

12.5 Literature

Since audit expectation gaps are predominantly addressed from the perspective of external auditing, the existing literature on expectation gaps mostly consists of studies focused on independent audits. This section first examines studies related to the expectation gap in external auditing and then discusses research on internal auditing.

Humphrey et al. (1993) revealed that unreasonable expectations, which are a major cause of the expectation gap, often stem from an audit expectation centered on fraud detection. Dixon et al. (2006) investigated expectation gaps from the perspective of financial statement users and found that there is a gap particularly regarding expectations about fraud and auditor judgment. Their study also suggested that expanding the scope of audits and improving education could help reduce the expectation gap.

Palaniappan et al. (2007), in alignment with previous literature, confirmed the existence of the expectation gap and emphasized not only unreasonable expectations but also deficiencies in regulation and auditor performance. Salehi and Azary (2008) demonstrated that bankers have strong expectations concerning fraud detection. Similarly, the studies by Noghondari and Foong (2009) claimed that bankers have differing expectations from the audit process. Hassink et al. (2009) arrived at similar conclusions. More recent studies by Ellul and Scicluna (2020) and Nguyen and Nguyen (2020) also confirmed the existence of expectation gaps in relation to fraud detection.

The study by Arrington et al. (1983), which focused on the psychological traits of audit users, suggested that this perspective could offer a better understanding of expectation gaps. Anderson et al. (1993) and Saha and Baruah (2008) similarly explored the relationship between users' various biases and the expectation gap, concluding that some expectations were indeed reasonable. Adeyemi and Uadiale (2011), in their research, confirmed the existence of expectation gaps and highlighted the significance of user perception on the issue.

Byington and Sutton (1991) pointed out the failure of the regulations introduced by professional accounting organizations to meet public expectations and reduce the expectation gap, predicting that similar criticisms would continue to arise in the future. Similarly, Otalor and Okafor (2013) emphasized the inverse relationship between the extent of the expectation gap and the reliability of financial information, arguing that an increase in auditor responsibility and better communication could help address this issue.

Leung and Chau (2001) stated that while the new auditor's report had positive effects, it would lead to greater expectations in the long run. Sarısoy and Kepçe (2019) examined stakeholder expectations during the initial implementation of the new auditor's report and found that an expectation gap still existed. Similarly, Olojede et al. (2020) asserted that despite the introduction of the new auditor's report to reduce expectation gaps, such gaps continued to exist.

Campbell and Mutchler (1988) found no significant expectation gap regarding the auditor's role, audit report, and audit opinion, suggesting that eliminating the expectation gap may not be as difficult as presumed.

A significant portion of the studies was conducted in countries with Anglo-Saxon legal traditions, focusing on judicial judges and juries. Lowe and Pany (1993) revealed that juries held an expectation gap, particularly concerning fraud detection. Gramling et al. (1996), in a study involving undergraduate students, found that the expectation gap diminished among those who had taken an auditing course. Similarly, Frank et al. (2001) sought opinions from juries and accounting students, concluding that while juries showed an expectation gap, students did not. Koh and Woo (2001), Mohamed and Zauwiyah (2004), Brown and Jones (2011), and Dinç and Gerakan (2014) all claimed that education reduces the expectation gap. Siddiqui et al. (2009), however, argued that while education reduces the gap, it may also generate new expectations.

Dewing and Russell (2002) and Zhang (2007) demonstrated the impact of oversight in reducing the expectation gap. Akther and Xu (2020) similarly suggested that oversight contributes to narrowing the gap, stressing the importance of preserving auditor independence and improving communication.

Gold et al. (2012) argued that the expectation gap is a persistent phenomenon. In line with this, Ruhnke and Schmidt (2014) also stated that the expectation gap is permanent. Dang and Nguyen (2021) contended that while the expectation gap cannot be entirely eliminated, it can be reduced.

Although there are few direct studies examining the expectation gap in internal auditing, several studies have investigated the views and perceptions of various stakeholders on internal audit services. These empirical studies are summarized below.

Hillison et al. (1999) proposed that internal auditors could act as a defense line against fraud within organizations, arguing that internal auditors are in a better position than external auditors to detect fraud. The study highlighted the role of internal auditors in fraud detection.

Sarens and De Beelde (2006), based on five Belgian case studies, qualitatively analyzed the expectations and perceptions between internal audit and top management. The results indicated that top management had a significant impact on internal audit and expected it to compensate for control loss due to increasing organizational complexity. On the other hand, internal auditors expected top management to take the initial steps to formalize the risk management system and to provide top-level support.

Memiş (2007) explored the internal audit profile in Turkey by gathering opinions from internal auditors. The study revealed that most companies employing internal auditors did not have an independent internal audit unit, all internal auditors had undergraduate or higher education, and internal auditors were able to operate independently with top management support. It was also noted that internal auditing was not sufficiently prioritized in Turkey and that legal and regulatory frameworks were inadequate.

Mohamed (2013), in his study aiming to propose improvements to fraud control in the context of financial statement audits, examined various interviews conducted with internal and independent auditors across two case companies to understand their roles and responsibilities. The study found a divergence in perceived responsibilities in detecting and controlling financial statement fraud, and it was determined that when company management solely relies on internal control systems to prevent fraud, an internal audit expectation gap arises.

Chambers and Odar (2015), in their study, explored how internal auditing can avoid being one of the corporate governance watchdogs that failed to prevent the global financial crisis. They concluded that internal audit services failed to operate effectively for their intended purpose and identified this as an area in need of improvement.

Özdoğan and Öncü (2016) aimed to present the current state of internal auditing from the perspective of internal auditors and to identify areas that require development. Their study emphasized the importance of properly structuring internal audit within a company and revealed that internal auditors perceive gaps between their roles and responsibilities and the level of certification and education received.

Kyburz (2016), in his research, claimed that conflicting demands from departments for which internal audit is responsible may lead to expectation gaps in internal audit. A comparative analysis of perceptions and expectations regarding internal audit revealed that there were no significant differences in perceptions and expectations among board members, executive representatives, and internal auditors.

Karcıoğlu and Kurnaz (2017) consulted public internal auditors to assess the current stage of risk-based auditing in the public sector. Their study concluded that the implementation level of risk-based internal auditing is low due to deficiencies in the risk identification and assessment process.

Labuschagne and Fourie (2018) examined whether the IIA's guidance statements provide sufficient guidance regarding stakeholders' expectations of the internal auditor's role in fraud investigations. Using a qualitative research methodology, they found significant discrepancies between the IIA guidance and stakeholder expectations concerning internal auditors' roles in fraud investigations. The study also stated that the IIA's guidance does not adequately cover the knowledge, skills, and competencies required for fraud investigations, and it suggested that internal auditors' roles and performance in such investigations should be explicitly included.

Demir et al. (2019) investigated the role of internal audit systems in fraudulent financial reporting by collecting the views of independent auditors in Turkey. The results indicated that internal audit plays an effective role in reducing financial fraud.

Adafula et al. (2019) examined the audit expectation-performance gap from the perspective of internal audit functions in developing economies by analyzing the views of four key stakeholders in the financial reporting chain (independent auditors, senior management, audit committee members, and professional bodies). The study found that there were no significant differences between stakeholders in terms of expectation-performance gaps.

Bircan (2020) investigated the changing role of internal audit, the transformation of internal audit activities, the evolving profile of internal auditors, and their perceptions and expectations. The study revealed structural changes and transformation in internal auditing, noting that while there is high awareness regarding the need for a mental shift and transformation, actual implementation of this awareness remains relatively limited.

El Nashar (2020), assuming that expectation gaps would be less in computer-assisted internal audits, applied decision tree and Bayesian theorem approaches to estimate internal audit expectation gaps among company management, investors, and financial statement users. The study concluded that strengthening internal audit would positively impact the reduction of the expectation gap.

12.6 Examination of Independent Auditors' and Internal Auditors' Expectations Regarding Internal Audit Services

This study aims to examine expectations regarding internal audit services. Expectation gaps in internal auditing may arise for all stakeholders of the service. In this study, the views of independent auditors—who generally have a relatively high level of knowledge about internal audit—and internal auditors—who carry out the internal audit service—were consulted. Since expectations are subjective expressions influenced by individuals' different characteristics, examining these expectations is only possible by presenting the relevant individuals' perspectives.

In the literature, studies examining expectation, perception, and awareness are generally conducted using survey or interview techniques. In this research, the in-depth interview technique, one of the qualitative research methods, was used.

12.7 Methodology

Individuals differ in how they understand, perceive, and evaluate phenomena and events, and it is acknowledged that learning about these differences is challenging. Therefore, researchers have shown interest in examining individuals' subjectivities regarding various issues (Türnüklü 2000: 545). These examination processes are conducted using specific scientific techniques.

Although both qualitative and quantitative research types are applied in practice, their approaches to existence and knowledge differ. Qualitative research is based on the assumption that "reality is human perception, which varies from person to person or culture to culture and may change over time," and for this reason, it is argued that qualitative research reflects reality more accurately (Sağlam and Kanadlı 2019: 4).

As illustrated in Fig. 12.3, the qualitative research process consists of eight stages. Similar to other research types, the process begins with the identification of the research problem, followed by an analysis of the problem and the determination of an appropriate research approach based on the nature of the problem. Subsequently, data collection is conducted using a suitable sample aligned with the chosen method, and in the next phase, the collected data is categorized and analyzed.

Compared to quantitative research, qualitative research has certain advantages as well as some criticisms. The main concerns involve reliability, validity, generalizability, and sampling. In qualitative research, validity refers to the accurate

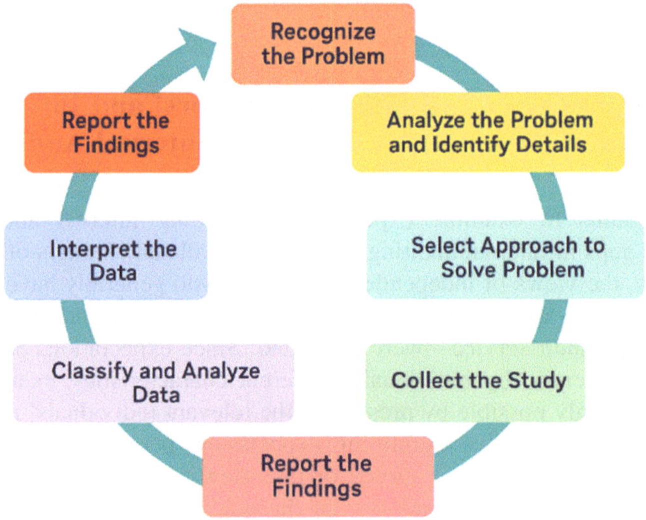

Fig. 12.3 The qualitative research process. *Source* Creswell (2002); Patton (1990); as cited in Baltacı (2019, p. 372)

representation of a social phenomenon, and it is evaluated through the detailed explanation of both the data collection process and the resulting findings. Reliability, on the other hand, is often assessed in social sciences using quantitative research principles. Although it is not feasible to perform a statistical reliability analysis in qualitative studies as in quantitative ones, the ability to replicate results under varying conditions is considered a sign of reliability. Nevertheless, due to the dynamic nature of social environments, it is acknowledged that similar results may not always be obtained (Korkmazyürek 2019, pp. 138–139).

In qualitative research, data is generally obtained concerning the environment, process, and perception. The most common methods for collecting such data include interviews, observations, and document analysis, with interviews being the most frequently preferred technique. Especially in uncovering emotions, perceptions, viewpoints, and experiences, the interview method is recognized as particularly powerful (Karataş 2015, p. 64). Due to its alignment with the objectives of this study, the interview method was chosen.

Another critical aspect in qualitative research is the sampling process. When it is not feasible to collect data from the entire population, a sample that can represent the broader population is selected using generalizable methods in quantitative research. In contrast, qualitative research focuses not on generalizing to the entire population but on explaining the topic in depth. Therefore, purposeful sampling methods that do not rely on probability theory are commonly used in qualitative studies (Baltacı 2019, p. 373; Korkmazyürek 2019, pp. 138–139). Sampling methods such as extreme or deviant case sampling, intensity sampling, maximum variation sampling, snowball or chain sampling, stratified purposeful sampling, and convenience sampling may be used in qualitative research (Baltacı 2019, p. 374). Given that interviews and observations are typically employed in qualitative studies, working with large samples is often not feasible due to time and cost constraints and the challenges posed during data analysis. For this reason, rather than seeking representativeness of the population, the relevance of the participants to the research topic is prioritized in sample selection (Karataş 2015, pp. 70–71; Yağar and Dökme 2018, p. 4; Tekin 2006, p. 104).

In this study, the snowball sampling method was preferred. Snowball sampling refers to a process in which a researcher reaches new participants through individuals already identified (Kılıç 2013, p. 45). It is particularly useful when information about the population is limited or when reaching individuals within the population is difficult. In this frequently used technique in qualitative studies, the researcher accesses new individuals through referrals from those already contacted (Evreni, 2021; Research Universe, Sample Selection and Measurement, https://www.bingol.edu.tr). In qualitative studies within the accounting and auditing fields, various methods such as snowball sampling, purposive sampling, and theoretical sampling have been observed (Segal 2019; Hansen et al. 2020; Roussy et al. 2020). There is no existing network providing contact information for independent or internal auditors to be interviewed for this study. While the names of independent auditors are disclosed by the Public Oversight, Accounting and Auditing Standards Authority (KGK), their contact information is not made public. Although some audit firms share contact details, this is not common practice. As there is no institution similar to KGK authorizing internal auditors, accessing their information is even more challenging. Furthermore, due to the timing of the study (fiscal year-end), the heavy workload of professionals, and the ongoing COVID-19 pandemic, limited response rates were anticipated. For these reasons, as in similar studies, the snowball sampling method was adopted. Additionally, in selecting participants, a minimum experience criterion of at least three years was established, considering the basic requirements necessary to hold the titles of internal or independent auditor.

In-depth interviews allow researchers to examine a subject from a broad perspective, enabling detailed responses to open-ended questions and capturing participants' feelings, knowledge, and experiences (Tekin 2006, p. 101). It is accepted that using flexible and open-ended interview questions enriches the data obtained (Roussy et al. 2020). In this study, interviews were conducted with independent and internal auditors to examine expectations and perceptions regarding internal audit. Internal auditors represent the providers of the internal audit service, while independent auditors represent the beneficiaries. According to ISA 610 (International Auditing and Assurance Standards Board (IAASB) (n.d.), independent auditors can utilize internal audit services under certain conditions. Of course, other stakeholders also benefit from internal audit. In other studies, the views of these stakeholders—such as business managers, creditors, and investors—can be examined.

To formulate the interview questions, a literature review was conducted. However, due to the limited number of studies specifically focusing on expectation gaps in internal audit, the questions were developed based on prior research on audit expectation gaps and the theoretical framework of internal audit. Seventeen open-ended questions were prepared. These were reviewed by two academics and one practitioner and finalized following their suggestions and corrections. After receiving ethics committee approval, the questions were piloted through an initial interview before being used with the remaining participants.[1]

The interviews were conducted online, via the program/method preferred by the participants, by scheduling appointments with those who agreed to participate, due to the Covid-19 pandemic. Some participants who initially scheduled an appointment later stated that they would not be able to attend the interview due to various personal reasons. In total, approximately six hundred minutes of interviews were conducted with twenty-two participants within the scope of the study. However, two participants were excluded from the scope of the research due to providing limited responses and not answering some questions. In the literature, it has been observed that several studies utilizing in-depth interviews were conducted with a similar number of participants. For example, Segal (2019) conducted interviews with twenty auditors; in another study, Roussy et al. (2020) conducted in-depth research on

[1] It was approved by the Ethics Committee of Istanbul Arel University in the meeting held on 06.08.2021, decision number 2021/11.

internal auditing with ten audit committee chairs and eight chief internal audit executives. Similarly, Schulte and Hallstedt (2018) conducted in-depth interviews with twenty-two participants on risk management.

Prior to the interviews, participants were not provided with the questions but were briefly informed about the scope of the research. Although some studies highlight various benefits of sending the questions in advance, not doing so was preferred in this case to allow participants to respond naturally without rehearsing their answers beforehand (Segal 2019: 479). Participants were reminded before the interview that their identities would remain confidential and that personal information such as name, surname, or company affiliation would not be requested. Some participants responded to multiple questions at once, which was interpreted by the researchers as an indication that the questions were well-designed. Some participants preferred not to express opinions on certain questions. In addition, although not initially included in the question set, follow-up questions were occasionally asked by the interviewer based on participants' responses. Although this study was carried out by two researchers, to ensure consistency in the interview process, all interviews were conducted by a single researcher.

12.8 Data Analysis

Following the completion of the interviews, the audio recordings were transcribed, and the coding phase began. In qualitative research, data coding involves examining the data, dividing it into meaningful parts, and attempting to identify the concepts indicated by these parts. Coding is a dynamic process that requires multiple reviews of the data set (Baltacı 2019: 378). There are various methods for coding data in qualitative research. In this study, the data were first subjected to **open coding**, followed by **axial coding**. Open coding represents the stage at which the initial categorization of the data is performed, producing smaller data sets from the broader body of information. Axial coding, on the other hand, involves reassembling the data in its new form to establish relationships between the categories (Erbaş n.d.).

The responses provided by the participants were grouped under each question and analyzed in a way that accurately reflects their thoughts. In addition, detailed responses from participants were specifically highlighted. The coding process was carried out independently by two researchers. Descriptive information about the internal auditors and independent auditors who participated in the study is presented in Table 12.3.

The participants have an average professional experience of 7.75 years, with 35% female and 65% male representation. Among the internal auditors, 40% are engaged in internal audit services in the public sector, while 60% work in internal audit roles within private sector companies.

Table 12.3 General characteristics of the participants

No	Code	Participant type	Gender	Experience (Years)	Sector
1	I01	Internal auditor	F	4	Private
2	I02	Internal auditor	F	8	Private
3	I03	Internal auditor	M	6	Private
4	I04	Internal Auditor	M	10	Private
5	I05	Internal auditor	M	13	Public
6	I06	Internal auditor	F	3	Private
7	I07	Internal auditor	M	5	Private
8	I08	Internal auditor	M	8	Public
9	I09	Internal auditor	M	12	Public
10	I10	Internal auditor	M	10	Public
11	B01	Independent auditor	F	7	-
12	B02	Independent auditor	M	10	-
13	B03	Independent auditor	F	6	-
14	B04	Independent auditor	F	7	-
15	B05	Independent auditor	M	8	-
16	B06	Independent auditor	M	12	-
17	B07	Independent auditor	M	8	-
18	B08	Independent auditor	M	6	-
19	B09	Independent auditor	F	6	-
20	B10	Independent auditor	M	6	-

Note "F" = Female, "M" = Male, "Private" = Private sector, "Public" = Public sector, "-" = Not specified

12.9 Findings

Regarding the differences in the working styles of internal auditors and independent auditors, three independent auditors and three internal auditors did not respond. In general, independent auditors emphasized the differences in objectives, working methods, and responsibilities between the two services. Internal auditors similarly referred to the differences in purpose between the services. They highlighted that internal audit focuses on areas beyond financial statements, emphasizing the importance of efficiency and effectiveness for internal audit services. One internal auditor (I01) stated that while independent auditors stand out in terms of independence, internal auditors have the advantage of being more familiar with internal processes within the organization. Based on the responses, differences between independent and internal auditors emerged particularly in terms of *working methods*, *objectives*, and *responsibilities*.

12.9.1 Interaction Between Internal and Independent Auditors

The ISA 610 outlines how independent auditors can make use of internal audit services during their audit engagements. Internal and independent auditors mutually benefit from each other's services. Regarding this interaction, all independent auditors stated that they utilize internal audit services.

One independent auditor (B05) expressed that they encountered resistance when requesting internal auditors' work and that internal auditors were reluctant to share their findings. In contrast, another auditor (B04) indicated that the presence of an internal audit unit in the audited company provided a sense of confidence and reduced their workload. Similarly, auditor B09 noted that internal audit work, under appropriate conditions, helped alleviate the auditor's burden.

Furthermore, five independent auditors (B02, B05, B06, B08, B09) emphasized that internal audit work particularly contributes to defining the audit scope and identifying the company's risk areas.

On the other hand, although all internal auditors similarly reported that they benefit from independent audit services, they did not elaborate on how or in which areas these services are utilized. Some internal auditors briefly mentioned the impact of independent audits on the scope and efficiency of their internal audit processes. One participant (I03) provided a detailed example regarding the interaction between internal and independent audits.

In conclusion, the responses suggest that for independent auditors, internal audit work is particularly valuable in defining the scope of the audit. Additionally, both services are mutually beneficial, although the depth of this interaction varies among practitioners.

12.9.2 Perceptions of Internal Audit's Role in Transparency and Institutionalization

Regarding the impact of internal audit on corporate transparency, nearly half of the independent auditors stated that internal audit services do not contribute meaningfully. The main reason cited was the influence of company management over internal audit functions. While some independent auditors admitted that internal audit could theoretically support transparency, they asserted that this is rarely achieved in practice. In contrast, most internal auditors believed that internal audit enhances transparency. Thus, while internal auditors generally agreed on the transparency benefits, independent auditors presented more divergent views. For independent auditors, the independence of internal auditors is central to transparency; internal auditors, however, emphasized proper execution of the function.

With regard to institutionalization, again, nearly half of the independent auditors agreed that internal audit could support institutionalization in theory, but expressed doubt about its practical application. Some auditors acknowledged that internal audit contributes to institutionalization only if effectively applied. A few also reported that the current implementations in certain organizations already offer such contributions. One auditor (B07) stated that the existence of an internal audit unit alone is insufficient for institutionalization: "*... a company cannot claim to be institutional just because it has an internal audit unit; it is also a matter of management's vision ...*"

Among internal auditors, all but three (I01, I03, and I04) believed that internal audit contributes to institutionalization. These three, however, also accepted that such contribution is only feasible when internal audit is properly maintained. Overall, internal auditors showed stronger consensus than independent auditors regarding institutionalization. While transparency received relatively less support, both groups appeared to agree that internal audit can theoretically enhance both institutionalization and transparency—provided that internal audit practices are implemented effectively and under the right conditions.

12.9.3 Internal Audit's Effectiveness in Risk Management

In evaluating whether internal audit services play an effective role in addressing risks that companies may face, both internal and independent auditors generally shared similar views. Six independent auditors stated that internal audit is effective in identifying risks and taking action. Three others noted that internal audit can make a contribution, provided it is implemented effectively. One auditor (B01) did not comment on the current effectiveness but rather focused on the conditions required for internal audit to be beneficial in risk management.

Among internal auditors, six participants stated that internal audit plays an effective role in managing risks. Two others indicated that internal audit may be beneficial only within a well-functioning system. Another two internal auditors acknowledged the theoretical benefits of internal audit but asserted that, in practice, it is not always sufficiently effective.

Beyond risk identification and mitigation, one internal auditor (I04) emphasized that expectations from internal audit vary across company managements, and these differences are even visible in job advertisements for internal audit roles. This participant noted that when management expects internal audit to focus on risk-related matters, the service is more likely to operate in alignment with that objective.

Overall, the responses reveal that internal audit can be effective in identifying and managing risks, but this depends significantly on how effectively the service is conducted and whether it is aligned with its intended purpose.

12.9.4 Alignment of Internal Audit Practices with Theoretical Framework

Independent and internal auditors presented differing views on whether internal audit services are conducted in line with their theoretical foundations.

Among the independent auditors, three participants (B04, B07, and B10) clearly stated that internal audit services are not being carried out as they should be. Additionally, two auditors attributed the shortcomings in internal audit practices to the unfavorable attitudes of family-owned businesses toward internal auditing. In contrast, six independent auditors emphasized that internal audit services are implemented properly in large and institutional firms. One auditor (B03) highlighted the positive impact of the Turkish Commercial Code No. 6102 on the development of internal audit services.

On the other hand, almost all internal auditors—except one (I02)—believed that internal audit services are not being carried out as they should be. Two internal auditors (I03 and I10) provided detailed explanations for this. One pointed out that the lack of a formal evaluation mechanism linked to the level of institutionalization prevents an accurate assessment of internal audit quality. Despite formal claims that companies listed under the Capital Markets Board have functioning audit committees, in practice, these committees are often inactive or symbolic. The responsibility to evaluate the effectiveness of internal audit falls to these committees, but due to their ineffectiveness, evaluations remain insufficient (I03). Another internal auditor (I10) noted a sectoral disparity, explaining that while internal audit services may function effectively in the financial sector, they are often inadequate in the real sector. In such contexts, systemic control mechanisms are lacking, and deficiencies are only identified after problems occur, prompting reactive changes.

In summary, compared to internal auditors, independent auditors were more inclined to believe that internal audit services are implemented appropriately—especially in corporate settings. Internal auditors, however, emphasized that internal audit is often viewed as a "bureaucratic requirement" rather than a function executed in accordance with its theoretical principles.

12.9.5 Compliance with Regulations and Ethical Principles in Internal Audit Practices

In terms of compliance with regulations, four independent auditors stated that they believe internal auditors act in accordance with regulations, while two auditors emphasized that such compliance is more likely observed in corporate enterprises. However, fewer affirmative responses were provided by independent auditors when asked specifically about compliance with ethical principles. Some independent auditors shared notable observations on this matter. One stated: "*... employees at every level sometimes bend the rules, but I think they act in accordance with* *ethical and moral standards. They may bend the rules with interpretation, but still behave ethically ...* " (B09). Another auditor highlighted differences between firm types: "*... in family businesses, things don't operate very smoothly because internal auditors may act inappropriately out of concern for their future. But in corporate firms, internal auditors act more professionally. They are aware that any potential losses in the business may reflect on them as well, and they care more about prestige than anxiety for the future ...* " (B10).

On the other hand, the majority of internal auditors reported that internal audit services are carried out in accordance with both regulations and ethical principles. One internal auditor (I04) refrained from expressing an opinion. Two others (I03 and I10) suggested that greater attention to regulations and ethics is observed in corporate enterprises.

One internal auditor provided a detailed explanation of the organizational factors affecting ethical compliance: "*... ethical principles are taken into account, but again, this is related to the level of institutionalization of the company. The degree to which the internal audit culture has been established within the company and the management's perspective on internal auditing are very important. If the management fully supports internal auditing in every aspect, the effectiveness of internal auditing and adherence to ethical principles will certainly increase. However, if there is no well-established institutional structure, if the audit committee does not measure or evaluate the effectiveness and quality of internal audit activities, if there is no established system within the company and if an environment with control weaknesses prone to misconduct exists, then internal auditors may drift away from ethical principles to avoid losing their jobs ...* " (I03).

In general, internal auditors expressed stronger confidence than independent auditors in the regulatory and ethical compliance of internal audit practices. These statements suggest that while unethical behavior may occur in practice, compliance with regulations and ethical principles is perceived to be higher in corporate enterprises.

12.9.6 Objectivity of Internal Audit Reports

Three of the independent auditors interviewed stated that internal audit reports do not contain objective information. Five auditors expressed that the reports could contain objective information if proper internal audit services are provided, and two believed that internal audit reports consist of objective information.

In general, independent auditors emphasized that internal audit reports are not sufficiently objective due to the internal audit function operating under the influence of management, which affects the information included in the reports.

Except for one internal auditor (I06), all internal auditors stated that internal audit reports objectively reflect the financial and operational status of the enterprise.

When compared with independent auditors, a significant difference in opinions is observed on this issue. Based on the perspectives of independent auditors, the "effective functioning of the internal audit service" emerges as a key factor for the objectivity of internal audit reports.

12.9.7 Independence and Objectivity in Internal Audit Services

Participants generally addressed independence and objectivity together when evaluating internal audit services. Nearly all independent auditors expressed the view that internal auditors are not sufficiently independent and objective. Only two independent auditors offered suggestions on the matter, while six recommended enhancing independence by affiliating the internal audit unit directly with the board of directors. Additionally, one independent auditor (B06) suggested that rotation could improve objectivity in internal audit services.

Internal auditors provided relatively more extensive views on this topic. About half of them stated that achieving independence and objectivity is not possible, while the other half indicated that it could be possible under certain conditions. Most internal auditors agreed that linking the internal audit unit to upper management could enhance these qualities. However, one internal auditor (I01) emphasized that independence and objectivity in internal audit services are not always achievable. Another internal auditor (I02) presented an alternative view, suggesting that outsourcing internal audit services to an external professional organization could improve independence and objectivity.

In conclusion, the feedback collected reveals that independence and objectivity in internal audit services remain concerning issues. Although affiliating the internal audit unit with upper management could contribute to improving these aspects, this concern may not be entirely eliminated in all circumstances.

12.9.8 Legal Obligation of Internal Audit in Certain Enterprises

Eight independent auditors stated that making internal audit services mandatory by legal regulation for certain enterprises would be beneficial. However, two auditors (B05 and B02) expressed that such an obligation is unnecessary. Additionally, several independent auditors (B01, B03, B06, and B07) emphasized that even if internal audit were mandatory, it would not serve its intended purpose unless businesses adopt an appropriate perspective toward internal audit.

Similarly, the majority of internal auditors (eight participants) supported the idea that internal audit services could be made legally mandatory for certain enterprises. Yet, they also stressed that effectiveness depends on whether the company's management has a proper attitude toward internal auditing. Some internal auditors also pointed out deficiencies in the current legal framework concerning internal audit and emphasized the need for improvements.

It was observed that both independent and internal auditors share similar views regarding the legal obligation of internal audit for specific enterprises. However, they also highlighted that in addition to legal enforcement, it is essential for company management to adopt a proper outlook toward internal audit for it to be truly effective.

12.9.9 Willingness of Enterprises to Establish Internal Audit Units Voluntarily

Nearly all independent auditors, except B02, emphasized that enterprises are generally not willing to establish internal audit units voluntarily, particularly due to cost-benefit concerns. Several participants noted that businesses other than large enterprises would be especially reluctant to form internal audit units.

Among internal auditors, six stated that large companies with a corporate structure are more likely to establish internal audit units voluntarily. However, they also noted that smaller enterprises often see internal audit as a cost factor and thus are less inclined to adopt it. One internal auditor (I06) highlighted that if enterprises were more aware of the benefits of internal audit services, they might be more willing to establish such units, but the current level of awareness remains low.

Overall, it can be concluded that internal audit units are largely viewed through a "cost" lens, that there is insufficient awareness about the benefits of internal audit, and that corporate enterprises are more likely to be willing to establish internal audit units.

12.9.10 Stakeholders Who Benefit the Most From Internal Audit Services

Participants were asked which stakeholder group benefits the most from internal audit services. The responses were distributed as follows (Table 12.4).

Some participants mentioned more than one group in their responses; the table reflects only the group each respondent believed benefits the most.

While there were similarities among the answers, noticeable differences also emerged. Independent auditors predominantly stated that internal audit services provide the greatest benefit to business management. In contrast, internal auditors mostly emphasized that the main beneficiary is the business itself.

One participant (I04) pointed out that the beneficiary may vary depending on the type of internal audit service provided. For example, they noted that "internal

Table 12.4 Primary Beneficiaries of Internal Audit Services

Benefiting group	Independent auditors (B)	Internal auditors (I)
Business management	4	2
Business and shareholders	2	-
Independent auditors	1	1
Business management and shareholders	1	-
Shareholders	1	2
Business	1	3
Business management and public sector	-	1
Economic system	-	1

audit's contribution to occupational health primarily benefits business management and the public."

In summary, internal audit services are perceived to provide the greatest contribution especially to **"business management"** and **"the business"** itself.

12.9.11 The Effect of Internal Audit Services on the Reliability of Financial Statements

Regarding the impact of internal audit services on the reliability of financial statements, six independent auditors expressed positive views, indicating that internal audit enhances financial statement reliability. One auditor partially agreed with this notion, while three auditors emphasized that internal audit services can positively influence reliability only when an effective internal control system is in place.

Internal auditors shared similar opinions. Five internal auditors stated that internal audit units have a positive effect on the reliability of financial statements, while two auditors believed internal audit is partially effective in this regard. Two others pointed out that internal audit services are only effective if they are conducted properly and function efficiently. One internal auditor (I06), however, expressed a different opinion, asserting that the presence or absence of internal audit does not have any effect on the reliability of financial statements.

In general, participants from both groups believe that internal audit services contribute to improving the reliability of financial statements. Nonetheless, this contribution is considered to depend significantly on the functionality and effectiveness of the internal audit system.

12.9.12 The Use of Internal or External Resources in Internal Audit Services

The question of whether internal audit services should be provided from within the company or through external outsourcing received the most extensive responses from participants. Among independent auditors, four stated that outsourcing internal audit services would be more effective, while three argued that providing the service from within the organization would be more efficient. Two independent auditors believed that a hybrid system is more effective. One independent auditor (B01) pointed out that both systems have different advantages and disadvantages, stating: "*... in outsourced services, it may not be easy to understand the business, identify risky areas, and perform analyses—being familiar with these issues and auditing effectively can be difficult. The external auditor has limited time. On the other hand, internal blindness can develop within the organization. Therefore, the quality of the resource used and proper planning are essential ...*" Another independent auditor (B03), who supported the hybrid model, explained: "*... combining the knowledge and experience of someone who knows the company with that of external professionals can produce more effective results. Bringing someone unfamiliar with the company to set rules and establish systems may create operational challenges, as internal employees may struggle to adapt, and without adaptation, the desired efficiency may not be achieved ...*"

Among internal auditors, four stated that external sourcing would be more beneficial, while three preferred internal sourcing. Two internal auditors noted that both systems have different strengths and weaknesses. One internal auditor (I05) stated that internal sourcing would be more beneficial for large companies. Another internal auditor (I01) emphasized that while internal audit should initially be outsourced, it should later be continued internally.

Overall, it can be stated that the perspectives of independent and internal auditors on this matter are largely aligned. The use of internal or external resources in internal audit services is considered to have distinct advantages and disadvantages, depending on the context.

12.9.13 The Role of Internal Audit in Detecting Fraud

When examining the responses of independent auditors regarding the role of internal audit in detecting fraud, one independent auditor did not respond, four stated that internal audit does not have an impact on fraudulent financial reporting, and three indicated that internal audit could be effective only if it operates efficiently. Most independent auditors emphasized that internal audit services are more effective in detecting and preventing employee fraud rather than fraudulent financial reporting.

In contrast, internal auditors demonstrated a stronger belief in the effectiveness of internal audit services in detecting fraudulent financial reporting compared to independent auditors. A divergence in opinion between internal and independent auditors was observed regarding the detection of fraud. Nevertheless, independent auditors generally perceive internal audit as more effective in identifying "employee fraud" rather than "fraudulent financial reporting."

12.9.14 Resources Allocated to Internal Audit and the Cost-Benefit Balance

All independent auditors stated that they believe the cost incurred for internal audit services is lower than the benefits obtained. Except for one, six independent auditors considered the resources allocated to internal audit in companies to be insufficient, while three noted that adequate resources are only available in large and institutional companies, and inadequate in others.

Among internal auditors, one participant (I01) did not respond, five internal auditors stated that the resources allocated were sufficient, and four found them insufficient. Except for one internal auditor (I09), all internal auditors expressed the opinion that the cost of internal audit is lower than the benefit obtained. These findings reveal a difference of opinion between independent and internal auditors regarding the adequacy of allocated resources.

One internal auditor (I01) highlighted the lack of awareness among company management, stating that if companies understood the potential benefits of internal audit, they might allocate more resources. Similarly, one independent auditor (B03) noted that companies, from a taxation perspective, tend to focus on legal compliance only and therefore do not allocate sufficient resources to internal audit.

Overall, it can be concluded that resources allocated to internal audit units are generally deemed "insufficient" outside of corporate enterprises, and internal audit is perceived as a "costly" function due to the management's misperceptions.

12.9.15 Competence and Adequacy of Internal Audit Personnel

Four independent auditors stated that the number of internal audit personnel in companies is insufficient, while two auditors (B09 and B10) emphasized that this inadequacy is more pronounced in non-corporate enterprises. Compared to the issue of quantity, fewer criticisms were directed at the competency of internal auditors. Additionally, seven independent auditors expressed that internal auditors should possess certifications. One of them (B03) elaborated on this view by stating: *"… nowadays, every profession, even cooking, has a school. Every job has its theory and experience, so I believe that having certain certifications improves the quality of the work produced. Therefore, I am one of those who think that people should go through specific certification processes ...*"

On the other hand, six internal auditors stated that the number of internal auditors in their organizations is sufficient. However, four of them expressed critical opinions regarding the qualifications of internal audit personnel. While four internal auditors believed that certifications are not very important, six others emphasized their significance. One internal auditor (I03) pointed out the high cost of the certification process and noted that the support of company management is essential in this regard. Another internal auditor (I01) stressed the importance of international certification rather than merely undergoing a bureaucratic certification process.

It is evident that there is a difference of opinion between independent and internal auditors regarding the "competence and adequacy" of internal auditors. Nevertheless, it can be generally stated that a system of "mandatory certification" for internal auditors is considered beneficial.

12.9.16 The Impact of the Covid-19 Pandemic on Internal Audit Practices

Independent auditors generally emphasized the negative effects of the Covid-19 pandemic on internal audit work. In particular, they highlighted issues such as the inability to conduct physical inventory counts, difficulties in obtaining certain types of audit evidence, and changes in business workflows. Nonetheless, some auditors also mentioned that the shift to remote work created by the pandemic offered certain advantages.

Internal auditors similarly addressed various challenges resulting from the pandemic-related disruptions. One internal auditor (I05) pointed out that during this period, the importance of information technologies was recognized, and that it might become necessary to develop specialization in data mining in the future.

12.10 Conclusion and Discussion

Audit expectation gaps arise due to the differing expectations and perceptions of various stakeholders in the audit environment. In the literature, audit expectation gap studies have predominantly focused on independent auditing; however, it is likely that similar gaps exist in other assurance services that cater to different user groups. Moreover, since expectations are influenced by the nature of the service and the interest groups involved, the characteristics of assurance services and the surrounding perceptions will vary accordingly. Expectation gaps are generally considered a negative phenomenon, as they hinder the fulfillment of the fundamental objectives of assurance services.

Various academic studies and regulatory policies have been proposed to reduce or eliminate these expectation gaps. Academic research has focused on the components and causes of expectation gaps and examined whether such gaps can be eliminated and which practices may contribute to their reduction. Regulatory bodies, on the other hand, have generally implemented changes through legislation to frame audit activities more effectively.

In general, expectation gaps are considered to arise from deficiencies in legislation, performance shortcomings of auditors, and unrealistic demands of certain interest groups. As assurance services strive to adapt to a rapidly changing business environment, regulatory bodies have increasingly focused on addressing legislative inadequacies. Additionally, oversight mechanisms have been established to improve auditor performance. Nevertheless, despite improvements in legislation and performance, many studies have shown that expectation gaps persist due to the influence of different stakeholder characteristics and the presence of some unrealistic demands.

As with independent auditing, expectations regarding legislation in internal audit can also lead to expectation gaps. Since internal audit services are not implemented in a standardized form like independent auditing, they tend to differ depending on the structure of the organization. Because unrealistic expectations often stem from demands that are unlikely to be fulfilled, it is important that internal audit activities are clearly defined and communicated

In this study, in-depth interview methodology, a qualitative research approach, was employed to explore the expectations of internal auditors and independent auditors regarding internal audit activities. The findings can be summarized as follows:

There are notable differences between internal auditors and independent auditors concerning the contribution of internal audit services to institutionalization, their execution in accordance with theoretical frameworks, compliance with regulations and ethical principles, the objectivity of internal audit reports, the independence and impartiality of internal auditors, and the role of internal audit in detecting fraud.

However, internal auditors and independent auditors exhibited similar perspectives on the impact of internal audit services on the reliability of financial statements, the cost-benefit balance of internal audit, certification requirements, the competence and adequacy of internal audit personnel, the obligation of internal audit in certain enterprises, and the role of internal audit in identifying risks the organization may face.

It is particularly important that internal audit services operate in an objective work environment to fulfill their intended purposes. Furthermore, the perception that internal auditors do not sufficiently comply with legal and ethical principles is noteworthy. Lastly, the view that internal audit is merely a cost, especially among non-corporate enterprises, and the presence of inappropriate management perspectives may hinder the success of internal audit activities.

While this research focuses on the perspectives of internal and independent auditors through in-depth interviews, it should be noted that expectation gaps can also exist among other stakeholder groups of internal audit and other assurance services. Future research could explore the expectations of different stakeholder groups to identify the sources of expectation gaps and propose possible solutions. Using different research techniques, expectation differences among various groups can be further investigated on selected themes.

References

Adafula B, Osei EM, Ofori IK (2019) Expectation–performance of internal auditors: examining views from Ghana. J Account Tax 11(5):79–88

Adeyemi SB, Uadiale OM (2011) An empirical investigation of the audit expectation gap (AEG) in Nigeria. Afr J Bus Manag 5(19):7964–7971

Ağdeniz Ş, Çetin C (2021) Uzaktan iç denetim ve uzaktan iç denetimin sınırlılıkları. Muhasebe Bilim Dünyası Dergisi 23(Özel Sayı):58–80

Ahlawat SS, Lowe DJ (2004) An examination of internal auditor objectivity: in-house versus outsourcing. Audit J Pract Theory 23(2):147–158

Akther T, Xu F (2020) Existence of the audit expectation gap and its impact on stakeholders' confidence: the moderating role of the Financial Reporting Council. Int J Financ Stud 8(1):1–25

Altuk VE (2021) Covid-19 salgınının iç denetim üzerindeki etkileri: bir çözüm önerisi olarak uzaktan denetim. Denetişim 22:15–26

Anderson JC, Lowe DJ, Reckers PM (1993) Evaluation of auditor decisions: hindsight bias effects and the expectation gap. J Econ Psychol 14(4):711–737

Arrington CE, Hillison WA, Williams PF (1983) The psychology of expectations gaps: why is there so much dispute about auditor responsibility? Account Bus Res 13(52):243–250

Aslan B (2010) Bir yönetim fonksiyonu olarak iç denetim. Sayıştay Dergisi 77:63–77

Bailey KE, Bylinski JH, Shields MD (1983) Effects of audit report wording changes on the perceived message. J Account Res 355–370

Baltacı A (2019) Nitel araştırma süreci: nitel bir araştırma nasıl yapılır? Ahi Evran Üniversitesi Sosyal Bilimler Enstitüsü Dergisi 5(2):368–388

Bierstaker J, Chen L, Christ MH, Ege M, Mintchik N (2013) Obtaining assurance for financial statement audits and control audits when aspects of the financial reporting process are outsourced. Audit J Pract 32(Supplement 1):209–250

Bircan NG (2020) İç denetimde yapısal değişim ve dönüşüm: iç denetçilerin farkındalığı ve beklentileri üzerine bir araştırma. Istanbul Üniversitesi Muhasebe Enstitüsü Dergisi – Journal of Accounting Institute 63:67–83

Bozkurt N (2012) Muhasebe Denetimi. Alfa Yayınları, İstanbul

Brown DL, Jones KT (2011) Graduate education and the audit expectations gap in the post-SOX era. J High Educ Theory Pract 11(3):67–82

Burton FG, Emett SA, Simon CA, Wood DA (2012) Corporate managers' reliance on internal auditor recommendations. Audit J Pract Theory 31(2):151–166

Byington JR, Sutton SG (1991) The self-regulating profession: an analysis of the political monopoly tendencies of the audit profession. Crit Perspect Account 2(4):315–330

Campbell DR, Michenzi AR (1987) Revising the audit report: a response to the expectation gap. CPA J 57(4):34

Campbell JE, Mutchler JF (1988) The 'expectations gap' and going-concern uncertainties. Account Horiz 2(1):42–49
Chambers AD, Odar M (2015) A new vision for internal audit. Manag Audit J 30(1):34–55
Creswell JW (2002) Educational research: planning, conducting, and evaluating quantitative. Prentice Hall, Upper Saddle River, NJ
Dang TA, Nguyen DKN (2021) Components constituting the audit expectation gap: the Vietnamese case. J Asian Finance Econ Bus 8(1):363–373
Demir M, Kısakürek MM, Arslan Ö (2019) İç denetim sisteminin hileli finansal raporlamayı önlemedeki rolüne yönelik bağımsız denetçiler üzerinde bir araştırma. Muhasebe Ve Finansman Dergisi 82:111–134
Dennis I (2010) What do you expect? A reconfiguration of the audit expectations gap. Int J Audit 14(2):130–146
Desai NK, Gerard GJ, Tripathy A (2008) Co-sourcing and external auditors' reliance on the internal audit function. Inst Int Audit Res Found 1–10
Dewing IP, Russell PO (2002) UK fund managers, audit regulation and the new accountancy foundation: towards a narrowing of the audit expectations gap? Manag Audit J 17(9):537–545
Dinç E, Gerekan B (2014) Denetimde beklenti farklılığı ve denetim eğitiminin beklenti farklılığı üzerindeki etkisine yönelik bir araştırma. Süleyman Demirel Üniversitesi Iktisadi Ve Idari Bilimler Fakültesi Dergisi 19(1):21–36
Dixon R, Woodhead AD, Sohliman M (2006) An investigation of the expectation gap in Egypt. Manag Audit J 21(3):293–302
El Nashar TA (2020) Internal audit expectation gap and auditing around the computer. SSRN. https://doi.org/10.2139/ssrn.3528088
Ellul L, Scicluna A (2020) An analysis of the audit expectation gap in the Maltese central government. Public Money Manag 1–12. https://doi.org/10.1080/09540962.2020.1769351
Epstein MJ, Geiger MA (1994) Investor views of audit assurance: recent evidence of the expectation gap. J Account 60–66
Erasmus L, Coetzee P (2010) The standing of the internal audit function within South African companies. Afr J Bus Manag 3:926–935
Erbaş H (n.d.). Araştırma, nitel araştırma. Online. https://slideplayer.biz.tr/slide/17140817/. Accessed 7 Feb 2021
Evreni A, Örneklem Seçimi ve Ölçüm. (2021). Online. https://www.bingol.edu.tr/media/210799/sayt-bolum12-Arastirma-Evreni-Orneklem-Secimi-ve-Olcum.pdf. Accessed 7 Feb 2021
Frank KE, Lowe DJ, Smith JK (2001) The expectation gap: perceptual differences between auditors, jurors and students. Manag Audit J 16(3):145–150
Giacomino DE (1994). Expanding the auditors' role to narrow the expectations gap. Bus Forum Summer(Fall), 31–35.
Glover SM, Prawitt DF, Wood DA (2008) Internal audit sourcing arrangement and the external auditor's reliance decision. Contemp Account Res 25(1):193–213
Gold A, Gronewold U, Pott C (2012) The ISA 700 auditor's report and the audit expectation gap–Do explanations matter? Int J Audit 16(3):286–307
Gramling AA, Schatzberg JW, Wallace WA (1996) The role of undergraduate auditing coursework in reducing the expectations gap. Issues Account Educ 11(1):131–161
Güldüler ES (2021) Kamuda İç Denetim ve Aşamlalarıyla Bir İç Denetim Uygulama Örneği. R. Kızılboğa Özaslan (Ed.), Kamuda Denetim Türleri (329–375. ss.). Ankara: Adalet Yayınevi.
Guy DM, Sullivan JD (1988) The expectation gap auditing standards. J Account 165(4):36–46
Hansen M, Fyall A, Spyriadis T (2020) From finance to adventure: using ERM as a framework in adventure tourism. Manag Sport Leisure 1–18
Hassink HF, Bollen LH, Meuwissen RH, de Vries MJ (2009) Corporate fraud and the audit expectations gap: a study among business managers. J Int Account Audit Tax 18(2):85–100
Hillison W, Pacini C, Sinason D (1999) The internal auditor as fraud-buster. Manag Audit J 14(7):351–363

Humphrey C (2007). Debating audit expectations. In Sherer M, et al. (eds) Current Issues in Auditing 3rd ed. Sage Publications.
Humphrey C, Moizer P, Turley S (1992) The audit expectations gap—plus ça change, plus c'est la même chose? Crit Perspect Account 3(2):137–161
Humphrey C, Moizer P, Turley S (1993) The audit expectations gap in Britain: an empirical investigation. Account Bus Res 23(sup1):395–411
IIA. (n.d.). About the profession. Online. https://na.theiia.org/about-us/about-ia/Pages/About-the-Profession.aspx. Accessed 9 Dec 2020
IIA (2017). Uluslararası İç Denetim Standartları: Mesleki Uygulama Çerçevesi Kapsamında Uluslararası İç Denetim Standartları. https://www.tide.org.tr/file/documents/pdf/UMUC-2017-updated.pdf. Accessed 7 Feb 2021
Ima JN (2015) Effective internal audit as a tool for fraud deterrence in Nigerian organizations. Humanit Soc Sci J 73–80
International Auditing and Assurance Standards Board (IAASB) (n.d.) ISA 240: the auditor's responsibilities relating to fraud in an audit of financial statements
International Auditing and Assurance Standards Board (IAASB) (n.d.) ISA 610: using the work of internal auditors and related conforming amendments
İSMMMO. (2015). İç denetime genel bir bakış. Online. https://archive.ismmmo.org.tr/docs/YAYINLAR/kitaplar/ic_denetim_2015.pdf. Accessed 10 Dec 2020
Johnstone KM, Gramling AA, Rittenberg LE (2014) Auditing: a risk-based approach to conducting a quality audit, 9th edn. South-Western Cengage Learning
Karataş Z (2015) Sosyal bilimlerde nitel araştırma yöntemleri. Manevi Temelli Sosyal Hizmet Araştırmaları Dergisi 1(1):62–80
Karcıoğlu R, Kurnaz E (2017) Türkiye'de kamu sektöründe risk odaklı iç denetim yaklaşımı: Kamu iç denetçilerine yönelik bir araştırma. Atatürk Üniversitesi İktisadi ve İdari Bilimler Dergisi 31(5):1087–1104
Kaval H (2005) Muhasebe Denetimi. Gazi Kitabevi, Ankara
Kılıç S (2013) Örnekleme yöntemleri. J Mood Disord 3(1):44–46
Kızılboğa R (2013) İç denetim sisteminde denetçilerin bağımsızlık ve tarafsızlığının önemi. Marmara Üniversitesi Sosyal Bilimler Dergisi 1(1):107–119
Koh HC, Woo ES (1998) The expectation gap in auditing. Manag Audit J 13(3):147–156
Koh HC, Woo ES (2001) The auditor-manager expectation gap in auditing. Manag Audit J 16(3):176–188
Koo CM, Sim HS (1999) On the role conflict of auditors in Korea. Account Audit Account J 12(2):206–219
Korkmazyürek Y (2019) Nitel araştırmalarda kodlama: "Psikolojik sözleşme algısı, örgütsel güven algısı ve profesyonel bürokrasi etkisi"ne yönelik bir örnek. Uluslararası İktisadi ve İdari Bilimler Dergisi 5(1):131–147
Kyburz A (2016) Internal auditing in Switzerland: stakeholder expectations versus self-perception : a theoretical and empirical analysis from a management perspective. University of St. Gallen
Labuschagne M, Fourie H (2018) Fraud investigation: an internal audit stakeholder expectation gap. South Afr J Account Audit Res 20:123–132
Lee TH, Ali AM, Bien D (2009) Towards an understanding of the audit expectation gap. ICFAI J Audit Pract 6(1):7–35
Leung P, Chau G (2001) The problematic relationship between audit reporting and audit expectations: some evidence from Hong Kong. Adv Int Account 14:181–200
Liggio CD (1974) The expectation gap: the accountant's legal waterloo? J Contemp Bus 3:23
Lowe DJ, Pany K (1993) Expectations of the audit function. CPA J 63(8):58–59
Marşap B, Kurt G, Uçma T (2012) Sürekli denetimin gerektirdiği iç denetim faaliyetleri açısından stratejik yönetim muhasebesinin gerekliliği. World Account Sci 14(4):1–18
McEnroe JE, Martens SC (2001) Auditors' and investors' perceptions of the "expectation gap". Account Horiz 15(4):345–358

Memiş MÜ (2007) Türkiye'deki iç denetim profilinin belirlenmesine ilişkin bir araştırma. Ç.Ü. Sosyal Bilimler Enstitüsü Dergisi 16(1):461–478
Miller JR, Reed SA, Strawser RH (1990) The new auditor's report: will it close the expectations gap in communications? CPA J 60(5):68–72
Mohamed N (2013) Financial statement fraud control: audit testing and internal auditing expectation gap. Int Proc Econ Dev Res 65:61–67
Mohamed NF, Zauwiyah A (2004) Audit expectation gap. The case of Malaysia. Manag Audit J 19(7):897–915
Mollaoğulları BF, Öncü S (2020) Denetim komitesinin iç denetim birimi çalışmalarına etkisi: türkiye'de iç denetim birimi yöneticilerinin algısı araştırması. Manisa Celal Bayar Üniversitesi, Yönetim Ve Ekonomi 27(3):405–424
Monroe GS, Woodliff DR (1993) The effect of education on the audit expectation gap. Account Finance 33(1):61–78
Munro L, Stewart J (2010) External auditors' reliance on internal audit: the impact of sourcing arrangements and consulting activities. Account Finance 50:371–387
Nguyen HT, Nguyen AH (2020) Audit expectation gap: empirical evidence from Vietnam. J Asian Finance Econ Bus 7(5):51–60. https://doi.org/10.13106/JAFEB.2020.VOL7.NO5.051
Noghondari AT, Foong SY (2009) Audit expectation gap and loan decision performance of bank officers in Iran. Int J Account Audit Perform Eval 5(3):310–328
Ojo M (2006) Eliminating the audit expectations gap: myth or reality? Munich Pers RePEc Arch 232:1–13
Okafor CA, Otalor JI (2013) Narrowing the expectation gap in auditing: the role of the auditing profession. Res J Finance Account 4(2):43–52
Olojede P, Erin O, Asiriuwa O, Usman M (2020) Audit expectation gap: an empirical analysis. Future Bus J 6:1–12
Otalor J, Okafor C (2013) Imperatives of bridging the audit expectation gap and enhancing the credibility of corporate financial information. Int J Bus Soc Res 3(5):125–138
Oussii AA, Taktak NB (2015) Internal audit function in Tunisian listed companies: an explanatory study. Res J Finance Account 6(19):92–103
Özbek Ç (2012) İç Denetim: kurumsal Yönetim, Risk Yönetimi, İç Kontrol. Türkiye İç Denetim Enstitüsü Yayınları, İstanbul
Özdoğan B, Öncü S (2016) Türkiye'de iç denetim mesleğinin güncel durumu: bir araştırma. Celal Bayar Üniversitesi I.i.b.f. Manisa. Yönetim Ve Ekonomi 23(1):19–33
Palaniappan AK, Lee TH, Gloeck JD (2007) The audit expectation gap: an empirical study in Malaysia. South Afr J Account Audit Res 7(1):1–15
Patton MQ (1990) Qualitative evaluation and research methods. SAGE Publications, Inc
Pierce B, Kilcommins M (1996) The audit expectations gap: the role of auditing education. DCU Bus Sch Res Pap Ser 13:1–32
Porter B (1993) An empirical study of the audit expectation-performance gap. Account Bus Res 24(93):49–68
Porter B, Gowthorpe C (2004) Audit expectation-performance gap in the United Kingdom in 1999 and comparison with the gap in New Zealand in 1989 and in 1999. Institute of Chartered Accountants of Scotland, Edinburgh, Scotland
Roussy M, Barbe O, Raimbault S (2020) Internal audit: from effectiveness to organizational significance. Manag Audit J 35(2):322–342
Ruhnke K, Schmidt M (2014) The audit expectation gap: existence, causes, and the impact of changes. Account Bus Res 44(5):572–601
Sağlam Y, Kanadlı S (2019) Nitel Veri Analizinde Kodlama. Pegem Akademi, Ankara
Saha A, Baruah D (2008) Audit expectations gap in India: an empirical survey. ICFAI J Audit Pract 5(2):68–83
Saladrigues R, Grañó M (2014) Audit expectation gap: fraud detection and other factors. Eur Account Manag Rev 1(1):120–142

Salehi M (2011) Audit expectation gap: concept, nature and trace. Afr J Bus Manag 5(21):8376–8392

Salehi M, Azary Z (2008) Fraud detection and audit expectation gap: empirical evidence from Iranian bankers. Int J Bus Manag 3(10):65–77

Salehi M, Mansoury A, Azary Z (2009) Audit independence and expectation gap: empirical evidences from Iran. Int J Econ Finance 1(1):165–174

Sarens G, De Beelde I (2006) The relationship between internal audit and senior management: a qualitative analysis of expectations and perceptions. Int J Audit 10(3):219–241

Sarısoy Ö, Kepçe N (2019) Bağımsız denetim raporunda kilit denetim konularına yer verilmesi ve beklenti farkları. Mali Çözüm Dergisi/Financial Analysis 29(153):39–66

Schulte J, Hallstedt SI (2018) Company risk management in light of the sustainability transition. Sustainability 10(11):4137,1–25

Segal M (2019) Key audit matters: insight from audit experts. Meditari Account Res 27(3):474–494

Shaikh JM, Talha M (2003) Credibility and expectation gap in reporting on uncertainties. Manag Audit J 18(6/7):517–529

Shalimova N, Zagirniak D (2020) The education impact on "expectations gap" in auditing and other assurance in specific industries. In 2020 IEEE Problems of Automated Electrodrive. Theory and Practice (PAEP), pp 1–6

Siddiqui J, Nasreen T, Choudhury-Lema A (2009) The audit expectations gap and the role of audit education: the case of an emerging economy. Manag Audit J 24(6):564–583

Sikka P, Puxty A, Willmott H, Cooper C (1998) The impossibility of eliminating the expectations gap: some theory and evidence. Crit Perspect Account 9(3):299–330

Spraakman G (2001) Internal audit at the historical Hudson's Bay Company: a challenge to accepted history. Account Hist J 28(1):19–41

Tekin HH (2006) Nitel araştırma yönteminin bir veri toplama tekniği olarak derinlemesine görüşme. İstanbul Üniversitesi Sosyoloji Dergisi 3(13):101–116

The Canadian Institute of Chartered Accountants (CICA). (1988, June). Report of the Commission to Study the Public's Expectation of Audits.

The Commission on Auditors' Responsibilities (COHEN). (1978). Report, Conclusions, and Recommendations.

TİDE. (n.d.). Uluslararası İç Denetim Standartları, İç Denetim Terimler Sözlüğü. https://www.tide.org.tr/uploads/IcDenetimTerimlerSozlugu.pdf. Accessed 6 Dec 2020

Türedi H, Zor Ü (2015) Risk odaklı iç denetim. Muhasebe Ve Finansman Dergisi 66:1–20

Türk Dil Kurumu Sözlük. (n.d.). Online. https://www.tdk.gov.tr/. Accessed 9 Dec 2020

Türnüklü A (2000) Eğitimbilim araştırmalarında etkin olarak kullanılabilecek nitel bir araştırma tekniği: görüşme. Kuram Ve Uygulamada Eğitim Yönetimi 24(24):543–559

Uzun AK (n.d.). İşletmelerde iç denetim faaliyetlerinin başlatılmasında başarı faktörleri. https://www.denetimnet.net/UserFiles/Documents/DeloitteMakaleleri/i%C5%9FLETMELERDE%20Ba%C5%9Far%C4%B1%20Fakt%C3%B6rleri.pdf. Accessed 7 Dec 2020

Wolf FM, Tackett JA, Claypool GA (1999) Audit disaster futures: antidotes for the expectation gap? Manag Audit J 4(9):468–478

Yağar F, Dökme S (2018) Niteliksel araştırmaların planlanması: araştırma soruları, örneklem seçimi, geçerlik ve güvenirlik. Gazi Sağlık Bilimleri Dergisi 3(3):1–9

Yurtsever G (2014). Türkiye İç Denetim Enstitüsü'nün yeni başkanı Gürdoğan Yurtsever: iç denetim işletmeler için hayati öneme sahip (Röportaj). https://www.tide.org.tr/uploads/Turcomoney_mayis_2014.pdf. Accessed 11 Feb 2021

Zhang P (2007) The impact of the public's expectations of auditors on audit quality and auditing standards compliance. Contemp Account Res 24(2):631–654

Chapter 13
An Examination of the Effects of the Pandemic Period on the Independent Audit Process Within the Scope of International Auditing Standards

Yasemin Ertan

Abstract The COVID-19 pandemic has had extensive and profound effects on independent audit processes, making it imperative for auditors to use their ethical responsibilities, professional scepticism and judgemental skills more effectively. The economic downturn caused by the pandemic, the widespread adoption of remote working practices, weaknesses in internal control systems and increased fraud risks have further increased the need for reliable financial information. During this process, it has been necessary to apply alternative audit procedures due to difficulties in obtaining audit evidence. Additionally, accounting estimates have become more complex and subjective under pandemic conditions, making the audit of such estimates more critical. The assessment of subsequent events and the going concern assumption has become one of the key focus areas of the audit process in the pandemic context. In conclusion, during the pandemic, auditors must act in accordance with independent audit standards while taking into account the extraordinary circumstances, support their obligation to collect sufficient and appropriate audit evidence with technological tools, and maintain audit quality.

Keywords Independent audit · Pandemic · Ethics · Professional scepticism · Professional judgement · Accounting estimates · Going concern

---

This chapter was previously published in Turkish by Gazi Kitabevi with the ISBN: 978-975-7727-16-7.

Y. Ertan (✉)
Faculty of Business Sciences and Economics, Bursa Uluda University, Bursa, Türkiye
e-mail: yasertan@uludag.ed.tr

G. Kurt, Ö. Sarısoy (eds.), *Recent Advancements in Auditing*, Accounting, Finance, Sustainability, Governance & Fraud: Theory and Application,
https://doi.org/10.1007/978-981-95-5811-7_13

13.1 Introduction

Pandemic is a general name given to infectious diseases that are effective worldwide or in a large area of the globe and threaten the health of people. The World Health Organization, which was established in 1948 within the United Nations in order to make all people physically, mentally and socially healthy, first declares an emergency and then, if necessary, a pandemic when diseases that threaten the international community occur (Türkiye Bilimler Akademisi 2020).

Humanity has faced various epidemics and pandemics throughout history. For example, the largest epidemic in history is the Spanish flu, which infected approximately five hundred million people (¼ of the world population) between 1918 and 1920 (Tavukçu 2020). The plague caused the death of approximately fifty million people in the fourteenth century (World Health Organisation 2020). The cholera pandemic, which is transmitted by water and food, emerged in 1817 and is considered to be the most lethal disease of the nineteenth century (Parıldar 2020, p. 23). On the other hand, humanity has faced many pandemics such as SARS in 2003, avian flu in 2006, swine flu in 2009, Middle East Respiratory Syndrome in 2012, and Ebola in 2014 (Türkiye Bilimler Akademisi 2020).

Today, a new pandemic is being fought. In December 2019, in Wuhan, China, the disease, which started with pneumonia cases of unknown cause, was named COVID-19. COVID-19, which affected the whole world within three months, was declared a pandemic by the World Health Organisation on 11 March 2020. In the following period, each country fought the pandemic by taking measures shaped according to its geographical and economic dynamics. Naturally, Türkiye has also been greatly affected by the COVID-19 pandemic. During the pandemic period, many measures have been taken to combat the pandemic. For example, measures such as stopping land and air transportation between countries and cities, closing schools for holidays, closing shopping malls and restaurants, restricting public events, introducing curfew restrictions, and encouraging working from home have been implemented.

These measures, which are inevitable for combating the pandemic, have brought some difficulties for all segments of society, especially businesses operating in sectors such as transport, tourism, food and beverage, and automotive. One of the areas most affected by the pandemic in social and economic terms has been consumer behaviour. During the pandemic, the consumption habits of individuals have changed significantly, and a tendency to decrease in discretionary spending has been observed. The decline in consumer demand naturally affected business activities, causing a drop in revenue for some businesses. For some businesses, the decrease in economic activities and even the cessation of economic activities from time to time made it more difficult to access financing sources. On the other hand, the measures taken to protect the health of employees in enterprises have led to an increase in costs. Another challenging factor for businesses in this process is the difficulties experienced in the collection of receivables (İstanbul Chamber of Certified Public Accountants

& İstanbul Ticaret University 2020: 8–9). In addition to all these negative aspects, sustaining their existence by struggling with the pandemic has required businesses to change the way they operate, remote working practices have started to be seen much more than before, and for many businesses, the transition to remote working practices has been a sudden change that has not been prepared before. This sudden change has made the design and effectiveness of the existing internal control systems of the enterprises inadequate.

Internal control systems are systems designed and operated to ensure that businesses achieve their objectives and prevent errors and fraud within the business. Changes in the internal and external conditions of the entities have increased the likelihood of errors and created a favourable environment for fraud. This situation has brought the need for accurate and reliable information to a different dimension; therefore, the role and responsibility of the independent audit have become more important in this period.

13.2 The Importance of Independent Audit in Pandemic Periods

Accounting, which is defined as recording, classifying, summarizing, analysing and interpreting the financial events occurring in the enterprise, is the language used by enterprises to explain their realities to themselves and their stakeholders. This feature makes the financial statements created by summarizing the accounting data an important tool for the whole society to understand the business. As mentioned above, the pandemic has caused many changes in the environment in which businesses operate, which has resulted in the differentiation of natural risks for businesses. In addition to the issues discussed in earlier sections, situations such as low productivity as a result of business employees working from home, key business employees becoming ill and unable to fulfil their duties, and the use of information technologies much more than before, may prevent accounting from fulfilling its responsibility to provide accurate and reliable information to the whole society.

However, the changes in the way of doing business brought about by remote working environments require the adequacy of internal control systems to be questioned.

Undoubtedly, accurate and reliable financial statements will enable the whole society to overcome the disaster caused by the pandemic with less damage. In this context, the mission of independent auditing to ensure the reliability of financial statements has evolved to rebuild investor confidence and serve as a mechanism to reinforce corporate accountability.

During the pandemic period, there have been changes in the way audit firms operate, as well as in the businesses audited. In this process, auditors had to work from home and experienced difficulties in accessing audited companies and their employees. In addition, the change and increase in the risks faced by the audited entities have made the audit activity more complex.

It is undeniable that the COVID-19 pandemic has affected all businesses across the globe to varying degrees. Although this difficult process is not the first for humanity, it will probably not be the last.

In this chapter of the book, the impacts of the COVID-19 pandemic on independent audit processes are systematically analysed within the framework of the "International Standards on Auditing (ISAs)". Additionally, this section examines the fundamental challenges faced by auditors in the context of uncertainties, access restrictions, ethical dilemmas, and increased risk levels created by pandemic conditions. It also explains how auditors' professional scepticism, judgement, and ethical responsibilities have evolved during the pandemic. It also focuses on critical accounting and auditing issues such as obtaining "audit evidence", evaluating "accounting estimates", "going concern" and "subsequent events".

13.3 The Effects of Pandemic Periods on the Independent Audit Process

The pandemic period has had different effects on businesses operating in various sectors. In particular, while the volume of activity in retail, tourism, food and beverage and service sectors based on physical retailing decreased significantly, significant increases were observed in the business volume of businesses operating in areas such as e-trade, digital platform services, cargo and logistics.

The risk-focused auditing approach, which emerged as an extension of the effects of the Enron scandal on the accounting and auditing profession and is widely applied today, has three stages: risk assessment, risk response and reporting. The scope and subject matter of independent auditing in Türkiye are regulated by Article 398 of the "Turkish Commercial Code No. 6102". The aforementioned article stipulates that auditing shall be conducted in accordance with the principles determined by the "Türkiye Republic Public Oversight, Accounting and Auditing Standards Authority". Within the framework of the authorization granted to the "Türkiye Republic Public Oversight, Accounting and Auditing Standards Authority" to issue auditing standards, it has adopted the strategy of referencing International standards issued by the "International Federation of Accountants" (Kamu Gözetimi, Muhasebe ve Denetim Standartları Kurumu, 2019e). Consequently, independent audits in Türkiye are being carried out in accordance with the "Independent Audit Standards", which are translations of the standards published by the International Federation of Accountants, and independent audits in Türkiye are based on a risk-oriented independent audit approach. These standards, referred to as "Independent Auditing Standards" (Bağımsız Denetim Standartları- BDS), facilitate the implementation of independent auditing in our country in accordance with international norms.

The chaos and uncertainty caused by the pandemic in business operations, as well as the extraordinary circumstances that arose in the performance of auditors' activities, made it necessary to approach the application of independent auditing standards from different angles during this period. In the following sections, specific challenges faced by auditors in the pandemic period, especially in the areas of compliance with ethical principles, professional scepticism and judgement, obtaining sufficient and appropriate audit evidence, evaluating accounting estimates, going concern and auditing of events occurring after the balance sheet date, will be examined and the issues to be considered in dealing with these challenges will be discussed.

13.3.1 Code of Ethics

Ethical rules are rules shaped by elements such as the experiences of society and moral and religious beliefs, which enable us to live together in harmony as a community. In addition to ethical rules that apply to the whole society, there are also professional ethical rules developed to ensure that professionals carry out their professions in a manner that benefits the whole society. One of the responsibilities of auditors in the audit process is to carry out their activities in accordance with ethical rules. Adherence to ethical principles is critical for the reliability and social benefit of the independent audit process. During the pandemic, changing conditions have added new dimensions to the ethical dilemmas that auditors may face. Auditors will only be able to perform their profession in a way that benefits society as a whole by focusing more than ever on ethical rules. In accordance with the code of ethics, auditors should act honestly, be impartial, comply with the principles of professional competence and diligence, keep the secrets of the entities they audit, and exhibit behaviours appropriate to the profession.

During this period, audit fees are one of the factors that could pose a threat to auditors' compliance with ethical rules. According to the Code of Ethics for Independent Auditors (Türkiye Republic Public Oversight, Accounting and Auditing Standards Authority (POA) 2019a), the failure of audited entities to pay audit fees for previous years poses a personal interest threat for auditors. Undoubtedly, this threat is not limited to the pandemic period. However, it is likely to become more prevalent during the pandemic period. During pandemic periods, businesses face a number of risks that do not exist when creating their plans and budgets, and the measures taken to overcome the pandemic process and demand decreases may cause businesses to experience financial difficulties. The fact that the enterprises do not pay the audit fee for the previous year due to these problems poses a threat to the auditors' compliance with the principles of independence and objectivity. Another self-interest threat that auditors may face in this period is related to the amount of audit fees. The entities may endeavour to reduce the audit fees by citing the difficulty and financial difficulties of the period. However, in cases where it may be difficult to perform the work in question in accordance with the technical and professional standards in practice due to the low audit fee, a threat of self-interest arises against the ethic principle of "professional competence and care" (POA 2019a).

Objectivity, which is one of the ethical rules, requires that biases and conflicts of interest should not influence the auditor's professional judgement and decisions. During this period, auditors should act in accordance with the principle of objectivity, even though they may have different and deeper concerns than in other periods regarding health, economic and financial issues. The pandemic period has also caused many changes in terms of auditors and audit activities. During the pandemic, auditors may have to work from home or audited companies may request auditors not to come to the company for health reasons. The principle of "professional competence and care", which is one of the ethical principles, requires auditors to keep their professional knowledge up to date in order to adapt to the changes in the field of accounting and auditing caused by current developments. The pandemic period has once again demonstrated the importance of this ethical principle. Many audit firms continued their work during the pandemic period by using technological tools more than before. On the other hand, this situation has increased the risk of information security. In accordance with the principle of confidentiality, auditors should take care to protect information about businesses while using technological tools (International Ethics Standards Board for Accountants 2020).

13.3.2 Professional Scepticism

Another responsibility of independent auditors is to maintain professional scepticism throughout the audit. Professional scepticism refers to "acting in an enquiring manner, being alert to conditions that indicate misstatement due to error or fraud, and evaluating audit evidence rigorously" (POA 2019b).

The high level of uncertainty caused by the pandemic, sudden changes in the way businesses operate, and potential weaknesses in the internal control systems of many businesses have differentiated and increased the risk of material misstatement. However, as explained in detail in the "3.5 1.1 Obtaining Sufficient and Appropriate Audit Evidence" section of this chapter, auditors faced some obstacles in obtaining audit evidence. In this context, maintaining professional scepticism has become a critical requirement. Auditors should critically evaluate the information obtained during the pandemic period and approach the events in a questioning manner. For example, in cases such as detecting contradictions between the audit evidence obtained, doubting the reliability of the information obtained from documents and inquiries, and sensing the possibility of fraud, further research should be carried out in accordance with professional scepticism, and necessary changes should be made in audit procedures.

13.3.3 Professional Judgement

Professional judgement is the auditors' use of their knowledge and experience while making decisions in the audit process. The pandemic has further increased the importance of professional judgement in audit practices, requiring auditors to make flexible and professional decisions by taking into account the current circumstances, especially in critical areas such as determining the level of materiality, assessing audit risk, and determining the scope, timing and nature of audit procedures.

BDSs contain detailed regulations that guide auditors in carrying out their activities during the audit process. However, due to the differences in the sectors and activity volumes of the enterprises, there are areas that cannot be expressed with precise rules and therefore require auditors to use their professional judgement. When using their professional judgement, auditors should act within the framework of BDSs, accounting standards and the code of ethics.

One of the issues requiring professional judgment in the audit process is determining the materiality threshold. If the absence or misstatement of information in financial statements would influence the decisions of financial statements users, the information is considered material. One of the auditor's responsibilities during the audit process is to identify material misstatements in financial statements, make efforts to correct them, and form an opinion accordingly. Due to the differences in the types of businesses, the sectors in which they operate, and their sizes, it is not possible to determine a single materiality threshold that would be generally applicable to all businesses, nor is it possible to propose a benchmark or specify a percentage to be applied to a benchmark. For this reason, BDSs leave the determination of the materiality threshold to the professional judgment of the auditor. During the audit process, one of the materiality thresholds determined is the materiality threshold for the financial statements as a whole.

Materiality for the financial statements as a whole is the amount that represents the maximum amount of misstatement that can be recognized in the financial statements. If the misstatements identified in the financial statements, whether individually or in the aggregate, are less than this materiality amount, an unqualified audit opinion may be expressed on the financial statements. Materiality, which is a critical element in planning and performing the audit, is generally calculated by reference to a specific benchmark and applying a percentage to that benchmark.

During the pandemic, auditors should assess whether there is a change in the focal points of the users of the financial statements while determining the materiality amount. For example, in normal circumstances, while the focal point of financial statement users for a commercial enterprise is the profitability of the enterprise, the uncertainty and crisis environment brought by the pandemic period may cause the focal points of financial statement users to change and evolve to issues such as liquidity, cash flow, solvency. If the items that financial statement users focus on in the financial statements have changed, it is useful to reconsider and evaluate the benchmark used in determining the materiality figure for the financial statements as a whole (Arnold 2020). The same applies to the determination of materiality on an account-by-account basis. Due to the pandemic, some accounts may have become riskier than before. In order to form a sound audit opinion, the materiality and risk levels of the financial statement items should be reconsidered when determining materiality at the account level.

Other matters requiring the use of professional judgement, such as the determination of audit risk, the scope, timing and nature of audit procedures to be performed, and the collection of sufficient and appropriate audit evidence, should also be assessed, taking into account the changes arising from the pandemic period.

13.3.4 Identification and Assessment of Material Misstatement Risks

"A system of internal control is a process designed, implemented and maintained by those charged with governance, management and other personnel to provide reasonable assurance regarding the reliability of financial reporting, the effectiveness and efficiency of operations, and compliance with relevant legislation to ensure that the entity achieves its objectives" (POA 2017a). One of the auditor's responsibilities in the audit process is to assess the control risk by examining whether the entity's internal control system is designed as it should be and whether it operates effectively. This allows the significant misstatement risks faced by businesses to be identified. During the pandemic period, there have been changes in the way businesses operate, some controls in existing internal control systems have become obsolete, and the need to add new procedures to the design of the internal control system may arise. For example, during this period, digital access, security, and data storage breaches have become among the important risks affecting the activities of enterprises. Auditors should take these factors into consideration when determining the control risk during the audit process.

One of the issues that auditors should pay particular attention to during the pandemic is the risk of fraud. According to BDS 315 Art. 25 (POA 2017a), auditors should identify and assess the risks of material misstatement due to fraud during the audit process. During the pandemic periods, the fact that businesses had to rapidly change the way they operate in order to adapt to the changing environment may have led to an increase in the risk of fraud. According to the fraud triangle theory, if there is pressure and threat in an environment and behaviours can be rationalized, there is a high probability of fraud in that environment. Many businesses were economically affected by the pandemic. The financial difficulties faced by businesses are a pressure factor in the direction of fraud. For example; employees of an enterprise experiencing financial difficulties may have been under pressure by management to make fraudulent entries in order to maintain the existence of the enterprise or situations such as the inability of the enterprise to fulfil the conditions of the loan agreements may be a pressure factor in the direction of fraudulent financial reporting. In addition, in this period, reasons such as the deterioration of the personal financial situation of the employees, the decrease in family income due to the unemployment of one of the employees' family members have become pressure factors that may lead employees to fraud. In this period, the fact that the controls put in place to ensure the financial reporting process did not work due to the fact that the employees did their work from their homes. And this situation may have led to different opportunities for committed fraud. In addition, employees may rationalize this fraudulent behaviour by thinking, "I am changing the numbers to help the company survive" or "I will pay this back when things return to normal" (Dohrer 2020). As a matter of fact, these and similar factors caused by the pandemic should also be taken into consideration in assessing the risk of fraud during pandemic periods.

In this context, it should not be ignored that pandemic conditions increase the risk of fraudulent financial reporting, especially in subjective areas such as accounting estimates. Accounting estimates, which are inherently uncertain, have become more complex and risky due to increasing economic pressures and weakening internal control systems. Therefore, accounting estimates should be evaluated with greater care during the audit process than in normal periods, and this area should be treated as an audit matter of special importance. During this period, potential indicators of management fraud should be analysed more carefully as well. For example, avoiding recognizing impairment losses on assets in order to overstate revenues or misstating assets and liabilities in order to meet contractual obligations may be potential indicators of fraud. In addition, employees working from home and internal control systems not yet fully adapted to this new organization weaken the effectiveness of controls over accounting estimates and make this area more susceptible to error or fraud.

13.3.5 Obtaining Sufficient and Appropriate Audit Evidence

In the independent audit process, one of the prerequisites for auditors to form their opinions reliably is to get sufficient evidence in sufficient quantity and of appropriate quality. In this context, it should be kept in mind that all information obtained during the audit is audit evidence, and even the unavailability of information is one of the issues that shape the audit opinion. Indeed, BDS 200 (POA 2019b) recognizes as one of the auditor's responsibilities the collection of sufficient appropriate evidence that the financial statements are prepared in accordance with the applicable reporting framework. Sufficiency of evidence refers to the adequacy of its quantity, and relevance refers to its quality. Auditors use their professional judgement when deciding on the sufficiency and appropriateness of evidence. In order to facilitate the auditor in obtaining sufficient and appropriate quality evidence, the management of the auditee is also responsible for the audit. During the audit, management is responsible for providing the auditor with the accounting records, underlying documents and all other information requested by the auditor, and for enabling the auditor to make unrestricted enquiries of persons whom the auditor considers appropriate (POA 2018a).

The pandemic period has shown to be a more challenging process for obtaining evidence compared to other periods. For example, due to travel and movement restrictions, auditors may not be able to obtain evidence of inventory counts. However, according to BDS 501 (POA 2014a), if the inventory item material in the financial statements, the auditors are required to participate in physical inventory counting in order to observe the counting procedures, examine the inventory, conduct test counts, and evaluate the procedures for recording and controlling the results of physical inventory counting. However, if it is not possible to participate in the inventory count, alternative audit procedures may be applied to obtain evidence about the status and availability of inventories (POA 2014a) BDS 501 does not specify the circumstances in which it may not be possible to participate in the inventory count, and the decision is left to the auditor's professional judgement. Auditors should use their professional judgement by taking into account the ethical provisions and professional knowledge, the explanations and restrictions imposed by public authorities, and the health of the audit team and the whole community.

In the pandemic period, auditors may encounter the following situations related to inventory counting (Grant Thornton Türkiye 2020):

- The audited entity continues its normal operations, but the auditor may not be able to participate in the inventory count due to various constraints.

In this case, auditors may focus on the partial count results to obtain evidence. If partial counts have been previously supervised, audit procedures may be applied to transactions that occurred between the date of the partial count and the period end. If auditors are unable to participate in a partial inventory count, another way to obtain evidence about the condition and availability of inventories is to enlist the assistance of internal auditors. In order to obtain the assistance of internal auditors, the organizational status and adequacy of the internal audit function in the entity should be assessed (POA 2014b) Another method that can be applied when it is not possible for the audit team to participate in the inventory count is to conduct video conferences with the auditee regarding the inventory count. There is no difference between video conferencing and physical participation in the inventory count for the purpose of the audit team. In order to increase the quality of the evidence obtained, it should be ensured that the video conference is conducted by an employee other than the warehouse employees, and the conference should be arranged to cover the entire counting process (such as the organization of the count, the separation of old and damaged stocks, the prevention of stock mobility that will cause stocks to be counted twice …). In order to reveal errors and fraud, the counting team may be requested to open the boxes containing the stocks during the video conference. The audit team should request copies of the completed inventory count records from management and assess whether the final inventory balance reflects reality. Recording the video conference and preserving it as audit evidence is important for the auditor to give an opinion in the audit report and to prove that the auditor has performed the audit properly.

In cases where it is not possible to participate in the inventory count by video conferencing, the audit team should assess why it is not possible, and the existence of fraud risk should be examined.

- The entity may have had to interrupt operations, and the year-end inventory count may not be performed.

In this case, when the entity performs an inventory count in the future, it may observe the count, and alternative audit procedures may be performed from the inventory count date to the end of the period. Another alternative in the event that an inventory count cannot be performed is to focus on the results of partial counts. If partial counts have been previously supervised, audit procedures may be applied to transactions that occurred between the partial count date and the period end.

- Inventory count will be carried out at the establishment, and the audit team may be allowed to attend.

In this case, the audit team should ensure that protective practices such as the use of masks, hand washing and social distancing are carried out during the period of supervision of the stocktake to avoid becoming ill.

A further issue that may be encountered in obtaining audit evidence during the pandemic period is examining the availability of fixed assets by visiting the entity's facility to test the completeness claim of management regarding tangible fixed assets. If auditors are restricted from accessing the entity's operational areas, digital photographs with time display or live video conferences can be used to obtain evidence on the existence and completeness of fixed assets.

The inability of auditors to receive responses to verification letters is another challenge that may be encountered in obtaining audit evidence during the pandemic. During this period, the parties for whom verification is requested may have resorted to working from home or may have fallen ill due to the pandemic. Therefore, verification requests may not be responded to. In this case, auditors should apply alternative audit procedures. In this context, for account receivable balances, evidence should be obtained by examining certain subsequent cash collections, delivery notes and sales made near the end of the period; for account payable balances, evidence should be obtained by examining subsequent cash payments or reconciliations with third parties and other records such as warehouse receipts (POA 2013).

Although the current process brings difficulties in obtaining audit evidence, the auditor's responsibility for obtaining sufficient and appropriate audit evidence continues. In this process, the auditor has to use their professional judgement to decide whether alternative audit procedures can be applied and, if applicable, whether the evidence obtained is reliable.

13.3.6 Accounting Estimates

Uncertainties inherent in business activities make it difficult to directly measure some financial statement items (such as doubtful receivables, impairment of inventories, fair value of financial assets and liabilities, useful life of depreciable assets); these items are determined by estimation and included in the financial statements. These estimates are based on the most recent and reliable data and judgments. Uncertainty, complexity and subjectivity, which are the main components of inherent risk, are at higher levels during the pandemic period compared to other periods. High uncertainty in the business environment increases complexity and subjectivity. In this process, the use of different assumptions and methods from previous periods, support packages implemented by governments, changes in legal regulations, and changes in contract terms may increase complexity. On the other hand, not knowing when the pandemic will end leads to an increase in estimation uncertainty. All these factors have made the audit of accounting estimates more challenging and complex than ever.

Although the pandemic period is more prone to errors in accounting estimates, it creates a favourable environment for fraud, and accounting estimates may be used for fraud. For example, business management may use loss amounts that they believe will be accepted as "normal" by stakeholders in order to cover up large clean-up accounting. The revenue figure may be understated by understating revenues and overstating expenses, or by recognizing losses and removing certain unproductive assets from the balance sheet. In this environment, it is important for auditors to maintain and even increase their professional scepticism in auditing accounting estimates.

Auditors' responsibilities regarding the collection of evidence also apply to accounting estimates and the disclosures required in relation to them. In this regard, BDS 540—Independent Audit of Accounting Estimates and Related Disclosures, revised after 31.12.2019, provides guidance (POA 2019c). As emphasized in the standard, auditors should assess the consistency of the methods, assumptions and data used in the formation of estimates with past periods, whether they have been revised according to current conditions and the appropriateness of these revisions. In addition, within the scope of internal control mechanisms, whether there are processes to review and approve estimates, how the validity of the data used is decided, and the effectiveness of the controls related to estimates should be questioned.

If uncertainty about accounting estimates has become significant during the audit and requires the auditor to use more than ordinary endeavours, it should be included as a key audit matter in the audit report. According to BDS 701 (POA 2019d), "key audit matters are those matters that, in the auditor's professional judgement, are of most significance in an audit of the financial statements". Therefore, auditors should clearly state in the audit report the matters on which they focus the most during the audit process.

If the audit process does not provide sufficient appropriate audit evidence regarding the accounting estimates, and if it is considered that this may lead to material misstatements in the financial statements, the auditor should express an opinion other than an unqualified opinion in accordance with BDS 705 (POA 2017c). In this framework, either a limited unqualified opinion or an unqualified opinion should be preferred, taking into account the prevalence of the misstatement in question.

13.3.7 Going Concern

Going concern, which is one of the basic accounting assumptions of financial reporting, is based on the principle that an entity will continue its activities for the foreseeable future and has no intention or obligation to liquidate or suspend operations. In accordance with this assumption, the financial statements should be prepared in accordance with the going concern principle. An entity's ability to continue as a going concern and the assessment of going concern are critical issues that are also of interest to auditors.

Various factors such as the sector in which the business operates, geographical region, financial status of customers and suppliers, and liquidity structure may affect the continuity of the business. Especially extraordinary situations, such as the COVID-19 pandemic, make it more difficult and important to make such assessments. The economic uncertainties experienced during the pandemic have had a serious impact on the ability of enterprises to continue their activities; therefore, it has made it necessary for both management and auditors to carefully consider the assessments regarding the going concern assumption.

In accordance with BDS 570 (Art. 10)—'Going Concern'—auditors must assess if there are any doubts about the company's ability to continue as a going concern, and if the company's management has assessed this ability as part of the risk assessment process (POA 2017b). The following section provides examples of events that may adversely affect an entity's ability to continue as a going concern during a pandemic:

- Due to the measures taken to combat the pandemic, businesses may have faced major market losses, may have lost important customers and/or suppliers, or may be experiencing difficulties in terms of human resources.
- Although business restrictions and demand contraction cause a decrease in the sales of the enterprise, the goods remaining in the enterprise's inventory may have deteriorated, or the goods may be outdated due to the sales shortage. Therefore, enterprises may be faced with significant amounts of inventory impairment.
- There may have been delays in launching new products and services due to declining demand and changing business patterns. This can be a problem for businesses whose continuity depends on new products being launched.

- Financial losses may arise from fluctuations in foreign exchange rates.
- Weakening of short-term and long-term payment capacity may cast doubt on the company's viability

In light of the audit evidence obtained, the auditor should use their professional judgement to determine whether the going concern basis of accounting is appropriate. As a result of this judgment;

- The use of the going concern basis is appropriate, but only if a material uncertainty exists:
  - The auditor may express an unqualified opinion if the uncertainty in the financial statements has been appropriately assessed by management and the plans developed in this context have been disclosed. However, there is an important point to be considered here. In accordance with BDS 570 (Art. 22), a separate paragraph titled "material uncertainty about going concern" should be included in the audit report that includes an unqualified opinion. In this paragraph, the uncertainty about going concern should be clearly stated, and reference should be made to the footnote disclosures in which this uncertainty is included.
  - If the financial statements do not provide sufficient and appropriate disclosures about the material uncertainties related to going concern, the auditor should express a qualified opinion or an adverse opinion in accordance with BDS 705—Opinion other than unqualified in the auditor's report. In this case, the paragraph supporting the opinion in the audit report should clearly state the uncertainty regarding the continuity of the business and emphasize that this uncertainty has not been adequately disclosed in the financial statements.
  - If the going concern basis of accounting is not appropriate, but the financial statements have been prepared on a going concern basis, a negative opinion is expressed.

13.3.8 Subsequent Events

"Subsequent events"include events that occur between the end of the reporting period and the date when the financial statements are authorized for issue, whether favourable or unfavourable to the entity (POA 2018b). Some of these events require adjustments to the financial statements. If there is evidence that the event in question existed at the balance sheet date, the event should be reflected in the financial statements; that is, the related amounts should be revised. On the other hand, if circumstances indicate that the event occurred after the balance sheet date, then no adjustment to the financial statements is required. However, if such events are material—in other words, if they have an impact on the economic decisions of users of the financial statements—the nature of the event and its estimated financial impact should be disclosed separately for each type of material event (POA 2018b).

COVID-19 was declared a pandemic by the World Health Organisation on 11 March 2020. As of 31 December 2019, no adjustments are required to be made to the financial statements since the developments caused by the pandemic belong to a period subsequent to the balance sheet date. However, in order for the users of the financial statements to make healthy decisions, the nature and possible effects of the event in question should be disclosed in the footnotes (POA 2019e). On the other hand, for entities whose accounting period falls after the pandemic declaration—for example, sports clubs whose accounting560 period starts on 1 June and ends on 31 May of the following year—developments related to the pandemic are considered within the scope of the event requiring adjustment after the balance sheet date and these effects should be reflected in the financial statements with the necessary adjustments.

Uncertainties and rapid changes caused by the pandemic have increased the likelihood of unforeseen events occurring in businesses. In this context, auditors are required to obtain sufficient appropriate audit evidence to confirm that all subsequent events up to the financial statements preparation date and the date of the audit report are appropriately reflected in the financial statements.

During the audit process, it is important for auditors to examine the effects of subsequent events on the entity and the manner in which these events are reflected in the financial statements. In this context, the auditor may make various inquiries to determine whether there are pandemic-related events that occurred after the balance sheet date. Through such enquiries, audit evidence may be obtained regarding events that may have occurred after the balance sheet date, particularly those exemplified below (POA 2018b):

- Whether new commitments, borrowings and sureties have been undertaken as a result of the pandemic
- Whether new asset purchases or sales have been made and planned as a result of the pandemic
- Whether there is an increase in capital instruments or debt instruments, whether there is a planned merger or liquidation
- Whether any support is provided by the government in the form of loans or grants
- Whether there is any change in contingent assets and liabilities
- Whether there are any unusual adjustments or closing entries

The auditor should ensure that all significant events in the subsequent period are identified and appropriately reflected in the financial statements within the framework of the existing conditions and that sufficient and appropriate quality evidence is obtained in this regard.

Until the date of the auditor's report, auditors should obtain sufficient appropriate audit evidence to confirm that subsequent events are accurately and completely disclosed in the financial statements. After the issuance of the auditor's report, it is generally not mandatory to perform audit procedures related to subsequent events.

However, in some cases, after the preparation of the report, the auditor may become aware of an event after the balance sheet date that may require modification of the report. In such a case, the auditor should consider whether the event in question requires restatement of the financial statements.

If the financial statements require adjustment and management makes the necessary changes, the auditor shall issue a new auditor's report on the new financial statements. However, if the financial statements need to be amended but management does not make such an amendment, the auditor shall express an opinion other than an unqualified opinion, unless the report has already been delivered to the entity. If the report has already been delivered, the auditor should warn the entity not to publish the financial statements.

In addition, if the auditor becomes aware of an event that may require modification of the report after the financial statements have been issued, they are required to decide if the financial statements require modification. If a modification is necessary, a new auditor's report should be prepared with reference to the modified financial statements. The scope and reason for the modification must be disclosed in the 'Matters noted' or 'Other matters' section of the new report, in accordance with BDS 706 (POA 2017d). If no changes are made, however, the auditor is required to take appropriate measures to ensure the continued reliability of the previous auditor's report.

On the other hand, if the results of the audit procedures indicate that the financial statements are materially misstated, or if the audit evidence is insufficient to determine whether a material misstatement exists, BDS 705 should be considered in forming the auditor's opinion (POA 2017c).

Finally, if the auditor obtains sufficient appropriate audit evidence regarding subsequent, it may be appropriate to report this event as a "Key Audit Matter" within the scope of BDS 701 or to include it in the "matters drawn to attention" or "other matters" paragraphs within the scope of BDS 706 (POA 2017d).

13.4 Conclusion

The COVID-19 pandemic has had a profound impact on independent audit processes, as in all areas of life, and has necessitated a re-evaluation of the basic concepts of the audit profession. Businesses are the building blocks of national economies. Accurate and reliable information on the financial status of enterprises is for the benefit of the whole society, especially for the enterprises themselves. In this period, the confusion due to the change in business activities and the uncertainty about the process increases the possibility of errors and may create a more favourable environment for fraud to occur than ever before.

The primary objective of independent auditing is to obtain reasonable assurance that financial statements have been prepared in accordance with the applicable financial reporting framework and to express an opinion on this subject. An independent audit is of great importance to ensure that the economic dimensions of the disaster caused by the pandemic do not deepen by enabling the entity to see its own realities and to obtain the information it needs for stakeholders to make their decisions correctly. In order to obtain this expected benefit from the independent audit, auditors should take into account the conditions arising from the pandemic while applying independent auditing standards in the audit process. In this period, auditors may face ethical dilemmas differently or more intensely than in previous periods. In these cases, they should act within the framework of the principle of independence and ethical rules. In the current period, both entities and auditors face many new events. Auditors should continue to maintain a reasonable level of professional scepticism during this period. Thus, it will be more successful in uncovering errors and fraud that may arise as a result of confusion and uncertainty. Auditors should make decisions in areas where they need to use their professional judgement during this period, taking into account the changes caused by the pandemic. Although there may be difficulties in obtaining evidence in independent audits conducted during the pandemic period, the auditor is responsible for obtaining sufficient and appropriate audit evidence. In this period, auditors should utilize technological developments in order to obtain sufficient and appropriate audit evidence. Auditors should maintain professional scepticism and act with professional care and diligence, taking into account the risk of fraud, when making assessments of going concern and examining the assessments made by management, when assessing whether accounting estimates are reasonable and properly disclosed, and when examining whether subsequent events are accurately reflected in the financial statements.

References

Arnold C. (2020) Summary of COVID-19 audit considerations. International Federation of Accountants. https://www.ifac.org/knowledge-gateway/supporting-international-standards/discussion/summary-covid-19-audit-considerations

Bilimler Akademisi T (2020) *COVID-19 küresel salgın değerlendirme raporu.* http://www.tuba.gov.tr/tr/haberler/akademiden-haberler/tuba-covid-19-kuresel-salgin-degerlendirme-raporu-kitaplastirildi

Dohrer B (2020) 4 key COVID-19 audit risks for 2020 year ends. J Accountancy https://www.journalofaccountancy.com/news/2020/jun/key-coronavirus-audit-risks-for-2020-year-ends.html

International Ethics Standards Board for Accountants (2020) Covid-19: Ethics And Independence Considerations. https://www.ifac.org/system/files/publications/files/IESBA-Staff-Q-A-COVID-19-Ethics-Independence-Considerations.pdf

İstanbul Chamber of Certified Public Accountants & İstanbul Ticaret University (2020) *COVID-19 salgın dönemi ekonomi anketi: İşletmelerde karşılaşılan sorunlar ve çözüm önerileri.* İstanbul, Türkiye

Parıldar H (2020) Tarihte bulaşıcı hastalık salgınları. *Tepecik Eğitim ve Araştırma Hastanesi Dergisi* 30:19–26

Tavukçu S (2020) *Salgın hastalıkların tetiklediği dünya tarihindeki güç ve düzen değişiklikleri.* Stratejik Düşünce Enstitüsü. https://www.sde.org.tr/sinan-tavukcu/genel/salgin-hastaliklarin-tetikledigi-dunya-tarihindeki-guc-ve-duzen-degisiklikleri-kose-yazisi-16688

Turkish Commercial Code No. 6102 (2011) Official Gazette dated 14/2/2011 and numbered 27846.

Türkiye GT (2020) Global Assurance Alert 2020/04: Covid-19 Inventory Observation. https://www.grantthornton.com.tr/globalassets/_markets_/tur/media/pdf/global-assurance-alert-2020-04-covid-19-inventory-observation.pdf

Türkiye Republic Public Oversight, Accounting and Auditing Standards Authority (POA) (2013) BDS 505- External Verifications. Official Gazette dated 30/12/2013 and numbered 28867 https://www.resmigazete.gov.tr/eskiler/2013/12/20131230m1.htm

Türkiye Republic Public Oversight, Accounting and Auditing Standards Authority (POA) (2014a) BDS 501- Independent Audit Evidence – Specific Considerations For Certain Items, Official Gazette dated 10/01/2014 and numbered 28878. https://www.resmigazete.gov.tr/eskiler/2014/01/20140110.htm

Türkiye Republic Public Oversight, Accounting and Auditing Standards Authority (POA) (2014b) BDS 610- Utilisation of the Work of Internal Auditors, Official Gazette dated 14/02/2014 and numbered 28913. https://resmigazete.gov.tr/fihrist?tarih=2014-02-14

Türkiye Republic Public Oversight, Accounting and Auditing Standards Authority (POA) (2017a) BDS 315- Identifying and Evaluating "Material Misstatement" Risks by Understanding the Business and Its Environment, Official Gazette dated 13/12/2017 and numbered 30269. https://www.resmigazete.gov.tr/eskiler/2017/12/20171213.htm

Türkiye Republic Public Oversight, Accounting and Auditing Standards Authority (POA) (2017b) BDS 570 Going Concern, Official Gazette dated 24/03/2017 and numbered 30017. https://www.resmigazete.gov.tr/eskiler/2017/03/20170324.htm

Türkiye Republic Public Oversight, Accounting and Auditing Standards Authority (POA) (2017c) BDS 705- Issuing an Opinion Other Than an Unqualified Opinion in the Independent Auditor's Report. Official Gazette dated 24/03/2017 and numbered 30017. https://www.resmigazete.gov.tr/eskiler/2017/03/20170324.htm

Türkiye Republic Public Oversight, Accounting and Auditing Standards Authority (POA) (2017d) BDS 706- Paragraphs on Matters Emphasised and Other Matters in the Independent Auditor's Report. Official Gazette dated 24/03/2017 and numbered 30017. https://www.resmigazete.gov.tr/eskiler/2017/03/20170324.htm

Türkiye Republic Public Oversight, Accounting and Auditing Standards Authority (POA) (2018a) BDS 210- Agreement on the Terms of the Independent Audit Agreement, Official Gazette dated 06.06.2018 and numbered 30443. https://www.resmigazete.gov.tr/eskiler/2018/06/20180606.htm

Türkiye Republic Public Oversight, Accounting and Auditing Standards Authority (POA) (2018b) TMS 10- Turkish Accounting Standard for Events After the Reporting Period (Balance Sheet Date). Official Gazette dated 06.06.2018 and numbered 30443. https://www.resmigazete.gov.tr/eskiler/2018/06/20180606.htm

Türkiye Republic Public Oversight, Accounting and Auditing Standards Authority (POA) (2019a) Code of Ethics for Independent Auditors. Official Gazette dated 22/09/2019 and numbered 30896 https://www.resmigazete.gov.tr/22.09.2019

Türkiye Republic Public Oversight, Accounting and Auditing Standards Authority (POA) (2019b) BDS 200- The General Objectives of the Independent Auditor and the Conduct of Independent Auditing in Accordance with Independent Auditing Standards. Official Gazette dated 31/12/2019 and numbered 30995 https://www.resmigazete.gov.tr/fihrist?tarih=2019-12-31

Türkiye Republic Public Oversight, Accounting and Auditing Standards Authority (POA) (2019c) BDS 540 Independent Audit of Accounting Estimates and Related Disclosures. Official Gazette dated 31/12/2019 and numbered 30995 https://www.resmigazete.gov.tr/fihrist?tarih=2019-12-31

Türkiye Republic Public Oversight, Accounting and Auditing Standards Authority (POA) (2019d) BDS 701- Reporting of Key Audit Matters in the Independent Auditor's Report. Official Gazette dated 31/12/2019 and numbered 30995 https://www.resmigazete.gov.tr/fihrist?tarih=2019-12-31

Türkiye Republic Public Oversight, Accounting and Auditing Standards Authority (POA). (2019e) *Bilgi notu: Türkiye denetim standartları hakkında genel açıklama.* https://www.kgk.gov.tr/Portalv2Uploads/files/Duyurular/v2/TDS/Bilgi_Notu_09_05_2019.pdf

World Health Organization (2020) Plague. https://www.who.int/health-topics/plague#tab=tab_

Chapter 14
Legal and Criminal Liabilities of Independent Auditors

Recep Güneş

Abstract This study examines the obligations arising from independent audit contracts and the liabilities of independent auditors toward both audited companies and third parties within the framework of the Turkish legal system. While independent audit contracts impose obligations on the parties, the responsibilities of auditors are broader in scope. These obligations are crucial for ensuring the reliability and safety of information for users. The principle of independence, which underpins independent auditing activities, is grounded in integrity, objectivity, and professional skepticism. The Turkish Commercial Code (TCC), the regulations of the Capital Markets Board (CMB), and the regulations of the Public Oversight Authority (POA) comprehensively regulate situations that may impair auditor independence. The liability of independent auditors toward third parties does not arise from the audit contract but is instead based on tort. Although Article 554 of the TCC addresses auditors' liability toward the company and its creditors, it contains no explicit provision regarding third parties. Nonetheless, considering the public nature of audit reports, it is widely accepted that liability may arise in favor of third parties who suffer damages as a result of such reports. For this liability to be established, the audit report must be flawed, publicly disclosed, actual damage must have occurred, and a causal link must be present. However, auditors should not be held liable without limits; a reasonable balance of liability must be maintained. Legal liability claims against independent auditors must be evaluated in terms of the prerequisites for filing a lawsuit, statute of limitations, competent and authorized courts, and the mandatory mediation process.

This chapter was previously published in Turkish by Gazi Kitabevi with the ISBN: 978-975-7727-16-7.

R. Güneş (✉)
Faculty of Business, Artvin Çoruh University, Artvin, Türkiye
e-mail: recep.gunes@artvin.edu.tr

G. Kurt, Ö. Sarısoy (eds.), *Recent Advancements in Auditing*, Accounting, Finance, Sustainability, Governance & Fraud: Theory and Application,
https://doi.org/10.1007/978-981-95-5811-7_14

Companies or third parties suffering damage during or following the audit process may seek compensation through liability lawsuits. However, such lawsuits are infrequent in Turkey. The main reasons for this include a lack of awareness among information users regarding their legal rights and normative fragmentation within the audit sector. This study also explores the legal and criminal liabilities of independent auditors under Turkish law. Auditors who breach auditing principles and standards may incur not only civil but also criminal liability. For criminal liability to arise, such violations must be committed intentionally. Under Decree Law No. 660 and Article 6(c) of the Turkish Penal Code, independent auditors, as they perform a public duty, may be sanctioned similarly to public officials. In conclusion, the liability of independent auditors arises from breach of contract in relation to the audited company and from tort in relation to third parties. The injured party may bring claims under any legal basis; however, double compensation for the same damage is not permissible. The competent court for liability lawsuits is generally the commercial court of first instance, although in some cases, civil courts of first instance may also have jurisdiction.

Keywords Independent auditor · Legal liability · Criminal liability · Audit contract · Mandatory mediation

14.1 Introduction

The definition of independent auditing is not explicitly provided in the Turkish Commercial Code; however, it is elaborated in detail in the regulations and communiqués, which serve as written sources for auditing. We believe it would not be appropriate to discuss independent audit firms' liabilities without first determining what independent auditing entails, the scope it covers, and the legal characterization of independent audit contracts. Therefore, in our study, we will examine what independent auditing is, what audit contracts should include, and the legal nature of such contracts. We will address the responsibilities of independent auditors and independent audit firms within the framework of practical issues and decisions of the Court of Cassation. The study aims to develop suggestions for a more effective system functioning, in light of recent developments in independent auditing, specifically focusing on the responsibilities of independent audit firms, where deficiencies have been observed in practice.

14.2 Independent Auditing

Although independent auditing is not defined in the Turkish Commercial Code, its definition is included in the relevant communiqués of the Public Oversight Authority and the Capital Markets Board. According to Article 4 of the Capital

Markets Board's Communiqué Serial X, No. 22, independent auditing is defined as:

"The process of auditing and evaluating enterprises' annual financial statements and other financial information, which is to be publicly disclosed or requested by the Board, through the application of all necessary independent auditing techniques as stipulated in independent auditing standards, to obtain sufficient and appropriate independent audit evidence to provide reasonable assurance regarding compliance with financial reporting standards and the accuracy of such information, and reporting the results based on the examination of the books, records, and documents."

In academic literature, auditing is generally defined as: "A systematic process of objectively collecting and evaluating evidence regarding economic activities and events, to determine the degree of conformity with predetermined criteria, and communicating the results to interested parties."

In banking regulations, independent auditing is defined as the activity of collecting and reporting evidence to inform relevant parties about the accuracy and reliability of accounts, recording systems, and financial statements.

14.2.1 History of the Auditing Activity and the Development of the Concept of Auditor Liabilities

When examining the concept of auditing, which is defined as "the process of collecting and evaluating evidence by a specialized unit to determine and report the compliance of information related to a public or private organization with predetermined criteria," historical research shows that the origins of auditing date back to around 3000 B.C. According to information obtained from archaeological findings, kings who ruled in ancient Mesopotamia authorized their scribes to conduct inventories of royal grain warehouses and to oversee the officials responsible for them. In this context, it is evident that the auditing of public accounts and activities within state governance essentially formed the core of early auditing practices (Bezirci and Karasioğlu 2011, pp. 572–574).

In 2001, 257 publicly traded companies in the United States filed for bankruptcy, followed by 191 companies in 2002. Audit reports issued for many of these companies before their bankruptcies provided positive opinions, and almost none of these reports mentioned any issues that might prevent the companies from continuing their operations in the years to come. This situation significantly damaged the public reputation of the accounting and auditing profession. In 2000, Enron ranked as the 7th largest company in the U.S., filed for bankruptcy despite a favorable audit report issued by its auditor, Arthur Andersen. The Enron scandal led to questions about the purpose of auditing itself; investors, shareholders, and the general public lost trust in auditors, and this loss of confidence became a major catalyst for the historical transformation of the auditing profession (Ergüden 2014, p. 186).

In France, the "Joint Audit" institution was established to ensure the independence of auditors and to protect the users of information who rely on audit reports. Under the Joint Audit system, audits of applicable companies are conducted by at least two completely independent auditors. This system aims to ensure objectivity in auditing and allows auditors to monitor each other. However, in cases where disagreements arise between auditors, the audit process may take longer and become more costly (Erdoğan 2014, pp. 103–104).

In Turkey, the establishment of the independent auditing institution and the profession of independent auditing, as well as their inclusion in the legal framework, do not date back very far. The first legal regulations were introduced for the banking sector, followed by regulations targeting the capital markets. After the Capital Markets Board (SPK), regulations were also introduced for the energy markets; however, these were not as comprehensive as the earlier ones (Sağlar 2015, p. 171).

14.2.2 Scope of Independent Audit

The term "audit" in its basic usage refers to the act of inspecting or examining, essentially involving the comparison between what currently exists and what should exist. In a broader sense, auditing is defined as an assurance service provided transparently and objectively to institutional stakeholders concerning their financial statements. In this context, the independent audit function can also be described as a defense mechanism (Meral 2019, p. 20).

According to Article 68, Paragraph 1 of the Turkish Commercial Code (TCC), traders are required to prepare financial statements. A trader must prepare financial statements showing the relationship between the company's assets and liabilities at the beginning and end of each fiscal period. The obligation to prepare financial statements falls under the responsibilities of the board of directors under Article 514 of the TCC. Financial statements must be prepared by Turkish Accounting Standards and must reflect the company's assets, debts, and liabilities completely, understandably, clearly, verifiably, accurately, and truthfully. According to Article 68/3, the balance sheet and income statement constitute the year-end financial statements. As per Article 397/4 of the TCC, the financial statements comparing the assets and liabilities of companies subject to audit are audited by an independent auditor by the Turkish Auditing Standards, which are compatible with international auditing standards and issued by the Public Oversight Authority (Falcıoğlu 2016, pp. 71–72).

Under the repealed Law No. 6762, the internal audit system did not achieve the expected level of independence and objectivity. Therefore, the legislator established the independent auditing system in Articles 397 to 406 of the new Law No. 6102. Under Article 397, Paragraph 4 of the TCC, independent auditing is a system in which the financial statements of the company and the annual activity report of the board of directors are examined for compliance with the Turkish Accounting Standards, the law, and the articles of association by independent and impartial experts and auditors who are entirely unaffiliated with the audited company (Yılmaz, 2018, p. 23; Özkorkut 2013, p. 194). According to Article 397/1 of the TCC, the term "independent auditing standards" refers to the Turkish Auditing Standards aligned with international auditing standards and defined by the Public Oversight Authority (Urkan 2016, p. 69).

Articles 397 and 404 of the Turkish Commercial Code No. 6102 regulate independent audits and independent auditing firms under the heading of auditing. Previously, the authority to determine which companies are subject to independent auditing was granted to the Council of Ministers under Article 397, Paragraph 4 of the TCC. However, with Decree-Law No. 700, dated July 2, 2018, Article 192 amended the phrase "by the Council of Ministers" in Article 397, Paragraph 4, to "by the President," and the phrase "prepared by the Ministry of Customs and Trade and approved by the Council of Ministers" in Paragraph 5 to "by the President." Consequently, the authority to determine the companies subject to independent audit has been transferred to the Presidency.

Article 397, paragraph five of the Turkish Commercial Code (TCC) stipulates that joint stock companies not covered under paragraph four may also undergo independent audits. The purpose of this regulation is undoubtedly to ensure the reliability of the financial statements of enterprises and to present them to information users through objective and independent audit reports. The last sentence of Article 397, paragraph five, of the TCC states: "... the provisions of the law regarding the responsibilities of the auditor shall also apply to audits conducted under this paragraph." With this, it is emphasized that, even in cases where independent audits are not mandatory, the legal provisions concerning auditor responsibilities will be applied by analogy to audits carried out voluntarily.

Under the current TCC system, only a small number of joint stock companies are subject to mandatory independent audits, despite the large number of such companies. The provision allowing non-mandatory audits was intended to provide control over the financial statements of these companies and to instill confidence in information users. However, in practice, this provision remains more of a recommendation than an enforceable mechanism (Falcıoğlu 2016, pp. 92–93).

The repealed Law No. 6762 included the audit body as one of the company's three mandatory organs. However, in practice, audit reports were often prepared without sufficient attention to independence and impartiality, and misleading information was provided to users. A convergence of interests emerged between the audit body and the management body of companies, leading to weaknesses in governance (Uzay and Bayat 2016, pp. 1507–1508). The Turkish Court of Cassation General Assembly has also stated: "... although the new TCC (Law No. 6102) identifies the general assembly and board of directors as the mandatory organs of joint stock companies, it does not clearly state whether the audit body remains an organ, thereby indirectly eliminating the audit body as a company organ. On the other hand, Articles 397 and subsequent articles of Law No. 6102 regulate that auditing activities shall be conducted by independent auditors, and it is stipulated that liability suits will henceforth be filed by the board of directors.

Court of Cassation General Assembly of Civil Chambers, Case No: 2017/105, Decision No: 2018/1936, Date: 13 December 2018. "*Although many individuals and institutions benefit from independent audits and audit reports, the main users are typically investors who lack expertise in accounting and financial statement analysis. The aim of this regulation is to protect the interests of third parties by ensuring the preparation of transparent and accountable reports by independent auditors who are entirely detached and impartial from the company.*"[1]

Today, due to growing needs in practice, the number of companies and their operational areas has expanded, bringing about various issues. Chief among these is the issue of trust in the financial information contained in companies' financial statements, especially by investors, foreign capital owners, and the state. Corporate scandals have intensified the need for accurate and impartial information (Aydoğan 2016, p. 771). Since a company's financial condition closely concerns its employees, investors, the state as a tax collector based on that financial condition, and competing businesses in the same industry, the auditing of financial statements is a matter of great importance and sensitivity (Çelik 2005, p. 57). Therefore, if the company's accounting information is not audited at all or is inadequately audited after an independent audit contract is signed, or if the auditor loses objectivity, the Liability of both the auditor and the audit firm will arise.

14.3 Independent Audit Agreement

According to Article 1 of the Turkish Code of Obligations No. 6098, a contract is established through the mutual and corresponding declarations of intent by the parties. Based on this definition, the constitutive elements of a contract are: the declaration of intent, the mutuality of these declarations, and the conformity of the declarations of intent. What is meant by the mutuality of intent is that the declarations of intent have been presented to the other party (Ayan 2016, pp. 151–152). For a bilateral legal transaction such as a contract to be valid, the parties must be competent, the subject of the contract must not be contrary to public order, general morality, or personal rights, the declarations of intent must conform, there must be no collusion, and the subject of the contract must not be impossible. The issue of individuals being legally competent to perform legal transactions is examined within the scope of personal law. Only a person can have rights, as a person refers to entities deemed capable of holding rights and obligations by the legal system—in other words, entities considered eligible to acquire rights and assume obligations (Ayan and Ayan 2014, p. 3).

[1] Court of Cassation General Assembly of Civil Chambers, Case No: 2017/105, Decision No: 2018/1936, Date: 13 December 2018.

If the legal outcome that the parties wish to achieve by concluding the contract is the creation of a debt, then a debt-incurring contract is in question (Oğuzman and Öz 2013, p. 43). In this context, an independent audit agreement is a consensual, bilateral, and reciprocal contract that gives rise to obligations.

The freedom to choose a contracting party, which is part of contractual freedom, does not apply in the case of independent audit contracts. According to Article 400 of the Turkish Commercial Code (TCC), only individuals holding the title of Certified Public Accountant (SMMM) or Sworn-in Certified Public Accountant (YMM), and who are authorized by the Public Oversight, Accounting and Auditing Standards Authority (KGK), or capital companies whose partners possess these qualifications, can carry out audit activities (Urkan 2016, p. 86). Regardless of whether the auditor is appointed by the general assembly, approved by the general assembly upon the recommendation of the board of directors, or appointed by the commercial court, an agreement must be concluded with the auditor (Arı 2019, p. 90).

Through the independent audit agreement, the audit firm undertakes the obligation to objectively examine the financial statements within the framework of Turkish Accounting Standards and to prepare a report, while the audited entity assumes the obligation to pay a fee. It is not possible to carry out an audit without signing an independent audit agreement. Indeed, the independent audit agreement may be considered as the constitution of the audit activity.

14.3.1 Form of the Independent Audit Agreement

As a rule, the Code of Obligations does not require any specific form when parties conclude a contract. In other words, the principle of freedom of form is adopted, and parties are free to determine how they express their intent. However, in some cases, contracts must comply with a specific form for their validity. The consequence of non-compliance with the required form is nullity. Since this constitutes a ground for objection, a judge can ex officio consider whether the transaction complies with the form, and it can be asserted by the parties at any time (Bilgili and Ertan 2018, p. 55).

The TCC does not impose a formal requirement for audit contracts. However, Article 29 of the Independent Auditing Regulation requires that the independent audit agreement be made in writing and sets this as a minimum condition. Due to the invalidity resulting from failure to comply with the required form, in contracts such as independent audit agreements that impose obligations on both parties, if the obligated performance has already been executed, the return of what was given may be requested via an unjust enrichment or restitution lawsuit (Eren 2014, p. 290). Obligations and penalty clauses based on such a contract will also be invalid due to non-compliance with the form, and compensation or performance benefits cannot be claimed based on the contract. It is important to emphasize that a party who knowingly or fraudulently signs the contract despite this deficiency cannot later claim the contract is invalid—such a claim would constitute an abuse of rights under Article 2 of the Turkish Civil Code. However, the deceived party may claim compensation for damages under Article 49/2 of the Turkish Code of Obligations (Cansel and Özel 2017, p. 211).

14.3.2 Qualification of the Contract

Liability arising from the failure to perform, or the improper performance of, the obligation under the agreement between the Independent Audit Firm and the audited entity pertains to contractual liability. The obligations arising from a contract are determined according to the legal nature of that contract. Therefore, determining the legal nature of independent audit agreements is important in terms of liability law.

Article 29 of the Independent Auditing Regulation issued by the Public Oversight Authority regulates the mandatory elements of independent audit agreements. According to this provision, the purpose, subject, criteria, and scope of the audit, the responsibilities of the parties, a clause stating that the audit will be conducted by Turkish Auditing Standards, a clause regarding access to necessary documents for the audit, and the audit fee must be included in the agreement; these are not subject to the discretion of the parties but are compulsory.

The independent audit agreement is a service contract that sets out the responsibilities of the auditor toward the company and vice versa. The work and processes starting from the auditor signing the audit agreement and assuming the role, to writing the report and submitting the audit opinion, include elements from contracts regulated in the Code of Obligations, such as contracts of work, agency, and service contracts (Topçuoğlu 2012, p. 92).

Upon examining the content of independent audit agreements, it is evident that they do not fully align with similar contracts, such as contracts of work, agency, or service contracts regulated in the Code of Obligations. Although the independent audit agreement is a type of service contract, it significantly differs from other service contracts. Therefore, categorizing the independent audit agreement under the scope of other service contracts would not align with the unique characteristics of such agreements (Çelik 2005, p. 67). For these reasons, the most appropriate solution would be to consider the independent audit agreement as an innominate contract with its distinctive structure.

14.3.3 Subject Matter of Independent Audit Agreements

The subject matter of independent audit agreements is regulated under Article 6 of the Public Oversight Authority regulation. According to this provision, the subject of independent audits includes the financial statements required to be audited under the TCC, annual activity reports, systems for early detection and management of risks, and other matters that are required to be audited or assessed by other legislation.

According to Article 514 of the TCC, the company's annual activity report is prepared by the board of directors and submitted to the general assembly. This authority is non-transferable under Article 375 of the TCC. Under Article 397 of the TCC, the scope of the audit is limited to verifying whether the financial information contained in the annual activity report is consistent with the audited financial statements and reflects the truth. Apart from this, no audit activity may be conducted on the financial report. Otherwise, it may be said that independent auditors are conducting performance audits (Urkan 2016, p. 168).

14.4 Obligations Arising from the Independent Audit Agreement

There are several obligations stemming from the independent audit agreement that both parties to the contract are required to fulfill. Although these obligations exist primarily to protect the parties and uphold the agreement, they also aim to ensure the security of information users who act based on the audit reports generated after the audit process. In independent audit agreements, which impose obligations on both parties, the responsibilities of independent audit firms are generally more extensive and detailed compared to those of the audited companies.

14.4.1 Obligations of Audit Firms and Auditors

The auditing activity generally begins with the signing of the independent audit agreement and ends with the auditing of the financial statements and the issuance of the audit report. However, the Liability of auditors starts even before the actual audit activity begins—during the negotiation phase of the agreement—and continues even after the audit report has been issued and the audit activity has concluded.

14.4.2 Obligation to Conduct Activities by Independent Auditing Standards

The obligation to act according to auditing principles and established standards is one of the most crucial responsibilities that independent auditors and audit firms must adhere to until the audit activity is completed. Essentially, this type of obligation encompasses other related obligations as well.

Article 3 of Part 31 of the Capital Markets Board's Communiqué Series: X, No: 22, states that the auditor must obtain appropriate and sufficient independent audit evidence regarding the conformity of the comparative financial statements with the financial reporting standards. Article 28 of Part 2 of the same Communiqué mandates compliance with the determined independent audit standards for the audit to be valid. Furthermore, Article 29 stipulates that auditors who issue audit reports will be jointly liable for any damage caused to audited companies and third parties due to non-compliance with the standards.

14.4.3 Duty of Care

The duty of care refers to the diligence and effort that a prudent auditor would show under similar circumstances. The standard of care required is full compliance with auditing principles, rules, and standards (Çelik 2005, p. 108). Due to this duty, auditors and audit firms are liable at all stages of the audit process.

14.4.4 Obligation of Independence

Article 22 of the Regulation on Independent Auditing by the Public Oversight Authority (KGK) stipulates that audit firms and auditors must perform the audit activity independently. Even at its most basic definition, independence is a fundamental element of both the auditor and the audit activity. The relationship between the auditor and the audited company is a contractual one, and there should be no other organic connection between the parties.

Although the Turkish Commercial Code (TCC) does not explicitly state whether auditing is a corporate body of the company, by listing the board of directors and the general assembly as the only compulsory bodies of a joint-stock company, it implicitly removes auditing from being considered a corporate organ. The law, in its effort to preserve independence, prevents the auditing function from being transferred to or evolving into a new company organ. This is also indicated in the justification of Article 397 of the TCC, which states that the audit function cannot be delegated, either wholly or partially, to another organ, nor can it be used directly or indirectly by another body (Uzay and Bayat 2016, p. 1508).

14.4.4.1 The Concept of "Independent" Auditing and Its Regulation in Turkish Law

The Turkish Commercial Code No. 6102 introduced more transparent and auditable practices compared to the former Code No. 6762 and provided legal guarantees for the independence of auditing in joint-stock companies. Thus, the aim is to ensure the delivery of impartial and reliable information to all stakeholders (Töre and Tanyeri 2016, p. 46).

Article 13 of the Draft Communiqué on Activities by the Capital Markets Board describes independence as a set of behaviors and understanding that ensures the professional activity is conducted honestly and impartially. Similarly, Article 22 of the KGK's Independent Auditing Regulation defines independence as the expression of an opinion free from influences that may adversely affect the auditor's professional judgment, ensuring they act with integrity, impartiality, and professional skepticism.

An auditor must carry out the audit independently and impartially, both in behavior and thought, and must evaluate the obtained data objectively before issuing the report. However, to achieve complete independence and impartiality, auditors are also expected to act with professional skepticism. The KGK regulation highlights this in its provisions outlining the purpose of auditing and the process of gathering audit evidence, stating that the auditor must act according to the Turkish Auditing Standards and with professional skepticism.

According to Article 22 of the KGK regulation, independence essentially means expressing an opinion that is free from any influence that could negatively affect professional judgment, while acting with professional skepticism. This term refers to evaluating the validity of audit evidence with a questioning approach.

Article 13 of Part 2 of the Capital Markets Board's Communiqué Series X, No: 22, states that if there is doubt concerning the independence of auditors or audit firms, independence shall be deemed to have been compromised. Due to the public interest nature of auditing and the sensitive balance it affects, the Board has set strict limitations on the auditor's objectivity, leaving no room for interpretation. No institution, person, or professional organization should interfere with the establishment and organization of independent audit firms. Any such interference may jeopardize objectivity and, consequently, independence. Given that the content and purpose of the Capital Markets Board's regulations relate to the maintenance of public order and market organization, they should not be assessed from a narrow perspective.

Article 400 of the TCC regulates the conditions under which an auditor may lose their independence and, therefore, be ineligible to act as an auditor.[2]

---

[2] Turkish Commercial Code—ARTICLE 400 (TTK-MADDE 400)

In the presence of any of the following circumstances, a sworn-in certified public accountant yeminli mali müşavir), a certified public accountant (serbest muhasebeci mali müşavir), and/or a capital company or any of their shareholders, or any person working for those mentioned in this

It is unlikely that these conditions can be exhaustively listed due to the unpredictability of real-life situations. Hence, even if a case is not listed in the Article, if there is doubt about the auditor's independence, it must still be considered compromised.

If the general assembly of a company appoints an auditor despite the existence of a circumstance that impairs independence, the legal nature of the independent audit agreement becomes significant. According to Article 27 of the Turkish Code of Obligations, if the general assembly decision is made in violation of the mandatory provisions of the TCC, the appointment of an independent and impartial auditor is null and void, and accordingly, the audit agreement between the company and the auditor is also null and void. In such cases, a declaratory action may be filed without being subject to any statute of limitations or preclusive period (Özkorkut 2013, p. 253).

Even if there is no concrete evidence casting doubt on the independence and impartiality of an appointed auditor, a new auditor may still be appointed by the Commercial Court of First Instance located at the company's registered office under Article 399 of the TCC, provided there is a strong suspicion and a justified reason. The court may only appoint a new auditor if it is convinced of the presence of a justified reason after hearing the auditor and the relevant parties.

According to paragraph 6 of Article 399 of the TCC, if the appointment decision is annulled, or the auditor resigns, becomes unable to perform their duties, or is obstructed, the Commercial Court of First Instance shall appoint a new auditor, and

---

sentence, or any person or persons who jointly practice the profession with them, cannot be appointed as an auditor in the relevant company.

Namely, if any of the persons mentioned in the previous sentence:

(a) Is a shareholder in the company to be audited,

(b) Is a manager or employee of the company to be audited, or has held such a position within the three years preceding the appointment as auditor,

(c) Is a legal representative, agent, board member, manager, or owner of a legal entity, commercial company, or commercial enterprise affiliated with the company to be audited, or holds more than twenty percent of shares in any of these entities, or is a relative by blood or marriage up to and including the third degree, or a spouse, of a board member or manager of the company to be audited,

(d) Works in a business affiliated with the company to be audited or in a company holding more than twenty percent of the shares in it, or provides any service to a real person who has more than twenty percent of the shares in the company to be audited,

(e) Has been involved in or contributed to the keeping of the books or preparation of financial statements of the company to be audited, apart from audit activities.

(f) Is the legal representative, agent, employee, board member, partner, or owner of a natural or legal person (or is the person) who is prohibited from being an auditor under paragraph (e) due to involvement in the company's bookkeeping or financial statement preparation apart from audit activities,

(g) Works for an auditor who is disqualified from acting as an auditor due to any of the conditions listed in subparagraphs (a) to (f),

(h) Has earned more than thirty percent of their total professional income from audit and consultancy services provided to the company to be audited or to companies in which it holds more than twenty percent of the shares within the last five years, and is expected to earn the same in the current year, may not act as an auditor.

the court's decision shall be final. In its decision No. 2016/1620, Case No. 2015/6870, the 11th Civil Chamber of the Court of Cassation ruled:

"... the lawsuit concerns the appointment of an independent auditor for a joint-stock company under Article 399 of the TCC. Although the decision dated 10.03.2015 was appealed by the plaintiff's attorney, court decisions either accepting or rejecting the appointment of an independent auditor are final according to Article 399/(6) of the TCC ... The appeal must be dismissed[3]". However, it should be concluded that the legislator intended only decisions regarding the appointment of auditors to be final. This is clearly stated in the article and its justification. In contrast, decisions rejecting the appointment should not be considered final, and general procedural rules should apply. Therefore, unless there is an explicit legal provision stating otherwise, it should not be accepted that decisions rejecting the appointment of an auditor are unappealable.

14.4.5 "Rotation" as a Measure to Ensure the Independence of the Auditor

Due to the professional relationship arising from the independent audit contract between the auditor and the audited company, a closeness and alignment of interests may develop. This unity of interests may compromise the independence of the auditor, either due to fees or other reasons, and may result in audit reports containing errors significant enough to mislead third parties. Criticisms suggesting that familiarity and acquaintance arising from human relationships between the audit firm partners and the audited company managers always harm the audit and make the objectivity of the report questionable are not well-founded. In fact, in practice, such familiarity can offer some operational convenience. However, if this familiarity gradually turns into a unity of interest, then it can be said that such a situation may create grounds for misleading third parties.

A long-term service contract between the auditor and the audited company, or a long-standing business relationship covering several reporting periods, may create a bond between the parties and compromise independence. Therefore, the legislator has adopted the rotation practice in Article 400 of the Turkish Commercial Code (TCC). According to the provision, "An auditor who has been appointed for the same company for seven years in total within ten years cannot be reappointed as an auditor for three years." This requirement, referred to as "rotation" in practice, prevents an auditor from auditing the same company continuously and without interruption. The Public Oversight, Accounting, and Auditing Standards Authority (KGK) is authorized to regulate the implementation principles and shorten the periods concerning this provision.

[3] Court of Cassation, 11th Civil Chamber, Case No: 2015/6870, Decision No: 2016/1620, Date: 17 February 2016, https://www.kazanci.com.tr.

The mandatory audit rotation practice is aimed to limit the closeness between the audit firm and the audited company, strengthening the independence of the audit, increasing the public perception of auditor independence, and reducing errors that might repeat due to routine operations by introducing a new perspective (Gönen and Rasgen 2016, p.1814).

If, contrary to the mandatory provisions regarding audit rotation, an independent audit contract is signed between the auditor and the audited company as a result of a general assembly resolution, such a contract cannot be considered valid. In that case, under Article 396/6 of the TCC, the commercial court of first instance where the company's headquarters is located appoints a new auditor, and the court's decision is final (Özkorkut 2013, pp.263–264).

14.4.5.1 The Impact of Fees on the Obligation of Independence

Under the independent audit contract, the audited company is obligated to pay a fee to the auditor. The audit fee is among the mandatory elements of the audit contract.

In a survey study involving participants working in the field of independent auditing, a significant number of participants expressed the view that deficiencies occur in the audit process due to inadequate fees, and 74% believed that audit quality is negatively affected by the inadequacy of audit fees (Meral 2019, p.85). Undoubtedly, the fee is an element that ensures the quality of the activity performed. Failure to pay the audit fee or improper payment may economically strain the audit firm and make it dependent on the audited company. Conversely, an excessively high fee may compromise the audit firm's objectivity. Therefore, to maintain a sensitive balance, organizations like KGK, which have sanctioning power, should increase their oversight regarding the determination and payment of fees and apply sanctions when necessary.

14.4.6 Obligation of Confidentiality

The concept of confidentiality refers to matters related to private or professional life that are intangible, must be kept secret, and are not known by everyone. For a matter to be considered confidential, the fundamental requirement is the intent to keep it secret. Whether a matter is confidential and whether it is regarded as such depends on whether it was learned during the performance of duties and must be evaluated based on the specifics of each case.

According to Article 404 of the TCC, "... the auditor and the special auditor are obligated to maintain confidentiality. They may not use, without permission, business and trade secrets related to the audit that they learn during their activities. Those who intentionally or negligently violate their obligations are liable to the company or, if they cause damage, to the affiliated companies. If there is more than one liable person, liability is joint and several." This provision outlines the responsibilities of auditors, special auditors, audit assistants, and, in the case of a capital company conducting the audit, the representative of the audit firm.

Paragraph 5 of the mentioned article establishes that liability claims are subject to a five-year statute of limitations. However, if the act giving rise to liability is subject to a longer statute of limitations under the Turkish Penal Code (TCK), then the longer period provided by the penal code shall apply.

Auditors may gain access to information and documents that may be considered trade secrets of the enterprise due to their broad powers granted by law during the audit process. This situation carries a risk of harming companies. Article 404 of the TCC prohibits auditors from sharing with third parties any business or trade secrets learned during their audit activities. Therefore, information not related to the audit activity or obtained outside the audit process is not covered by this provision (Yılmaz 2018, p.38).

If the information and documents obtained during the audit constitute a criminal offense, the obligation of confidentiality does not apply. In this context, the sixth paragraph of Article 404 of the TCC states that the provisions in the penal code regarding crime reporting are reserved.

14.4.7 Obligations of the Audited Entity

Since the independent audit contract is bilateral, in addition to the obligations of the audit firm, the audited company, as the client, also has obligations. The company's main obligation under the contract is to pay the fee. The fee can be freely agreed upon by the parties but must be included in the contract.

To conduct a lawful audit, the auditor may request the company's financial statements. Under Article 401, first paragraph of the TCC, the audited company must promptly provide the financial statements and the board of directors' annual activity reports to the auditor. Moreover, the company's board of directors must provide the auditor with access to the company's books, receivables and payables, negotiable instruments, and inventory so that an audit report can be prepared.

14.5 Liability of the Independent Auditor

Although independent auditors and audit firms do not act as guarantors of the proper management of businesses, their responsibilities largely stem from the opinions expressed in the financial statements and reports they issue. Accordingly, the legal liability of independent audit firms does not arise from providing guarantees, but from the failure to carry out the necessary actions related to their audit activities (Bozkurt 2018, pp. 30–39).

Auditors and audit firms have responsibilities toward both the audited company (as their client) and third parties who are users of the information. Article 63 of the

Capital Markets Law states: "Independent audit firms are liable, within the scope of their duties, for any damages arising from the failure to audit financial statements and reports by the regulations, jointly with those who signed the report. Independent audit firms and credit rating and valuation firms are liable for damages caused by incorrect, misleading, and incomplete information included in their reports." This provision holds auditors jointly liable for not preparing audit reports at all or not preparing them properly. Similarly, Article 29 of Section II of the Capital Markets Board's Communiqué Serial X, No:22 parallels Article 63 of the Law, stating that auditors who sign audit reports will be jointly liable for damages to clients and third parties arising from failure to conduct audits in compliance with auditing standards. These provisions indicate that the auditor's liability arises essentially from the audit process and the reports prepared as a result of such activity, and not from a performance audit of the company's management, nor is such a Liability imposed.

The reasons behind fraudulent or erroneous financial statements, which may be intentionally prepared to influence users' perceptions of the company's performance and profitability, include meeting market expectations, minimizing taxes, and securing financing (Uzay and Kaya 2018, p. 725). The auditor's opinion presented in the audit report offers reasonable assurance to information users. Although reasonable assurance is a high level of assurance, it does not equate to absolute assurance. Independent auditors can achieve reasonable assurance by reducing audit risk to an acceptably low level (Aydın and Çürük 2017, p. 236).

14.5.1 Liability Toward the Audited Company

The primary party to whom audit firms may be liable during independent audit activities is, without doubt, the audited company—i.e., the party to the audit contract. If the audit firm fails to perform the contract at all or properly, it will be subject to contractual liability. Breach of contract is the fundamental type of liability, but auditors may also incur liability under tort law beyond contractual breaches. If, due to wrongful acts outside the scope of the contract, auditors cause harm to the company, tort liability may arise.

For tort liability to arise, there must be a fault, an unlawful act, resulting damage, and a causal link between the unlawful act and the damage. Damages to the audited company may appear as loss of profit, potential loss, or consequential damages. For tort liability to apply, the wrongful act must not arise from failure to perform the contract properly. If the damage results from a breach of contract, the case falls under contractual liability. In both types of liability, the goal is not to punish the wrongful act but to compensate the injured party.

If the auditor's conduct constitutes both a breach of contract and a tort, the injured company may face the question of which legal basis to rely on. In such cases, the prevailing view in doctrine and practice allows the injured party to choose between competing liabilities, but they cannot claim compensation twice for the same damage (Oğuzman and Öz 2013, pp. 445–446).

From the perspective of the injured company, it is generally more advantageous to claim under contractual liability than under tort. This is because, in contractual liability, the debtor must prove the absence of fault and cannot escape liability for the acts of auxiliaries (Oğuzman and Öz 2013, p. 448).

Fault-based liability is essential in auditors' Liability to clients. Recognizing strict liability would broaden the auditor's responsibilities and could negatively impact audit activities. The standard for determining auditor fault is the "due professional care" expected in the profession. Minimum care means full compliance with auditing principles and rules. Any deviation from these standards results in liability. However, if the auditor is found to have fully complied and proves to be faultless, no liability arises. Even if the auditor has fulfilled their duty of care, if the financial statements fail to reflect the truth, no liability will arise (Çelik 2005, pp. 161–162).

Article 554 of the Turkish Commercial Code (TCC) holds auditors liable for damages to the audited company, shareholders, and creditors due to their faulty conduct. Even if this article were not in place, liability could still be based on the Turkish Code of Obligations. However, Article 554 provides a specific legal foundation for auditors' liability to third parties, and it must be emphasized that this article is the primary source for auditors' liability to the audited company (Urkan 2016, p. 283).

14.5.2 Relationship Between Contractual Liability and the Concept of Default

Default refers to the failure to perform an obligation within the agreed-upon time. According to Article 117 of the Turkish Code of Obligations: "A debtor of a due debt falls into default upon the creditor's notice." This article sets out two conditions for default: the debt must be due (mature), and the creditor must have issued a notice.

In addition to maturity and notice, performance must still be possible, and the creditor must be willing to accept performance (Oğuzman and Öz 2013, p. 471). If the performance date is determined by agreement, no notice is required. Also, if the notice is unreasonable under the principle of good faith (TMK Article 2), the debtor may fall into default without notice. For example, if the debtor is expected to know the performance date better than the creditor, default arises without notice (Oğuzman and Öz 2013, pp. 476–478). If the creditor is not ready to accept performance, the debtor cannot be in default even if the due date has passed.

Since audit contracts are bilateral, the audited company also has obligations. If the company fails to provide the requested documents, refuses to accept the report after it is ready, or unnecessarily delays the process, the auditor cannot be considered in default.

According to Article 29 of the Public Oversight, Accounting and Auditing Standards Authority (KGK) Regulation, an audit contracts must include the audit's start and end dates and the report delivery date. Therefore, when the performance date is contractually specified, no notice is needed for default. In any case, under the principle of good faith, the auditor is expected to know and follow the performance date and thus falls into default without notice if they fail to comply.

In the event of default, the creditor may demand specific performance and compensation for delay, maintain the contract and seek positive damages, or terminate the contract and seek negative damages (Oğuzman and Öz 2013, pp. -525–528). Independent audits are essential and mandatory for companies. According to TCC Article 397/2, financial statements not audited are considered not prepared. In such cases, the company cannot distribute dividends or use the financial statements in monetary transactions, leading to significant losses. Thus, delivering the report late provides no practical benefit.

Termination and rescission are distinct concepts. Rescission has a retrospective effect, while termination applies prospectively. In rescission, partial performances must be returned, and no further performance occurs. Therefore, rescission is only possible in one-time performance contracts. Since audit contracts involve continuous obligations and the auditor's responsibilities extend beyond the contract term, rescission is not applicable (Urkan 2016, pp. 298–299).

14.5.3 Liability of Independent Auditors Toward Third Parties

The fact that financial statements have been audited constitutes a significant basis for investment decisions by third parties acting as information users. Therefore, the damages caused by the negligence of independent auditors may go beyond the audited entity and also affect third parties. Hence, it is not acceptable to consider independent auditors as entirely free of liability toward third parties. It is accepted that independent auditors may be liable to third parties whom they do not personally know and whose number cannot be limited. However, it would not be fair or reasonable to impose liability on auditors toward every third party without limitation, and such an approach would negatively affect the auditing process, potentially bringing it to a halt. This raises the question of who qualifies as a third party. Third parties may include investors, employees of the audited company, creditors, customers of the audited company, and the state.

The independent audit contract is concluded between the audit firm and the audited company, and third parties are not parties to this contract. Therefore, in the event of a dispute, due to the principle of privity of contract, the contract will only be valid between its parties. Third parties cannot make claims against the audit firm based on the audit contract. The liability of the audit firm toward third parties can only arise from tort.

For audit firms to be held liable in tort toward third parties, the auditor must have prepared a misleading, incorrect, or incomplete audit report through fault or negligence; this report must have resulted in damage; and there must be an appropriate causal link between the auditor's conduct and the damage. For tort liability to arise, the audit firm or auditor must have issued a misleading, incorrect, or incomplete audit report, and this report must have been disclosed to the public (Urkan 2016, p. 337). Given that audit reports function in some respects as public disclosure documents, auditors cannot be held liable to third parties for audit reports that were not publicly disclosed.

Although Article 554 of the Turkish Commercial Code (TCC), which governs the liability of auditors, stipulates that auditors who act negligently in performing their duties while auditing a company's financial statements and reports shall be liable to the company's shareholders, the company itself, and the company's creditors, it contains no provision concerning liability toward third parties. However, the absence of a specific provision in the law does not mean that auditors are exempt from liability for damages caused to third parties. In such cases where there is no specific regulation, general provisions must be applied. Therefore, third parties who suffer harm due to the actions of independent auditors or audit firms may demand compensation for their damages under the provisions of the Turkish Code of Obligations (TCO) concerning tort liability (Topçuoğlu 2012, pp. 196–207).

The principles of the Turkish Auditing Standards (TDS) Code of Ethics establish that independent auditors must act not only in the interest of the audited company but also in the public interest, which defines one of the most distinguishing features of the auditing profession. When examining the liability of auditors to third parties (due to fraud, gross negligence, or ordinary negligence), it becomes apparent that such liability arises from violations of fundamental ethical principles (Erdoğan 2016, p. 71).

In the Turkish legal system, the auditor's liability is not limited to the audited entity. Among the relevant provisions, only Article 404 of the TCC restricts who may assert claims. In contrast, other legal regulations do not impose such a limitation on the claimant side, and there is a trend toward expanded liability. Since the auditing regulations in our legal system have been shaped by adopting provisions from various foreign legal systems, it is important to ensure coordination among the different norms (Göktürk 2017, pp. 406–407). Article 404 of the TCC, which adopts the principle of limited liability toward the company, constitutes a special provision. For full and effective coordination with Article 554 of the TCC, a legislative amendment is undoubtedly necessary.

Denying the auditor's liability toward third parties would contradict the fundamental purpose expected from an audit. However, in the absence of any limitations on liability, the auditor would, in effect, serve as a kind of guarantee fund (Göktürk 2017, p. 413). The audit report, being the source of damage in every dispute, would become a potential point of defense. It is evident that in situations where auditors are held to unlimited liability toward third parties, the auditing function cannot be performed fully or effectively. Therefore, the liability of the auditor should be balanced in a way that does not hinder the sensitive functioning of the auditing activity while still providing reasonable assurance to third parties.

If third parties fall outside the scope of the audit firm's liability and still initiate a liability lawsuit, the case should be dismissed on procedural grounds due to the absence of legal interest, by Article 114(h) of the Code of Civil Procedure (CCP). According to Article 115(1) of the CCP, this lack of legal interest as a prerequisite for filing a lawsuit may be examined by the court at any time, and the parties may also raise this issue at any stage of the proceedings. Legal interest refers to the presence of a legally protectable interest at the time of the lawsuit to safeguard the plaintiff's potential subjective right.

14.6 Situations Where the Independent Auditor is Not Liable

Even if there is a consultancy-like relationship between the audit firm and the audited entity, the audit firm cannot be held liable if it is understood from the circumstances that no audit obligation was undertaken under an independent audit agreement. This situation can only be determined based on the contents of the contract. If the audit agreement imposes an obligation on the audit firm to conduct an audit, the auditor's liability may only arise if they fail to comply with auditing principles and standards and therefore issue a biased and inaccurate report. Accordingly, the auditor can avoid liability—even if damage occurs to the audited company or users of the information—by proving that they acted by auditing principles and standards.

Article 32 of the Capital Markets Law states that "compensation claims arising from inaccurate, misleading, or incomplete public disclosure documents cannot be made if the purchase or sale of capital market instruments is not based on such a document." It is therefore explicitly regulated that if the transaction causing the plaintiff's alleged damage was not based on an audit report that qualifies as a public disclosure document issued by the defendant auditor, the compensation claim will be rejected.

If the damaged plaintiff acted despite knowing that the audit report cited as the basis for their lawsuit was inaccurate, misleading, or incomplete, and consequently suffered a loss, they cannot claim compensation for that loss. In such a case, the plaintiff must bear the damage themselves. The burden of proof lies with the defendant audit firm or auditor to demonstrate that the plaintiff company or third party knew that the audit report was inaccurate, misleading, or incomplete, and nevertheless carried out the damaging transaction. The defendant may prove this with any type of evidence (Urkan 2016, p. 373).

For the audited company or third parties to hold the independent audit firm liable for damages arising from the report it issued or from its actions during the audit process, they must demonstrate an adequate causal link between the report that was prepared in violation of auditing principles and standards and the damages they suffered.

14.7 Liability Lawsuit

During or after audit activities, the company or third parties who have suffered damages must seek compensation through a liability lawsuit. In practice, there are very few lawsuits related to the liability of auditors and audit firms. The reasons for this are that information users and companies are not fully aware of their legal rights and that the regulations regarding auditor liability are insufficiently applied in practice. Various laws, regulations, and communiqués contain numerous provisions related to independent auditing that may apply to liability lawsuits. As a result, this causes a situation of inapplicability due to the conflict of norms. It would not be wrong to state that there is a multi-headed structure in the field of independent auditing in Turkey. At this point, the Public Oversight, Accounting, and Auditing Standards Authority (KGK) must fully assume its umbrella role in the field of independent auditing. The institution has a major Liability in establishing a controlled and solid foundation for the infrastructure related to independent auditing (Karakoç 2013, 36). Undoubtedly, seminars and panels organized by KGK in cooperation with chambers, universities, and independent audit firms to raise awareness about liability will not only reduce disputes in practice but will also be important in terms of helping the injured party learn and exercise their rights in case of unresolved disputes.

The defendants in a liability lawsuit are independent audit firms and auditors. The plaintiffs are either the audited company, which can be considered the client, or third parties. Since audited companies are parties to the independent audit contract, there is no dispute regarding their right to file a lawsuit in the event they suffer damages due to the auditor's fault. However, accepting that every third party can file a lawsuit against the audit firm would render audit activities impracticable and is therefore not acceptable. Third parties who suffered damage and benefited from the audit reports—documents that essentially serve as instruments for informing the public—at the time the lawsuit was filed, in their capacity as information users, may file a liability lawsuit.

14.7.1 Time Limits and Statute of Limitations in Liability Lawsuits

According to Article 560 of the Turkish Commercial Code (TCC), the liability lawsuit must be filed within two years from the date the audited company learns of the liable party, and in any case, within five years.

Article 404 of the TCC regulates the obligation to perform the audit impartially and honestly, as well as the duty of confidentiality. Paragraph five of this article provides a five-year statute of limitations, stating that this period starts from the date of the audit report. However, if the act giving rise to liability is subject to a longer statute of limitations under the Turkish Penal Code (TPC), the same longer period shall apply to liability lawsuits seeking compensation for damages. In this context, the starting date for the five-year limitation period should be the date on which the duty of confidentiality was breached, not the report date. Otherwise, trade secrets learned during the audit process would be protected only for five years following the publication of the audit report. If the secret is disclosed after this period, claims for damages based on TCC Article 404 would be barred due to the statute of limitations (Yılmaz 2018, 57).

One important point to consider when filing a liability lawsuit is that the statute of limitations varies depending on the legal basis of the plaintiff's claim. If the plaintiff files the lawsuit based on a breach of contract and relies on TCC Article 554, the statute of limitations periods outlined in TCC Article 560—two years and five years—will apply. However, if the plaintiff files the lawsuit based on tort, as regulated in Articles 49 and following the Turkish Code of Obligations (TCO), then the statute of limitations periods set out in TCO Article 72—two years and ten years—will apply.

14.7.2 Competent and Authorized Courts in Liability Lawsuits

There are no specific legal provisions regulating which court has jurisdiction in disputes between audit firms and their clients. Therefore, general jurisdiction rules apply, and the provisions of the Code of Civil Procedure (CCP) become applicable. According to Article 6 of the CCP, the court of general jurisdiction is the court located in the domicile of the real or legal person who is the defendant at the time the lawsuit is filed. Since independent audit firms can be organized as joint stock companies and, under Article 51 of the Civil Code, the domicile of a company is the place where the company's business is managed—that is, the place where its headquarters is located—the competent court for lawsuits against independent audit firms is the court of the place where the company's headquarters is situated.

Lawsuits for compensation of damages brought against independent audit firms are civil lawsuits by nature. Disputes considered commercial and therefore adjudicated in commercial courts are civil lawsuits (TCC Art. 4/1). Civil lawsuits arising from matters regulated in the Turkish Commercial Code (TCC) are considered commercial, regardless of the parties' statuses and whether the dispute relates to their commercial enterprises (Arkan 2019, p. 108). According to Article 4 of the TCC, civil lawsuits arising from matters regulated under the Commercial Code and involving both parties' commercial enterprises are considered commercial cases. In lawsuits filed against company auditors, the competent court varies depending on whether the case is commercial. As a rule, commercial cases are heard in commercial courts. The law makes a distinction between absolute and relative commercial cases (Şener 2016, p. 139). Liability lawsuits filed based on provisions of the TCC are considered absolute commercial cases and fall under the jurisdiction of the Commercial Courts of First Instance. For example, lawsuits arising from breaches of confidentiality obligations must be filed under Articles 404 and 554 of the TCC in Commercial Courts of First Instance (Kocabıyık 2018, p. 282). Since independent audit firms are organized as joint stock companies and legal persons, merchants do not engage in ordinary business; a dispute concerning both parties' commercial enterprises is a relative commercial business, and the lawsuit should be considered commercial. Furthermore, even if the audit firm is not organized as a capital company, independent auditing is regulated under the TCC and is therefore an absolute commercial business, falling under the jurisdiction of the Commercial Courts of First Instance.

However, it is also possible for lawsuits against independent audit firms or auditors not to be commercial and thus not fall within the jurisdiction of the Commercial Court of First Instance. This would be the case for lawsuits based solely on tort claims and not on the TCC, brought by shareholders or creditors who do not have the status of merchants. In such cases, the competent court is the General Civil Court of First Instance (Kocabıyık 2018, p. 282).

If a lawsuit arising from an independent auditing contract and having a commercial nature is filed in a general civil court despite the presence of a commercial court in that location, or if a non-commercial case is filed in a commercial court, the court must, ex officio and without the need for either party to raise the issue, refer the case to the competent court. This is because the relationship between Civil Courts of First Instance and Commercial Courts of First Instance is not one of division of labor but one of jurisdiction, and jurisdiction rules are of public order. However, in places where no Commercial Court of First Instance exists, the failure to raise jurisdictional rules in commercial cases does not necessitate a ruling of lack of jurisdiction, and the Civil Court of First Instance may proceed with the case (Arkan 2019, pp. 121–122).

Whether a dispute arising from independent auditing is considered commercial is also important in terms of the law of evidence. Although the submission of evidence in commercial cases is also subject to the provisions of the CCP, some additional evidentiary tools are available in commercial cases. For instance, commercial books can be used as evidence in commercial cases; invoices and confirmation letters can be used as evidentiary tools and create a rebuttable presumption (Bahtiyar 2016, p. 84).

14.7.3 Liability Lawsuits Within the Scope of Mandatory Mediation in Commercial Cases

Except for non-contentious judicial proceedings of a commercial nature, applying to a mediator before filing a lawsuit is a procedural requirement in commercial cases that involve claims for the payment of a certain amount of money, such as debts and compensation claims (TCC Art. 5/A). Therefore, the plaintiff must attach the original or a signed copy of the final report indicating the failure to settle the mediation process to the statement of claim. If a lawsuit is filed without applying to a mediator, the commercial case will be dismissed due to the lack of a procedural requirement (Arkan 2019, p. 117). However, even though mediation is a procedural requirement, this obligation only extends to initiating the mediation process. The course and outcome of the mediation process—whether successful or not—are governed by the parties' autonomy (Yavuz 2019, p. 54).

Lawsuits regarding the liability of auditors are considered commercial cases under the Turkish Commercial Code. Lawsuits brought against auditors are essentially related to claims for damages and receivables. As such, they fall under the scope of Article 5/A of the TCC, which lists monetary receivables and claims for damages as matters requiring mandatory mediation before litigation. Accordingly, if a lawsuit is filed against an independent audit firm without first applying for mediation, the lawsuit will be dismissed on procedural grounds, even if the plaintiff is substantively justified.

The party applying for mediation may be shareholders of the company, members of the board of directors, or third parties who have suffered damages. In lawsuits filed without fulfilling the procedural requirement of mediation, the absence of mediation may be identified at any stage of the proceedings, and the lawsuit may be dismissed on procedural grounds (Atasoy and Bilgin 2019, p. 135).

In our view, if the audited company files a lawsuit against the independent audit firm for compensation of damages, such a case is undoubtedly commercial and involves monetary receivables and claims for damages. Thus, applying for mediation is unquestionably a procedural requirement. However, if auditors not organized as capital companies file lawsuits against the audited business for unpaid fees, even if the claim is for a sum of money, it should be considered an ordinary debt collection lawsuit, heard by the Civil Courts of First Instance, and should not be subject to the mandatory mediation requirement.

14.8 Criminal Liability of Independent Auditors

The failure of independent audit firms to conduct audits by auditing principles and standards can lead not only to legal liability but also to criminal liability. However, unlike legal liability, for criminal liability to arise, the auditing principles and standards must have been violated intentionally (Çelik 2005, p. 195).

According to Article 6, paragraph (c) of the Turkish Penal Code (Law No. 5237), a public official is defined as a person who, through appointment or election or by any means, permanently, temporarily, or periodically participates in the execution of public activities. In light of this provision, anyone involved in the execution of public activities will be considered a public official under the substantive criminal law. Those considered public officials may commit crimes that are legally possible for public servants to commit, and crimes committed against them will be deemed as committed against public officials.

Under Decree Law No. 660, since the duties carried out by independent auditors are public, independent auditors should be regarded as public officials. Accordingly, for crimes committed during or due to the execution of these duties, independent auditors must be punished as public officials by Article 6/c of the Turkish Penal Code (Özdek 2017, pp. 491–496).

14.9 Conclusion

According to Article 68 of our Commercial Code No. 6102, merchants are obliged to prepare financial statements. This duty falls under the Liability of the board of directors. While preparing financial statements, the board of directors must act in accordance with auditing standards and present the company's assets and liabilities in a clear, understandable, and complete manner. However, in practice, the expected objectivity in preparing financial statements is often not achieved. Therefore, the aim of the independent auditing system in our legal framework is to ensure the auditing of companies' financial statements.

Before the enactment of this provision in our law, the audit body was one of the mandatory organs of the company. However, due to the unavoidable alignment of interests between the audit and management bodies, management weaknesses emerged, leading to misleading information for users who relied on financial statements for investment decisions. Consequently, the audit body was removed. For all these reasons, it has been aimed that the accounting information of businesses be audited by independent auditors who have no organic ties with the audited company, thus allowing users of this information to make investment decisions in a secure environment.

The independent audit contracts signed between the auditors and the audited companies are bilateral contracts with mutual obligations, subject to a written form requirement, and can be characterized as sui generis contracts for work (innominate contracts). These contracts impose various obligations on both the auditor and the audited entity. Failure to comply with these obligations will undoubtedly result in certain sanctions.

Independent auditors have obligations stemming from the contract, such as compliance with auditing standards, the duty of care, the duty of independence, and the duty of confidentiality. If auditors fail to fulfill any of these obligations, liability will arise. They will not be absolved of liability if they either fail to prepare the required audit reports or do not prepare them properly.

Auditing ultimately provides users of financial information with reasonable assurance through audit reports. However, reasonable assurance should not be construed as absolute assurance. Therefore, auditors will not be held liable for inaccuracies in their audit reports, provided they have fulfilled their obligations with due care and have not acted intentionally.

Auditors may be liable to both the audited company and third parties for failure to comply with their obligations. Since there is a contractual relationship between the auditor and the audited entity, liability will arise in the form of a breach of contract. However, in the absence of a contractual relationship between auditors and third parties, liability can only arise through tort. Denying auditors' liability toward third parties would hinder the realization of the objective benefits expected from auditing. Therefore, if third parties suffer damages as a result of auditing activities, they may seek compensation under the provisions of tort liability in the Turkish Code of Obligations.

The cause of liability toward the audited company may be either a breach of contract or tortious conduct. In such cases, both contractual and tortious liability may coexist. The claimant may choose to base their lawsuit on either legal ground, but the same damage cannot be compensated twice under both.

Parties claiming to have suffered damage during or after auditing activities must file a liability lawsuit to claim compensation. The competent and authorized court for liability lawsuits is the commercial court of first instance located at the company's headquarters. However, not every liability lawsuit will be commercial and thus may fall outside the jurisdiction of commercial courts. For example, claims based solely on tort and not grounded in the Turkish Commercial Code, brought by claimants who are not merchants, fall under the jurisdiction of civil courts of first instance.

For commercial lawsuits involving monetary claims such as compensation or debt recovery, applying to a mediator is a procedural requirement before filing a lawsuit. If a lawsuit is filed without first applying to a mediator, it will be dismissed due to this procedural deficiency. Since lawsuits filed against auditors fall under commercial law and typically involve compensation claims, they are considered commercial lawsuits and are therefore subject to mandatory mediation.

However, if the auditor filing a compensation claim is not organized as a capital company, and the lawsuit merely involves a simple debt recovery, then it should be considered an ordinary debt lawsuit. In that case, the competent court would be the civil court of first instance, and mediation should not be treated as a mandatory prerequisite.

References

Arı Z (2019) Anonim Şirketlerin Denetimi. Ekin Yayıncılık, Bursa

Arkan S (2019) Ticari İşletme Hukuku (25. Baskı). Banka ve Ticaret Hukuku Araştırma Enstitüsü, Ankara

Atasoy ÖA, Bilgin BO (2019) Anonim Şirket Yönetim Kurulu Üyelerinin Sorumluluğu Konusunda Açılacak Ticari Davalarda Zorunlu Arabuluculuk Uygulaması Ve Sorumluluk Davasına Etkisi. İstanbul Aydın Üniversitesi Hukuk Fakültesi Dergisi 2:111–165

Ayan M (2016) Borçlar Hukuku(Genel Hükümler) (11. Baskı). Seçkin Yayıncılık, Ankara

Ayan M, Ayan N (2014) Kişiler Hukuku (5.Baskı). Mimoza Yayınları, Konya

Aydın A, Çürük T (2017) Bağımsız Denetçinin Finansal Tablolara İlişkin Görüş Oluşturma ve Raporlama Standardından Kaynaklanan Yükümlülükleri. Çukurova Üniversitesi Sosyal Bilimler Enstitüsü Dergisi 26(2):226–238

Aydoğan S (2016) Türkiye'de Bağımsız Denetimin Yeni Türk Ticaret Kanunu Çerçevesinde Değerlendirilmesi. Uluslararası Yönetim Iktisat Ve Işletme Dergisi, (30 ICAFR 16 Özel Sayısı) 771–785

Bahtiyar M (2016) Ticari İşletme Hukuku (17.Baskı). Beta Yayınları, İstanbul

Bezirci M, Karasioğlu F (2011) Türkiye'de Denetimin Tarihsel Gelişimi. Sosyal Ekonomik Araştırmalar Dergisi 11(21):571–592. Erişim tarihi, 21.06.2020 https://dergipark.org.tr/tr/pub/susead/issue/28414/302397

Bilgili F, Ertan D (2018) Borçlar Hukuku Genel Hükümler. Dora Yayıncılık: 12.Bası.

Bozkurt N (2018) Muhasebe Denetimi (8.Baskı). Alfa Yayıncılık

Cansel E, Özel Ç (2017) Borçlar Hukuku Genel Hükümler. Seçkin Yayıncılık, Ankara
Çelik A (2005) Bağımsız Denetim Kuruluşlarının Sorumluluğu. Seçkin Yayıncılık, Ankara
Erdoğan A (2014) 6102 sayılı TTK'ya Göre Sermaye Şirketlerinin Bağımsız Denetimi. Erciyes Üniversitesi Hukuk Fakültesi Dergisi 9(1):81–105
Erdoğan S (2016) Bağımsız Denetçilerin Üçüncü Kişilere Karşı İhmal Kapsamındaki Sorumluluğu. Mali Çözüm Dergisi 26(133):57–79
Eren F (2014) Borçlar Hukuku Genel Hükümler (17. Baskı). Yetkin Yayınları, Ankara
Ergüden E (2014) Yeni Türk Ticaret Kanunu ile Birlikte Anonim Şirketlerde Bağımsız Denetim. Bahçeşehir Üniversitesi Hukuk Fakültesi Dergisi 9(117–118):183–196
Falcıoğlu Ö (2016) Anonim Şirket Finansal Tablolarında TTK 515 Kapsamında Dürüst Resim İlkesine Uygunluk ve İlkeye Aykırılığın Sonuçları. Bahçeşehir Üniversitesi Hukuk Fakültesi Dergisi 11(137):69–102
Göktürk K (2017) Denetimden Doğan Hukuki Sorumluluk. KGK Muhasebe Ve Denetim Sempozyumu-istanbul Bildiriler Kitabı Içinde 384–414
Gönen S, Rasgen M (2016) Bağımsız Denetimde Zorunlu Denetçi Rotasyonu. Insan Ve Toplum Bilimleri Araştırmaları Dergisi 5(7):1809–1822
Karakoç M (2013) Türk Ticaret Kanunu ile Bağımsız Denetimde Meydana Gelen Gelişmeler. Muhasebe Ve Finansman Dergisi 59:17–37
Kocabıyık S (2018) Bağımsız Denetçinin Üçüncü Kişilere Karşı Hukuki Sorumluluğu (1.Bası). Seçkin Yayıncılık, Ankara
Meral E (2019) Ücretin Denetim Bağımsızlığı Üzerindeki Etkisi. İstanbul Işık Üniversitesi
Oğuzman K, Öz T (2013) Borçlar Hukuku Genel Hükümler Cilt-1 (10. Baskı). Vedat Kitapçılık, İstanbul
Özdek V (2017) Denetimden Doğan Cezai Sorumluluk. KGK Muhasebe ve Denetim Sempozyumu-İstanbul bildiriler kitabı içinde. İstanbul
Özkorkut K (2013) 6102 Sayılı Türk Ticaret Kanunu Açısından Anonim Şirketlerde Bağımsız Denetim (1.Bası). Banka ve Ticaret Hukuku Araştırma Enstitüsü Yayınları, Ankara
Sağlar J (2015) Türkiye'de Mevzuatlar Açısından Bağımsız Denetime Bakış. Karahan Kitabevi, Adana
Şener OH (2016) Ticari İşletme Hukuku (Birinci Ba). Seçkin Yayıncılık, Ankara
Topçuoğlu M (2012) Türk Ticaret Kanuna Göre Bağımsız Denetçinin Sorumluluğu. Seçkin Yayıncılık
Töre İ, Tanyeri A (2016) Şeffaflığa Etkileri Açısından 6102 Sayılı Türk Ticaret Kanunu'nda Bağımsız Denetim. Hukuk Ve Iktisat Araştırmaları Dergisi 8(2):34–47
Urkan E (2016) Sermaye Piyasalarında Bağımsız Denetim Sözleşmeleri ve Sorumluluk. Yetkin Yayınları, Ankara
Uzay Ş, Bayat SB (2016) 6102 Sayılı Türk Ticaret Kanununun Bağımsız Denetim Alanında Getirdiği Yenilikler ve Tartışmalı Konular. Süleyman Demirel Üniversitesi Iktisadi Ve Idari Bilimler Fakültesi Dergisi 5(21):1503–1513
Uzay Ş, Kaya P (2018) Hileli Finansal Raporlama ve Bağımsız Denetçinin Sorumluluğu. Muhasebe Bilim Dünyası Dergisi 20(Özel Sayı):721–740
Yavuz M (2019) Ticari Davalarda Dava Şartı Olarak Arabuluculuk. Gümrük Ve Ticaret Dergisi 5(15):52–61
Yılmaz A (2018) Anonim Şirketlerde Bağımsız Denetçilerin Türk Ticaret Kanunu Madde 404 Hükmünün ihlalinden Kaynaklanan Hukuki Sorumluluğu. Banka Ve Ticaret Hukuku Dergisi, C. XXXIV, S. 3, pp. 21–60

Index

G. Kurt, Ö. Sarısoy (eds.), *Recent Advancements in Auditing*, Accounting, Finance, Sustainability, Governance & Fraud: Theory and Application,
https://doi.org/10.1007/978-981-95-5811-7

MIX
Papier aus verantwortungsvollen Quellen
Paper from responsible sources
FSC® C105338

If you have any concerns about our products,
you can contact us on
ProductSafety@springernature.com

In case Publisher is established outside the EU,
the EU authorized representative is:
Springer Nature Customer Service Center GmbH
Europaplatz 3, 69115 Heidelberg, Germany

Printed by Libri Plureos GmbH
in Hamburg, Germany